World Yearbook of
Education 2004

World Yearbook of Education 2004

Digital technology, communities and education

Edited by Andrew Brown and Niki Davis

Routledge
Taylor & Francis Group

LONDON AND NEW YORK

First published 2004
by RoutledgeFalmer

Published 2022 by Routledge
2 Park Square, Milton Park, Abingdon, Oxon OX14 4RN
605 Third Avenue, New York, NY 10017

*Routledge is an imprint of the Taylor & Francis Group,
an informa business*

First issued in paperback 2011

Typeset in Times by
Florence Production Ltd, Stoodleigh, Devon

British Library Cataloguing in Publication Data
A catalogue record for this book is available from
the British Library

Library of Congress Cataloging in Publication Data
A catalog record for this book has been requested

ISBN13: 978-0-415-33493-8 (hbk)
ISBN13: 978-0-415-50105-7 (pbk)

Contents

List of illustrations   ix
List of contributors   xi
Series editors' introduction   xiii

Introduction   1
ANDREW BROWN AND NIKI DAVIS

PART I
Digital transformations   13

1 **Learning, a semiotic view in the context of digital
   technologies**   15
   GUNTHER KRESS

2 **Networking and collective intelligence for teachers
   and learners**   40
   BERNARD CORNU

3 **Multimedia learning in the digital world**   46
   JOSÉ L. RODRÍGUEZ ILLERA

4 **Children's concepts of ICT: pointers to the impact
   of ICT on education within and beyond the
   classroom**   57
   BRIDGET SOMEKH

5 **(Dis)possessing literacy and literature: gourmandizing
   in Gibsonbarlowville**   74
   SOH-YOUNG CHUNG, PAUL DOWLING AND
   NATASHA WHITEMAN

6 **Rethinking and retooling language and literature
   teaching**   95
   RONALD SOETAERT, ANDRE MOTTART AND
   BART BONAMIE

PART II
Learners and teachers   113

7 Playing and learning with digital technologies –
   at home and at school   115
   TONI DOWNES

8 Learning and teaching adult basic skills with digital
   technology: research from the UK   131
   HARVEY MELLAR AND MARIA KAMBOURI

9 Teachers and teaching innovations in a connected world   145
   NANCY LAW

10 Teaching with video cases on the Web: lessons learned
    from the Reading Classroom Explorer   164
    RICHARD E. FERDIG, LAURA R. ROEHLER, ERICA C. BOLING,
    SUZANNE KNEZEK, P. DAVID PEARSON AND AMAN YADAV

Part III
Intercultural interactions   177

11 Digital technology to empower indigenous culture
    and education   179
    PAUL RESTA, MARK CHRISTAL AND LORIENE ROY

12 Refugee children in a virtual world: intercultural online
    communication and community   196
    LIESBETH DE BLOCK AND JULIAN SEFTON-GREEN

13 The role of local instructors in making global e-learning
    programmes culturally and pedagogically relevant   211
    MICHELLE SELINGER

14 Case method and intercultural education in the digital age 225
    MARSHA A. GARTLAND, ROBERT F. MCNERGNEY,
    SCOTT R. IMIG AND MARLA L. MUNTNER

15 Intercultural learning through digital media: the
    development of a transatlantic doctoral student
    community   234
    ANDREW BROWN AND NIKI DAVIS

PART IV
Building communities 249

16 A cross-cultural cadence in E: knowledge building with
networked communities across disciplines and cultures 251
ELSEBETH K. SORENSEN AND EUGENE S. TAKLE

17 Telecollaborative communities of practice in education
within and beyond Canada 264
THÉRÈSE LAFERRIÈRE, ALAIN BREULEUX AND
GAALEN ERICKSON

18 Informatics teacher training in Hungary: building
community and capacity with tele-houses 277
MÁRTA TURCSÁNYI-SZABÓ

19 Building communities of practice in 'New' Europe 289
CHRISTINA PRESTON AND LAURA LENGEL

20 A systemic approach to educational renewal with new
technologies: empowering learning communities in Chile 299
PEDRO HEPP, J. ENRIQUE HINOSTROZA AND ERNESTO LAVAL

Index 312

Illustrations

Figures

1.1	This is a car	18
1.2	Onion cells: theory	21
1.3	Onion cells: eye-piece	22
1.4	Georgia's drawing	24
1.5	Blood circulation: diary	27
1.6	Blood circulation: concept map	29
1.7	Blood circulation: teacher's drawing	30
1.8	Institute of Education prospectus: contents page and page of text	36
1.9	Institute of Education web site: home page	37
4.1	Wendy's concept map	58
4.2	Stephen's concept map	60
4.3	Fiona's 2000 concept map	69
4.4	Fiona's 2001 concept map	70
7.1	A framework of children's use of computers	124
9.1	Innovativeness diagram for scientific investigation case study	158
11.1	Technology use with respect to the social functions described by the Anishinabe clan system	187
20.1	The Enlaces programme: yearly expansion 1992–2006	301

Tables

4.1	Students' awareness of computers in their world	66–7
4.2	Summary of Fiona's 2000 and 2001 concept maps	68
7.1	Classification of children's use of computers	122–3
9.1	The pedagogical roles played by teachers	151
9.2	K-means cluster analysis of teachers' roles	154
9.3	Cross-tabulation of teachers' role clusters and innovative practices	155

9.4   Innovative practices and teachers' role clusters by
        world regions   160
9.5   Emerging practices and emerging pedagogies by
        world region   161

Contributors

Liesbeth de Block, Institute of Education, University of London, UK

Erica C. Boling, Rutgers University, USA

Bart Bonamie, Ghent University, Belgium

Alain Breuleux, McGill University, Canada

Andrew Brown, Institute of Education, University of London, UK

Mark Christal, Smithsonian Institution, National Museum of the American Indian, USA

Soh-young Chung, Sogang University, Seoul, Korea

Bernard Cornu, University of Grenoble and La Villa Media, France

Niki Davis, Iowa State University, USA, and Institute of Education, University of London, UK

Paul Dowling, Institute of Education, University of London, UK

Toni Downes, University of Western Sydney, Australia

Gaalen Erickson, University of British Columbia, Canada

Richard E. Ferdig, University of Florida, USA

Marsha A. Gartland, University of Virginia, USA

Pedro Hepp, Universidad de La Frontera, Chile

J. Enrique Hinostroza, Universidad de La Frontera, Chile

Scott R. Imig, University of Virginia, USA

Maria Kambouri, Institute of Education, University of London, UK

Suzanne Knezek, Michigan State University, USA

Gunther Kress, Institute of Education, University of London, UK

Thérèse Laferrière, Université Laval, Canada

Ernesto Laval, Universidad de La Frontera, Chile

Nancy Law, University of Hong Kong, China

Laura Lengel, Bowling Green State University, USA

Robert F. McNergney, University of Virginia, USA

Harvey Mellar, Institute of Education, University of London, UK

Andre Mottart, Ghent University, Belgium

Marla L. Muntner, University of Virginia, USA

P. David Pearson, University of California-Berkeley, USA

Christina Preston, Mirandanet, UK

Paul Resta, University of Texas at Austin, USA

José L. Rodríguez Illera, University of Barcelona, Spain

Laura R. Roehler, Michigan State University, USA

Loriene Roy, University of Texas at Austin, USA

Julian Sefton-Green, WAC Performing Arts and Media College, London, UK

Michelle Selinger, Cisco Systems, UK

Ronald Soetaert, Ghent University, Belgium

Bridget Somekh, Manchester Metropolitan University, UK

Elsebeth K. Sorensen, Aalborg University, Denmark

Eugene S. Takle, Iowa State University, USA

Márta Turcsányi-Szabó, Eötvös Loránd University, Hungary

Natasha Whiteman, Institute of Education, University of London, UK

Aman Yadav, Michigan State University, USA

Series editors' introduction

The *World Yearbooks of Education* have dealt with topical educational issues for well over fifty years now. Many of the topics covered in recent volumes would have been familiar to the original editors since many educational issues stay constant – the management of schools and vocational education would be two examples. At first glance, the topic of this *Yearbook* would appear to be novel, for both the speed of development in digital technology and its impact on education almost appear to have suddenly sprung upon us. But this is not really the case. Like vocational education and the management of schools, the impact of new technologies on education has also been a recurring topic. The 1982 *World Yearbook: Computers and Education* and the 1988 *World Yearbook: Education for the New Technologies* demonstrate a continuing concern for the way in which education faces up to the rapid development of new technologies. This volume continues this process. What is new is that digital technologies are really beginning to make dramatic changes to education in ways that were only glimpsed at in those earlier volumes.

As this current volume makes clear, a real revolution in the way in which we conceptualize and practise education and learning is taking place. Revolution is not too strong a word as both the pace of change and its impact on education are truly remarkable. This volume goes further than merely describing this rapidly changing educational context, seeing digital technologies as emancipatory for teachers, learners and the communities to which they belong, including new virtual communities, while at the same time warning of the dangers of a 'digital divide' both within states and between them. The volume is appropriate to the *Yearbook* series not only because its contributions cover a wide range of states, but also because the authors recognize that digital technology and its impact on education are major aspects of the wider process of globalization. Several chapters are indeed forerunners of next year's volume on globalization.

It is no longer a specialist field, although the contributors are all specialists. Anyone with an interest in the current rapid changes in education must take on board the issues raised by this book. Consequently, we are grateful to Andrew Brown and Niki Davis for collecting together such a wide-ranging set of perspectives, ground-breaking case studies and radical analyses.

David Coulby and Crispin Jones
Bath, 2003

Introduction

Andrew Brown and Niki Davis

Writing on the educational and social potential of new technologies is interspersed with imagined cyber-utopias and cyber-dystopias. Commentators have been preoccupied with, on the one hand, the emancipatory potential of technology to empower individuals and groups and, on the other, the potential of technology for surveillance, oppression and constraint. Similarly, in relation to cognitive development, new forms of technology are frequently presented as either enabling (providing additional tools and contexts in which learners can develop new skills and understandings) or limiting (engaging users in routine tasks and procedures that dull creativity and impede problem solving activity). In the meantime, practitioners and researchers across the world, in a variety of institutional settings and social, cultural and economic conditions, are using new technologies in anticipated and unanticipated ways, with both anticipated and unanticipated consequences.

This *World Yearbook* sets out to explore the manner in which digital technology is used by individuals and groups in both their own learning and in the development of communities of practice which act as contexts for learning and interaction. In doing this, the editors and authors recognize that we are dealing with a diverse set of technologies and a wide range of communities. The technologies in question range from communication media such as email and the Internet through to production media such as digital video. These media are, however, converging and the separation between communication and production, between distribution and content, becomes ever less tenable. At the same time the division between formal and informal educational settings and between leisure activities and learning has also been eroded. It is for these reasons that we have chosen to focus on 'digital technology' rather than 'information and communication technology' (ICT), the term used predominantly in the UK, or 'technology', the preferred term in the US. 'Digital technology' as a term is sufficiently broad and free of limiting connotations and is internationally recognizable.

The notion of community is key to the chapters in this *Yearbook*. Digital technologies have provided a means for the creation of new virtual communities, for instance around particular social or cultural interests, and for the reproduction, reassertion or reinvention of identity of spatially displaced communities, such as refugee groups. It has also enabled groups and individuals to interact with each other through new media and highlighted the need to address issues of intercultural communication and understanding.

As well as considering different forms of digital media and their use in different social, cultural and economic conditions, the chapters cover a range of different forms of community, forms of cultural identity, and forms of communication, understanding and relations between different cultural groups as they are facilitated and mediated by the use of digital technologies. These issues are variously addressed by authors both with respect to relations within and between their own 'local' communities and wider international and intercultural relations in the global arena. In the process of doing this, the issue of 'digital equity' and the differential access to digital technologies and skills is brought to the fore.

The apparent lack of boundaries when using digital technologies leads to the reconsideration of the relationship between what have conventionally been considered formal and informal modes of education. Online learning and teaching, the emergence of new 'communities of practice' beyond the school and college and the active engagement of particular cultural and interest groups, including parents, have generated a range of new sites for pedagogy and learning. This collection explores the effects of this diversification of pedagogic sites on how we think about learning and teaching, on educational institutions, on the preparation of teachers, on the development of new educational media and on strategies for development and change. In reflecting on these effects, the authors adopt a range of approaches and a variety of perspectives. Descriptions are given of initiatives designed to increase access to and participation in education, an outcome urgently pursued by international agencies, including the United Nations Educational, Scientific and Cultural Organization (UNESCO), which also strive to work in ways that respect local cultures and diversity (Haddad and Draxler, 2002).

Yearbook structure

This *World Yearbook of Education* is unusual. The structure and content of the book reflect Castells' (1996) suggestion that, with the advent of the 'network society', it is necessary to rethink spatial distinctions to recognize the importance of both the virtual 'space of flows', created through the interlinking of digital information and communications systems in distant locations, and the physically bounded 'space of places', locales which provide the setting for much of the day-to-day experience of social agents. The approach we have taken in compiling the collection also recognizes the creation, within the network society, of a 'Fourth World' of exclusion that crosses national boundaries and other established distinctions such as First/Third World and 'developed'/ 'developing' economy. This reinforces our concern for 'digital equity' and the consequences of the 'digital divide'.

We have not attempted to provide an overview of the use of digital technologies in education in the world today by presenting an array of distinct national, regional or other geopolitically defined perspectives. Instead the authors, drawn from twelve countries and five continents, reflect on the ways in which digital technologies serve to link cultures and disciplines within and across locales to build or reinforce communities in the enhancement of learning and teaching and in the production and reproduction of knowledge. To achieve this, we have attempted to combine analysis with the presentation of empirical research and description of specific experiences, projects and initiatives. The chapters also move from consideration of general issues across contexts to the specific concerns of particular groups, the perspectives of children to the professional development of teachers and relations within communities and interactions between culturally diverse groups. In this way we strive to get a sense of how people are thinking about the relationship between digital technology, communities and education and what groups and individuals are doing with these technologies within conditions of complexity, diversity and flux.

The chapters in the collection are organized as four interrelated sections. The first, *digital transformations*, deals with the impact of digital technology on educational thinking and practice in formal and informal settings. The second section moves on to consider the central social agents of education, *learners and teachers*. In the third section the focus is on the *intercultural interactions* that are facilitated by the use of digital technology. The final section presents a number of examples of the use of digital technology in *building communities*, concluding with a paper on the restructuring of education in Chile, which provides an example of how carefully planned collaborative support with digital technology can foster change in complex settings subject to changes in local, regional, national and global political climate.

Digital transformations

Digital technology is both a key element in the production of late modernity and a product of it. It both shapes and is shaped by contemporary circumstances. In relation to education, digital technology fuels change in and an increased demand for formal education, whilst motivating fundamental questions about what constitutes learning, where and how learning takes place, and the effects of interaction using digital technology on the reproduction of social and cultural relations.

However, whilst 'ICTs have revolutionized the world economy', educa-tion, it appears, remains relatively unchanged (Haddad and Draxler, 2002: 6).

In the first chapter, *Gunther Kress* adopts a semiotic view of learning in the context of digital technologies and develops a theoretical perspec-tive that has the potential to address current demands for education to 'produce' 'young people who have dispositions towards creativity, innovation and ease with change'. He notes that the rearrangement that has taken place 'in the constellation of modes of representation and media of dissemination – from writing and book to image and screen – is having profound consequences for meaning-making and hence for learning'. Currently dominant learning theories were developed in a more static era when a society's rules and officially sanctioned know-ledge could more easily be identified and critiqued. The social semiotic approach to meaning taken by Kress asserts the inseparability of the sign from the sign-maker's motivation. He explores the implications of this by using a number of examples. Learning, from this perspective, is about the making of meaning and, in the light of this, it is necessary to rethink educational processes. New media have fundamentally changed relations between author and reader and offer new possibili-ties for multimodal production. Authority relations with respect to knowledge production have subsequently, Kress argues, been inverted and groups and individuals can now take responsibility to gain and create the knowledge they require. As a consequence Kress urges us to view education in the age of digital technology as design rather than transmission. This requires us to provide support for learners to ask: 'How can I implement my desires, given these historically shaped resources, the structure of power in this environment, these character-istics of my audience?'

The concerns of other authors in this and other subsequent sections of the book frequently address and overlap with the issues raised by Kress. *Bernard Cornu* also argues that there is a need to view education in a fundamentally different way in the light of digital technology. In particular he presents an innovative view of the potential role of educa-tion in facilitating the development of 'collective intelligence'. Cornu traces successive conceptions of learning and intelligence, from the view that learning is individual to an understanding of learning as collabo-rative and subsequently to a contemporary view of learning as networked and intelligence as collective. He states: 'Collective intelli-gence is a third step, more complex, made of networks of intelligences and which includes a collective dimension in the knowledge, in the prob-lems to be solved and in the way intelligence is activated.' He urges educators to explore this new concept and develop the necessary tools to enable learners and teachers to work collectively in our networked society. He suggests that our conception of a teacher needs to develop beyond the now established transition from 'sage on the stage to guide on the side' to a collective mode of operation that facilitates collaboration with learners in the achievement of collective intelligence.

The increasing incidence of 'multimedial' texts in formal educational and everyday settings raises questions about how we understand the relationship between different modes of communication and how, in the light of these understandings, we approach instructional design. *José L. Rodríguez Illera* demonstrates the difficulty of identifying a coherent unified descriptive language from current research on multimodal communication. He argues that, in pedagogic terms, the 'multimediality' of programmes, materials or environments has no necessary positive value in its own right. Furthermore, the move to the Internet as the dominant mode for the delivery of educational multimedia has imposed limits on the richness and interactivity of programmes. In order to construct pedagogically effective multimedia environments we need, he argues, to understand the specificity of different modes and how they work together, and to integrate this understanding into a broader theory of learning. Adding additional modes or media to pedagogic texts achieves nothing in itself, and, indeed, can be detrimental to learning, he argues. Whilst digital technology opens up new possibilities for pedagogic design, it is our understanding of pedagogy and learning that must guide this design, not the fetishization of multimediality.

Children's understandings of ICT are central to the realization of the potential of digital technology in education. *Bridget Somekh*, drawing on a comprehensive national study of the impact of ICT on education in the UK (BECTA, 2003), provides evidence of the complexity of children's concepts and of the transformation that has taken place in the domestic world and out of school activities of children. Whilst this research in notable for being the first large-scale study to show a statistically significant positive impact of ICT on learning, it is striking that the informational and communicative connectedness evident in children's out of school activity cannot be matched by their use of digital technology in school. This prompts another call, from another direction, for the transformation of schooling in the light of the impact of digital technology. It also reminds us again of the need to be aware of variation in access to digital technology and the importance of actively attending to 'digital equity'.

In a paper written collaboratively using hypertext-authoring software, *Soh-young Chung, Paul Dowling* and *Natasha Whiteman* examine the transformative potential of community and individual activities in cyberspace for the institutions of formal education. Literature and literacy are conventionally 'possessed' by formal education: Chung, Dowling and Whiteman explore the ways in which this is challenged by the increased visibility, facilitated by the Internet, of the popular production and consumption of literacy in the areas of both popular and conventionally elite culture. The spaces and communities created, recreated and transformed by the increasing accessibility of new media are not socially neutral, however. As in all areas of social practice there are principles of exclusion and inclusion, and the potential for territorialization and struggle over possession, whilst offering the possibility of new alliances and topographical reconfiguration.

The future of literature and literacy in the light of increasing accessibility of digital technology is also a central concern for *Ronald Soetaert, Andre Mottart* and *Bart Bonamie*. Their particular focus is the exploration of the successive paradigms that have informed the practices of language teaching and that provide conceptual frameworks for understanding the positioning and identity of the members of a particular professional community, language teachers. They reject the quest for a single paradigm and propose a critical rhetorical approach to all modes of communication, not only spoken and written language, but also visual, audio and gestural modes, which recognizes the 'inherent rhetoricity' of electronic and other forms of discourse. They look to the transformation of the relationship between the arts brought about by digital technology, and in particular, as Chung, Dowling and Whiteman have indicated, the potential erosion of difference between the visual arts and literature as writing, to signal ways in which language teachers might 'rethink and retool' in the face of the pervasiveness and potential of 'digitization' in formal education and popular culture.

Learners and teachers

In shifting attention specifically to learners and teachers, the central themes of the previous section are extended and contextualized. In relation to the transformation of education through the use of digital technology, *Toni Downes* states categorically that 'if there is any potential for digital technologies to be used in homes and schools to transform children's lives, it will require a significant and fundamental shift in how we conceive of childhood, learning and schooling' and that until this has been achieved 'it is hard to see how the complex learning that is afforded by digital technologies in the home can also be a reality in schools, and the new learning that children bring from home can find recognition and authenticity in school'. To explore this disjunction between home and school uses of digital technology, she draws on national demographic data from Australia and the US and from a major Australian study of children's use of computers in homes and later UK research. She stresses that children should not be seen as 'workers' in their use of digital technology, but as involved in playful and purposeful activity in which they exercise control over technology and learning. This contrasts with the oft-mundane uses of digital technology in schools, with tight control over time, pacing and forms of activity. As Chung, Dowling and Whiteman observe, school seems set to become 'an increasingly dour place to be'. Downes draws attention to the variation in levels of access between nations and between social and cultural groups, and points out that the effects of low levels of domestic access to digital technology are frequently compounded by poor facilities in neighbourhood schools. As Castells has emphasized, with the increasing internal diversification of the Third World and the generation of social exclusion within the boundaries of First World nations, the network society has led to the

> emergence of a Fourth World of exclusion, made up not only of most of Africa, and rural Asia, and of Latin American shanties, but also of the South Bronx, La Courneuve, Kamagasaki, or Tower Hamlets of this world. A fourth world that . . . is predominantly populated by women and children.
>
> (Castells, 1997: 7)

Harvey Mellar and *Maria Kambouri* present research into the use of digital technology to address the social exclusion of adult individuals and groups who are lacking the basic skills, principally numeracy and literacy, that are seen as essential for employment and participatory citizenship. Their research covers a range of settings and communities, including prisons and refugee groups, and a variety of initiatives, including 'learning shops' and the use of computer games in adult learning designed to reach groups who are alienated from formal education. They observe that the use of digital technologies in these settings is leading to changes in what constitutes 'basic skills', which now includes skills relating to ICT use, and in the occupational and work aspirations of individuals. As in the earlier chapters, the potential of particular forms of provision to exclude as well as include is demonstrated. For instance, the use of computer games to enhance literacy and numeracy can draw in particular groups whilst alienating others. They also identify the experience and approach of tutors as being central to the success of initiatives. The persistence of 'old pedagogies' can lead to the reproduction of the digital divide as a learning divide.

The transformation of pedagogy is the focus of the research presented and discussed by *Nancy Law*. She provides an overview of a 28-country international study of innovative pedagogical practices using ICT, conducted to explore the impact that governmental investment in ICT in education is having on teachers and teaching. The case studies presented illustrate ways in which teachers are incorporating ICT and digital technologies into their practice. The findings also indicate that teachers as professionals have become more connected, working collaboratively with colleagues and members of the broader community to bring about more challenging and more fruitful learning experiences for their students. It is also clear, however, that whilst there is evidence of changing practice, the transformation of underlying pedagogy, essential, Law argues, to achieve sustained change in education, is somewhat more problematic. The transfer of 'emerging practices' from one setting to another achieves little without the creation and adoption of 'emerging pedagogies'.

The use of digital technology in teacher education to facilitate the development of effective pedagogy is at the heart of the work presented by *Richard E. Ferdig, Laura R. Roehler, Erica C. Boling, Suzanne Knezek, P. David Pearson* and *Aman Yadav*. They describe the use of multimedia case studies of the teaching of reading, which include online videos of practice in US classrooms presented within a searchable database and linked with an online asynchronous conferencing facility. Hypermedia programs like Reading Classroom Explorer use the potential of digital technology to provide teachers with opportunities to experience, explore and discuss good practice in an environment that brings together theory and practice, and for trainee and novice teachers they act to link coursework and field experience. The chapter explores the potential of digital tools and resources like these to supplement, interact with and transform established pedagogic approaches and enable the development of communities of reflexive and reflective practitioners.

Intercultural interactions

The digital transformations discussed in the first section of the book, together with the changing experiences, practices and perspectives of learners and teachers considered in the second section, lay the foundation for the discussion of research and development on intercultural interaction presented in the third section. Digital technology provides tools for individuals and communities to (re)present themselves and for intercultural interaction in virtual spaces. The increasing accessibility of these spaces, and the facility to author and interact within them, raises new questions about the relationship between cultures and individual and collective identities, and the need for greater 'intercultural competence' in digital environments.

Paul Resta, Mark Christal and *Loriene Roy* explore the ways in which Native people in the United States are re-developing their culture, heritage and education, and the manner in which they have adopted and adapted Western technology. They seek to overcome the tendency for digital technology to become an expression of cultural imperialism and develop its potential to improve the lives of indigenous people in a way that is congruent with the indigenous worldview. Their suggestion that other indigenous cultures and nations should explore the development of appropriate protocols and strategies clearly relates to discussion elsewhere in the collection of the relationship between digital technology and education within and between diverse communities and cultures. Their powerful argument clearly generalizes to other contexts and communities.

The notion that communication technologies can support the learning of, and give voice to the experience of, displaced and potentially excluded people is clearly appealing. The experience of using digital technology with refugee children across Europe presented by *Liesbeth de Block* and *Julian Sefton-Green* leads us, however, to be less sanguine and pay greater attention to complex local social contexts in and through which children establish their identities. They stress that, while there is potential to use communication technologies to connect diaspora over time, displaced children's day-to-day priorities relate to the demands of their immediate social environment. The chapter thus emphasizes the more general point that effective application of digital technologies is always challenging because they need to be embedded within diverse local contexts. In addition, we need to be clear that our aspirations as adults, and the aspirations of policy makers, frequently do not match the priorities and circumstances of children. For the children in this project, the virtual contacts appeared to have greatest potential when they related to current shared popular culture rather than past experiences.

From a corporate perspective, *Michelle Selinger* considers what constitutes culturally appropriate pedagogy. Currently an education consultant for Cisco Systems, an international corporation specializing in Internet networking technology, Selinger draws on her experience as a teacher educator and distance education specialist to survey the Cisco Academies. These were established by Cisco Systems to educate people in over 150 countries worldwide in the use of networking technologies. She argues that the translation of global e-learning into local cultural terms and the use of appropriate pedagogies by local instructors is crucial in making training effective. On the basis of this, she recommends the further development of communication technologies to engage instructors more fully, as a community of learners themselves, in the improvement of the quality of pedagogy and resources to address the diversity of cultures and languages worldwide. The commercial corporate context addressed by this chapter is important because companies are diversifying opportunities in education and, as Haddad and Draxler (2002) note, there is an increasingly urgent need to respond to increasing demands for education worldwide.

Marsha A. Gartland, Scott R. Imig, Robert F. McNergney and *Marla L. Muntner*, like Ferdig and colleagues in the previous section, have created resources to put digital technologies to work. They, too, use case studies and have developed a 'case method' for intercultural education in the digital age. Simulations are known to be effective uses of digital technologies in education and this chapter extends simulation to intercultural teacher education. The chapter provides more than a description of a multimedia project: it also explains the pedagogical approach in some depth and helps us appreciate the ingredients of a good case that incorporates engagement with intercultural issues.

The project to create a transatlantic community for doctoral students conducting research on ICT and education, discussed by *Andrew Brown* and *Niki Davis*, provides a transition between consideration of the challenges of intercultural communication and the development strategies for community building through digital technology, addressed in the final section. It was in building this transatlantic community, motivated by the same factors that stimulate the study of intercultural communication including an imperative of peace (Martin and Nakayma, 2000), that Davis came to realize that the idea of culture shock, normally associated with physically living within an unfamiliar 'foreign' community, has much to offer our understanding of intercultural interaction in online communities. Their project aims to develop the intercultural competence of the next generation of leaders in educational digital technologies, both through opportunities to travel to become physically part of an unfamiliar research community in other countries and through Web based learning with doctoral students from other settings and cultures. In this way it is intended that students and their university tutors can come to know themselves and others professionally and personally from multiple perspectives.

Building communities

The chapters in this section provide specific instances and realizations of the themes introduced and explored in preceding sections. The purpose is to provide insight into particular examples of the use of digital technology in building communities.

Elsebeth K. Sorensen and *Eugene S. Takle* have developed a complementary transatlantic partnership between their courses, such that Sorensen's Danish students, who are specialists in the use of digital technologies, advise and critically reflect on the ongoing development of Takle's digitally enhanced meteorology course on global change. The collaboration over the years has permitted them to compare their academic cultures, which vary in both in terms of location and discipline. They also bring together intercultural challenges and the building of communities. As with other projects, there is an important social semiotic dimension to their analysis.

Thérèse Laferrière, Alain Breuleux and *Gaalen Erickson* have been working across universities and schools to build large telecollaborative communities of practice in education within and beyond regions of Canada. They describe a synergy, and possibly another instance of collective intelligence, between the groups of actors that include teacher educators, student teachers and school pupils.

Chapter 18 by *Márta Turcsányi-Szabó* on the use of tele-houses in rural Hungary to support education, demonstrates how careful theory-based planning can increase capacity. This chapter provides further examples of activities designed to bridge the digital divide and bring resources into regions challenged by their geography and place in society. Turcsányi-Szabó brings a systemic view to planning and strategic development in the use of digital technologies to raise the profile of marginalized and disenfranchized communities. Her quote from a participant is particularly revealing in relation to the two-way communication that digital technologies allow: 'It is not only our eyes that have been opened, but that of the world too, to see us.'

Christina Preston and *Laura Lengel* have also been supporting development in the 'New Europe' that includes Hungary. Their chapter describes the way in which two communities of professionals who lead ICT in education can enhance the work of each other using communication technologies by building communities of practice between the old and the new Europe.

The final chapter of this *World Yearbook* presents a complex and systemic approach to the renewal education in Chile facilitated by ICT. *Pedro Hepp, J. Enrique Hinostroza* and *Ernesto Laval* present an overview of the Enlaces (which translates into English as 'Links') project, which has been held up as a model by several world agencies including UNESCO and the World Bank, and won the Society for Information Technology in Teacher Education 2003 award for Digital Equity in Technology in Teacher Education. The project is noted for the quality of its systematic planning, which recognizes the need for shared leadership and local interpretation of the teacher education and school support components of the initiative. It is also a story that starts with indigenous people and ends with a visionary aim to connect with 100 per cent of the school population in Chile, including the most remote school in Antarctica. This systemic approach to educational renewal catalysed with new technologies provides us with many clues for the integration of digital technologies in the service of education worldwide and the development of our collective intelligence in this area.

Digital technology, communities and education in 2004

The 2004 *Yearbook of Education* presents a range of perspectives, from key researchers and practitioners in the field, on the use of digital technologies in formal and informal educational settings in and across diverse cultures and communities. In doing so, a number of common themes, outlined in the preceding discussion, have emerged. Authors have repeatedly emphasized that technology must be situated in existing social, cultural, political and economic conditions and systems. They have also stressed the importance of the recognition of complexity (Davis, 2002) and the need for respect for diversity. Digital technology is seen as offering, but not determining, a range of possibilities for the development of learning and teaching and in the creation and enhancement of communities, including communities of learners and teachers. Our intention has been to present a culturally nuanced and informed account of current thinking and practice in an area that is in the throes of rapid change and development, and in doing so make a timely contribution to international debate and literature in the field.

References

BECTA (2003) [accessed 2 September 2003] ImpaCT2 The impact of information and communication technologies on pupil learning and attainment, ICT in schools research and evaluation series, number 7, British Education and Communication Technology Agency, London [Online] http://www.becta.org. uk/page_documents/research/ImpaCT2_strand1_report.pdf.

Castells, M. (1996) *The Rise of the Network Society*, Blackwell, Malden.

Castells, M. (1997) An Introduction to the Information Age, *City*, 1 (7), pp. 6–16.

Davis, N. (2002) Leadership of information technology for teacher education: a discussion of complex systems with dynamic models to inform shared leadership, *Journal of Information Technology for Teacher Education*, 11, pp. 253–71.

Haddad, W. and Draxler, A. (eds) (2002) [accessed 2 September 2003] *Technologies For Education: Potential, parameters and prospects*, UNESCO and Academy for Educational Development [Online] http://www.aed.org/publications/TechEdInfo.html.

Martin, J. N. and Nakayama, T. K. (2000) *Intercultural Communication in Contexts*, 2nd edn, Mayfield Publishing, Mountain View, CA.

Part I
Digital transformations

1 Learning, a semiotic view in the context of digital technologies

Gunther Kress

'Learning'

One of the currently focal concerns – and not just in education – is that of 'learning'. By this I mean that the term and the issue have acquired a degree of public presence, and maybe fashionability that goes well beyond the clearly necessary constant interest in the issue in education. It is reflected in such phrases as 'the learning society', 'the learning organization', 'life-long and life-wide learning', etc. That degree of interest itself requires explanation, for whenever a term gains such currency, something is going on reaching deeper than the focal issue itself. That, however, is not the concern of this chapter.

Here I want to make a rather different argument for a necessary rethinking of theories of learning, founded on a new theory of meaning. I do this for two reasons: one, in order to be able to deal with another current preoccupation, namely the call for education to 'deliver' creativity, innovation, and so on, or to express this better, for education to 'produce' young people who have dispositions towards creativity, innovation and ease with change. The other reason is that current social, political, economic, cultural arrangements are such that dispositions of this kind will indeed be essential for the young to deal with that world in productive participation in social life. Current theories of learning are founded on theories of meaning developed in an era constituted entirely differently, around the assumptions of stable systems, replicability of forms, processes and actions, of adherence to convention and its rules, whether in language or other modes of representation, or in social, economic and cultural practices much more generally.

These theories are unable to meet these demands. To characterize them briefly: they are based on language as the (central, major) means for making meaning; they stress the centrality of the system (of language), with its entities and rules. They focus on competence as the user's understanding, knowledge of, ability and adherence to the use of the system according to its conventions. Hence the stability of the system, guaranteed by convention (as the expression of the application of social power) is the central issue. Neither creativity nor innovation are features of the system as such; rather they exist as transgressions of its normal functioning and as such they are permitted to rare, socially sanctioned individuals – poets, advertisers – or they are illegitimately engaged in by others – rock-bands, stylistically marginal groups such as punks, and so on.

Theories of meaning inform and underpin conceptions of learning. To stay with language just for a moment: my task as a user of language is to adhere to the rules, the conventions of the system of language; equally, as a learner of language (whether as a child learning a first language or as an adult learning (another) language) my task is to 'adapt' myself to the conventions, to the entities and rules of the system. That is what is seen as gaining competence. What is the case with language is so with other social–cultural resources and practices – whether cooking, gardening, singing, or learning chemistry or maths. The still dominant conception of meaning and learning is founded on an acceptance of the authority of the system (of language, of practices, etc.) and its conventions over the actions and desires of an individual. In that sense it is authoritarian; and in that sense it is the very opposite to the means for engendering dispositions towards innovation, creativity, ease with change. It is in that respect that we need a theory of meaning which is apt both for the new social, cultural and economic givens, and as the basis for requisite apt theories of learning.

As a specific instance of the new givens, a fundamental rearrangement has been taking place in the area of representation and communication, which is having its impact on ways of making meaning and on possibilities for learning. It concerns both the modes for representation – hitherto seen largely as that of language – and the media of production and dissemination – hitherto dominantly the media of print and paper, the book foremost among them. To put it briefly at this point: the mode of image is taking over the role hitherto held by the mode of writing, in many domains of public communication, those of education at all levels included; and the medium of the screen is taking over the place that had hitherto been occupied by the book. This rearrangement in the constellation of modes of representation and media of dissemination – from writing and book to image and screen – is having profound consequences for meaning-making and hence for learning.

These are developments that are everywhere tied into developments at larger levels, those of globalization (to use a current shorthand for a vast and complex range of phenomena) and of its effects being at the forefront.

In this context I will now give a brief sketch of a semiotic view of learning, focusing on: (1) a brief (and unorthodox) theory of signs; (2) the notion of modes of representation and of their logics; (3) their interrelation with 'shapes of knowledge'; (4) the issue of multimodality;

(5) the new forms of semiotic engagement with the world of representation and communication; (6) the facilities of the new media; and
(7) the notion of design and its interlinking with changed dispositions
towards information and knowledge.

Signs: 'interest', transformations and 'signs of learning'

The unit of semiotic production and analysis is the sign, an entity in
which meaning and form are fused. (This is in contrast to linguistic
approaches in which grammatical and syntactic entities are seen as separate from semantic entities – syntax dealing with formal arrangements,
semantics with those of meaning. It is also in contrast to certain psychological approaches which deal with the notion of 'concept', an entity
which has existence in the 'mind', but without specific physical/material
realization.) One traditional account of the sign assumes that meaning
and form – signified and signifier – are linked arbitrarily and by convention. The example used by Saussure is that of a sign like that of the
French word 'arbre', where there seems no particular reason why the
signifier/sound shape /a:bre/ should be linked with the signified 'tree'
(or, in English, the sound shape /tri:/ should be linked with the signified 'tree'). If in a game of chess for instance, a piece is lost, say a pawn
or a castle, we can use a button to replace it – there is, it seems, an arbitrary relation between the form of the piece and its 'meaning/function'.
However, if it was the black pawn that was lost, and we had one white
and one black button, it is likely that we would use the black button to
stand in for the black piece – even though the white button would do.

The choice of black would not have been arbitrary; the decision to
allow a button to stand for a chess piece would rest on the convention
that my chess-partner and I had devised, and adhered to. Had we lost
two black pieces, say a pawn and a castle, and we had two buttons of
different sizes, I assume that we would use the bigger button to stand
in for the piece with the higher value. That choice would not have been
an arbitrary one: in this case, the size of button standing in for 'size'
(i.e. the value) of the piece. But had both of us lost a piece, then the
choice of colour would become pretty well fixed and non-arbitrary: we
would be unlikely to want to replace a white piece with a black button
and vice versa.

Let me now use a real example, one that has become criterial for me.
A three year old, sitting on his father's lap, draws a series of circles,
seven to be exact. At the end he says 'this is a car'. The result is shown
in Figure 1.1. The question arises as to how this is or could be a car.
While drawing he had said, 'Here's a wheel, here's another wheel, that's
a funny wheel. ... This is a car.' In other words, for him the criterial
feature of a 'car' was that it had (many) wheels. His sign was a representation of that which was criterial for him about the car, its 'wheelness'.

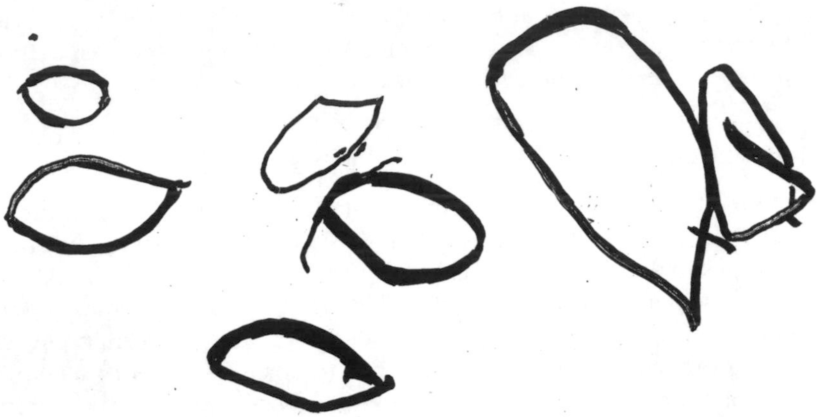

Figure 1.1 This is a car

Wheels, the signified, were represented by circles, the signifiers; and 'car', the signified, was represented by the arrangement of seven circles. To represent wheels by circles rests on the process of analogy: wheels are like circles. The result of the analogy is a metaphor; and similarly with the representation of car by many circles. Hence in this case the sign is a (double) metaphor: wheels are (like) circles, and many circles are (like) a car.

We might further ask why for this child wheels could be the criterial feature for 'car'. If we imagine the height of a three year old, looking at the family car (in this case a 1982 VW Golf, with its very prominently visible wheels, especially at that eye-level) we might conclude that this sign-maker's position in the world – literally, but also psychically, affectively – might well lead him to see cars in that way. His sign therefore represents his 'interest', his position in the world at that moment vis-à-vis the object to be represented.

I want to draw out a number of features from this: it is the interest of the sign-maker which determines what is regarded as criterial about an entity to be represented; that which is criterial determines what is to be represented about that entity; and only what is seen as criterial is represented. Hence representation is always partial: and that is the case about this car as much as it is the case about the representation of a car in an advertisement. The sign-maker chooses the most apt means for representing that which is to be represented – in this case circles are apt signifiers for wheels. There is a relation of motivation, we might say an iconic relation, between form and meaning. It is in no way an arbitrary relation. In this instance, the sign is established on the basis of an analogy between form and meaning; the form is an apt means for representing the meaning. The sign is a metaphor which expresses how the sign-maker sees that which he wishes to represent. Above all, the sign is newly made, on the basis of how the sign-maker sees the world and wishes to represent it. The sign expresses the sign-maker's interest. This sign is new: it is an innovation, and it is creative, in the usual sense of those words. The sign is as much an indication of the sign-maker's place in the world (in relation to this entity that he represents); it is about him as much as it is about the entity itself. It expresses his interest vis-à-vis the entity to be represented, and it expresses his place in the world.

In the semiotic theory of signs which I have sketched here, a social semiotic theory, I take this instance as paradigmatic of all sign-making, and assume that the features which I have drawn out here apply and are active in all sign-making: signs are always newly made on the basis of the interest of the maker; they are metaphors that represent the maker's stance in relation to that which is to be represented and of the maker's place in the world; the relation of signifier to signified is never arbitrary; it aptly realizes the maker's criteria in representation.

If we look at this from the point of view of learning, the following might be said: the sign which the child has made gives us an insight into his 'stance' in the world, with respect to this specific entity. But as a general principle we can take signs to be just that: an indication of the 'interest' of the sign-maker, in relation to the specific bit of the world that is at issue. It is an indication of the 'shape' and the characteristics of his interest and engagement with the world, and an indication of his experience of the world. The sign made is a sign of all that.

In fact, we can go a step further. The circles made by the child have a history: from energetic circular tracings with whatever instrument had been to hand, to a gradual and increasing regularity in the circularity of the traces, to the making of individual circular shapes. This describes a history of some 18 months, in which time there was a constant transformation of these shapes towards the regularity of the circles. The use of the individual circles in an arrangement, as here, was the most recent transformation in that sequence. In that constant and ceaseless transformation the child was constantly transforming his resources for outward representation; but at the same time, each time, also transforming his 'inner' resources for representation. At the point marked by the production of this sign he used these resources to make a representation of an object in the world – a gain in terms of his inner 'capacities' and in his resources for representing. He had gradually taught himself to make circles, and he had used that resource for this act of representation. He had learned to make circles, and he had learned how to use this resource for representation.

The sign of the car is a sign of that learning. In my view, signs made outwardly are the best evidence that we have for learning. Of course, 'learning' is not a term that belongs in semiotics; 'sign-making' is. Learning belongs in psychology. However, 'learning' is the name given to an inner transformation in resources as a result of sign-making, and to its outer consequences in terms of the resources for representing now available to the sign-maker. Learning is conceptual and cognitive change when it happens in a pedagogical environment in the presence of a curriculum, that is, of a (formal or informal) schedule for engagement with specific knowledge in order to produce such change. Sign-making and learning are two sides of one piece of paper, as Saussure might have said: one side regarded from the point of view of semiotics, the other from that of pedagogy and psychology.

Here is another example, this time from a science classroom; the sign-makers are 13-year-old girls. They have been studying plant cells over four lessons; now they have been asked by their teacher to prepare a slide of an onion's epidermis, view it under the microscope, and then to report what they did: the teacher has asked them to 'write what they did' and 'to draw what they have seen'. The teacher asked that they should put their written report first, at the top of the page, with the drawing underneath, and not to use colour pencils in their drawing. Four girls were working around the one microscope having made the one slide. Two of their reports and drawings are shown in Figures 1.2 and 1.3.

Apart from the fact that the first does have the drawing at the top, there are startling differences, if we remember that they had sat through the same lessons, and had prepared and looked at the same slide. I won't go into detail here, having discussed the differences and their significance in some other places (see, for instance, Kress 2001, 2003; Kress and Van Leeuwen, 2001). However, what is clear is that each has made very different selections from all the masses of material offered during the lessons, and the discussions among the four girls, and transformed them in their specific ways. What had appeared in the mode of writing on a handout sheet ('the cells will look like bricks in a brickwall') appears in the different mode of image; what had appeared in the mode of speech by one of the girls as talk around the microscope also appears in the different mode of image ('it looks like a wavy weave').

The teacher's instruction to 'write what you did' is transformed in a specific way by each of the two: once as 'report', and once as 'procedure'. In the examples the notion of transformation is clear: something presented is taken up in specific ways, and is re-presented in relation to each sign-maker's interest: one girl's interest is to stay close to the prediction of the handout, but in that she also prefers to present what she saw in a theoretical form – 'this is what it is like in theory'. The other girl's interest is to stay close to what the teacher might have said about the virtue of accurate observation, as essentially 'scientific'.

<u>Looking at onion cells</u>   <u>26/11/9?</u>

What was the magnification?
Can you label any of the parts?

26 November 199

<u>Looking at cells</u>

<u>What I did.</u>   ✓

At first Amanda and I collect
all the equipment. Amanda peeled
the skin off the onion, while
I got the microscope. Amanda
put the onion-skin on the slide,
then I put a drop of iodine
on the onion the we put a
cover slip on top of it. We then
sorted the microscope out then

We put the slide under neath
on the stage.
We then looked in the ey
piece. It was an ~~moving~~ inter ✓
to look at and ~~draw~~.
draw.

Good but make sure you copy
up missed work.

Figure 1.2 Onion cells: theory

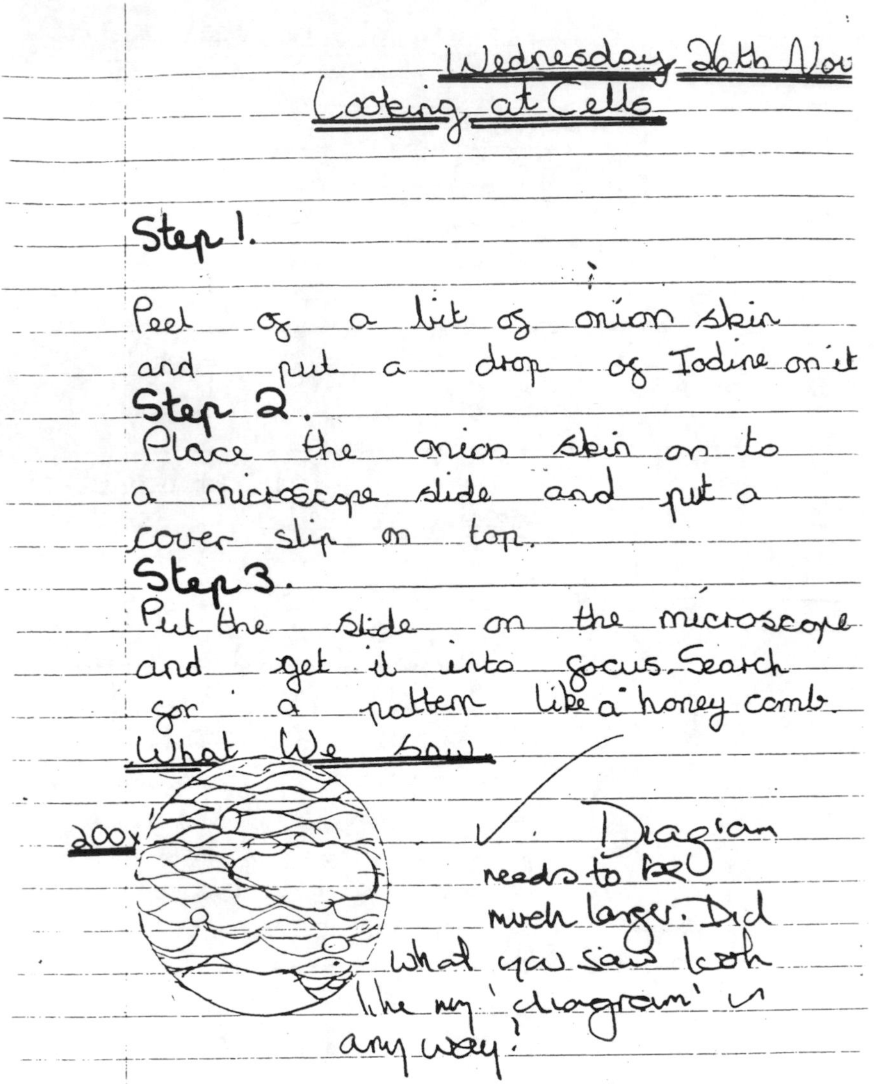

Wednesday 26th Nov

Looking at Cells

Step 1.

Peel of a bit of onion skin
and put a drop of Iodine on it

Step 2.

Place the onion skin on to
a microscope slide and put a
cover slip on top.

Step 3.

Put the slide on the microscope
and get it into focus. Search
for a pattern like a honey comb.

What We Saw

200x

✓ Diagram
needs to be
much larger. Did
what you saw look
like my 'diagram' in
any way?

Figure 1.3 Onion cells: eye-piece

One takes 'write what you did' to mean 'report accurately what you actually did'; the other takes it to mean 'present a regularized account of what should happen'. The complex signs made by each are the result of complexes of transformations, each reflecting the interests of each girl, their sense of what 'being scientific' might mean. Both are signs of learning: they are precise accounts of what the result of the girls' engagement with the lessons and their demands had been.

A teacher who is interested in learning – rather than in testing what has been absorbed/acquired in an older sense of learning – would, using this approach, be able to discover much about the students' engagement with the subject, their understanding, the similarities as well as the differences in their sense of what being scientific is, in short, get a real sense of their learning. The texts are precise records of just that. They are signs of learning.

Modes of representation: materiality, logics and affordances

In the 'cells examples' just discussed, writing and image are each used in quite specific ways, to do specific tasks. Without being too detailed, writing is used to represent what happened – actions and events in sequence, once in the genre of report and once in the genre of procedure, and image is used to represent what was visually present in the world observed. The two modes were, it seems, used for differential engagement with the world, and for differential representation of the world. This might seem obvious, except that, as I just mentioned, on the handout the look of the cells had been represented using writing, and in the girls' discussion around the microscope it had been represented in speech. In other words, there is a choice of what mode to use, and therefore a question as to which mode might be better, and for what reasons, and what the effect of the choices might be. In order to establish this I wish to use the notion of 'logics' of modes.

Speech happens in time, and that which is represented in speech has to be represented in temporal sequence, willy-nilly. It is impossible to escape this logic of temporal sequence. One sound follows another, one word another, one clause another. In that sequence order is established: something has to be first, something else second, and something has to be last. Meaning attaches to being first, to being second, to being last, and so on. Cultures will make their choices as to what 'last' is to mean; that is open to the culture. In my culture to say 'Amanda married Josh' means something different to 'Josh married Amanda'. The meaning of that difference is not entirely fixed – it might be that I am Josh's friend, and signal that by making his name thematic or topical in my utterance. It might be that Amanda is the sort of woman whom I judge to

Figure 1.4 Georgia's drawing

go out to get her man, and so I mention her name first to suggest that she was the agentive one in that process. What is not open is that 'lastness' will be significant, and will differ from 'firstness'. Temporal sequence – unfolding, happening in time – is conceptually close to action-ality, to event; and so it is little surprise that narrative should be both such a dominant genre, and should be represented among all human cultures – all those which rely on speech as their most significant repre-sentational mode. The logic of speech is organized and founded on the logic of time, and of sequence in time.

Image, by contrast, is organized by the logic of space. That which I wish to represent has to be depicted in space, and the relations between the elements that I wish to depict have to be displayed through the semiotic means of space. In the image in Figure 1.4 the relations between Georgia (age 4) and her parents, and her sense of her place in her family, are handled through the affordances of space: where she places herself in the image, the size at which she represents herself, the framing struc-ture that she constructs, the relative size of her parents, and so on.

Georgia could have depicted herself next to her mother, on the left of the image; the meaning of the image would have been a quite different one. The logic of space and spatial relations organizes the possibilities of meaning: it is one of the basic – may be the most basic affordance of the image, just as that of time and sequence is for speech.

Of course with the mode of image come other features, for instance that of colour and its use to make meaning. In speech there is not only sequence but also the many features of sound: pitch variation to produce the 'melody of the voice', intonation; energy in articulation to produce accent and rhythm; the modulation of sound by the speech organs to produce sound qualities, etc. All of these material aspects of mode are available for making meaning, and are used in different cultures in quite specific ways. In English, for instance, intonation is used in the meanings of affect, but is also used to make grammatical/syntactic meaning – the voice rising at the end of a speech-unit conveying the meaning 'openness', 'incompleteness', 'hesitation', which has become conventionalized in one form as 'question'.

Modes have materiality; and that materiality leads to potentials for making meaning used differently in the histories of different cultures. The affordances of modes are always the product of the material and its inherent logics, and of the work of cultures, often over very long historical periods with that materiality and its logics.

Modes and the shaping of 'knowledge'

If we wished to present the meaning of Georgia's depiction of herself in her family in speech or writing, the task would be one not just of translation – that is, of a restatement, a re-presentation in the same mode with its affordances – but one of a fundamental re-conceptualization of that meaning through and in the affordance of a different mode: that which had been represented through the logics of spatial arrangement has to be recast in the logic of the fundamentally different logic of temporal sequence. That which had not depended on the relation between nouns by a verb now has to be represented in that manner: 'I am standing between my Mum and my Dad'. Apart from the utter flatness of this utterance compared to its meaning in the image, Georgia did not have to name – to lexicalize – the relation between herself and her parents in the image; in speech or writing she would have to do so. Something that is represented as a relation in space now has to be given a name – 'standing between' – and has to be represented as relation of action between nouns, in time. Knowledge is profoundly differently configured in the two modes.

I use the term transduction for this entirely ordinary activity of re-expressing something that had been represented in one mode and its terms and meanings, in the terms of another mode and its meanings. In that process the shape – the ontological and epistemological configuration of that which we call knowledge – is always changed. Each mode brings with it epistemological commitments of quite specific kinds, commitments which cannot be avoided if I use the mode. Georgia, in drawing her image, has to place her depiction of herself somewhere, she cannot avoid that – to one side of her mother, or of her father, or, as she did, between them. But having made the choice, a specific meaning attaches to that choice; it cannot be avoided. In speech, on the other hand, some element has to be first, another second, another third, and another last. Meaning attaches to these placements; in languages such as English, first position brings with it the meaning of topic or theme, and in nearly all cases, even if weakly so, the meaning of 'agent of the action named by the verb'. In such languages, first position of noun tends to imply causal initiation; if there is a sequence of clauses, the first clause tends to be interpreted as causally related to the following clause: 'Jane came into the room, and Fred left.'

In Figures 1.5 and 1.6 I present an example from a different science class, also of 13 year olds, and a different topic, that of blood circulation. These examples also come at the end of a sequence of lessons on blood circulation. In the first case they are homework, where the teacher had asked the children to write 'a story' imagining their journey as a red blood cell around the body. Given that the task was vaguely specified – a 'story', the children responded with a wide range of genres – diary, scientific report, medieval fairy tale, James Bond adventure and others. However, that is not my point here; rather it is to show up the difference in the shape of knowledge between the representation in a mode organized according to temporal logic, writing and one of its genres, as against the representation in a mode organized according to spatial logic, image and one of its genres. That is illustrated in the concept map, a task the children performed working in pairs, in class. In the 'diary' the relevant entities are organized by temporal sequence and the stages of the journey of the blood cell, leaning on reality, within the possibilities of the particular genre used; in the concept map the order is not provided by the real world but is constructed and imposed by the maker of the map. This order is one of a hierarchy devised by the children. Entirely different principles are at issue here: not those of the real world (even though mediated) as in the diary, but those of the world of science mediated by theory.

The significant point is the differing forms which that which we regard as 'knowledge' necessarily assumes when it is realized in any specific mode. This is crucial from the perspective of learning, as it shapes the possibilities of human engagement with knowledge. Materially and physiologically – which senses are engaged? Semiotically and socially – what representational preferences do the students have, speech and narrative or image and display? Ontologically and epistemologically – which representation seems most apt, or connects most with the students' position in their world? And so on.

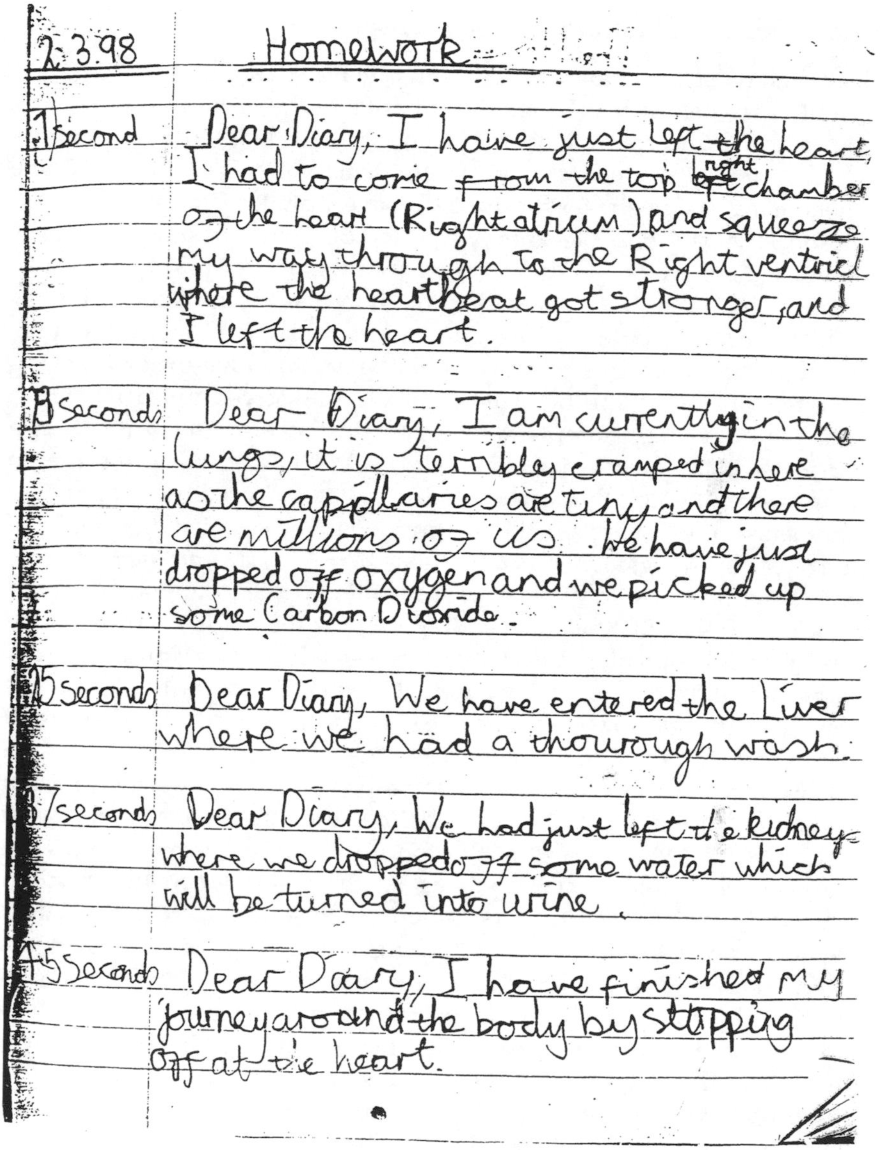
2.3.98 Homework

1 second Dear Diary, I have just left ~~the~~ heart, I had to come ~~from~~ the top ~~left~~ right chamber of the heart (Right atrium) and squeeze my way through to the Right ventricel where the heartbeat got stronger, and I left the heart.

13 seconds Dear Diary, I am currently in the lungs, it is terribley cramped in here as the capillaries are tiny and there are millions of us. We have just dropped off oxygen and we picked up some Carbon Dioxide.

25 seconds Dear Diary, We have entered the Liver where we had a thourough wash.

37 seconds Dear Diary, We had just left the kidney where we dropped off some water which will be turned into urine.

45 seconds Dear Diary, I have finished my journey around the body by stopping off at the heart.

Figure 1.5 Blood circulation: diary

Multimodality: looking at modal ensembles

In the onion cell example, the text consisted of image and writing: it is a multimodal ensemble. I suggested that there are reasons for choosing the modes as the young women did, basically in line with the inherent and cultural affordances – writing for temporally existent, event-like phenomena, and image for those which have spatial existence and organization. It is now possible to move to two different questions: one asks whether there are what I have called functional specializations in this, and whether in any message-entity, text information and knowledge are differentially distributed between the modes, what I have called the functional load in a text; the other question begins to move towards asking how this interacts with the facilities of the new screen-based media.

In the onion cell example we might say that that which is the real curricular issue – what is a plant cell (like)? – is realized in the drawn images, even though the teacher seems to have focused, judging by his comments, much more on the writing. I would say that the mode of image carries the greater functional load. We can become more specific in this: writing is used to deal with scientific procedure; image is used to deal with scientific fact. Depending on how the teacher – or we – see this, we can then make evaluations of greater subtlety about the matter of functional load. It is not inconceivable after all, that a teacher might assume that what makes science science is precisely its concern with procedures and their characteristics.

If we take another example, more complex, we can go further. Earlier in the sequence of lessons on blood circulation, the teacher had drawn a circle on the white board; at the top of the circle a symbol indicated the heart. This image/diagram was on the board when the children entered the classroom after a break. In the lesson the teacher modified the circle several times: by drawing arrows on it as he suggested the direction in which the blood was moving and which organs it was 'visiting'; by adding a second loop on the top (as seen in Figure 1.7) to indicate that the structure was in fact more complex. However, he also 'modified' the diagram in other ways, not visible afterwards, by gesturing with his hand over the diagram, for example moving his hand over it in the direction of the blood's circulation and placing his hand lightly on the diagram at various points to indicate the organs visited: 'It goes to the lungs ... to the small intestine ... to the cells ... to the heart ....' This gestural overlay modified the diagram, just as did his actions/gestures '... it needs something to start pumping ...' accompanied by bellows-like action with the elbows and arms pressing into the body; or contracting gestures with his hands made into fists, to indicate the squeezing action of the heart, a gesture made several times in quick succession.

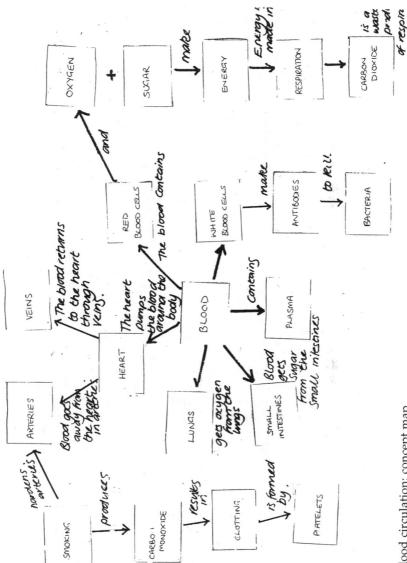

Figure 1.6 Blood circulation: concept map

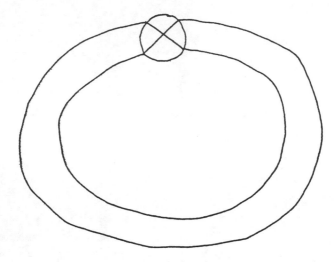

Figure 1.7 Blood circulation: teacher's drawing

Here we have several modes – speech, diagram, gesture, also the teacher's positioning – used in an orchestrated fashion by the teacher. It becomes more complex to understand what the functional specialization of the modes are here, or their functional load, and the effect of their interrelation and interaction in the teacher's orchestration. I will briefly mention two aspects: the hugely abstracted representation of 'blood circulation' remains on the board throughout the whole lesson, even later when the teacher places a 3D model onto the bench in front of him, or takes a text-book and shows, towards the end of the lesson, how all this is represented in canonical form in a book. In that way, that large abstraction forms the constant backdrop to the teacher's gradual building up of detail: constantly there, and yet constantly modified from moment to moment. Neither speech nor writing could fulfil that task. The gestural overlay over this image serves the function of beginning to add detail of a specific kind; yet once the gesture has been made, it is also gone – no real trace of it remains. This has great advantages for the teacher: the lungs are not actually 'there' where the gesture had placed them, nor is the small intestine 'there' next to the lungs on that circle. Nor for that matter are the cells either an organ in the way the lungs are, nor 'there' where the gesture had placed them.

Here we see, briefly, one function of speech – as before to name, to lexicalize – the cells everywhere in the body are given a name (as a noun) like that of other organs, and thus classified as the same, and like other organs, with a specific location. In this part of the lesson sequence speech tends to have that function: to follow the other modes, giving names to actions, processes, entities which have been established through image or gesture or action. If the teacher had actually drawn the organs onto the circle that would have been a problem in two ways: through the epistemological commitment given – 'the lungs are there' – when plainly they are not; and through the classification of cells as an organ like other organs, when plainly they are not. The transience of the gesture serves well in that respect: it makes the point that needs to be made, and then it is gone. The classificatory act of naming serves its purpose, differently: it brings an entity into existence following the gesture, but gives it no visible form. As a 'word' it is not a problem here, but an image would be; the word can be dealt with later, whereas as an image would be unsustainable epistemologically, and its use would undermine the credibility of the whole performance.

From here I can go on to begin to answer the second question, and make some suggestions about the relation of this representational aspect of communication and the facilities of the new media, and their joint effects on the possibilities for learning. The two cultural technologies, those of representation – writing, image, gesture, speech – and those of dissemination – book, magazine, TV, the 'new media' – are of course always intricately linked and yet also separate. From the perspective of learning, the new media do two things first and foremost: they change the relations of author and reader in fundamental ways; and they make possible much greater and freer use of modal ensembles – they are more open to fuller multimodal representation than the page and print based media were and still are.

Here I will focus on that second aspect for a moment, and return to it in a following section. The new media make possible a wider use of modes, and therefore open up in quite different ways the possibilities of choice of modes in relation to the wishes of 'authors' and their sense of their relations both to what is to be represented, and to the needs and characteristics of their audience. To put it differently, the new media are rhetorically much more open, more flexible, and permit something much closer to the rhetorical action of the teacher in the classroom than did the older media, especially those of the page. If the teacher's actions were finely adjusted to the learning needs of the children in the classroom, then we might expect that the new media permit much more of this, with consequences for learning.

Media and reading paths: the new forms of semiotic engagement with the world of representation and communication

At this point I want to change tack for a moment or two, to come at this issue from a different angle. Ostensibly it concerns the question of how we read (and produce) texts, though it goes, as I will attempt to

show, even wider, to larger social questions of authority, and epistemological questions around the production of knowledge. I want to start by
considering the relations of modes and media – of writing and book and
of image and screen. The book and writing have shared a history, in
Western Europe, for some 500 years, so much so since the use of move-
able type that at times the technology of writing and its uses and fortunes
have been identified with the medium of the book. Writing had shaped
the (look of) the page, so much so that the manner in which pages
had been constructed and were to be read had become 'naturalized': from
top left to bottom right each line in turn (or in the Arabic or Hebrew
alphabetic cultures, from top left to bottom right with changes also to the
directionality of pages in the book themselves). This reading direction
– a reading path – was so naturalized that its existence attracted no
attention; it was not noticed.

Images have, with some exceptions (such as images constructed
around timelines, flowcharts, etc.), no necessary or obvious reading
path. In Georgia's image, there is no reason to start with her own
figure; though if we did, we are not then required to move either to
the figure of her mother or to that of her father next. In the onion cells
examples, we can start from the written part of the text or from the
image part; and this openness – or indeterminacy – is a feature of most
images. To put it differently: on the traditional page the reading path
is set and fixed by the author, and by the conventions which author
and reader alike adhere to; with most images that is not the case. The
reader/viewer constructs the reading path, and does so according to
criteria arising out of their interest. The book was the site of writing;
the screen is the site of image – it is the contemporary canvas. If the
book and the page were structured and dominated by the logic of
writing, in many different ways, the screen is structured and dominated
by the logic of the image. The consequences of this for reading is beginning to become more and more apparent, both because writing is
becoming shaped by the image logic ruling the screen, and because
of the facility for multimodal text production, which leads to texts no
longer like those of the traditional written page. As the screens are becoming simultaneously the sites of multimodal texts, these are becoming
read in accordance with the spatial logic of image.

With the 'old' page and writing the task of the reader is to follow
along the line, adhering to the rigidly fixed order of the elements on the
line, one after the other in their sequence, as well as adhering to the
syntactic ordering of the elements. The order of elements on the line is
absolutely fixed; that of the elements in the syntax is also, more rather
than less. Hence the reader has no freedom as far as the order of elements
is concerned; however, the elements themselves – let us call them 'words'
somewhat too informally – are not fixed. Indeed words are quite vague,
not filled with meaning, but waiting to be filled with the user's meaning.

Words as names are vast generalizations. Hence each word/element needs to be filled with meaning by the reader, and to be made precise to the context of reading, in an act of interpretation. So reading of writing is adhering to rigid order, and to interpret the open and general elements within that rigid order: it is the paradoxical activity of interpreting 'open' elements lodged in a fixed order.

The image(-like) text is different: here the elements are full of meaning, but most often they exist in an open order, or in an order to be established by the reader/viewer. The depicted elements in a picture are 'plain with meaning': what is shown is what is meant to be seen, nothing more and nothing less. However the relationship of the depicted elements to each other is to be established and/or fixed by the reader. Depicted elements are always specific, rather than being general like words.

On the traditional page the world is ordered for the reader; with the new image(-like) texts the world is ordered by the reader. From elements available on the page the reader has to design their order: hence my slogan that the reading of new pages is reading as design. But in designing the new page in their reading, readers are creating their own text, expressing their interest through this (de)sign; they have become authors. That authorship may express itself in an immediate outwardly focused re-writing of the text, or it may exist as the inwardly focused production of the text. The reader designs the world of the text according to her or his interest: and that characterizes new forms and practices of reading.

Media and the facilities of the media: multimodality and authoring

When every reader is an author, authorship is no longer rare, so that which led to authority through and in texts before will no longer do so now. The social structures that existed to make authorship into authority do not exist for the texts produced with the new media. Hence while one facility of the new media has its positive aspects – making authorship available to all who have access to the technology, it has – seen from the former perspective – negative consequences, in separating authorship and authority. The older book relied on the author to work on behalf of the reader whose world and life and needs the author was assumed to know and understand, a knowledge which enabled them to produce the knowledge which readers would need to solve the problems in their lives. In a book first published in 1920, *The Boy Electrician*, the author says in his preface: 'if left to himself (the boy) will make things of such material as he has to hand . . . at seven he will wire the whole house with his telephone system . . . his elder brother will improve on this by purchasing a crystal' (Sims, 1920: 5).

The date of publication of my copy of the book is 1948; and indeed that notion of authorship remained current until very recently. The contents pages set out in stately order what the boy electrician will find in the book. It is knowledge gathered and organized for the needs of a specific audience. The author knows; he has knowledge for whose production (in some way) he is responsible. He has worked on behalf of the reader to assemble this knowledge. Each chapter is a large and coherent 'body of knowledge' in this ordered assemblage, in which the order of the chapters matters as much as the order of the pages in gaining access to this knowledge. The reader's task is to 'acquire', to 'absorb', not even to interpret so much as to faithfully decode. The author has worked on behalf of the reader, and it is the reader's responsibility to respect the author's work in every way.

The author not only knows what he presents, but also knows – as here – sufficient about the reader's circumstances, about their social and cultural positioning, the demands of their lives, to be confident that in some significant way his book and the knowledge it contains will answer to some real purpose in that life.

In this environment 'reading' is the task of following the order established by the author entirely, to be familiar with the code which the author has used in order to 'decode' the meaning which the author exposes in the text. This order goes from the ordering of the (word) elements on the line, following that order, following the order of the lines, of the paragraphs and pages, and the chapters. Order and authority are absolutely interwoven.

If we take a later book by contrast – a Dorling Kindersley fact book for the same age group – we find an entirely different organization. It is not that the author (usually now a design team) has not given thought to the reader, but it is the reader's less knowable interest which supplies the major organizing principle for this (usually double) page – now no longer chapters. In this double page spread most information is realized in image and the function of language is to gloss, to label, perhaps to expand and to link. It seems a page for 'browsing' – except that that term obscures what is in fact now a different manner of reading, as much as a quite different attitude to information and knowledge. This mode of reading originates not with the author's informed organization for the reader, but with the reader's own interest: what seems like browsing is the reader's principled search on the page for that which can become information in order to be transformed into knowledge by the reader in accordance with their interests. The pages of this book – in any case not only very differently organized – have no chapters, no page after page of slow development of a coherent, orderly presentation of knowledge. These double page spreads are resources for presenting material that might become information and be transformed by the reader into knowledge.

The process here is that the reader scans what is presented on the page – at that point it may not even have the status of information for the reader – selects what might serve as information in relation to a specific interest and question, and integrates and transforms that into what for them then becomes knowledge. In the earlier case knowledge is that which is assembled and produced for the reader by an author who knows the reader's needs; in the latter case knowledge is what the reader produces for themselves out of what they have selected as information.

To give one more example of this: the contents page and a page of text from the 1992 prospectus of the institution where I now work are presented in Figure 1.8. In many ways the similarities with *The Boy Electrician* are apparent: the institution as author sets out what it knows that the reader of this prospectus needs to know, in the order determined by the institution – in this case determined very much by the internal organization of the institution: its departmental structure, its courses, and so on. The institution knows what the reader will need, and it sets out the knowledge according to its own principles of order. If we think of the process of reading, the reading-path which the reader must take is clearly established. There is no possibility of deviation from it: it is laid out according to the institution's principles of organization, which provides the sense of what the reader will need.

If we look by contrast at the web site of this institution (Figure 1.9), we find an entirely different organization. Whereas the printed prospectus had a clear order for the reader to follow, here the ordering principle is entirely different. Now there are about 12 or 13 'entry points' to this home page, not one fixed point of entry. The ordering principle rests on an attempt to imagine the varying interests of those who will be 'visitors' to this site. From these entry points, oriented to these imagined interests, the visitor can go in any number of directions, guided by their interests. They are looking at the materials, seeking that which can become information in relation to their own purposes, which they will then transform into the knowledge that becomes the tool to solve their specific problem.

This is an inversion of the earlier situation; its consequences for practices are enormous; and that must be acknowledged and built into any new curricular design.

Here is the definition of knowledge which encapsulates this new situation: 'information is material which is selected by individuals to be transformed by them into knowledge to solve a problem in their life-world' (Boeck, 2003). This definition allows us to acknowledge what has always been the case, namely that knowledge relates to problems that arise in specific social domains – Schutz's 'life-worlds'. The fact that this was not – or less – recognized and admitted before is due to changed assumptions about power: in the era of the dominance of the state the

Contents

Foreword 7
History of the Institute 11
The Institute
School of the University 12
Objects 13
International Student Policy 13
Anti-Racist Practice 13
Equal Opportunities 13
Government and Structure 13
Student Numbers 14
The Institute Building 16
Courses of Study 17
The Departments 23
Centres 42
Research 47
Arts Centre 55
The Library 56
Publications 57
Educational Media (Services) 57
Student Information:
Fees 58
Grants Information 58
Studentships and Other Awards 59
Advanced Students Research Account 60
Secondment and Other Assistance to
Teachers 60
Tutorial and Advisory Arrangements 60
Data Protection 61
Universities' Statistical Record 61
Applicants with Physical Disabilities 61
Day Nursery 61
Union Society 62
Community Charge 62
Accommodation 62
Health Service 63
Chaplaincies 64
Map of Area 66
Cross-sections of Building 66
Overseas Student Information 67

Initial Teacher Education
Introduction 72
General Notes 73
Postgraduate Certificate in Education 76

BEd, Diploma and Short Courses
Introduction 88
BEd Honours Degree for Serving Teachers 89

General Notes on Diploma Courses 92
Diploma in Education 94
Diploma in Professional Studies 99
Courses for the BEd, Diploma in Education
and Diploma in Professional Studies 100
Specialist Diploma Courses
General Notes; Index of Diploma Courses 107
Associateship/LEA Teacher Fellowships 126
Short Courses of Study 128

Higher Degrees
Introduction 133
General Notes on Higher Degree Studies 134
Taught Master's Courses
List of Courses 136
General Notes 138
Master's Degrees in the Faculty of Education 140
Master's Degrees in Other Faculties 172
Research Degrees
MPhil in the Faculty of Education 174
MPhil in Other Faculties 175
PhD in the Faculty of Education 175
PhD in Other Faculties 177
Special Courses and Research
Opportunities 177

Postgraduate Certificate in Education

Senior Tutor responsible for Initial Training:
Michael Naish, MA

The Institute provides a one-year full-time course of professional training leading to the award of University of London Postgraduate Certificate in Education. Students pursuing the course will be training to teach in primary schools, or secondary schools, including sixth-form colleges, colleges of further education, or tertiary colleges.

Qualifications For Entry

The course of study and subsequent examination are open to graduates of the University of London, or other approved universities, and holders of the Diploma in Technology (Dip. Tech) or of a degree awarded by the Council for National Academic Awards which is accepted as an appropriate qualification or of a qualification giving graduate status which is acceptable to the University.

In accordance with DES Circular 9/78 all persons who become eligible to join the teaching profession on and after September 1984 must before entry to their course of teacher training have obtained a Pass (for examinations held before June 1975) or Grade A, B or C (for examinations held in and after June 1975) at GCE Ordinary level in English Language and in Mathematics (or its approved equivalent. A Grade A, B or C at the GCSE examinations is accepted as equivalent to a pass at GCE Ordinary level. Further details may be obtained from the Deputy Registrar.

Students without the necessary GCE Ordinary level (or equivalent) qualifications who apply for a PGCE (secondary age range) place after the last date for entry to the GCSE examinations and are provisionally offered a place, may apply to the Institute to sit a special qualifying examination in English Language and/or Mathematics. The cost of such an examination in 1989-90 is £35 per subject. The special qualifying examination will take place in the first week in September.

Candidates with general or pass degrees, or with honours degrees including more than one main subject, or in subjects not normally figuring in the school curriculum, can be considered for acceptance by the Institute.

How to Apply

Before making an application, all applicants should be familiar with the general notes on pp 73-5 above.

Both home and applicants from overseas* who wish to teach in the United Kingdom after they qualify should apply through the Graduate Teacher Training Registry, from whom forms of application and vacancy information are available from 1 September in the year preceding admission. The address is:

Graduate Teacher Training Registry,
3 Crawford Place,
London W1H 2BN.

In order to accelerate the despatch of GTTR literature all applicants are asked to enclose a self-addressed envelope, 10 x 7 inches, stamped 24p for second class, 30p for first class, or any equivalent postal tariff announced by the Post Office. (In the case of applicants applying from overseas the equivalent in international reply coupons should be sent.) Applications as early as possible after 1 September in the year preceding admission is strongly advised. Applicants who are offered a place will be required to confirm acceptance or refusal of the offer within a fortnight.

The Course of Study

The course of study, designed to prepare students for work in any of the three stages of education, primary, secondary and further (1944 Acts), will be based on partnership with schools and practising teachers and close integration

---

*Commonwealth applicants (but not those from Australia, Canada, New Zealand or Sri Lanka) who wish to return to their own country to teach, whether applying from overseas or from the United Kingdom, should not apply through the GTTR scheme, but should apply with the aid of their national education officer or the British Council in their own country

of theory and practice. The course will be school and Institute based and will include the following four elements:

1 Curriculum Subject Teaching
2 An Education component, which will draw on constituent disciplines
3 A Further Professional Option
4 Practical Training in Teaching

Each of the components seeks to elucidate the application of principles to practice and to help students to see the principles arising from the practical situations and problems they will encounter. The components are based on close co-operation with practising teachers, and seminars will be held in schools and the Institute giving students the opportunity to discuss questions raised in lectures, and to voice their own questions arising out of practical work in schools.

Every student is allocated to tutorial groups, each of which is looked after by a member of staff. Tutors have the role of helping students in all matters concerned with the course, and students are encouraged to turn to their tutors if they have any problems or difficulties.

During the course of the year all students will gain experience of using computers.

1. Curriculum Subject Teaching

Candidates will study to an advanced standard the methods of teaching their special subject or subjects in the context of primary, secondary or further education. The areas of study will be:

(i) methods of teaching a particular subject or subjects and the contribution of this subject or subjects to the curriculum as a whole;
(ii) the planning of learning experiences;
(iii) classroom management;
(iv) the use of educational aids;
(v) evaluation and assessment.

Such other areas as may be determined by the Institute.

A critical analysis will be undertaken of the nature of the subject(s) or of the teaching programme for an age group, and of the philosophical, sociological and psychological problems involved. Aims and purposes of teaching particular subjects or groups of subjects; principles of curriculum and syllabus construction; studies requiring the use of appropriate apparatus, aids and materials for the learning of particular subjects or

topics in a school. Particular attention will be paid to the implementation of the National Curriculum.

The following courses are available:

Art and Design Education Graduates in any field of art and design are eligible to apply for this course, the main purpose of which is to prepare students for teaching posts in secondary schools. It is desirable that all candidates should have a broad experience of art and design. Those qualified in the history of art and design and allied disciplines will be considered for this integrated course in which practical workshops are an essential part. All candidates are required to bring to interview evidence of recent involvement in practical work. The department is committed to a broad-based approach to art and design in education which requires teachers to be flexible in their thinking and wide-ranging in their practical skills. Students are helped to develop personal rationales for teaching which are rooted in a deepening awareness of their own creative processes and an understanding of current curriculum issues. Throughout the course major London museums and galleries are used as a rich resource for learning. (Admissions Tutor: Roy Prentice, BEd MA FRSA)

Business Studies This course is specifically designed for those who wish to teach the integrated TVEI, GCSE and A and AS level courses in Business Studies. It provides a good grounding in a wide range of business education courses, and includes applications of technology and business education with technology as a core component of the National Curriculum. Those applying should have good degrees in Business Studies or closely related subjects. Other candidates will be considered, particularly those who have significant and relevant business experience. The ability to handle basic statistics and other numerate data crucial to business decisions is essential, although this does not mean that such topics should have been part of the applicant's degree course. Applicants with no business experience are recommended to undertake a period of direct contact with a firm or organization as a part of their course work. (Admissions Tutor: D H Dyer, BSc(Econ)

Business Studies, Economics and see under Economics and Business Studies.

Computing, Mathematics and see under Mathematics and Computing.

Economics The course is intended to provide training for teaching economics in secondary

Figure 1.9 Institute of Education web site: home page

ruling myth told us that there was just the one relevant life-world. Now with the dominance of the (niche) market, we know that that is not the case and indeed it never was. The social and cultural diversity/ fragmentation which characterizes the present era means that we cannot pretend to know the needs and requirements of others.

Significantly, the directionality of authority in relation to knowledge and knowledge construction has reversed: individuals now have the responsibility to gain and produce the knowledge needed to deal with problems in their lives. Previously knowledge was 'dispersed' by those with power to those without; now knowledge is brought into being as the result of the transformative action of individuals acting on the world of information in relation to problems they encounter in their life-worlds. Of course, 'problem' here includes everything that is essential to the maintenance of the individual or a group, and not only rare, significant, remarkable events.

To return to reading just for one moment: in the former situation, reading aimed to gain truth to the original authority of the text, which

---

Figure 1.8 Institute of Education prospectus: contents page and page of text (see opposite)

delivered knowledge; now reading aims for a truth which arises out of the individual's interest. The former is now unlikely to deliver relevant knowledge; the latter can. Indeed, reading is now close to the making of the text: it is sign-making on the basis of engagement with materials 'in the world'. Reading itself – just as much as the 'originating' production – has become the activity of design.

The role of multimodal representation in all this is complex and profound. The media of the new screens provide, simultaneously, means for the production of text and for its dissemination. Given the facts of social diversity, the disappearance, or attenuation, or absence of central power, and above all the displacement of the state by the market as the telling source of power, there is now no longer a canonical mode of representation. Rather, the characteristics of the audience (now in any case no longer seen as citizens but as consumers), their needs, wishes and their real or attributed desires move into the foreground. Representational mode becomes a matter of design: does this group prefer image or writing? Moving image or still? What ensemble of modes will serve best my rhetorical needs vis-à-vis this audience? We might ask, from that perspective about the genre and the placement of the image on the Institute of Education home page, its lighting and use of colour, and its reading by the imagined diverse group of 'visitors' to that site.

But the facilities of multimodal representation also have their epistemological uses and consequences, as I mentioned earlier. These can now be seen to be part of the ordinarily available rhetorical resources of representation and communication in the context of digital technologies.

Design: changed dispositions to information and knowledge

What emerges from this is the new centrality of the notion of design as an educational aim, as a consequence of social, economic, political, semiotic and technological changes. 'Competence', the aim of the former era, as much as 'critique', that of the more recent past, are both lodged in social and epistemological environments of stability – of social and semiotic stability, underpinned by power expressed as convention. 'Competence' aimed at full understanding of the resources, and of their appropriate use; 'critique' engaged with agendas of others' making and asked in whose benefit they worked. In that respect 'critique' necessarily looks to the past, even though it has the aim of unsettling social givens. 'Design' sees individuals in their present environments and asks about their needs and desires, and the possibilities of their implementation given the resources available in this environment, now. On the basis of a full understanding of the potentials of available resources, the constraints of present social environments, 'design' looks forward; it has an agenda for the future. The question of the designer is, 'How can I implement my desires, given these historically shaped resources, the structures of power in this environment, these characteristics of my audience?'

Structures, systems and the conventions that support them were central in conceptions of competence; human agency was marginal in many different ways. Notions of learning were shaped in these environments; now they have to be rethought in the different, perhaps more complex, contemporary givens. Theories of learning rest on theories of meaning. Both underpin practices that lead to the shaping of human dispositions, in all ways. Both underpin theories of knowing and knowledge. These are crucial in thinking about relevant notions of education. Semiotics does not deal with learning; it does deal with meaning. Therein lies its potential for contributing to this debate.

References

Boeck, M. (2003) Information, wissen und medialer wandel (Information, knowledge and the changing media), *Medien Journal*, 27 (1), pp. 51–65.

Kress, G. R. (2000) A curriculum for the future, *Cambridge Journal of Education*, 30 (1), pp. 133–45.

Kress, G. R. (2001) 'You've just got to learn how to see': Curriculum subjects, young people and schooled engagement with the world, *Linguistics and Education*, 11 (4), pp. 401–15.

Kress, G. R. (2003) *Literacy in the New Media Age*, Routledge, London.

Kress, G. R. and Van Leeuwen, T. (2001) *Multimodal Discourse: The modes and media of contemporary communication*, Edward Arnold, London.

Sims, J. W. (1920) *The Boy Electrician*, George G. Harrap, London.

2 Networking and collective intelligence for teachers and learners

Bernard Cornu

A few years ago, researchers were studying and discussing the influence of computers on education, teaching and learning. Computers were considered as wonderful new tools, able to enrich the resources available for teaching and to improve teaching and learning, through 'computer aided' devices, through appropriate software and through a more individualized way of learning. But the development of information technologies and of communication technologies, and their merging into ICT (information and communication technology) brought major and profound changes across the whole of society and education. Information is now digitalized, information technologies process digitalized information, and communication technologies transport digitalized information. One can digitalize texts, images, sound, videos, leading to multimedia digitalized information. One can communicate with others more and more easily; one can access any kind of information anywhere in the world in a few seconds. Digitalized information is more accessible, more interactive, easier to access, transport, store and process. One speaks about 'digitalized society' or 'information society'. Such a society, which is now appearing, has specific characteristics, and profound changes are occurring.

In this chapter, two main ideas linked with the emergence of the digitalized society will be addressed: networking and collective intelligence. These two ideas are closely linked, and they will certainly influence education profoundly. We are at the very beginning of the development of such concepts, and in this chapter we will stay at a general level, raising issues and questions that will have to be more deeply addressed in the future.

A networked society

The first major change in society is the development of networks and structuration in networks. Networks bring considerable change in education and in the role of the teacher. We are used to linear structures, and to pyramidal or hierarchical structures ('tree type'). This is the way our world is organized and our social systems are organized. For example, just look at the organization chart of a company, a government ministry or a university. It is typically a pyramidal structure. Look at the organization of a book; the table of contents is a linear structure, but allows a hierarchical use of the book, through the titles, subtitles, paragraphs, etc. This is just one of many possible examples.

A network is a set of interlinked points, or nodes. It is a complex structure that has interesting properties. The networks of most interest are generally those made of people and information: linking people with people, people with information, information with information. In a network, there are generally many possible paths from one node to another; in contrast, in a pyramidal structure most of the time there is a unique path (we sometimes call it the hierarchical or official channel). In a network, there is often the possibility of creating new links. A network includes sub-networks. A network therefore creates new proximities, new hierarchies.

The example most often quoted is, of course, the Internet. It is a huge network, constantly becoming more complex and enriching. A web site is generally built according to a pyramidal, or 'tree', structure; some of them are in a more networked form, hypertext-links enriching the tree structure. But the set of all web sites has a much more complex structure. There are links between web sites, or even between pages or items in web sites. It is always possible to create new links. Circulating in such a network is not easy, and tools have been designed for that purpose: 'search engines', portals, etc. Behind web sites, there are individuals, groups of people and organizations. The network links not only web sites; it links people and information. The fact that now people and information can be connected in a networked form changes profoundly the relationship between people, and between people and information.

Let us look at some examples. New networks allow new kinds of communication between people. Of course, one can always communicate with the people one already knows. But accessing someone in a certain hierarchy, in an organization, now becomes possible without following the traditional official channel. It is easier now to find people's email addresses than their telephone numbers; one can access people through their function, through their name and through other kinds of criteria. We really are in a new era of communication between people: networked communication.

Accessing information in a book has also changed. We are used to 'pyramidal' access, through the bibliography, through the title and the author's name, through the table of contents, the chapter titles, etc. Accessing information in a book was a kind of a circulation in a tree structure. But the new networks, such as the Internet, enable us to access information in books in new ways. We can go directly to a word, to an item of information, even without first knowing the author's name or the title of the book. We can move from one book to another one, we can link information from different books, we can circulate in books in a 'networked' form.

The organization chart of a company or an institution shows its hierarchical structure: heads, sub-heads, etc. A networked structure creates new links between the different components of an institution, creates new hierarchies and enables adaptation of the structure to solve different kinds of problems. In a world of networks, hierarchies in institutions cannot stay in the pyramidal form; they will have to evolve, adapt and take a networked form, more compatible with the network environment.

The case of education is particularly important. Since society is more and more networked, schools must prepare the pupils for this networked society. This implies an adaptation of the contents and, more importantly, the methods of education. Knowledge is now available and distributed in a networked form. The school is the place where pupils both gain knowledge and learn how to access and acquire knowledge. Therefore, schools must use the networks, be part of the networks and teach the networks. The traditional lesson, in which the knowledge circulates only from the teacher to the pupils, must change into a form where the knowledge is considered in a networked form and circulates in a networked way. The way in which resources, such as textbooks, libraries and distance materials, are used must take into account the networked form of knowledge. The school must be organized and designed in a more network-compatible form: pupils must be able to work in networks, teachers must work in networks and school administration must be more networked. Internal networks can be made available in schools (for instance, as 'intranets'), and schools must of course be linked to the Internet, so that networked work with other partners, such as other schools, other countries and other institutions, is made possible. Practitioners must consider all the consequences of the networked form of the society and imagine the changes these may bring about in schools and in education.

One of the most pyramidal organizations, in a country like France, is the educational system itself. In a networked society, where education and schools should be at the centre of the networks, it is vital to imagine new forms of organizations for educational systems, better adapted to networks and facilitating the role of education in the networks.

Collective intelligence

A second major change in society is the emergence and the development of a more collective form of intelligence. We are traditionally used to intelligence as a personal and individual quality. School aims at developing the individual intelligence of the pupils. But groups, institutions and societies need a form of collective intelligence. Collective intelligence is not only the addition and juxtaposition of individual intelligences. There is a specific form to collective intelligence.

Let us look at a typical example: ants. One ant is a very simple animal, with very few competencies and a very limited intelligence. Its capacity for action and for communication is limited. But a group of ants, an ant-hill, is a very intelligent group: it is able to determine the shortest way from one point to an other, it is able to build bridges, it is able to overcome obstacles, it is able to carry very heavy loads. This kind of intelligence does not come from a hierarchical organization: there is no leader among the ants, there is no one knowing better than the others and explaining or showing the others, or coordinating the work (the role of the 'queen' is of a different nature). The ability of a group of ants comes from a collective behaviour through the 'stygmergy'. Ants produce a special smelling substance, a pheromone, which facilitates collective intelligence. For example, the time it takes for the smell of pheromone to disappear along a path and the amount of pheromone linked to the number of ants that have gone through this path, will enable the ants to determine the shortest path. Collective intelligence includes cooperative work and cooperative intelligence, but there is something more than just cooperation. Other groups of creatures, for example bees, also have a form of collective intelligence.

The collective intelligence of human beings is complex and takes many different forms, including collective knowledge, cooperation, collective work, collective thinking, group activities, enrichment and capitalization of knowledge and intelligence, and collective training. The current keywords associated with human collective intelligence are cooperation, transmission and hierarchy. But new information and communication technologies make available new networks, new ways of storing and accessing knowledge and resources and new ways of communicating with people and with groups. They create the possibility of a new form of collective intelligence, which may in turn substantially increase the collective capacity and competence of human beings. This collective intelligence is made of a network of individual intelligences. Individual intelligences are not only juxtaposed, but linked and interrelated in ways which make them complementary, which enrich them, in order to solve problems and address questions that need a collective form of intelligence.

Collective intelligence is emerging in many aspects of social life. Citizenship in a networked society could become more and more collective, and based on a collective intelligence. Science and technology demand more and more collective intelligence. Industry, business and work in general, require more and more collective intelligence. The way people work has evolved. We have moved from an individual to a cooperative mode: working together, sharing tasks and using teamwork.

Collective intelligence adds a new dimension, since it brings into action new collective characteristics of human intelligence. Preparing students for collective intelligence and related competencies will be a necessity in the networked society.

Education is the privileged field for the development of collective intelligence, and the classroom is the first place where collective intelligence should be addressed, developed and improved. Learning has mostly been considered as an individual task. But we should now think in terms of collective learning: learning through collective tasks and activities, in order to develop not only individual but also collective knowledge and collective abilities. Once we have defined the aims of education in terms of collective knowledge and abilities, it is necessary to design and adapt activities in order to facilitate collective learning. New information and communication technologies make numerous activities available for the development of collective intelligence and learning.

Teaching has also to address these collective dimensions. New teaching content and methods must be elaborated and developed for this purpose. This means that the classroom, students and teachers must be considered as a collective entity, with specific characteristics, in which specific activities can be set up in order to reinforce collectivity. This is again a new challenge for education in the networked society.

Teachers are, of course, the main agents of changes in education. Collective intelligence should first be developed for teachers. Traditionally, the teaching profession is a very lonely profession: teachers are alone in front of their pupils; teachers are alone for marking homework and papers; teachers are alone for preparing their lessons. A lonely profession, it could be said, can only lead to individual competencies and intelligence for the pupils. Establishing collective professional behaviour for teachers is necessary in the networked society. Teacher education has to take this into account, both in the content and in the methods of teacher education. Methods are important in teacher education: teachers tend not to act in the way they are told, but to reproduce, more or less consciously, the way they are taught and trained. Therefore, we do not only need courses about collective abilities and collective intelligence, but we need collective activities in teacher education. Developing a collective intelligence for teachers is a new task for teacher training institutions.

A new agenda

Such ideas need to be deepened and much work remains to be done. Some key points must be considered and acted upon. There is a need to define and study more precisely what collective information is, what collective knowledge is and what collective memory is. Collective knowledge cannot be reduced to a collection of individual knowledge.

Collective knowledge is made of knowledge and links between knowledge. Collective knowledge is not a list of subject knowledge; there is a trans-disciplinary and global dimension to such knowledge.

There are different steps in the emergence of collective intelligence. Individual intelligence is not totally isolated, and it aims at solving problems and acting in a society. But individual intelligence is structured, acquired and evaluated in an individual way. The second step is the one of cooperative intelligence, which makes people able to work together, cooperate and solve problems they would not have been able to solve alone. Collective intelligence is a third step, more complex, made of networks of intelligences and which includes a collective dimension in the knowledge, in the problems to be solved and in the way intelligence is activated.

Collective intelligence needs new and adapted tools. Information and communication technology tools are necessary for collective intelligence. The World Wide Web is a very good example of a product and a tool for collective intelligence. But certainly we are at the very beginning of the tools and resources for collective intelligence, and we will have to imagine and design adapted tools for collective intelligence.

Collective intelligence needs collective communication. Communication has evolved from one-to-one communication, to one-to-all communication and information and communication technologies allow a kind of 'all-to-all' communication. It is an essential component of collective intelligence.

Collective intelligence aims at addressing collective tasks and problems. Future reflection must include the question of which problems and which tasks are appearing in the networked society and need a form of collective intelligence.

Collective intelligence is a relatively new concept. Clearly, we have to explore it in its multiple facets, and to reflect on its consequences for education. But this concept is closely linked to networks and their development. The society of tomorrow will probably be a more collective one in terms of knowledge, intelligence, information and communication. Technically, researchers have progressed greatly in the development of 'collective informatics'; they have enabled computers to work collectively and they have defined and designed 'intelligent agents' as a model of collective activity. For education in the networked society, it is necessary for us to build on this, to be able, as human beings, to work collectively and develop collective skills.

3 Multimedia learning in the digital world

José L. Rodríguez Illera

This chapter will review the current situation of what is commonly called 'multimedia learning'. This type of teaching–learning, which uses computer applications that offer different coding systems and forms of representation such as text, sound, images and animation, has become commonplace in the last few years, even though there is not much research available on the subject. In the first part of the chapter, current practice in multimedia learning is reviewed, the difficulties in finding a unified descriptive language are considered and the main developments in research discussed. In the second part, some of the diverse fields that have started to incorporate the potential offered by multimedia learning are discussed, and the necessity of developing a unified approach proposed.

Multimedia learning

Multimedia learning and its associated problems

Over the last few years, the development and use of multimedia applications for education has been undergoing a shift in two contrary directions. On the one hand, the use of multimedia in education has become less and less visible, in the sense that many applications have been incorporated into normal everyday use, from word processors or presentations to interactive multimedia applications themselves. In this respect, the idea of 'multimediality', which arose at the end of the 1980s for the then new capabilities of computers (Ambron and Hooper, 1988, 1989), has been gradually disappearing. People no longer talk about 'multimedia computers' because they all are now. Multimedia has become a given, and now it is unusual to see applications that do not incorporate a variety of different media. From the descriptive point of view, multimediality has lost its discriminating value.

On the other hand, many applications have been transferred from CD-ROM to the Internet. The difference in architecture, the reduction in costs, the progressive increase in bandwidth and constantly improving access to telecommunications are the main reasons for this shift. As well as being technological, this has been fundamentally social. This second shift, however, has brought with it a decrease in the degree and complexity of interaction, as well as a much lower integration of the different media than was prevalent at the start of the last decade.

This double tension has had various consequences. First, it postpones the promise that many authors saw in CD-ROM as a vehicle capable of offering complex interactivity (Smith, 1999). In reality the vehicle is not the key factor for interactivity, although in the case of CD-ROMs sufficient read speed was reached to enable media to be loaded almost instantaneously, giving the sensation of responsiveness and interactivity. The technological problem has now become one of reducing the forms of interaction and the forms of composition to those permitted by the standard Internet application: the Web browser. The language browsers used for multimedia composition (limited by HTML and JavaScript) and for navigation, in which the semantic value of the link is the same as the navigational jump (Burbules, 2002), have considerably reduced the potential for interaction, because some standardized actions included, whilst important, are limited. Fortunately, other programming languages, such as Flash, allow more complex forms of interaction, although almost always within the interface imposed by the browsers.

It should not be forgotten that the Internet is not only a protocol and a type of application based on browsers, even though these are specialized in displaying information. Gaskin (2003) shows this on trying to distinguish between uses: 'Tasks like word processing, graphics production, and other media-creation tasks provide a useful distinction for the domain of dedicated applications: they involve *creating* data. In contrast, successful browser applications are more commonly oriented toward the *viewing* of data.'

Second, the double tension postpones the production of a new unified language. As Plowman (1994) states, following Burch's concept, we are in a phase similar to the 'primitive representation mode' of cinema, in which the search is still on for a unification of the multimedia elements, as well as 'institutional' forms of its syntax and meaning. In contrast to cinema, multimedia applications are interactive, so that their meaning does not depend solely on the structure of the message and on the interpretative activity of the receiver; the very actions of the receiver change the content of the message. On the other hand, multimedia applications always carry a significant multimodality (Kress and van Leeuwen, 1996), in such a way that it is difficult to construct a unique and standard interpretative language.

On the contrary, educational applications have opted, in many cases, to simplify both the multimedial diversity as well as the compositional forms of the different media, in such a way that the richness of the media has declined in favour of messages that are more easily interpreted. This has been the route chosen for various applications produced in different universities in Spain and other countries (see Hepp, 2003, for a general Latin American overview). In the TEAM Project (Rodríguez Illera and Suau, 2003) more than fifty teams of teachers from the Universitat de Barcelona have participated in developing multimedia materials in many different disciplines. In some cases these materials are very complex with thousands of different screens with hypertext and links. What stands out is that multimedia and interactive complexity has given way to simpler interfaces and environments, in many cases based on web sites or on the use of standardized virtual campuses (such as WebCT).

This simplified multimedia language has not been well researched either. Perhaps the most important problem with multimedia applications will continue to be understanding why a multimedia message is better, from an instructional point of view, than a 'monomedia' message. The question is broad and complex. It relates in the first place to the idea that it is possible to consider that the media are 'in themselves' educational. This is a question that is considered difficult or impossible to answer adequately as it is impossible to separate the effects of the different media from the effects of the different structuring of the instructional messages, which are not directly comparable due to the inherent specificity of the media.

However, pedagogical reflection is lacking on this idea of specificity of the media, which so evidently results from looking at the media from a non-specialized perspective. Although the media cannot be said to be intrinsically educational, nor the technology, it is also difficult to assert that it is possible to consider them mere 'media', neutral vehicles for a pre-existing educational message. If we take the distinction between learning with and learning from, the media and the technologies in general appear as an environment through which we communicate and express ourselves, but with which we also act. The distinction between the technological environment and the system or agent that is 'located' within that technological environment is not clear in many cases. That is to say that this is an analysis that entails the integration of the technological environment as part of the message produced in a specific situation. For this reason the question does not seem to be so much whether the media are educational, which effectively they are not because they are only media, but to see how they condition the characteristics of the educationally structured message.

Although the question of the advantage of multimediality has been displaced, there are basic aspects of this that remain unclear from the point of view of the processing of the information involved. Why are two media, or three or four, better than one? Is it always this way? Are some media better than others? And, if it is this way, why are they better? Or, on the contrary, does every medium impose a significant communicative specificity that makes it different to the other media? In short, the questions can multiply and each one leads to more questions.

Basic research on multimedia learning

One approach that tries to answer these questions about multimediality stems from the bringing together of cognitive psychology and information processing. Although the type and scale of analysis is very different to other theoretical frameworks, it is important as an approach because it aims to understand why the different media generate different representations and so influence the receiver. Furthermore, when the question is posed as to whether multimedial messages are more effective, which hardly happens at all in scientific literature, often the sole, and often vague, reference is to Paivio's Dual Coding Hypothesis. Paivio (1986) states that there are two specialized perceptive-cognitive sub-systems in the processing of different stimuli: one for audio stimuli, especially spoken language, and the other one for visual stimuli. Both systems complement each other, but the processes that they carry out are differentiated, especially in short-term memory and in the verbal or image models that they use. Paivio's idea may appear simple, but in the cognitive psychology tradition both systems have been treated separately. Many studies concentrate on one or the other, but rarely on both at the same time. Double codification states that our perceptive processes almost always use both sub-systems simultaneously.

This theoretical background provides the basis for the experimental approach developed by Mayer (2001) and is used, to a lesser extent, by others such as Rouet *et al.* (2001) and Dijkstra *et al.* (2001). Mayer has carried out a systematic analysis that has enabled him to construct a theory of multimedia learning in which the very idea of 'multimedia' is thought of classically as a mode of presentation (textual and visual representations), or as a form of sensory modality emphasizing more the role of the receiver and the necessary codifications. What is important is how these ways of thinking of multimedia are related to models of what multimedia learning is. Mayer uses the distinction, also classical, of conceiving of learning as an acquisition of information or as a construction of knowledge, making him fall back onto conceiving of multimedia learning as a technological issue (that is to say, how technology enables a better structuring of a presentation of information), or else as a cognitive issue, which sees the student as an active subject, implicated in the construction of knowledge from the data and information that the student processes. Both approaches would also be involved when establishing the role of the teachers. In the first case the teacher is a source of information, who structures and improves the access to it, while in the second case the teacher is more a figure who guides the student in the cognitive process of assimilating and constructing knowledge.

Beyond simply considering that Mayer's opposite positions are part of a continuum and that they are situated ideally as the two extremes of the continuum, the positions are clear and respond to a current vision of how to envisage the process of teaching and learning. The learning objectives must be added to this. Basically they are divided into capacity to remember and capacity to understand. The first one enables the reproduction of taught information, while the second one would be closer to significant learning, that is to say the capacity to establish connections between what is learnt and previous knowledge. Both objectives are based on differentiated cognitive capacities that can be measured using tests: retention and transference. From all this it can be deduced that there are various types of learning results: an absence of learning, learning routines and significant learning.

In spite of saying that the differences are very general, they represent a map on which many options can be situated. Thus the vast majority of educational programs can be easily placed in a specific position, and those that are not in any specific position are examples of more complex forms or are examples that are situated at some point in the continuum. Furthermore, these distinctions are habitual in scientific literature and they take us back to more conventional questions of educational psychology and pedagogy, such as asking ourselves what we learn for. It is not obvious that multimedia programs always look for profound knowledge, nor that they promote the capacity to transfer what has been learnt, but it is obvious that often they are limited to showing multi-coded information, emphasizing more the support in different media than the learning strategies and learning objectives.

In practice the problem of multimedia learning is to understand how the multi-coded arrangement of the diverse elements promotes better learning or not. But to be able to understand this question, learning (not just 'multimedia') must be placed in a theoretical perspective that provides a reference framework for the subsequent analysis. In the case of Mayer, the theoretical framework has three general principles: Paivio's Dual Coding Hypothesis, which has been referred to above, the limited capacity of humans to process information and the recognition that the subjects are active at the moment of constructing their learning.

The fact that the capacity for processing information is limited is well known. It is difficult even to remember a long list of numbers. The same occurs with advertising messages that in a couple of seconds may mix dozens of images. And, in some way, the same thing happens with multi-media products that use a wide range of media simultaneously: we can only remember some essential aspect of a narrated text (as it develops over time), or we focus our attention on a graphic or on an animation, without paying the same attention to the text that is shown. What we do is to process the total cognitive load that we can manage in our short-term memory, but the cognitive load that is presented often surpasses our limited processing capacities.

The cognitive load, related to the difficulty of the messages presented, can be either intrinsic or extrinsic. Some messages intrinsically require maximum concentration to be processed, since the topic that they deal with is, in itself, complex, or because attention must be paid to the different forms of representation (for example, what is explained verbally is different to what appears in video, or in some images). The extrinsic load refers to the form in which the message has been designed: in a simpler or more complex manner, with more or less redundancy, visually or narratively complex, etc. This complexity of the message format is the responsibility of the teacher who has designed it.

Mayer introduces the question of the activity of the subject who is learning. The idea at the heart of this is that the best learning results are produced when the subject is cognitively active. This assumes that there is an attempt to understand the conceptual structure of the material taught, that an attempt is made to create a mental model in which this conceptual structure is included. Meaningful learning would require this internalization, which in its turn would be a consequence of the cognitive operations and processes that the subject carries out in an active manner. These processes would basically be three: selection (words and images), integration (into the respective mental models) and the organization of both with respect to each other and in relation to previous knowledge. Therefore this concept of multimedia learning assumes that there are five steps, splitting the processes of selection and integration according to the channel.

Ultimately these cognitive differences lead to what is called the 'Multimedia Principle', which states that learning is better if two channels (verbal and graphic) are presented instead of just one. Its experimental basis is to be found in studies that refer to the effect of illustrations in textbooks and subsequently in studies that make a comparison between instruction with on-screen text and instruction with animations or graphics to illustrate what is being taught. From the point of view of the instructional designer, the question is centred on how to structure the different media that make up a multimedia message (for which Mayer states seven principles: multimedia, spatial contiguity, temporal contiguity, redundancy, coherence, modality and individual differences).

Mayer's work on multimedia learning is without doubt the broadest and most systematic carried out to date. It also clearly distinguishes multimedia from other similar but different digital phenomena like hypermedia and variants on hypertext (McKnight *et al.*, 1993; Rouet *et al.*, 1996). It is not, however, any more than an analytical approach, which clearly brings its own methodological and other limitations, often the result of deliberate decisions designed to enable tight experimental design and control.

First, the idea of multimedia that is used is over-simplified and limits generalization of the results obtained. The products designed and produced are normally much more complex than just having graphics and simple animation included to support informational text. It is a very analytical approach and uses a reduced conception so as not to be overloaded by the complexity of an 'authentic' multimedia application or environment. But this minimal methodological self-limitation still generates a certain paradox, since the very object of study is almost outside the model after such a dramatic simplification.

Second, what happens with other studies of more complex products? And, in any case, what do we truly understand by 'multimedia'? Is multimedial complexity needed for an application to be 'truly' multimedia? On the one hand, it seems clear that the very idea of 'multimedia' comes more from the information technology and software industries than from academic research. On the other hand, as we have already shown, a lot of the interest in multimedia, from both users in general and researchers, comes from a certain 'promise' of a new technology that would facilitate the access to complex forms of expression and communication, making learning simpler at the same time (Smith, 1999). This perceived promise has a lot to do with the anticipation of a new media to replace 'old' writing formats and techniques, bringing new capacities for narration, not least the capacity for the reader to influence the development of the text. For the moment, such promises are seriously limited by the difficulties that arise in developing applications that really can be adapted to the user and change their internal narrative. Despite this, there is a growing field of 'adaptive multimedia' that has this aspiration (see Kinshuk, 2002). Whatever, increased data storage capacity, processing speeds and Internet bandwidth make the production and use of sophisticated multimedia texts, combining a variety of media and complex narrative, more and more accessible.

Third, there are limitations associated with the explanatory format of cognitivism. No matter how much Mayer and other authors echo constructivist approaches, it is clear that all their experimentation is guided by cognitive principles. As in conventional instructional design, greater emphasis is placed on the design of the messages than on students' activities. Although this is consistent with what teachers can do (i.e. design better multimedial messages) and probably with what they should do, it continues to pose its own problems when isolating very simple messages. It also continues to assume an artificial teaching/learning situation. The descriptions Mayer and colleagues give indicate the use of highly decontextualized learning situations, which are completely removed from what happens in classrooms and other everyday pedagogic settings. There are neither group activities nor questions for teachers. Teaching consists of presenting information in different formats and checking later on how certain aspects have varied (retention or transference). As with research on the difference between different media, the content cannot be separated from how it is dealt with, and, in this case, from its ecological validity which seems to be very limited. In general, the implicit model of teaching/learning does not match current practice, and is more appropriate to very traditional and formal educational contexts.

Finally, interaction is absent from these experimental approaches. The comparison is made between an application that offers a text to be read and another one that adds a graphic, audio or a small animation to complement the text; that is to say both forms are non-interactive media. The role of the user seems to be limited to reading a text or to looking at some complementary materials, but not to interact with the text or materials. This certainly has to do with a methodological decision again, for instance to find the simplest way of distinguishing between a textual message and a multimedial one. Although this decision has a logic which enables the conditions for the presentation of the stimuli to be changed, what is certain is that this refers more to static media (such as a billboard or a text book) than to interactive media like those which characterize the idea of 'multimedia'. As many authors have stated, it is within the idea of interaction that the promises of new media converge, as much as or more than in multimediality.

To summarize: although the idea of multimedia learning is clearly an advance on stating a problem that has been explored little, some of the methodological decisions taken for its study have imposed severe limitations. The specifics of interactive media have been sacrificed in order to compare messages composed of one or more media, normally in a very simplified manner, and at the same time the learning situation has been reduced to an experimental situation far removed from real life. Whatever our doubts about the ecological validity of this research, fundamental ideas on the composition of simple multimedia messages have started to arise.

The social uses of multimedia learning

Beyond this basic research, the applied problems of interactive multimedia learning continue to be important, especially because of the technological and representational standardization reasons stated at the beginning of this chapter, but also because of the absence or the confusion of the pedagogical designs of many applications. There are various routes at this junction that are being traversed simultaneously, although not always together.

Perhaps the main route is through communities of practice and of learning. Along with its theorization (especially Wenger, 1998; Barab and Duffy, 1999; Brown and Duguid, 2000), a large number of practical experiences have arisen, linked in many cases to virtual spaces and to educational portals as a way to channel virtual learning. Many of these communities are full of 'lurkers', peripheral members although not always clearly legitimate, if we follow the terminology of Lave and Wenger (1991). There are some doubts as to whether these virtual encounters really constitute communities of practice or are rather 'pseudocommunities' as Hung and Nichani (2002) state, being limited by the characteristics of the electronic medium. However, the most interesting aspect of the communities is, curiously, their fundamentally linguistic character. The forums and email systems hardly incorporate multimedia elements at all. Written language (or new linguistic genres that are appearing, see Cassany, 2003) and dialogue, as well as the forms of collective debate, and, in general, what we can call interpersonal electronic interaction, are dominant.

Other routes that are traversed are the many different forms of 'personalization' of the interaction. A substantial number of approaches have contributed to this. These have emphasized a concept of learning based on socio-cultural principles in the broad sense, from learning and situated cognition, problem based learning and case studies, to methodologies with other theoretical approaches like adaptive educational multimedia (Kinshuk, 2002). In some way in all of these an attempt is made to construct learning situations that make sense for the learners and that intrinsically motivate them, independently of whether multimedia elements are used or not.

In third place (in a list that could be longer) is the creation of systems for help or for interaction based on the translation of the Vygotskian concept of 'zone of proximal development' from interpersonal interaction to person–machine interaction. Some recent interactive learning environments, such as The Ecolab which helps children aged 10 and 11 years to learn about food webs and chains (Luckin and du Boulay, 1999) and the creation of intelligent help agents, clearly go in this direction.

These routes are not exclusive, although they have seemed to be so far. If multimedia has to 'make itself invisible' by being present in all developments, and if it has to be integrated into the different approaches stated, it is worthwhile questioning its utility as an analytic category. If everything is multimedia, what falls, or will fall, outside as 'monomedia'? In some way this multimedial line of thinking entails going back to the primacy of the relationship between the media over the meaning of each medium taken separately. But it is evident that the forms of meaning of every medium (text, image, audio, the moving image) have their own logic and language, and it is not easy to find a hierarchy to decide in what order to read them. It is not as simple as thinking that the graphical nature of screens subordinate text to its visual composition as Kress (2003) suggests, because the way of differentiating meaning of both the image and the written language means that often it is the text that accompanies an image that in the end decides the meaning of the image (Vilches, 1987).

Despite the theoretical question of the place of multimedia (as a language, but also as an educational application) remaining open in a digital environment where everything is, in some way, 'multimedia', the practical consequences of this new digital environment and its generalized use are very important. For example, when posing the question again of what the basic forms of digital literacy are, as has been suggested (The New London Group, 2000; Snyder, 2002), not only the different media that together form a message but also the interactive component that digital technologies introduce have to be considered and that is the nucleus of the idea of multimedia. Digital literacies and how they are used are closely linked to learning, but not to the point where it is not possible to separate them. For this reason the questions posed by Mayer and other authors continue to be important. This is also the case even from the applied point of view: how should multimedia elements be integrated into the communicative space of digital communities, or into forms of individual help? It is clear that there are many questions that affect its semantic aspects, as well as pragmatic ones, and these constitute an authentic research programme.

Finally, from an educational point of view, multimedia learning is at a crossroads where it has to decide whether to mix multimedia into the applications and forms of educational communication, and to concentrate on learning, without presupposing that just by adding media learning will happen. Almost the opposite can also happen with multimedia, as occurs with navigating the Internet, an effect of cognitive dispersion that is the opposite of what is desirable for learning to occur.

References

Ambron, S. and Hooper, K. (eds) (1988) *Interactive Multimedia*, Microsoft Press, Redmond, WA.

Ambron, S. and Hooper, K. (eds) (1989) *Learning with Interactive Multimedia*, Microsoft Press, Redmond, WA.

Barab, S. and Duffy, T. M. (1999) From practice fields to communities of practice, in *Theoretical Foundations of Learning Environments*, eds D. H. Jonassen and S. M. Land, pp. 25–55, Lawrence Erlbaum, London.

Brown, J. S. and Duguid, P. (2000) *The Social Life of Information*, Harvard Business School Press, Cambridge, MA.

Burbules, N. C. (2002) The Web as a rhetorical place, in *Silicon Literacies: Communication, innovation, and education in the Electronic Age*, ed. I. Synder, pp. 75–84, Routledge, London.

Cassany, D. (ed.) (2003) *Los Nuevos Géneros Electrónicos*, special issue of the journal *Cultura y Educación*, Madrid.

Dijkstra, S., Jonassen, D. and Sembill, D. (eds) (2001) *Multimedia Learning*, Peter Lang, Berne.

Gaskin, R. (2003) [accessed 30 August 2003] Beyond the browser: rediscovering the role of the desktop in a Net-centric world [Online] http://www.fourth-world.com/embassy/articles/netapps.html.

Hepp, P. (ed.) (2003) [accessed 30 August 2003] *Latin American Perspectives on Educational Multimedia*, special issue of the journal *Interactive Educational Multimedia* [Online] http://www.ub.es/multimedia/iem.

Hung, D. and Nichani, M. (2002) Differentiating between communities of practice (CoPs) and quasi-communities: can CoPs exist online? *International Journal on E-Learning*, 1 (3), pp. 23–29.

Kinshuk (ed.) (2002) [accessed 30 August 2003] *Adaptative Educational Multimedia*, special issue of the journal *Interactive Educational Multimedia* [Online] http://www.ub.es/multimedia/iem.

Kress, G. (2003) *Literacy in the New Media Age*, Routledge, London.

Kress, G. and van Leeuwen, T. (1996) *Reading Images: The grammar of visual design*, Routledge, London.

Lave, J. and Wenger, E. (1991) *Situated Learning: Legitimate peripheral participation*, Cambridge University Press, Cambridge.

Luckin, R. and du Boulay, B. (1999) Ecolab: the development and evaluation of a Vygotskian design framework, *International Journal of Artificial Intelligence in Education*, 10, pp. 198–220.

Mayer, R. E. (2001) *Multimedia Learning*, Cambridge University Press, Cambridge.

McKnight, C., Dillon, A. and Richardson, J. (eds) (1993) *Hypertext: A psychological perspective*, Ellis Horwood, London.

The New London Group (2000) A pedagogy of multiliteracies designing social futures, in *Multiliteracies: Literacy learning and the design of social futures*, eds B. Cope and M. Kalantzis, pp. 9–37, Routledge, London.

Paivio, A. (1986) *Mental Representations: A dual coding approach*, Oxford University Press, Oxford.

Plowman, L. (1994) The 'Primitive Mode of Representation' and the evolution of interactive multimedia, *Journal of Educational Multimedia and Hypermedia*, 3 (3/4), pp. 275–93.

Rodríguez Illera, J. L. and Suau, J. (eds) (2003) *Tecnologías Multimedia para la Enseñanza y el Aprendizaje en la Universidad*, Edicions de la Universitat de Barcelona, Barcelona.

Rouet, J. F., Levonen, J., Dillon, A. and Spiro, R. J. (eds) (1996) *Hypertext and Cognition*, Lawrence Erlbaum, London.

Rouet, J. F., Levonen, J. and Biardeau, A. (eds) (2001) *Multimedia Learning: Cognitive and instructional issues*, Pergamon, Amsterdam.

Smith, G. (ed.) (1999) *On a Silver Platter: CD-ROMs and the promises of a new technology*, New York University Press, New York.

Snyder, I. (ed.) (2002) *Silicon Literacies: Communication, Innovation, and Education in the Electronic Age*, London, Routledge.

Vilches, L. (1987) *Teoría de la Imagen Periodística*, Paidós, Barcelona.

Wenger, E. (1998) *Communities of Practice*, Cambridge University Press, Cambridge.

4 Children's concepts of ICT

Pointers to the impact of ICT on education within and beyond the classroom

Bridget Somekh

The impact of ICT on the culture of children's homes

Between 1999 and 2002 the Internet became embedded in British society and British children acquired knowledge of the Internet, at home and at school, just as they learnt about other things, often without any sense of its 'newness'. In one important way, however, ICT frequently offered children a new kind of social power since, as with an earlier generation during the 1980s, many adults regarded children's ease of use of ICT with admiration and deferred to their knowledge. In homes, during this later period, increasing numbers of children and adolescents were given access to powerful computers with Internet access, often for extended periods of time and sometimes for their exclusive use. The Internet quickly rivalled television as the favourite media by which young people of all ages immersed themselves in popular culture within their homes, moving back and forth between family culture and youth culture in an integrated 'real' and 'virtual' environment in the family living room or their bedroom. Some of these young people are now using their computer for a kind of multi-tasking activity quite unlike anything known to pre-Internet generations, for example, simultaneously researching a topic and producing a word-and-image-processed text about it for homework, while chatting to friends using an IRC (Internet relay chat) system such as MSN messaging, listening to downloaded music and every now and then 'minimizing' their homework to take a few minutes relaxation with a computer game (either on CD-ROM or online).

Researching children's concepts of ICT: an overview and two examples

During this period I have been engaged in two research projects which collected data systematically on children's concepts of ICT by means of an image-based form of concept mapping produced with large (A3) sheets of paper and pens. In the REPRESENTATION project,[1] 180 British children aged 9–11 from six schools in Yorkshire were asked to draw

concept maps of 'Computers in My World' to communicate their ideas
to the researchers and also to other children in France, Spain, Greece,
Denmark and the Netherlands. The task was administered twice, in
October 1999 and June 2000, and on the first occasion was accompanied
by a written task to 'describe a computer to an extra-terrestrial being
... who has no knowledge of such things' (Pearson and Somekh, 2003).
In the ImpaCT2 project[2] a slightly different version of the same task was
again administered twice, this time to 2,000 children/adolescents from
three age cohorts (10–11, 13–14 and 15–16) in June 2000 and June 2001,
and in February 2001 a sub-sample of 35 children/adolescents were interviewed about the concept maps they had produced eight months
previously (Mavers *et al.*, 2002).

The example that follows was produced by a 10-year-old girl, Wendy,
for Project REPRÉSENTATION. Figure 4.1 shows her concept map,
and an extract from her writing describing a computer to 'an extra-
terrestrial who knows nothing of such things' is also given (spelling
corrected and ... introduced to indicate sentence breaks; (. . .) indicates
a cut in her text).

Wendy's writing

A computer is a television with a board with buttons (. . .) a computer
tells you stuff to do ... you can buy computers from shops they

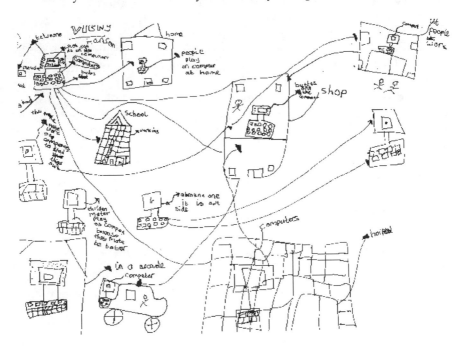

Figure 4.1 Wendy's concept map

are a lot of money to buy (. . .) computers can be in museums and arcades too . . . some computers might be broken so they might be in the bin. Some computers are really truly good because they tell you about animals and people on television. On computers there is a network on that you can play games, write stories coney [?] faxes and phones and maths and money work and geography. On computers there is a lap top . . . on that you can play games and there is some jigsaws and (. . .) the alphabet for the little children . . . for the big children there is books (. . .)

It is clear that when producing this concept map in October 1999, Wendy already knows quite a lot about computers, for example that they are used in many places (home, school, arcades, work and the hospital). She draws a shop, possibly as the place where a computer can be bought. There are at least ten pictures of computers in her map, all with a typical work station shape (no laptops) and several with very detailed depictions of keyboards and buttons. It seems that Wendy does not know the term 'monitor' and may actually be confused about the difference between a television and a computer. Her enthusiasm for computers is clear, however, both from her drawing and her writing. The interlocking lines at the bottom right hand corner seem to depict the computer network. There are also lines connecting many of the computers, but no email or Internet symbols, no icon of the spinning globe and no pictures of mobile telephones (these featured much more frequently in the maps produced eight months later in June 2000, having become more widely owned in the preceding six months). We can certainly be sure from this map and her writing that Wendy has not yet used the Internet.

It is interesting to compare the map drawn by Stephen (also aged 10), produced in a nearby school at the same time as Wendy's – see Figure 4.2. Like Wendy he draws a number of locations where computers are used (home, hotel, school, flats, work, bank, building society and 'chatas' – could this last be a local company?). But this time there is evidence of more detailed knowledge of different kinds of computers and specific knowledge of their role in providing access to information. There are three computers in the map directly linked with each other by 'the world' icon which is clearly meant to represent the Internet. Two of them are drawn with considerable care and have 'slots' for both CDs and floppy discs as well as speakers and keyboards. The one labelled 'my computer' is also labelled 'pentium' and connects to almost all the other drawings in the map.

The one labelled 'most complex I think' is linked to his home computer as well as to a car and the Internet, perhaps meaning that it operates in a different sphere from his own everyday life. There are no drawings representing email or chat, suggesting that Stephen does not yet have

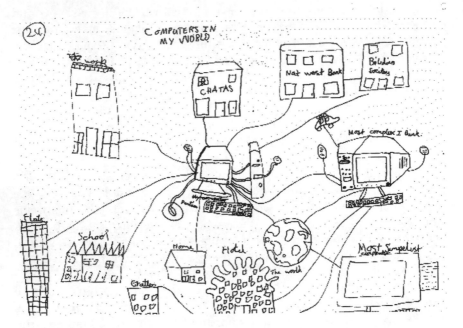

Figure 4.2 Stephen's concept map

knowledge of how computers are used for communications. His writing for the extra-terrestrial confirms these interpretations of his concept map, displaying his technical knowledge of computers, emphasizing the Internet as a source of information and making no mention of people using computers to communicate.

Stephen's writing

Computers are very handy (. . .) when you need information you can log on to the internet. They are very very very very powerful . You can play games and they have c d drives in computers. There are lots of thing to do on a computer. People put passwords on computers so people can't get on the computers (. . .) The computers are good for learning times tables as well as information. The games are fun [lists 10]. My best is AGE OF EMPIRES because it is like an army game and you fight other men. (. . .) The internet is a big web site so you can find out more about tv programs like Southpark and www warzone. My favourite is cheats you can get them as well. (. . .) People like computers a very lot. I wish I had a laptop because they're easy to carry (. . .) I have a pentium.

Interpreting the concept mapping data

The concept mapping data collected from children/adolescents in both these projects were qualitative in nature. They provide a rich picture of how each individual represented his or her ideas about ICT through drawing images/icons and linking them together with lines to show connections. The production of these concept maps took just 30 minutes, including the time to list the items drawn (or label the drawings). A brief discussion took place in advance to demonstrate the idea of drawing two images and linking them with a line (no more than two to avoid modelling a structure), and children were asked to try out the method on another topic such as 'my school' or 'holidays', but there was no attempt to instruct the children in the process of drawing a concept map to show their conceptual understanding as described by Novak and Gowin (1984). In many senses these image-based concept maps were akin to the mind-mapping described by Buzan (1993) but rather than being a planning tool or a form of note-making, children were told that their purpose was 'to tell the researchers your ideas through drawing a mind map instead of writing' so they should not be influenced by other students' drawings; and that the quality of the drawings was not important so they should try to draw quickly. Drawing the concept maps thus allowed children to externalize their mental representations of ICT at that particular time. They did not in any sense measure children's knowledge about ICT, and they were not comprehensive in terms of giving a total picture of their concepts of ICT.

Nevertheless, despite the qualitative nature of the data, it was possible to use quantitative as well as qualitative methods of analysis. This was useful to explore trends in the way that children represented 'computers in my world', particularly across the very large data set of 2,000 maps collected on each of two occasions in ImpaCT2. These data were, therefore, collected systematically, with the teachers who administered the task using an agreed 'script' of instructions for the children involved. They were then analysed both quantitatively and qualitatively, but the quantitative analysis depended upon the use of categories which had previously been developed through detailed qualitative analysis of a small number of maps.

The maps suggest that children/adolescents enjoyed doing this task and took great care with it. They provided the evaluators with a very large amount of information presented in a visual form which was readily accessible to analysis. Although there was some degree of ambiguity in the drawings and links, other problems such as anxieties over spelling and handwriting might have inhibited students in a writing task; although students were inevitably influenced by recent experiences to include some objects and not others, this phenomenon would have occurred in the same way in their writing; furthermore, drawing and writing enable different conceptualizations to be communicated so the drawings added new insights, which would not otherwise have been available (Kress *et al.*, 2001). Some advantages of collecting drawings rather than writing appeared to be: the students' positive attitude to the task; the amount of information that they were able to give the researchers in a very short time; and the ability of all students to participate equally without some being disadvantaged by poor spelling and handwriting.

The drawings were analysed slightly differently in the REPRÉSENTATION and ImpaCT2 projects, partly as a result of the very different sizes of the cohorts. In the former project it was possible to include a category for 'map type' (unconnected, linear, one-centred, several-centred and spaghetti) which required qualitative judgment and was no longer feasible when coding 2,000 maps. In ImpaCT2, on the other hand, a method was developed which enabled quantification of the links in even the most complex maps (which in REPRÉSENTATION had been classified as 'spaghetti' and not fully quantified). However, in both cases, there was no attempt to assess the correctness of the images or the links as the aim of the quantitative analysis was to access the extent of students' conceptualizations not to test their formal knowledge.

The number of objects (nodes) drawn, and the number of links between objects were counted in both projects. In ImpaCT2, the latter were counted in two stages, first by counting the number of links emanating from each node, and second by totalling the number for all nodes. This enabled us to count extremely complicated maps accurately. The ratio of nodes to links (the 'connectivity' score) was then determined by dividing the number of links by the number of nodes. This resulted in a ratio of 2:1 for the two simplest structures of maps (one central node linked to all other nodes; and all nodes linked to two others in a linear or circular form) and up to 7:1 or higher for maps with complex linkages between multiple objects. The latter could be said to bear a greater resemblance to the actual structure of networked technologies, suggesting more developed knowledge. The contents of the maps were then coded within two categories which emerged from an initial qualitative analysis of a sample of 60 maps carried out by two researchers. The analysis was grounded in the phenomenographic approach developed by Marton and Booth (1997) and involved the classic 'grounded theory' method of in-depth study of individual maps, followed by listing of conceptual labels, and constant comparisons between maps as further conceptual labels were developed and then grouped into categories (Strauss and Corbin 1990). The two category codes that emerged were: 'spheres of thinking' (SoT) and 'zones of use' (ZoU). The SoT included sub-categories of 'information', 'communication', 'advanced control mechanisms', 'technical details about computers', 'games', 'music', 'images' etc. The ZoU included 'home', 'school', 'workplace', 'shopping', 'transport' etc. Drawings were allocated to these sub-categories by the researchers and SoT and ZoU scores awarded to each map on the basis of the number of sub-categories identified within it. The list of SoT and ZoU was revised during the first phase of analysis to include, as far as possible, all types of drawings produced by the students. Since the variety of the drawings was very considerable, the category 'other' was retained for any which might still be outside the predicted categories. The team worked together to develop rules to ensure reliable coding, following which inter-rater reliability was checked across the six researchers and considerably surpassed the level recommended by Marton (1994: 5), that is, agreement between raters in at least two-thirds of the cases on first coding and agreement on two-thirds of the remaining cases after discussion.

Emerging patterns of students' concepts of ICT in their world

Phenomenographic analysis, using a combination of quantitative and qualitative methods, was used to identify patterns of students' awareness of computers in their world across the age cohorts. Phenomenography, as developed by Marton and Booth (1997), suggests that awareness of any concept or body of knowledge is always subject to variations of perception which derive from the individual and are shaped by prior knowledge, experience and other factors such as attitude and motivation. There is always a 'focal point' of awareness, in much the same way as a photograph presents some images in focus. This is surrounded by a 'field of awareness' in which other features/details are less well defined. Finally, there are 'fringe' awarenesses which are there in the background but may be only half-remembered. The starting point for phenomenography is the collection of individual perceptions – either in interviews or in this case concept maps – and analysis begins with the individual. However, phenomenography is primarily concerned with eliciting the emerging trends and patterns of awareness across a cohort, rather than with the awareness of individuals. Marton predicts that 'whatever phenomenon or situation people encounter, we can identify a limited number of qualitatively different and logically interrelated ways in which the phenomenon or the situation is experienced and understood' (Marton, 1994: 34). One aspect of qualitative analysis of the concept maps was, therefore, concerned with seeking for these patterns in young people's awareness of computers in today's world. The quantitative analysis had already shown large variations in terms of the extent and complexity of their awareness. While coding the maps, the researchers also became aware of strong patterns emerging within the SoT and ZoU categories, with most students drawing many more objects relating to some sub-categories than others.

The aim of the interviews was to determine the ways in which each student experienced computers in their world, in terms of: their *core focal awareness* (the aspects of personal knowledge of computers that come into the student's mind first and with greatest apparent significance); their *field awareness* (the aspects of personal knowledge of computers that are of slightly secondary importance and prominence); their *fringe awareness* (the aspects of personal knowledge of computers, if any, that are more hazy and distant). The second part of the interview was used to ask more specific questions about parts of the map that had not been discussed earlier as a further check on the validity of these data.

Since phenomenographic analysis derives the interviewee's awareness of phenomena from what he or she has communicated, it is essential that the interview questions influence the responses as little as possible. The map produced by the child/adolescent was the starting point in all cases. The interviewer asked questions about the map, to encourage the interviewee to talk about it, but as far as possible did not direct attention to any specific aspect of the map. The interviewers required considerable skill since the interviewees were conditioned by schooling into particular ways of responding to questions from adults: this is because teachers normally ask questions to test students' knowledge and have a 'right' answer in mind, rather than seeking a student's views and opinions; and students normally answer very briefly – or not at all since they can expect the teacher to answer the question themselves after a relatively short pause (Altrichter *et al.*, 1993: 138). These problems were overcome by modelling a different pattern of interaction: for example by clearly explaining the purpose of the interview, waiting for as long as was necessary for a student to respond, and consistently indicating interest in the student's responses (Mavers, Somekh and Restorick, 2002: 199–202).

The questions were as follows:

1 I found your concept map really interesting. Please could you tell me about it?
2 Is any part of your map especially important? Why?
3 Where did you start to draw and why did you start there? What did you do next and why (age 10–14)? Can you explain the order in which you drew your map (age 15–16).
4 Can you tell me how you know all of these things?
5 If you had had more time, would you have drawn anything else?
6 Why have you joined your pictures in this way?
7 Can you talk about the different ways computers are used in our world?

8 Can you tell me about the different places where people use computers and new technologies?

9 Would you like to add anything?

10 Have you done anything like this before in school? Can you tell me about it.

This was the planned order for asking the questions, but it was sometimes necessary to change the order to allow the students greater flexibility.

The analysis of each interview was carried out alongside the map upon which the responses were based. Grounded theory methods, similar to those used in the original analysis of the maps from which the categories of SoT and ZoU were derived, were then used to identify the focal, field and fringe awarenesses across the combined data set. In the majority of cases the interviews confirmed the original interpretation of the map, although frequently additional ideas were introduced in the interview (due in part at least to the passage of nine months between the two events). The reasons behind the drawing of particular objects were clarified in the interview in a way which generally reinforced and deepened the original analysis.

It was unfortunately not possible, given the ImpaCT2 resources of time and research personnel, to carry out a full quantitative analysis of the patterns of the sub-categories within SoT and ZoU across such a large number of maps. Therefore a supplementary study was carried out with a sub-sample of 34 students, involving more detailed coding of the sub-categories within SoT and ZoU (recording how many images were present for each sub-category as well as the overall number of sub-categories), and follow-up interviews to validate the original interpretation of the maps. The interviews related to the June 2000 concept maps and took place in March 2001, after a gap of nine months. Phenomenographic analysis was carried out on the combined interview and concept map data from each student.

Phenomenographic theory does not suggest that students will fit exactly into one of the 'types', but that they will present a pattern of awareness of computers in their world that identifies them more with one type than any of the others. The 'types' are therefore 'ideal types' drawn from what Marton and Booth (1997: 133) call the 'pool of meaning' derived from the cohort as a whole. To illustrate this process the analysis is given below for 12 students: four aged 10–11, four aged 13–14 and four aged 15–16. Their patterns of awareness of 'computers in my world' are presented in Table 4.1.

Six of the twelve have a core focal awareness of one of the sub-categories of SoT: Paul (aged 10) of the technology itself; Natalie (aged 10) of games; Heather (aged 15), Sally (aged 15) and Rob (aged 13) of

Table 4.1 Students' awareness of computers in their world

Pseudonym	Age group	Focal awareness	Field awareness	Fringe awareness
Paul (M)	10–11	Technical/electrical Networked computers	Games Music Communications	TV Information Images Home (only ZoU)
Charles (M)	10–11	Computer power Games Images	Music Information Communication	Library (only ZoU)
Natalie (F)	10–11	Games	Computers	School Home Information
George (M)	10–11	Computers Games Communications The workplace		Information Home Hotel
Liz (F)	13–14	Advanced control Computers The Internet	TV School Communications	Music Mobile phones Games Workplace Banking Shopping Transport
Ruth (F)	13–14	Computers/Technical Stockmarket (ZoU) School Bill Gates/Vendors Home	Communications Advanced control Information Workplace	Games Weather forecast Banking Shopping

Name	Age			
Tom (M)	13–14	Wide range of ZoU (8 in all) Transport (ZoU, 4 images)	Advanced control Computers School Workplace	Police Hospital Home
Rob (M)	13–14	Information (the net) Social institutions/people Computers School Shopping	Music Advanced control Home Workplace Banking	Communications TV Transport
Sally (F)	15–16	Information (the net) Communications Home	Images Computers School Shopping	Games Banking University/college
Heather (F)	15–16	Computers Social impact/access Commercialization Communications	Games Advanced control School Workplace Shopping	TV Mobile phone Information Banking Home Hospital
Mary (F)	15–16	Workplace (father's business, ZoU) School (9 images, ZoU) Games	Information Communications Computers	Library Music
Lisa (F)	15–16	Information (the net) Advanced control School (6 images)	Communications Computers Workplace Banking Library	Music Images Games Hospital

M = male; F = female

social uses including the Internet; and two have a combined focal awareness of advanced control mechanisms and the Internet: Liz (aged 13)
and Lisa (aged 15). Two others have a core focal awareness of ICT being
used in different locations (ZoU): Tom (aged 13) and Mary (aged 15).
Charles and George, both aged 10, do not fall into any sub-category.
Although this sub-sample is small it compares fairly well with other
samples used in phenomenographic research. It is likely that similar
patterns of awareness would emerge from a larger sample, and it might
then become clear which kinds of focal awareness are most common in
particular age groups and whether these are related to factors such as
gender. The strength of this analysis lies in the triangulation between
two types of data: concept maps and interviews. Most phenomenographic research relies on just one data source.

Fiona, one of the older students, produced two concept maps for the
ImpaCT2 project, at ages 15 and 16. In the first map she mainly used
text rather than drawing, an option that was available to older students
in case they found the need to draw inhibiting. In the second map,
produced immediately following her final examination paper for the
GCSE (the General Certificate of Secondary Education, taken by all
students at the end of Year 11), she ignored most of the concept mapping
instructions and as a result her scores for nodes, links and connectivity
are low – see Table 4.2.

Fiona's June 2000 map is shown in Figure 4.3. It is packed with detail
and the nodes mainly consist of words rather than drawings. Three
computers, probably those she herself uses most frequently, are drawn
as the largest objects, with the same attention to detail of keyboards and
'slots' seen in the drawings of younger children (see Figures 4.1 and 4.2).
At the top left hand corner and on the same scale as the other computers
the Internet symbol of the spinning globe has been fitted into the shape
of a heart plugged into the same kind of socket as the laptop, suggesting
that it is in fact a fourth representation of a computer. The label 'The
world is better with computers' may be either serious or jokey in intention. The rest of the design has been organized into zones representing
different kinds of computer use, the eye being drawn to the Internet
node highlighted with rays like the sun and close to the symbols for
Yahoo and chat and the email 'hub' node (i.e. a central node with other
nodes arranged around it).

Table 4.2 Summary of Fiona's 2000 and 2001 concept maps

Fiona, girl	Nodes	Links	Connectivity	Spheres of thinking	Zones of use
June 2000	83	167	2.01	7	5
June 2001	36	38	1	6	4

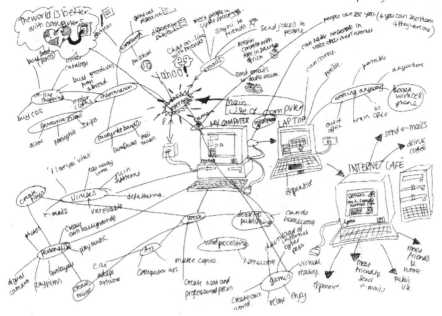

Figure 4.3 Fiona's 2000 concept map

The June 2001 map – Figure 4.4 – is image-based and appears to be an expression of enjoyment and exploration that would be consistent with post-examination euphoria. It is of great interest as a representation of the role of computers within family life and youth culture, highly personal, funny, giving the overall effect of creativity and youthful energy. The reduction in the number of nodes reflects the reduction in detail by comparison with the 2000 map, but the number of SoT and ZoU remain almost the same indicating that the *range* of coverage is very little reduced. Both maps present computers being used by people for a wide variety of purposes and in many locations, indicating in their different ways that Fiona has a very wide-ranging knowledge of their role in today's world. The emphasis is on social uses of computers; neither map includes much technical detail or reference to the use of computers for control, indicating that these aspects of ICT are not part of Fiona's focal awareness.

Fiona's concept maps initially attracted special attention because of their design qualities, and we then further noted the striking disparity of scores between 2000 and 2001. Their unusual nature then led us to seek out other data she had produced in response to other ImpaCT2 tasks. For example, a large number of students had kept a log of their computer activities at school and at home over the course of one week. Fiona's log complements and extends her representation, in the two

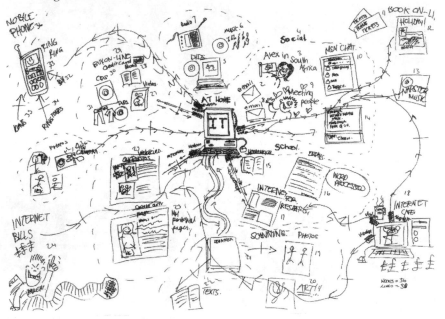

Figure 4.4 Fiona's 2001 concept map

concept maps, of her awareness of computers in her world. It was completed in April 2001, during the period leading up to public examinations. During that week she used a computer in two English lessons to research on the Internet for a presentation. She also used the Internet in two lessons in Art to research for GCSE and undertook further research for English in a CLAIT lesson. At home she records that she has two computers – a Compaz Preseno and a Dell. During the same week, she spent nearly five-and-a-half hours using the computer for homework: two hours researching for English using a search engine (Yahoo!); two hours typing out coursework for Graphics (Art) using a word processor and DTP; one hour getting information about Tracey Emin from the Tate Modern site for Art; and 20 minutes using Ask Jeeves to find out about GM (genetic modification) producers for science.

In general, the picture that emerges from Fiona's log is of considerably more use of the computer at home than at school. For example, she used a word processor to do school work at home for three hours and for a further four hours for her own interests, whereas at school she used a word processor for just two minutes. She had also used CD-ROMs at home for three hours (one hour for school work and two hours for her own interests) and an art package (two hours) and a music package – CD-rewriter – (two hours) for her own interests. This pattern was continued with online activities. Out of a total of 25 hours of online use recorded in the log, only five hours were for school work (searching for and exploring web sites and processing transferred Web information). For her own interests she spent six hours on email, four hours on preparing email attachments, three hours surfing the Internet and an hour processing the information, two hours creating web pages and four hours using MSN (personalized) chat rooms. Her other leisure activities involved using a hi-fi for about the same amount of time as the computer (27 hours, some of this time possibly simultaneously), watching television for 12 hours, talking on a mobile phone for just under two hours spread across five days and text messaging on a mobile phone for two hours (one hour each on Monday and Friday). In the course of these activities she reported using an electronic diary, a digital camera and a scanner. She listed the resources she found most useful for school work, in order, as the Internet, word processing, a scanner, DTP and CD-R. For her own leisure use she said she most enjoyed using the Internet and email/chat, followed by a scanner and CD-R.

Coda: implications for the future impact of ICT on education

There has not been space in this chapter to present sufficient examples from the concept mapping data to demonstrate the progression in children's concepts of ICT in their world over the period 1999–2002. To do that it would have been necessary to present a number of maps by children of the same age, spanning the time period. Nevertheless, the four sets of concept maps from the two projects do provide such evidence, at its simplest through the absence from the later data of the kind of confusion of function and/or terminology between a television and a computer monitor in Wendy's concept map, and more broadly through the evidence in the June 2001 maps that almost all the children in our sample of 2,000 had had actual experience of using the Internet including email, and a significant number had used these technologies extensively and frequently at home. These data suggest that the impact of ICT is currently considerably less on education within the classroom than on informal learning at home, and this seems to be due to a number of factors, some still beyond the control of schools and others necessitating changes in school culture that could be very difficult to achieve. An example of the former is the need for personal computer ownership by all students, which at present is generally regarded as an unrealizable dream, although it is acknowledged to be an essential feature of creative and effective use of ICT by adults. The latter can be summarized as the need to open the culture of the school to the enthusiasm of young people for exploratory use of the Internet. Whether and how this might be done is unclear, since downloading music and images, inventing new identities in interactive chat environments and playing extended online games appear to have little in common with the kind of planned learning that schools are funded by society to provide. The direction of movement to maximize impact is clear, however. As personal computer ownership is extended to more and more young people, they need to be given opportunities to take more control of their own learning, planning programmes of study within a curriculum that offers a considerable degree of choice. This implies the need for school structures that are radically reorganized to circumvent the barriers of very short time-frames, and allow for sustained learning through projects of varying length and kind that capture students' imagination.

Notes

1   REPRÉSENTATION, 1998–2000, was led by FORTH, IACM, Crete, Greece. The partners were INRP France, The University of Amsterdam, Orfeus Denmark, the University of Huddersfield England, the University of Crete Greece, Universite de Pompeu Fabra, Catalonia, and MAC Ireland. Associate partners were IUFM de Creteil France and the University of Mons-Hainaut Belgium. Further information is available on the project website at http://hermes.iacm.forth.gr.

2   The ImpaCT2 project, 1999–2002, was funded by the Department for Education and Skills and managed by the British Educational Communications and Technology Agency. It was directed by Colin Harrison, University of Nottingham, co-directed by Bridget Somekh, Manchester Metropolitan University, and Peter Scrimshaw, Open University. Researchers were Diane Mavers, Cathy Lewin, Kaye Haw and Tony Fisher. The ImpaCT2 publications can be found at: http://www.becta.org.uk/page_documents/research.

References

Altrichter, H., Posch, P. and Somekh, B. (1993) *Teachers Investigate Their Work*, Routledge, London.

Buzan, T. (1993) *The Mind Map Book: Radiant thinking – the major evolution in human thought*, BBC Books, London.

Kress, G., Jewitt, C., Ogborn, J. and Tsatsarelis, C. (2001) *Multimodal Teaching and Learning: The rhetorics of the science classroom*, Continuum, London.

Marton, F. (1994) Phenomenography, in *The International Encyclopedia of Education*, eds T. Husen and T. N. Postlethwaite, pp. 4424–29, Pergamon, Oxford.

Marton, F. and Booth, S. (1997) *Learning and Awareness*, Lawrence Erlbaum, Mahwah NJ.

Mavers, D., Somekh B. and Restorick, J. (2002) Interpreting the externalised images of pupils' conceptions of ICT: methods for the analysis of concept maps, *Computers and Education*, 38, pp. 187–207.

Novak, J. D. and Gowin, D. B. (1984) *Learning How to Learn*, Cambridge University Press, New York.

Pearson, M. and Somekh, B. (2003) Concept mapping as a research tool: a study of primary children's representations of information and communication technologies, education and information technologies, *Education and Information Technologies*, 8 (1), pp. 5–22.

Strauss, A. and Corbin, J. (1990) *Basics of Qualitative Research: Grounded theory procedures and techniques*, Sage, London.

5 (Dis)possessing literacy and literature

Gourmandizing in Gibsonbarlowville

Soh-young Chung, Paul Dowling and Natasha Whiteman

Begin

Some time ago the founder of the Electronic Frontier Foundation, John Perry Barlow, penned *A Declaration of Independence of Cyberspace*, reconfiguring Gibson's dangerous dystopia as the liberal paradise once dreamed of by Jefferson and de Tocqueville (and look where we are now); a paradise beautifully realized in Gabriel Axel's film, *Babette's Feast*. Here, the elders of the dour Protestant community can share with the gourmet general a table prepared by the finest chef de cuisine ever to delight Paris and all can depart sated by the certain knowledge that their principles have been upheld, that they have righteously abstemiously or rightfully indulgently or right creatively possessed the feast and, in doing so, denied no one. The feast, of course, was – at least subsequent to its preparation – inanimate and so indifferent to possession. There was, furthermore, quite enough to go around. Formal education, however, is centrally concerned with the possession of individuals and with the establishing of scarcity through its careful distribution of places and menus at its table: below the salt, literacy; above the salt, literature. All of course on the basis of merit. The question with which we are concerned here is, to what extent can the very highly visible and accessible (at least to those of us above the salt in the metropolis) activities in Gibsonbarlowville and its villages work transformatively on the institutions of formal education?

We are three authors with, respectively, backgrounds in literature, mathematics and then sociology, and film and media. This essay began life in the hypertext authoring environment, Storyspace (by Eastgate Systems, http://www.eastgate.com). This is the environment in which the first hypernovel, *afternoon: a story* by Michael Joyce was written and is available. The essay had to be rendered in a form suitable for conventional print publication and so moved to Microsoft Word, but has retained, we hope, a few of the features commonly to be found in hypertext writing. It is produced in comparatively short sections – mostly a little longer than *lexia*, perhaps – which are to a degree self-contained. Writing in this way has meant that we have been able to author our delegated sections separately – though in discussion and with some overall editing – so they may retain clear style signatures. We hope also that there is just enough tension between the three strands of the essay and perhaps between sections within these strands to retain at least some of the openness in its reading that its hypertext rendering might have allowed. Nevertheless, the linearizing of the essay has privileged one particular line of argument that considers the juxtaposition of bureaucratizing practices in the school, academic community activity and several cases of community and individual activity that are tangled with developing digital media. This line asks the question that was posed above, but we will provide only a general and not a specific answer to it.

The possessive school

Schooling works differently in different educational systems and varies between systems and in time in terms of its strength of possession and in terms of the visibility of its possessive strategies. In the UK, the era in which the Conservative Minister for Education referred to the 'secret garden' of the school curriculum (Lawton, 1980) allowed the fostering of creative writing in the English curriculum and the rolling back of prescriptive grammar. Times have changed. However strong or weak its hold, a formal curriculum with its associated assessment and evaluation and management strategies effects a claim to the possession of the principles of evaluation of academic performances. These possessive strategies construct *pedagogic relations* between the school author and student audience of the curriculum (Dowling, 2001a, 2001b, in press; Dowling and Brown, 2000). In the field of literacy, these principles of evaluation are constituted as competencies to be transmitted to students so as to provide access to literate performances in diverse areas that include everyday practices such as the private consumption and production of popular and elite cultural forms. This access is mythical, however, particularly in relation to the everyday. The incorporation of the everyday into the formal curriculum always entails a recontextualization that is to a greater or lesser extent transformative. The construction of literacies is always a context-dependent affair (see, for example, Street, 1993, 1999) whereas the curriculum must of necessity provide not only abstracted generalizations, but generalizations that are also organized into a sequence. This second aspect of the relation between everyday practices and curricular literacy is perhaps well illustrated by the relationship between a hypertext and any particular reading which, however engaging, is of necessity a severe reduction. Here is not the place to discuss the transformative effects of the recontextualization of everyday practices by the school, but see Moss (2000) on media literacies and Dowling (1998, 2001b, 2001c) on numeracy.

Possession and privacy

The possessive power of the school is sustained by formal curricula which are institutionalized, generally, by state bureaucratizing strategies, public examinations and so forth; that of the academy in respect of literary studies is sustained by international alliances that are realized in the journals and in the conference circuits. Whilst there may be substantial divergences across the territory as a whole, at any given point the institution constitutes a domain of literate or of literary competence over which it claims possession. This competence comprises the principles by which literate or literary performances are to be evaluated. If the competence may be referred to as the esoteric domain of literacy or literary knowledge, then what this competence recognizes as legitimately literate or literary performances comprise its public domain (cf. Dowling, 1998; 2001a, 2001b, 2001c, in press; Dowling and Brown, 2000). It is through their reading of the story in the literacy hour in the UK National Curriculum or through their perusal of the exemplary letter of application or their engagement with Jane Austen or James Joyce or Michael Joyce that the student is – at least potentially – able to enter the esoteric. Confronting this public domain are the everyday literate and literary practices that occur outside the school, frequently in private but generally under conditions of comparatively weak institutionalization which can pose little threat to the hegemony of the possessive regime of formal education.

Private possession

The acknowledgement and study of the social, collaborative activities surrounding media texts is not new. When private and domestic in scope and context, these practices have remained relatively invisible. Wilbur notes (in the context of romantic fiction):

> we suspect that there is something like a community of readers who share particular tastes and concerns ... sometimes this potential community shows itself as something more solid, in the form of magazines like *Romantic Times* which chronicle its existence, or at conferences for romance readers and writers.
>
> (Wilbur, 2000: 52)

But this privacy is not to avoid the gaze of the academy. In the 1980s and 1990s a surge of ethnographic approaches to fan and audience reception studies attempted to address this suspicion and:

the question of how historical subjects actively engaged with the mass-produced representations available to them . . . this work made an effort to ask whether media consumers were determined in their response to mass-produced significations by the character of their formal properties, or whether those consumers could make those representations into something more specific that they themselves could use.

(Radway, 1996: 236)

Radway describes how the methodological response to this challenge involved a transition away from demographic approaches to the study of audience, towards highly localized focuses on sites of practice/activity. This shift resulted in the generation of descriptions of specific confrontations between types of texts and categories of viewers (Ang, 1996) such as popular romance readers (Radway, 1984), *Star Trek* fans (Jenkins, 1992) and soap opera audiences (Brunsdon, 1983; Geraghty, 1991). More recently, the objectification and 'showing' of 'singular fan cultures' or 'narrow intertextual networks' (Hills, 2002: 89) has been criticized, with the gaze being drawn instead toward the fluctuating and shifting involvement of individuals in 'multiple fandoms of varying intensities at different times' (Hills, 2002: 89; see also Baym, 2000).

Active possession

Private audiences may nevertheless be active in productive auditing. The 'active audience' model is founded upon a vision of media consumers as producers, nomads (Deleuze and Guattari, 1984), and poachers (De Certeau, 1988) It is at the heart of a 'cultural studies orthodoxy' built 'around the assumption of the creativity and skilfulness of active audiences and consumers' (Featherstone, 1995: 11), which has been particularly influential in legitimizing the study of activities surrounding popular culture texts such as soap operas and horror films. This model celebrates the housing of realization principles with the reader/viewer and problematizes the possessive regime. It involves a 'blanket extension of productivity' (Hills, 2002: 30) to include a range of activities with different degrees of visibility and regulation; including 'work' by fans (the creation of fan fiction, fanart etc.), talk and gossip, and the act of reading/viewing itself (see Hills, 2002).

The transition to the study of hypertext environments has involved even more explicit claims about dispossession and agency. Aarseth, for example, highlights the limitations of the productive capacity of the conventional reader (and by association the viewer) who 'however strongly engaged in the unfolding of a narrative, is powerless. Like a spectator at a soccer game, he may speculate, conjecture, extrapolate, even shout abuse, but he is not a player' (Aarseth, 1997).

Aarseth's 'cybertext reader' engaged with 'machines for the production of variety of expression', such as hypertexts, MUDs (Multi-User Dungeons, or Domains), adventure games and some print fictions, is claimed to be more 'truly' productive, dealing not only with 'interpretation' but 'intervention' (Aarseth, 1997). In a similar way, Landow bestows upon hyptertext the creation of 'an active, even intrusive reader' and describes the 'near merging of roles' between reader and writer (Landow, 1997: 90). He argues that hypertext offers an electronic enactment of poststructuralist conceptions of textuality (1997: 91), shattering previous notions of monolithic authority/authoring of the text, and highlighting the illusory centre within the stability of linear forms of writing.

Electronic visibility

In the UK the possessive nature of the school has been increasing apace since the landmark of the 1988 Education Reform Act (see Dowling and Noss, 1990; Flude and Hammer, 1990). Essentially, state intervention has decimated and linearized and objectivized the school curriculum performances that are measured against standardized assessments and regular, published inspections. Similar bureaucratizing activity is now moving into higher education in the form of quality assurance. Cost efficiency exercises as well as the quest for commensurability across and within institutions has seen the modularization of undergraduate and postgraduate degrees. English teacher educators are now required to record up to 800 competencies in trainees over the 10-month period of a Postgraduate Certificate in Education course. Even doctoral studies in the UK are coming under pressure from state funding agencies to normalize completion times and to include approved and generic research methods (research literacy) programmes. Research output is regularly measured in a 'research assessment exercise' which determines funding distribution. In the UK institution in which one of us is a full-time academic (as well as in many others) a currency has been devised which renders commensurable academic outputs in the form of publications, teaching, and administrative practices such as dealing with admissions; in the future, all of these and other activities will be measured against actual monetary income.

All of these bureaucratizing developments have been facilitated by the development of digital technologies which enable the input, storage, super-fast manipulation, output and publication of vast amounts of information which, to be comprehensible, is generally organized into comparable forms. One result has been to raise the visibility and measurability of the activities of formal educational institutions. Another, many academics would claim, has been the severe weakening of what we have called the esoteric domains of many (not yet all) spheres of academic practice from the elementary school to research in universities. At the same time, demands for 'relevance' in research and in the school curriculum are encouraging more and more activity in the public domains comprising recontextualized literate and literary performances.

In some tension with these moves is the potential, via the Internet in particular, for both the expansion and strengthening of existing academic alliances on a global basis and for the generation of new alliances including alliances between weaker, minority positions that may seize the opportunity to establish a critical mass. In some tension also is the potential of these global digital environments to facilitate alliances in the popular consumption and production of popular and elite cultural forms, thus raising the visibility of hitherto private practices onto a world stage.

Audiences online

Online, the 'showing of self' of privatized 'real world' activity is played out on a large scale, and within the public sphere. Although the activity may remain for specialist interest only, it is theoretically visible to anyone able to access the Internet. The transition to online environments has generated new empirical sites for investigation by media theorists, such as the 'viewer mastery' demonstrated on the Usenet alt.tv.twinpeaks (Jenkins, 1995), the newsgroup activities of X-Philes (Clerc, 1996), and the newsgroup rec.arts.tv.soaps (devoted to the American soap opera *All My Children*), the story of how 'a collection of previously disconnected individuals took their shared interest in a pop culture text and transformed it into a rich and meaningful interpersonal social world' (Baym, 2000: 21).

The increasing visibility of Internet-based fan involvement and immersion within fictionalized environments described in these studies has coincided with an apparent transition from reading (and writing) to a multiplicity of (re)readings and (re)writings. Janet Murray uses the Internet fan activity surrounding TV dramas to demonstrate 'the suitability of epic-scale narrative to digital environments' (Murray, 1997: 84), an environment which she describes as offering 'writers the opportunity to tell stories from multiple vantage points and to offer intersecting stories that form a dense and wide-spreading web' (Murray, 1997: 84).

Murray's 'story webs' are particularly pertinent to fans' expansion and transformation of canon universes (see Penley, 1992) and the processes of deterritorialization and reterritorialization of media products and fictional environments demonstrated online. The authority of these privileged media products is both built up (through celebration) and destabilized via a multitude of paths, performances and gateways, both exploratory journeys through Internet sites (of journalism, marketing, fan culture etc.) and the imaginings of fictional, narrative paths within fan production. Both types of 'hypertextual' participation are linked explicitly to an immersion/surrender to an imaginative world (Murray, 1997: 110) previously described by Henry Jenkins in his discussion of fan production: 'Fans seemingly blur the boundaries between fact and fiction as if it were a tangible place that they can inhabit and explore' (Jenkins, 1992: 18).

The incident on *The West Wing*

The West Wing, Season 4, Episode 22, US screen date 7 May 2003

Throughout its four seasons to date, the American television workplace drama series *The West Wing* has flirted around the romantic pairing of two of its characters, the arrogant yet lovable Deputy Chief of Staff Josh Lyman and his sarcastic and super-capable assistant Donna Moss. Ancillary characters such as the brittle Amy Gardner – introduced as a love-interest for Josh in the third season – only served to highlight the fact that within this fictional universe, Josh and Donna are 'meant' to be together. Unrequited and repressed love affairs in television serials have always proved powerful conduits for fan interest and Josh and Donna's (J/D's) relationship has spawned a number of dedicated sites on the Internet. These sites examine and attribute significance to both textual and subtextual material. They scour over the snatches of dialogue and glances between the couple that suggest the possibility of movement towards union, a movement that is tantalizingly delayed by the constraints of the narrative.

The fourth season saw this movement gathering some momentum, with an increasing explicitness of references to the relationship. One moment in particular was to cause great excitement within J/D communities. This scene involved a superficially casual, but emotively loaded, confrontation between Donna and Amy and the asking of a crucial question. A transcript posted online a few days after the episode was aired offers a neat description of the final minutes of the scene:

> Amy gently pushes a beer bottle around on the table and replies, 'You said, you have to get Josh.' Donna, looking madly through a little red book, says, 'Yeah . . . that was. . . .' She hesitates, wondering how to crawl out of this: 'I didn't mean to say that you don't . . . get him . . .' Amy casually asks, just before taking a sip of beer, 'You in love with Josh?' Even though Amy can't see her face, Donna manages to control it. Cornered. She smacks the book shut and the

camera cuts away as the lyrics to the song continue: 'To love you love you love you love you love you love you . . .'

(Deborah's recap for episode 4–22 Commencement,
http://www.televisionwithoutpity.com)

Yahoo! Groups

Yahoo! Groups is a 'free website and email group service' provided by the Internet portal Yahoo! and promoted as 'a convenient way to connect with others who share the same interests and ideas' (http://help.yahoo.com/help/us/groups/groups-01.html). Messages emailed to the groups are archived on their web sites and are accessible by a numbered archive system, which is used in references in this paper. The web sites thus house permanent catalogues of preceding communication which can be dipped into at will. For some of the sites, including the two discussed below (JDTalk and JoshDonnaFF) it is necessary to register by emailing the site administrators in order to gain access and contribute to the archives.

JDTalk

The Yahoo! Group JDTalk (http://groups.yahoo.com/group/Jdtalk) is the domain of a number of television fans united by their choice of a particular show, and within this show, of two characters. It is a space for asynchronous chat and discussion about *The West Wing* and its cast, but most importantly, offers a communal support system for Josh/Donna fans.

The first posting to the group to react to the incident on *The West Wing* contained the confirmation by one member – after the obligatory spoiler warning announcing upcoming plot revelations – of what had taken place during the episode and excitement that previous speculation had been proved correct.

Exchanges between those who had and had not seen the episode contained shared anticipation as well as anxiety that the issue had been put so firmly on the line:

> wow, Amy and Donna do have a scene and a slightly tipsy Amy asks . . . wait for it . . . She asks Donna if she loves Josh! I so knew that question would be asked. And I am revelling in the glory that I knew Amy would ask Donna!
>
> (posting 14545, 7 May 2003, 8.38pm)

This was the first of a series of responses in which the moment was communally digested:

Yes, but do you know what her answer is? I mean we all know what the answer is, but will she admit to it out loud and to Amy?

(posting 14547, 7 May 2003, 8.43pm)

I gotta say, after I read that, I was practically euphoric. I screamed. My sister thought someone had died. But then my super-worrying side took over. And since you've seen it, I've gotta ask, what does Amy ask that Donna responds, 'He's past it.' (or am I getting my spoiler eps mixed up?) help! I can't WAIT to see this!

(posting 14565, 7 May 2003, 11:45pm)

The scene was celebrated as a move towards potential realization and fulfilling of these fans' investment in the relationship, and outside sources (such as quotes from the actors and Aaron Sorkin, *The West Wing*'s 'creator') were pulled into the debate in order to inform speculation of potential future events. At the same time, a range of online resources were used to convey the scene for those who had not seen it, both dramatically (through detailed descriptions and links to fan fictions from their sister-group JDFF that involved similar confrontations between Amy and Donna) and visually (via screencaps from the episode).

Within the diversity of responses on JDTalk, *The West Wing* is configured as a closed, authored space. The activity maintains a respectful stance in relation to the show, aiming instead for the mastery of its text via complete understanding/creation of a perfect, total version of it. JDTalk constructs what Michael Joyce (1996) has described as an 'exploratory hypertext'; a site for exploration and interpretation of textual material that is, in this case, possessed by the reality of the show, its official participants (authors, actors, etc.) and associated secondary and tertiary texts (Fiske, 1987) that might assist in interpretation.

JoshDonnaFF

JoshDonnaFF (JDFF) (http://groups.yahoo.com/group/JoshDonnaFF) is a Yahoo! Group built upon the exchange of fan-written fictions (fics) concerning Donna and Josh and feedback on these stories. Although JDFF is in many ways highly regulated – moderators banning abusive/flaming/negative criticism and enforcing a no-NC-17 classification (which bars descriptions of explicit sex/violence) – individual performances are relatively unrestricted and authority is located with the fans-as-authors. The group's activities demonstrate a transformative extension of the authored, canon text to include space in which readers can play, making public inscriptions upon the canon and rendering it an ergodic text (Aarseth, 1997). Some fics are closely tied to the frameworks of screened episodes, offering post-episode denouements, filling gaps, developing possible storylines and adding backstory/future events to the chronology of the canon text. Others are more fantastical, involving shifts from canon to alternate universes where Donna could be Josh's boss, and crossover fictions such as Cindy Brewer's 26-part CSI/West Wing crossover fic series 'Gone'.

The response of JDFF authors to the incident on *The West Wing* was to assimilate, develop and extend the critical moment, providing parallel readings (what if Josh overheard the discussion) and continuations which provide the answer (and satisfaction) that the TV viewer was denied. Fictions were posted shortly after the episode was screened (on 7 May 2003): Jo March's 'Twenty Questions' ('Why do you ask, Amy? Are *you*?' Message 16381, posted 8 May 2003); Misha's 'The Question' ('I look her straight in the eye as I answer the question, "Yes, I am."' Message 16374, posted 8 May 2003); and Mary Dell's 'Question and Answer' ('"Before you called earlier, Amy asked me a question. I didn't get a chance to answer her before the agents came through. I couldn't have told her the answer, but I do need to tell you." She paused and took in another deep breath before saying, "Josh, I love you. I'm in love with you."' Message 16384, posted 9 May 2003).

This merging of official and unofficial authoring within these fictions involves a weakening of the possession of the canon text which is extended and opened up by individual authors' fictive trajectories. When individual requests and monthly challenges for fics incorporating specific scenarios are posted on the site, the authorized text is transformed into a pliable, bespoke environment. Within this multiplicity of remakings, stability is constructed at the level of character; it is in plot and story that particularity and breaches from implicit canon are demonstrated. Replication of 'authentic' aspects of the show's 'voice' is constructed via the emulation of the stylistics of the show's dialogue (particularly the rapid-fire screwball-comedy style patter of the show). This capturing and creating of textual, partial verisimilitude is apparent even in those fics that reimagine the textual universe in radically different ways.

Such ties to the canon text suggest certain modes of competency that are made more explicit in modes of evaluation which enable the certifiable hierarchizing of authors and fics, and particularly in the site's annual fanfic awards and monthly challenges (www.geocities.com/ joshdonnachallengearchive/Welcome.html). The fanfic awards' different categories and genres of competency (such as Canon, Non-Romance, Alternate Universe and Best Humour) may constitute a repossession of the textual space in terms of verisimilitude, but one which remains weakly defined, as awards are voted for by members.

Hypertextualizing literature

Prior to the development of globalized digital environments, literature was (and still is) widely consumed outside the academy in trains, planes, armchairs, beds and book clubs. Here, there is scope for unlimited dispossession of the academy; if you want to leave out all of the poems when you read Byatt's *Possession* because you decide that they do not advance the storyline, then you can (although you will still have to pay for the now redundant 195 pages or so). But the invisibility that enables this smooth reading space (cf. Deleuze and Guattari, 1988; Nunes, 1999) also serves to privatize it so that it poses no threat to the academy. However, the broadening of Internet access – still limited, of course, to regions of affluence outside of Castell's (1996, 1997) 'Fourth World of exclusion' – radically raises the visibility of hitherto minority and privatized reading in the formation of new communities.

An example of such communities is The Republic of Pemberley, a web site dedicated to Jane Austen, her novels and adaptations of the novels. Membership of the community is acquired by self-claiming an 'obsession with things Austen'. The forum section titled 'Jane Austen Novels and Adaptations' is the site where members post their readings of Jane Austen's novels and adaptations. The space is highly regulated and strongly classified (Bernstein, 1996; Dowling, 1999). The poster of anything adjudged irrelevant to the novels and adaptations is admonished. Subsections dedicated to specific novels are strictly defined and the scope of discussion delimited. Comparisons among the works or discussion that is not concerned with a specific novel are confined to the section 'Austenuations'. Sequels of the novels can be talked about here. Members' readings of the novels range from a brief comment on a single character to lengthy, analytical writing on a novel. The site maintains strong possession over principles of recognition, but dispossesses literary theory and tradition and the readings are smoother reader celebrations.

The site also provides a space – 'Bits of Ivory' (BoI) – for fanfiction. Here, readers can begin to dispossess Austen. But the nature of the fanfiction is strictly regulated. The vision statement of the board clearly indicates that characters and their basic traits and plots remain in Austen's possession.

> The stories at *Bits of Ivory* are intended to present Jane Austen's characters behaving as she wrote them in scenes we might wish she had an opportunity to write herself. We may describe what happens before or after the events in the novels, re-tell parts from the point of view of another character, or elaborate scenes which she, in her wisdom, did not describe in great detail. In this, the guide is Jane Austen's own sense of taste and humanity.
>
> (http://www.pemberley.com/derby/guidenew.html,
> last accessed 03/07/03)

The contributor guidelines provide more specific rules: a story should be faithful to the original conception of Austen's characters; the story must be set in the same historical year as Austen's; and so on. In effect, the canonized space of Austen's oeuvre is opened to include BoI, animating it as a living textual space that thrives on interaction with its readers/writers. Yet the reconfiguration is carefully guided not to commit 'ontological violation'; authorship is limited to extrapolation, which essentially contributes to celebration of Austen's work. There is to be no evolution of the species, only cloning. Crucially also, discussion of fan fiction is limited to *BoI* itself. A reminder posted by one of the committee members advises:

> we do not discuss fan fiction on the boards here at Pemberley. If you liked a particular *BoI* story, you can comment on that board or contact the author of the story directly. (This wording has now apparently been replaced by the simpler, 'Please do not discuss BoI stories or fan fiction on the other discussion boards'.
>
> (Messages posted on 'Austenuations' at
> http://www.pemberley.com)

Readings are placed in a hierarchy not by the manner or their presentation, but by their object text. Discussion about novels and adaptations are regarded as primary texts. Interestingly adaptations are possessed by their literary sources, a feature evidenced in that films are introduced without directors' names. Then sequels of the novels, which have been published in print, are privileged over fan fiction. The former may be discussed in 'Austenuations', which is one of subsections of Jane Austen Novels and Adaptations; fan fiction is restricted to BoI which belongs to 'Slightly Off the Austen Track'.

Affiliation to the academy is established on 'Special Austen Pages', which includes links to collections of academic articles and quotes from famous literary figures. It even includes Shakespeare resource pages. However, these affiliations hardly serve to lock readers into the conventions of literary studies. The hypertext markup language (html) of the web site levels the significance of each affiliation to diverse sites outside Pemberley. The link to the Internet bookshop and the link to Shakespeare are democratized as equals. But all of these off-world links are marginalized as slogans or logos; the whole of the site is dominated by the celebration of the readers' performances and discussions. The possessive principles of recognition of what can legitimately be posted on this site achieve a bureaucratizing structure for what are now weakened principles of realization relative to the academy. But unlike the academy, perhaps, possession here is not itself bureaucratic. Whereas the academy must effect an objectifying distance from its canon, possession by the canonized author is here established and succoured by passion. The paradigm of literary study is destabilized by the crack that is opening between its sustaining cultural surface and its shifting social structure.

The possessive academy

Antony Easthope proposed five features that characterize what he regarded as the onanistic paradigm of literary study:

> (1) a traditionally empiricist epistemology; (2) a specific pedagogic practice, the 'modernist' reading; (3) a field for study discriminating the canon from popular culture; (4) an object of study, the canonical text; (5) the assumption that the canonical text is unified.
>
> (Easthope, 1991: 11)

Thus literary study is territorialized as an extrasemiotic and ontological space. Both the text and the manner of its reading are in the possession of the academy and literary education has been preoccupied with the presentation of the canon text and the transmission of the means of accessing its essential experience. The principles of recognition of the text reside in the official canon and the principles of its realization reside in the official pedagogy constituting a highly possessive regime. This self-closing aesthetics of literary study has survived a sequence of theoretical interventions.

For Matthew Arnold and F. R. Leavis, the literary work was a source of aesthetic and moral integrity that was opposed to, and so should be deployed as a defence against, mass civilization and industrialization. Since a literary work is the embodiment of its author's humanistic vision, it or rather the authors of literature can be placed in a hierarchy according to the intensity and profundity of their 'awareness of the possibilities of life' (Leavis, 1948: 10). New Criticism continues the reverence towards the literary work regarding it as an organic and harmonious whole, a 'well wrought urn' (Brooks, 1968). Literary texts bear superior values that transcend the impact of their social and historical context on their own structure. They are even detached from their authors and become autonomous objects in an ultimate, formal aesthetics of truth. Despite their clear differences, as the focus of critical interest moves from authors to effectively authorless texts, the possessive regime is sustained.

Reader-oriented theories introduce a disruptive move by apparently problematizing the possession of the modes of textual realization by enfranchizing the reader as meaning maker. Literary texts are no longer insulated from readers' responses to which attention is now drawn. Various theoretical frames are deployed to explain them: psychoanalytical (Holland, 1975), hermeneutic (Fish, 1980), phenomenological (Iser, 1974), and so forth. However, the initial moves by these theories to privatize readings – to dispossess the academy – have failed because the theories ironically install themselves as guarantors of legitimacy that they invest in specified subject positions. Readers are given more options than in the Leavisite and New Critical paradigms that fashion them to ideals. But each subject position remains locked into its reading. Two, at least, of Easthope's defining features – an empiricist epistemology and a modernist reading – are shaken yet quickly re-stabilized as literary texts are re-possessed by the academy.

Poststructuralist theories disrupt the field for the object of study announcing the death of author and at the same time annihilating the boundaries of a text (Barthes, 1977, 1981; Foucault, 1977). Now, the meaning of a text is produced through the ways that it connects with other texts, so they are perpetually open to new meanings. No hierarchical distinction between texts is possible so that the distinction between the canon and popular culture is invalidated. Non-canonical works, as well as conventional 'literary' texts, are dealt with in the literature department. Such a state of affairs seems to challenge all of Easthope's conditions, radically dispossessing the academy: the paradigm of literary study seems untenable. However, poststructuralist intervention affects literary study not so much in terms of its practice as in terms of its identity. Now a more or less explicit fluency with poststructuralist theory takes over as the competence legitimating readings, establishing repossession of the principles of evaluation of critical performances. Furthermore, possessive strategies reinstate hierarchical principles in, for example, the privileging of literary texts over their film adaptations that now find their way in the academy, but as the 'cultural bastards' (Kempley, 1993) of the canon (see also Reynolds, 1993; Pellow, 1994; McFarlane, 1996). As was the case with earlier forms of literary theory, the strongly possessive regime is reasserted.

Literary hypertext

The primary textual feature of a hyperfiction is its manner of presentation. A hyperfiction is in essence a collection of blocks of writing, lexias, which can be assembled in diverse ways. A narrative is produced as a reader selects paths through lexias. Furthermore, the interpretation that a reader will make of any lexia will depend – sometimes strongly – upon the route that they have taken in getting to it and, indeed, the number of times that they have got to it before. So readings of hyperfictions vary logistically, and because of this they are far less predictable than readings of conventional fiction that at least invite us to turn pages sequentially. Since, commonly, the reader is not given access to a map of the work as a whole there may be no certainty that all available lexia have been encountered. Thus even the point of completion of a reading is open. Many hypertext theorists have pointed out that the instability and transmutability of narrative have already occupied a large part of literary discourse and that experimentation with the textual form has also been done before. So the first and one of the most widely discussed hypernovels, *afternoon, a story*, by Michael Joyce, is placed in:

a long tradition of experimental literature in which one of the main strategies is to subvert and resist narrative. The novel ('the new'), from Cervantes to the Roman Nouveau, has always been anti-genre, and *Afternoon* is but its latest conformation.

(Aarseth, 1994: 71)

But the devolution of authorship to the reader in hypertext has a different significance from that in those literary theories that are concerned with the transaction between texts and readers that are essentially subliminal to the literary text, the materiality of which is unmoved. The dynamics of aporia and epiphany in conventional literary work is played out in reading space, while in hypertext it is played in both reading and writing space as the reader's meandering is instantly enacted in the formation of a narrative 'self-organization' (Hayles, 1999). Joyce describes this feature of hypertext: 'Hypertext is the confirmation of the visual kinetic of rereading' (Joyce, 2001: 132). Each reading is a new reading or an un-reading of the previous one.

The inevitable entanglement of the reader with the text, the immediate merge of writing and reading spaces interrupts the possessive process of establishing any conventions of reading, apparently cancelling the space for critics. The immediacy and unseen possibilities of a variety of narrative denies an intensified and unified gaze of any theory. There are only readings, no interpretations. Every individual performance is a version (Bolter, 2001). Critics are no longer able to act as a posteriori investigators, but should be like 'the participant observer of social anthropology ... [who] must make it happen – improvise, mingle with the natives, play roles, provoke response' (Aarseth 1994: 82).

Bolter's use of the term 'performance' signals the dispossession of the author in favour of the audience in the hypertext mode, yet his counting of *individual* performance, like the nominalizing of 'reading', invokes closure as well as openness. In *The End of Books – Or Books Without End? Reading interactive narratives*, J. Yellowlees Douglas (2001) reads and re-reads this ambiguity in classroom activities with print text – in its 'original' form and cut into segments – and with hypertexts and in the readings of critics and theorists and, of course, in her own readings of, amongst other works, Joyce's *afternoon, a story*. Douglas reaches the point at which she feels she can 'close the book on *afternoon*' (2001: 101) after her fourth 'reading' had reached a conclusion on what happened to the wife and child of the main protagonist, Peter, and thus 'satisfied one of the primary quests outlined in the narrative' (2001: 101). But this alone does not account for her sense of closure:

I am not, for example, absolutely certain that Peter didn't simply see his ex-wife keeping company with his employer, swerve and strike another car, carrying an unknown woman and child in it. That would certainly account for the 'investigator finds him at fault' as well as the bodies stretched out on the grass, but not his son's school paper, blowing about on the grass – just as it would also leave Peter's search for Lisa and Andrew as open-ended as it was when I first began reading *afternoon*. Which makes all the more intriguing the reasons for my closing *afternoon*, feeling satisfied with the last version of the text I read, and accepting the approximate, albeit stylized, type of closure I reached at that last 'I call.'

(Douglas, 2001: 101–2)

Douglas identifies the lexia, 'I call', and another, 'white afternoon', as key 'places' and her sense of their very particular placements in the topography of the hypertext that combines with her having arrived at what she feels is an optimal interpretation of the mystery posed by the novel that, for her, stimulated her sense of closure.

The absence of an obvious last page in this form of hypertext may well have stimulated Douglas's intrigue represented in the main title to her chapter, 'just tell me when to stop'. Certainly her approach resembles, in a sense, that of the participant observer advocated by Aarseth although here the author/reader is under her own observation. But fundamentally, what she has done in this auto-ethnography is to find a way of returning to the author of the novel – in this case, Michael Joyce – an authorial voice that may otherwise be lost in the celebration of open readings. We might not ask 'just tell me where to stop' of a painting which generally has a frame to define its spatial boundaries. In material terms, the conventional novel defines temporal rather than spatial boundaries. The hypertext is, to use Bolter's term, 'topographic writing':

Whenever we divide out text into unitary topics, organise these units into a connected structure, and conceive of this textual structure spatially as well as verbally, we are writing topographically. Many literary artists in the 20th century have adopted this mode of writing.

(Bolter, 2001: 36)

But of course, many visual artists in the twentieth and twenty-first centuries are doing much the same thing. These and other developments such as the 'technotexts' that are read by N. Katherine Hayles (2002) would challenge the visual arts/literature distinction. In demanding of a work of literature 'just tell me where to stop', Douglas casts a distinctly literary and perhaps distinctly temporal gaze onto the hypertext in a strategy that, in effect, repossesses that which rightfully belongs to the literary critic.

Conclude

Literacy and literature are possessed by institutions of formal education in different ways. Literacy is possessed in the school – at least in England – by totalizing curricula, assessments and inspections that regulate the public domains of literacy activities that are generated in classrooms. This possession is now rendered more effective and more visible by digital technologies including the hypertext environment of the World Wide Web on which the curricula and inspection reports are published. Insofar as they are also possessed by these structures, teachers are bureaucratized. But the World Wide Web and the Internet more generally also raise the visibility and accessibility of the popular production and consumption of literacy in the areas of popular culture itself (*The West Wing*) and in conventionally elite forms (Jane Austen). We might expect particular sites to undergo transformations precisely because of their open access and this is poignantly illustrated in Nancy Baym's (2000) revisiting of the site of her participant observation some years after her initial study. We will also expect that new sites will emerge and some old sites will disappear. Previously, though, the public domain of school literacy was confronted by highly localized and generally invisible popular culture authoring and audience practices, now readers of the school have access to a visible public field of audience authoring that will inform their readings. The question then is, what does school literacy look like from the perspective of JDTalk, JoshDonnaFF and The Republic of Pemberley?

In the cases presented in this essay we have described at least two modes of audience authoring. The participants of JDTalk construct a site for exploration and interpretation that is possessed by the reality of the show and by its official participants (authors, actors, etc.). The game is the collective completion of a hypertextual space differentiated only by the shift from information about what has already occurred to speculation on what may occur. The past in this sense imposes stronger possession than the future. Because the show runs to different schedules in the US and elsewhere, the past may be defined differently via the use of spoilers and spoiler warnings. JoshDonnaFF constitutes a more constructive hypertext (to borrow from Joyce, 1996, 1998), which is ergodic (Aarseth, 1999) and is very weakly possessed by the show which now stands primarily as a reservoir of resources. Here, the past/future distinction is established only in terms of the availability of resources provided by the show. The Republic of Pemberley also includes fan fiction, but unlike JoshDonnaFF the fiction is probably better interpreted as itself an exploration of Austen in which fans try on her clothes, so to speak. Through its spotlighting of an officially canonized author and her work, Pemberley constitutes a potential dispossessing of the school if not of the academy in respect of the location of principles whereby modes of engagement with the canon might be regulated.

Higher education is generally not yet bureaucratized to the same extent as the school. Its practices are regulated via academic alliances and oppositions. The apparent democratization of access to global networks that is facilitated by the Internet may lead to the formation of new alliances and the subsequent redrawing of the map of literary studies. It seems clear that developments within the media of artistic endeavour are resulting in radically new environments. One result may be the potential erosion of the distinctiveness of the visual arts and literature as writing increasingly becomes topographic and multimedia and as the visual arts increasingly explore these new multimedia, hypertextual environments. As Hayles (1999) points out, it has always been misleading to regard the artistic content of a work as somehow separable from its material form. This error aligns with the Cartesian dualism of mind and body that is the problematic of a range of popular culture works including Gibson's *Neuromancer*, Dick's *Do Androids Dream of Electric Sheep* and its filmic realization in *Blade Runner*; these works, of course, now attract literary attention. New media, then, entail new artistic forms that the academic community will work to territorialize. The evidence of Douglas's readings of even 'first generation hypertexts' (Hayles, 1999) suggest that at least a part of this process will be constituted as some form of rearguard action directed, however imaginatively, at restoring literary authority to the literary critic.

So what of the impact of the denizens of Gibsonbarlowville on literacy and on literature within the institutions of education? Contrary to Barlow's naïve optimism (see Dowling, 1996) territory new or old is always precisely the terrain of struggles for possession, dispossession and repossession, for the formation and dissolution and transformation of communities. Contrary to Gibson's rather more imaginative pessimism, the struggles for free expression in cyberspace are not over before they begin. Advancing bureaucratization seems set to make the school an increasingly dour place to be and obstructive conservatism in departments of literature is also a grim prospect. Doubtless, the bureaucrats and Luddites will present a sour face to the feast of exciting new literate forms and communities that is emerging with the new electronic technologies, much to the amusement or irritation of the digital gastronomes. But this is definitely not *Babette's Feast*; there will be resolution. As interested participants, we await it with eager trepidation.

References

Aarseth, E. (1994) Nonlinearity and literary theory, in *Hyper /Text /Theory*, ed. G. P. Landow, pp. 51–86, The Johns Hopkins University Press, Baltimore.
Aarseth, E. (1997) [accessed 25 June 2003] *Cybertext: Perspectives on ergodic literature* [Online] http://www.hf.uib.no/cybertext/Ergodic.html.

Aarseth, E. (1999) Aporia and epiphany in *Doom* and *The Speaking Clock*: the temporality of ergodic art, in *Cyberspace, Textuality: Computer technology and literary theory*, ed. M-L Ryan, Indiana University Press, Bloomington.

Ang, L. (1996) *Living Room Wars: Rethinking media audiences for a postmodern world*, Routledge, London.

Barlow, J. P. [accessed 1 July 2003] *A Declaration of the Independence of Cyberspace* [Online] http://www.eff.org/~barlow/Declaration-Final.html.

Barthes, R. (1977) The death of the author (S. Heath, trans.), in *Image-Music-Text*, pp. 142–48, The Noonday Press, New York.

Barthes, R. (1981) Theory of the text (I. McLeod, trans.), in *Untying the Text: A poststructuralist reader*, ed. R. Young, pp. 31–47, RKP, London.

Baym, N. (2000) *Tune In, Log On: Soaps, fandom, and online community*, Sage, Thousand Oaks, CA.

Bernstein, B. B. (1996) *Pedagogy, Symbolic Control and Identity*, Taylor & Francis, London.

Bolter, J. D. (2001) *Writing Space: Computers, hypertext, and the remediation of print*, 2nd edn, Lawrence Erlbaum, Mahwah, NJ.

Brooks, C. (1968) *The Well Wrought Urn: Studies in the structure of poetry*, Dobson, London.

Brunsdon, C. (1983) Crossroads: notes on a soap opera in *Regarding Television*, ed. E. A. Kaplan, pp. 76–83, University Publications of America, Frederick, MD.

Byatt, A. S. (1991) *Possession: A romance*, Vintage, London.

Castells, M. (1996) *The Rise of the Network Society*, Blackwell, Malden.

Castells, M. (1997) An introduction to the information age, *City* 1 (7) pp. 6–16.

Clerc, S. J. (1996) DDEB, GATB, MPPB, and Ratboy: The X-Files' Media Fandom, Online and Off, in *Deny All Knowledge: Reading the X-Files*, eds D. Lavery, A. Hague and M. Cartwright, pp. 36–51, Faber and Faber, London.

De Certeau, M. (1984) *The Practice of Everyday Life*, University of California Press, Berkeley.

Deleuze, G. and Guattari, F. (1988) *A Thousand Plateaus: Capitalism and schizophrenia*, The Athlone Press, London.

Dick, P. K. (1982) *Do Androids Dream of Electric Sheep?*, Ballantine Books, New York.

Douglas, J. Y. (2001) *The End of Books – Or Books Without End? Reading interactive narratives*, The University of Michigan Press, Ann Arbor.

Dowling, P. C. (1996) [accessed 9 July 2003] *Baudrillard 1 – Piaget 0: cybernetics, subjectivity and The Ascension* [Online] http://www.ioe.ac.uk/ccs/ccsroot/ccs/dowling/1996.html.

Dowling, P. C. (1998) *The Sociology of Mathematics Education: Mathematical myths/pedagogic texts*, Falmer, London.

Dowling, P. C. (1999) [accessed 1 July 2003] Basil Bernstein in frame: 'Oh dear, is this a structuralist analysis?', paper presented to the School of Education, Kings College, University of London, 10 December 1999, [Online] http://www.ioe.ac.uk/ccs/dowling/kings1999.

Dowling, P. C. (2001a) [accessed 1 July 2003] *Social Activity Theory* (Working Paper) [Online] http://www.ioe.ac.uk/ccs/dowling/sat2001.htm.

Dowling, P. C. (2001b) School mathematics in late modernity: beyond myths and fragmentation, in *Socio-Cultural Research on Mathematics Education: An international perspective*, eds B. Atweh, H. Forgasz and B. Nebres, Lawrence Erlbaum, Mahwah, NJ.

Dowling, P. C. (2001c) Reading school mathematics texts, in *Issues in Mathematics Teaching*, ed. P. Gates, Routledge-Falmer, London.

Dowling, P. C. (in press) Language, discourse, literacy: stability, territory and transformation, in *Culture and Learning: Access and Opportunity in the Curriculum*, ed. M Olssen, The Greenwood Press, Westport.

Dowling, P. C. and Brown, A. J. (2000) A grand day out: towards a mode of interrogation of non-school pedagogic sites, *The Curriculum Journal*, 11 (2), pp. 247–71.

Dowling, P. C. and Noss, R. (eds) (1990) *Mathematics versus the National Curriculum*, Falmer, London.

Easthope, A. (1991) *Literary into Cultural Studies*, Routledge, London.

Featherstone, M. (1995) *Undoing Culture: Globalization, postmodernism and identity*, Sage, London.

Fish, S. (1980) *Is there a text in this class?: The authority of interpretive communities*, Harvard University Press, Cambridge, MA.

Fiske, J. (1987) *Television Culture*, Routledge, London.

Flude, M. and Hammer, M. (eds) (1990) *The Education Reform Act 1988: Its origins and implications*, Falmer, London.

Foucault, M. (1977) What is an author? in *Language, Counter-memory, Practice* ed. D. F. Bouchard, pp. 113–38, Cornell University Press, Ithaca, NY.

Geraghty, C. (1991) *Women and Soap Opera*, Polity Press, Cambridge.

Gibson, W. (1984) *Neuromancer*, Ace, New York.

Hayles, N. K. (1999) *How We Became Posthuman: Virtual bodies in cybernetics, literature and informatics*, The University of Chicago Press, Chicago.

Hayles, N. K. (2002) *Writing Machines*, MIT Press. Cambridge, MA.

Hills, M. (2002) *Fan Cultures*, Routledge, London.

Holland, N. (1975) *5 Readers Reading*, Yale University Press, New Haven.

Iser, W. (1974) *The Implied Reader: Patterns of communication in prose fiction from Bunyan to Beckett*, The Johns Hopkins University Press, Baltimore.

Jenkins, H. (1992) *Textual Poachers: Television fans and participatory culture*, Routledge, New York.

Jenkins, H. (1995) 'Do you enjoy making the rest of us feel stupid?': alt.tv. twinpeaks, the trickster author, and viewer mastery, in *Full Of Secrets: Critical approaches to Twin Peaks*, ed. D. Lavery, pp. 51–69, Wayne University Press, Detroit.

Joyce, M. (1992) *afternoon, a story*, Eastgate, Cambridge, MA.

Joyce, M. (1996) *Of Two Minds: Hypertext, pedagogy and poetics*, The University of Michigan Press, Ann Arbor.

Joyce, M. (1998) New stories for new readers: contour, coherence and constructive hypertext, in *Page to Screen: Taking literacy into the electronic era*, ed. I. Snyder, Routledge, London.

Joyce, M. (2001) *Othermindedness*, The University of Michigan Press, Ann Arbor.

Kempley, R. (1993) [accessed 5 July 2003] Ethan Frome, *Washington Post*, 17th September 1993 [Online] http://www.washingtonpost.com/wp-srv/style/longterm/movies/videos/ethanfromepgkempley_a0a367.htm.

Landow G. P. (1997) *Hypertext 2.0: The convergence of contemporary critical theory and technology (parallax – re-visions of culture and society)*, The Johns Hopkins University Press, Baltimore.

Lawton, D. (1980) *The Politics of the School Curriculum*, RKP, London.

Leavis, F. R. (1948) *The Great Tradition*, Chatto & Windus, London.

McFarlane, B. (1996) *Novel to Film: An introduction to the theory of adaptation*, Clarendon Press, Oxford.

Moss, G. (2000) Informal literacies and pedagogic discourse, *Linguistics and Education*, 11 (1), pp. 47–64.

Murray, J. H. (1997) *Hamlet on the Holodeck: The future of narrative in cyberspace*, The Free Press, New York.

Nunes, M. (1999) Virtual topographies, in *Cyberspace, Textuality: Computer technology and literary theory*, ed. Ryan M-L, Indiana University Press, Bloomington.

Pellow, C. K. (1994) *Film as Critiques of Novels: Transformational criticism*, The Edwin Mellen Press, Lewiston.

Penley, C. (1992) Feminism, psychoanalysis and the study of popular culture, in *Cultural Studies* eds L. Grossberg, C. Nelson and P. Treichler, Routledge, London.

Radway, J. (1984) *Reading the Romance: Women, patriarchy, and popular literature*, University of North California Press, Chapel Hill.

Radway, J. (1996) The hegemony of 'specificity' and the impasse in audience research: cultural studies and the problem of ethnography, in *The Audience and Its Landscape*, eds J. Hay, L. Grossberg and E. Wartella, pp. 235–62, Westview Press, Colorado.

Reynolds, P. (ed.) (1993). *Novel Images: Literature in Performance*, Routledge, London.

Street, B. (1993) The new literacy studies, guest editorial, *Journal of Research in Reading* 16 (2), pp. 81–97.

Street, B. (1999) New literacies in theory and practice: what are the implications for language in education?, *Linguistics and Education* 10 (1), pp. 1–24.

Wilbur, S. P. (2000) An archaeology of cyberspaces: virtuality, community, identity, in *The Cybercultures Reader*, eds D. Bell and B. M. Kennedy, Routledge, London.

Films

Babette's Feast (Babettes Gæstebud) (1987) Gabriel Axel (Dir.).
Blade Runner: The Director's Cut (1991) Ridley Scott (Dir.).

6 Rethinking and retooling language and literature teaching

Ronald Soetaert, Andre Mottart and Bart Bonamie

Introduction

With the increasing use of digital technologies in everyday life, teachers today are confronted with the declining importance of existing literacies, and the growing importance of new kinds of literacies. For some this is promising. For others it augurs a deep crisis. Teachers are seen as 'at loss as to how to bridge this huge gulf between lived experience outside the school and the formal requirement of participation and achievement in the classroom' (McCarthy, 1997: 133). Indeed teachers, and especially language teachers, are challenged by new concepts of identity as classrooms become sites of multiliteracies. For or against, teachers should understand these literacies in order to develop skills and content in helping their students with the literacy tasks they want to accomplish.

But the new literacies are also part of our whole culture. We need an analysis, a critique and an evaluation of problems and possibilities appearing in the vectors of media, culture, technology and, of course, education. In trying to understand these new literacies we should also analyse the complexity of the new economy, society and culture in the making (Castells, 1996), and education in general and language teaching in particular.

Where do we begin our thinking? We suggest that the concept *literacy* creates an interesting perspective to start our reflection about what is happening today, certainly in (language) teaching. But we also need a broader perspective to describe what is at stake. We suggest three major concepts: new economy, digitalization and globalization. Although we do not deal with it here, we also want to signal the biotech revolution, exemplified by genetic engineering, as a major trend in our culture.

We want to stress the interdependence of these different concepts; they all are deeply intertwined and historically embedded. For example digitalization shapes our lives but is at the same time shaped by life. Technological determination presents a false dilemma 'since technology *is* society, and society cannot be understood or represented without its technological tools' (Castells, 1996: 5). This will be a central tenet in our thinking about culture and education: literacy is constructed by technology because it is embedded in the use of certain tools. Vygotsky (1978) described the importance of tools for the development of our intelligence; so, inevitably, modern technological tools will also deeply influence our ideas about education. Egan (1997) tried to describe educational evolutions by focusing on technological revolutions. Therefore, we need to take into account the emergence of a new economy and emerging globalization because both trends will deeply influence the skills and the content we should teach, the institutions in which we teach and of course the way learning is organized.

In what follows we would like to explore how digitilization has influenced our culture in general and the teaching of language and culture in particular, from the perspective of changing literacies triggered by changing tools. Teachers are not technocrats; we need a critical literacy.

Language teaching: state of the art

Although our profession is said to be in crisis, there is also good news for all language teachers. Nobody will deny the importance of language learning in our society: for personal development or/and social contact; for economic reasons or/and cultural exchange; for travel or/and for reading and for many specific purposes. All these needs refer to a particular literacy. When the needs change, the literacies change with them and the methodologies should adapt. From the perspective of literacy we can describe the functions of language as part of particular literacies, and these functions inspire and construct particular methodologies for language teaching. To understand what is happening with digitalization we can gain a lot by understanding how older media have influenced language teaching.

Tradition

In a pre-industrial, and even an emergent industrial, society with hardly any regular international contact there are different functions for foreign languages. The international contact was through texts, and the main activities were focused on translating and interpreting. So it is quite obvious that careful translation was an important skill. The Grammar-Translation method (with a focus on careful translation and interpretation of written texts) dominated language teaching of that era.

Such a traditional perspective on teaching was embedded in a classical-humanist view of education deeply inspired by the model of Latin and Greek: studying grammar and vocabulary in order to read/translate the classical texts. Such a classical education delivered the symbolic capital of a cultural elite. Such a traditional literacy was focused:

> on language only, and usually on a singular national form of language at that, which conceived as a stable system based on rules such as mastering sound-letter correspondence. This is based on the assumption that we can discern and describe correct usage. Such a view of language will characteristically translate into a more or less authoritarian kind of pedagogy.
>
> (The New London Group, 1996: 64)

Indeed, schooling was a way of standardizing national languages, imposing national standard language over dialects and constructing a national identity. The New London Group stated that the focus was centred 'on language only' but we should also be aware of the import-ance of *literature* in traditional language teaching. Literature was the ultimate aim of all language teaching because it was considered the best the language could offer. And it was the best way the nation could present, represent and reproduce itself. But all these traditional concepts have been problematized: the literary canon, the nation, the standard language. And with them we have also problematized the hidden agenda that inspired, and the methodology that structured, the pedagogy.

Communication

From the very moment Western society became more industrial, the international face-to-face contacts became more frequent and important. So, the audio-lingual method and the communicative approach to language teaching were constructed as a methodology fit for new needs and new literacies.

The communicative turn was introduced as a major revolution in language teaching because it posed a very simple question: how does our language teaching fit with the language needs of society in general and our pupils in particular? A sense of purpose became a central issue. Knowing a language is a question of competence and performance. Language skills became the new *content* although not as a product but as a process: meaningful language use was considered more important than abstract grammar rules. Language materials became contextualized in real-life situations, in situated discourses.

Education became pupil-centred and motivation, creativity and autonomy were the new buzzwords. While teachers were busy creating material based on these communicative principles, older teaching methodologies did not disappear. In order to compensate for perceived limitations in the communicative approach, drill, grammar, rehearsal and overt instruction were maintained. Probably the weakest aspect of the communicative turn was the neglect of the importance of *content*. Although the methodology stressed the importance of function and understanding, for traditional teachers *understanding* was the weak point. What did students learn? A lot of practical skills but is it possible to be functionally literate without cultural literacy? 'Back-to-Basics' criticism, inspired by nostalgia for an idealized past constructed around cultural consensus, put literature and grammar back on the agenda (Bloom, 1987; Hirsch, 1987; see Soetaert and Van Kranenburg, 1998).

The weakness of the whole communicative turn was thus seen as the lack of content and the assumption of the existence of a shared cultural grammar. Not only traditional teachers were worried about the lack of culture or content on the curriculum. Others were concerned that the approach failed to account 'for language in its totality and therefore has become, in today's Global Village, an inadequate learning paradigm' (Boylan and Micarelli, 1998: 60). Boylan and Micarelli argue that learning a language *is* learning a culture, and that learning a culture is more complex than the communicative approach suggests. Glossing Shank (1990), they define learning a culture as 'acquiring the capacity to assume even if only temporarily, a sensibility and a mind-set (or Weltanschauung, world-outlook) consonant with the society whose languages one wishes to assimilate' (Boylan and Micarelli, 1998: 63).

The argument here is that the communicative approach should take into account the cultural aspects of communication and the intercultural dimensions of language use. Boylan and Micarelli plead for a cultural communicative competence, which they claim has become an imperative in our post-industrial societies. Linguistic needs have changed, so our teaching methodologies have to adapt. Not only have *linguistics* and *language* needs changed; the concept of *culture* has also been transformed. Before dealing with this aspect of language learning and teaching, we want to focus briefly on some aspects of the contemporary search for the ideal methodology.

Post-perspectives

Today we are aware of the perceived strengths and weaknesses of prior approaches, so the debate between the traditional or communicative approaches is no longer a fundamental issue. On the other hand, we are confronted with lots of new ideas, concepts and methodologies that cannot be brought under any one new unifying paradigm. Different trends are emerging, giving rise to practices and approaches such as task-based learning, content-based learning, process-based learning, collaborative learning, learner autonomy and lifelong-learning.

All these trends can be described as a kind of post-modern echo in language teaching. Not only have 'grand narratives' disappeared; we no longer strive for discovery of the 'one-and-only methodology'. The idea that all perspectives have particular strengths and limitations is widely accepted. The communicative approach stressed learners' needs and more or less decided which needs were relevant, and certainly made prescriptions about the methodology. By taking needs seriously, however, we should take different learning styles, methodologies, motivations and functions, content, culture and subcultures seriously. In this multiliterate, multicultural world needs are changing and these needs are very diverse and even contradictory. Sometimes you need passive skills in a language, sometimes you need active ones; sometimes you need communicative skills, sometimes you need traditional literacy; sometimes you need drill, sometimes you need situated practice. Why we learn a language will deeply influence why we choose a particular methodology. From such a perspective, based on needs, we can also realize that different learnerstyles require different methodologies. Indeed, this is a very complex agenda. For some, digitalization is seen as helping to create such new methodologies.

Digital technology

Digital technology has certainly influenced the debate about language teaching. We can describe what is happening by looking closely at the buzzwords and the discourse in which language teaching is described. As Soetaert and Bonamie (1999) have noted, CALL (computer assisted language learning) has been replaced by TELL (technology enhanced language learning) which in turn has been now been superseded by TILL (technology integrated language learning). The transformation from *assisted* to *integrated* is revealing. The first term signifies a concern with how to fit digital media into learning and teaching. This is replaced by a major concern with how to fit our learning and teaching into a digital environment. Technology has become more than an *add-on*. But we may also say that there are two kinds of applications. Type One makes it easier, quicker, more efficient to continue teaching in traditional ways, whilst Type Two makes new and better ways of teaching available, which would not be possible without technology (Maddux, 1994: 133).

Cyberspace constitutes an environment in which we can use, and learn, a language. In the communicative approach it was recommended that practice in the classroom should be brought as close to genuine communication as possible. While teachers are using all kinds of materials to achieve this aim, technology has created an environment in which: 'Children will read and write on the Internet to communicate, not just to complete some abstract and artificial exercise . . . The Internet provides a new medium for reaching out to find knowledge and meaning' (Negroponte, 1995: 202).

If the particular kinds of literacy in any given society shape teaching methodology, then the moment we are confronted with electronic environments, in which barriers of space and time change fundamentally, we are confronted with a new kind of literacy, and our methodologies should change accordingly. New literacy practices and new functions for languages are a direct result of the rise of a new kind of globalized information society. Alongside CALL, TELL and TILL, Kern and Warschauer (1999) introduce a fourth acronym: NBLT (Network-Based Language Teaching), a new way of using computers in which human-to-human communication is central. They claim:

> That learners can communicate either on a one-to-one or a many-to-many basis in local-area network conferences further multiplies their opportunities for communicative practice ... the fact that computer-mediated communication occurs in a written, electronically-archived form gives students additional opportunities to plan their discourse and to notice and reflect on language use in the messages they compose and read.
>
> (1999)

In all likelihood, the C (of computers) or the N (of networks) will ultimately disappear in the acronyms, as the digital electronic *screen* becomes ubiquitous in the same way that the *book* has became ever-present and more or less invisible.

Perspectives for/on the future

In addition to social and cultural transformations that reconfigure the meaning of literacy and contexts for language use and acquisition, there are theoretical developments and perspectives that are inspiring new approaches for language teachers. These include constructivism (as a major perspective unifying the post-trends discussed above), discourse analysis, cultural studies and rhetoric. And, of course, all these trends are deeply influenced by the digital turn.

Constructivism

In our reconstruction of the debate about language teaching methodologies we are confronted with the fact that it is difficult to identify a new ruling paradigm. Yet, we can distinguish a common inspiration and belief in a constructivist approach. Such a perspective deals with more than language teaching. It reconfigures our ideas about culture and education, and it focuses on the construction of knowledge in all disciplines and situations. Cultural behaviour is described as a particular instance of communicative behaviour: we literally create the world in which we live by living it (Maturana and Varela, 1987). This has some major consequences, not least making problematic the ontologically conceived dichotomy of 'real' and 'unreal' and its replacement by more pragmatic concepts. This paradigm shift can be described as a contextual revolution in the human sciences; or as a *linguistic turn,* because of the importance of language in constructing culture.

Meaning is said to be *constructed* or *negotiated* in interactions between persons constituting their standard practices with artefacts and tools. Much of the literature of this contextual revolution reads like discourse analysis, cultural studies and even literary criticism. If culture is described as a product of history rather than of nature, culture becomes the world 'to which we had to adapt and the tool kit for doing so' (Bruner, 1986: 12). As far as language learning is concerned, this process can no longer be described as 'a question of a 'natural' mind simply *acquiring* language as an additive' (Bruner, 1990: 12). These thoughts, common sense ideas in anthropology, can be translated for education. Anthropology teaches us that 'there is no such thing as human nature independent of culture' (Geertz, 1973: 49).

This cultural shift leads to the idea that our ways of life 'depend upon shared meanings and shared concepts and depends as well upon shared modes of discourse for negotiating differences in meaning and interpretation' (Bruner, 1990: 25). In such a theory it is possible to link functional literacy and cultural literacy, but in this process both concepts are transformed through the central claim of constructivism: truth claims depend on the perspective we have chosen to assume.

This interpretative and linguistic turn strips philosophy from its foundational status. Asking this pragmatist's question is not the same as implying that anything goes. Such a question confronts us with a very practical problem: 'How does this view affect my view of the world or my commitments to it?' (Bruner, 1990: 27). The changing world we are living in confronts us with the complexity of prediction of commitments and values. Bruner (1986, 1990) and Rorty (1989) defend the viability of willingness to negotiate differences in worldview as a keystone for a democratic society. It is essential, however, to have a good working definition for open-mindedness: 'a willingness to construe knowledge and values from multiple perspectives without loss of one's own values' (Bruner, 1990: 30). For some the digital technology is welcomed as an ideal space in which multiple perspectives can be realized and brought into contact through multiple links and networks.

Cultural studies

In traditional language teaching the core content was literature, the literary canon. Culture was defined in a nineteenth century discourse as: 'the best that has been thought and known in the world', or at least 'the best of the West'. The turn inspired by cultural studies broadens this definition towards a more democratic, more anthropological understanding of culture as 'a whole way of life'; what we do with the tradition that we are handed, what we take up, what we reject (Hoggart, 1958; Williams, 1976).

Through a perspective based on cultural studies, combined with an analysis of discourse, we can deconstruct the historically based definitions of disciplines in education. If we realize that disciplines are only tools or constructions and not natural categories, we can deconstruct certain practices and positions, such as demonstrating that the reference to literature as an autonomous field is a nineteenth century construction.

A more sociological perspective on culture describes the ideological basis of so-called neutral definitions of culture. A cultural studies approach makes problematic the mechanisms of social and cultural reproduction. Culture is not seen as a having a fixed character but as a process of transformation. A traditional rationale for the cultural canon is based upon a hierarchy where cultural objects are ranked. In cultural studies this ranking game is questioned. Cultural activities are described as a set of activities developed within asymmetrical relations of power. Such a perspective should be reflected in the curriculum, seen as a kind of contact zone or 'social spaces where cultures meet, clash, and grapple with each other, often in contexts of highly asymmetrical relations of power, such as colonialism, slavery, or their aftermaths as they are lived out in many parts of the world today' (Pratt, 1991: 34; see also Bizzell, 1994). Within these spaces, texts can be studied as efforts of rhetoric (Soetaert, Top and van Belle, 1995; Soetaert and Mottart, 1999). So our profession can redefine its object of study and use its techniques to interpret and evaluate 'a variety of cultural texts' and zones (Bérubé, 1998: 25).

The digital screen, creating a multimedia environment, and the Internet, creating an interactive space, seem better tools for realizing such a contact-zone. Technology has the potential, for instance, to invite students to become agents in the production of cultural and social practices.

Teachers should see themselves as active participants in social change, as active designers, as makers of social futures. A key concept of the New London Group is education as design, 'in which we are both inheritors of conventions of meaning and at the same time active designers of meaning' (New London Group, 1996: 65). From such a perspective teachers are more than transmitters of knowledge, they are mediators, go-betweens between the life-world of their students and their specialized discipline, between the classroom, the workplace and society (Giroux, 1999).

Cultural studies might deliver theoretical tools to move within and across disciplinary positions and cultural artifacts to address the challenges presented within multiple public spheres. Critical pedagogy joins cultural studies in raising questions about how culture is related to power. It calls for resistant readings and the development of oppositional practices, so it also calls for teachers to be resistant intellectuals. The main aim is to make each claim provisional, 'not to elude the burden of judgment, meaning, or commitment but to enable cultural workers to challenge those forms of disciplinary knowledge and social relations that promote material and symbolic violence' (Giroux and Shannon, 1997: 6). All this is inspired by the need for people to speak affirmatively and critically of their own histories, traditions, and personal lives.

Such a critical perspective makes problematic the cultural model of Hirsch's cultural literacy. It rephrases the slogan 'what all Americans need to know' into what 'all Americans also need to know but are prevented from knowing' (Macedo, 1999: 118). Compatible with this argument is the idea that some traditional concepts of *Landeskunde* as national cultural myths should be questioned in the language curriculum, because we need a non-essentialist view on culture.

Discourse analysis

The *linguistic turn* has, or at least should have, an impact on our thinking about education. In discourse analysis we hope to find a major perspective for thinking about a new kind of curriculum. We use *discourse analysis* as the general approach, realizing that very often we find similar perspectives in pragmatics, speech act theory, and semiotics.

Discourse analysis has outgrown its original agenda: analysing language above the level of the word or the sentence. More and more discourse analysis focuses on the problem of how people use language. So discourse analysis has enlarged its field of study: from the study of language, mainly texts, toward the study of cultural practices (Fairclough, 1992b). What do we learn?

Language makes no sense outside discourse:

> There are many different 'social languages' connected in complex ways with different Discourses. There are many different sorts of literacy – many literacies – connected in complex ways with different Discourses. Cyberpunks and physicists, factory workers and boardroom executives, policemen and graffiti-writing urban gang-members engage in different literacies, use different 'social languages', and are in different Discourses.

> (Gee, 1996: ix)

This realization was inspired by a major critique aimed at the dominant discourse voiced in poststructuralist feminist and postcolonial theory, and today in the discourse of cyberculture. These voices can no longer be silenced so the need is growing for spaces for confrontation and emancipation. As our culture and life-world becomes more divergent, we realize that

> the central act of language becomes the multiplicity of meanings and their continual intersection. Just as there are multiple layers to everyone's identity, there are multiple discourses of identities and there are multiple discourses of recognition to be negotiated. We have to be proficient as we negotiate the many lifeworlds we encounter in our everyday lives. This creates a new challenge for literacy pedagogy.
>
> (New London Group, 1996: 71)

There is a growing consensus that we should shift the terms of the discussion 'from the notions of elitism toward an acceptance of the fact that *everyone* has different knowledge and belongs to (many) different discursive communities' (Hutcheon, 1994: 97).

We learn about the asymmetries of power between consumers and producers, referring to an unequal access to resources and competencies. Discourse analysis highlights the processes by which official education can act as a gatekeeper of mastery of discursive resources. School subjects and disciplines can be described as discourse communities. To be part of a discipline means to ask particular questions, to use a particular discourse. So all teaching can be described as a socialization into a discourse. Human knowledge:

> is initially developed as part and parcel of collaborative interactions with others of diverse skills, backgrounds, and perspectives joined together in a particular epistemic community, that is, a community of learners engaged in common practices centered around a specific (historically and socially constructed) domain of knowledge.
>
> (New London Group, 1996: 82)

Combined with a broader sociological perspective we learn more about the way literacies are constructed and reconfigured from and as cultural capital. We are confronted with the regulatory effects of schooling and educational language. Describing implies prescribing.

Indeed, important for education is the fact that in classrooms we can construct and deconstruct what counts as knowledge, or what kind of interpretations and evaluations count as legitimate. For instance, ethnomethodological studies of classroom talk detail many of the typical discourse moves and techniques with which teachers regulate classroom knowledge. In its constructive moment, critical discourse analysis can be used as the basis for the teaching of 'critical language awareness' and 'critical literacy' to students (Fairclough, 1992a). Such a perspective is important because when teachers learn to juxtapose different languages and discourses they gain 'meta-cognitive and meta-linguistic abilities to reflect critically on complex systems and their interactions' (New London Group, 1996: 69).

For the New London Group meaning is structured by 'order of discourse':

> the structure or the set of conventions associated with semiotic activity (including use of language) in a given social space – a particular society, or a particular institution such as a school or a workplace, or more loosely structured spaces of ordinary life encapsulated in the notion of different lifeworlds.
>
> (1996: 74)

The concept 'order of discourse' refers to the fact that discourses may be related to each other, discourses shape and are shaped by each other. Schools can be described as sites in which orders of discourse are interrelated: the school subjects or disciplines can be described as discourses, teacher and pupils have particular discourses, classrooms create a particular discourse and of course all (sub)cultures are structured by discourse.

Discourses produce, reproduce and transform people. Different people can belong to different orders of discourse, different networks. Various semiotic systems are structured through a kind of grammar. We would like to replace the idea of *grammar* by the concept of *rhetoric*. Again, we will argue that the emergence of digital technology has paralleled the return of rhetoric as an important discipline.

Rhetoric

Revival

Rhetoric can be described as a rich source and discipline in which the basic ideas of Western society have been developed regarding how language and communication function. But before going on we should make problematic a few concepts in this plea for the revival of rhetoric. Rhetoric has been despised as a 'discipline of deception' or has been trivialized as a 'bag of tricks' to embellish language. Rhetorically this was done by opposing *rhetorical strategies* with *true, honest, natural language*.

It is likely that the obsession with trivializing rhetoric as 'embellishment' is inspired by the idea that we can find some basic information in a text, that there is a naked truth. What we are focusing on here, however, is meaning and so the way words and information are organized and presented is crucial. A rhetorical perspective makes us aware of the fact that rhetoric is deeply embedded in all culture and all discourse. In this sense, interpreting rhetorical strategies implies understanding a culturally specific context; rhetoric is embodied and embedded in a situated environment. Realizing this implies that we are confronted with a basic realization in Western philosophy: Western rhetoric is only one model. Even in Western society itself there are different models although some have been silenced because of the dominance of a particular supermodel: the Aristotelian perspective.

We were told that *ornatus* in Latin not only means ornament but also tool. So rhetoric can be described as an important tool kit we need in a kind of society in which truth has been problematized. Indeed, as Lanham argues, because rhetoric has been despised it was difficult to realize what it really was: an information system (Lanham, 1993: 57). But it is even more than that, Lanham argues:

> Rhetoric defines itself as a counter-system to the Platonic political order by admitting stylistic, ornamental behavior, by acknowledging that such behavior lies at the heart of human life, is what human politics is all about. If stylistic behavior is acknowledged as part of the complex human 'reason' then rhetoric becomes the systematic attempt to account for this complex 'reason'.
>
> (1993: 57).

This rhetorical turn is inspired by linguists who have stressed a continuum between orality and literacy and the existence of 'multiple literacies' and multiple intelligent ways to use language (Heath, 1983; Scribner and Cole, 1981; Labov, 1972). More and more the superiority of an, or any, elitist culture, language or discourse has been challenged. Kaplan (1966) coined the concept of 'contrastive rhetoric' to describe how people differ in the way they put arguments together. In English, and in the dominant Western culture, the linear, hierarchical, straightforward mode has become the governing model.

This linguistic turn can also be seen as an anthropological turn: different cultures reflect different ways with language, different 'ways with words'. In a fascinating essay Villanueva (1999) illustrates how even one's linguistic ancestry is displayed in the way one uses words. He explains how the Latino's ways with words have been influenced by several rhetorical styles, with different patterns than traditional rhetoric (with its roots with the Sophists of fifth century Athens). Also in other languages – his case study is English – he traces a history older than 'the Aristotelian ways we think of as 'right' in the late twentieth century. Villanueva argues:

It is Aristotle's way with words that comprise the code that students must come to learn. We know it, even subconsciously. We have been book-folks. That is how we came to be teachers. Getting through college is being exposed to the ways with words of academics. We must, to become teachers, but I would argue we need to know a little more. We need to look at Aristotle himself – his rhetoric, a short work, and his logic a little longer.

(1999: 118)

His conclusion for language teaching is deeply post-modern: there is no 'right' nor 'wrong'. 'There is, however, switching codes, adjusting the language to fit the situation' (1999: 117). What does this mean for the classroom? 'It means we should become discourse analysts, rhetorical critics' (1999: 117).

Multimedia

Rhetoric – as most of us know it today – is mainly concerned with spoken and written language; but other modes of communication can and should be added: visual, audio and gestural modes. Disciplines such as critical discourse analysis, pragmatics, stylistics, cultural studies and semiotics also focus on the competencies that are an extension of linguistic competence. Of course this turn is embedded in what happened to the mass media in our society.

But the digital revolution confronts us with the fact that *all* modes of communication appear on the computer screen. What happens when text comes from page to screen? Lanham relates this translation from one medium to another to the rhetorical tradition: 'First, the digital text becomes unfixed and interactive. The reader can change it, become writer. The center of Western culture since the Renaissance ... the fixed, authoritative text, simply explodes in the ether' (1993: 31). So for Lanham we are moving back in time, toward the world of rhetoric, 'where gestural symmetries were permitted and sound was omnipresent' (1993: 74–5) and where image and word were closely intertwined. In recent theory, this idea that screens are inherently rhetorical has become a central perspective for research. A central tenet for Welch, for instance, is that 'historical rhetorical and writing practices must be reperformed (rewritten and reenacted) in our scholarly, teaching and everyday lives. This move acknowledges the inherent rhetoricity of all symbol systems, including the electronic forms of discourse' (Welch, 1999: 21). Indeed, computers force us to see how all texts and images and sounds – in fact, life itself – are deeply and essentially rhetoric. Rhetoric is re-established as the 'Queen of the Curriculum', it replaces literature as the 'King's Road to Language Learning'. Yet it does not abolish literature but it suggests rhetoric as a 'general theory for all the arts, and, as well, the structure for a central curriculum in the arts and letters' (Lanham, 1989: 16). And for the whole of education, we would like to suggest. But the good news for our profession, as language teachers and researchers, is that we can lead the dance; not only from a linguistic perspective, but also from the perspective of art.

Art

What is happening and probably what lies ahead can be seen in how art has dealt and is dealing with traditional and new media:

> Nowhere does technological pressure fall more intensely than on the relation between the arts. Digitalization gives them a new common ground, a quasi-mathematical equivalency that recalls the great Platonic dream for the unity of all knowledge. Digitalization both desubstantiates a work of art and subjects it to perpetual immanent metamorphosis from one sense-dimension to another.
>
> (Lanham, 1989: 273)

For Lanham and others, post-modernist art supplied the aesthetic of electronic display half a century before we started processing our words electronically.

De Kerckhove (1997) has stressed the idea that the Internet is undoubtedly also a cultural technology, so we should turn to the avant-garde arts to learn what is happening to us. A new chapter of art history is about to be written, and we should carefully read this story. Art has always been a very important measure for human achievement: 'The presence or absence of 'true art' defined as free creation unfettered by functional requirements, could be used as a kind of litmus test of the level of civilization a group of people had supposedly achieved' (Phillips and Steiner, 1999: 7). Art has a task: 'to give shape to possibilities and questions about this socio-economic shift and its emerging cultural form that are not raised by virtual environments produced and designed for instrumental purposes or for entertainment' (Morse, 1996: 198). This leads us towards the curriculum as a post-modern work of art:

> a participatory drama in which students must take part, a drama which is set in a stage but not set in concrete, with dialogue which is there to revise and a plot which licenses us to collaborate with chance – all these together aiming to teach not only knowledge but the way knowledge is held. And this, of course, is how Whitehead defines wisdom.
>
> (Lanham, 1986: 141)

This wisdom should inspire the curriculum.

Rethink and retool

In this chapter we have tried to analyse how the digital revolution has influenced language and culture by focusing on the case study of language and literature teaching. How can we re-think and re-tool what we are doing? One way of revising the function of new technological tools for education could be 'to re-position common theoretical questions, asking not how education might use these new tools, but instead asking what, educationally, they might offer' (de Castell *et al.*, 2002: online, no page number).

As we have tried to argue, the history of the introduction of media – books, television, computers – has a common story-line: we start using the media as a tool but the tool starts creating a culture. Indeed, cyberspace will become our 'contact zone'. The main focus could become an *educational* theory of technology. A theory from which we 'learn from our tools even as we endeavor to rethink, not just their uses, but more fundamentally the prospects of digital technologies for reconceiving the very idea of a truly *public* education' (de Castell *et al.*, 2002).

Therefore, we need 'to denaturalise and make strange' what we have learned and mastered (New London Group, 1996: 86). Indeed, become students of our own changing culture and language.

References

Bérubé, M. (1998) *The Employment of English*, New York University Press, New York and London.

Bizzell, P. (1994) Contact zones and English studies, *College English*, 56 (2), pp. 163–9.

Bloom, A. (1987) *The Closing of the American Mind*, Simon & Schuster, New York.

Boylan, P. and Micarelli, A. (1998) Learning languages as 'culture' with CALL, in *CALL, Culture and the Language Curriculum*, eds L. Calvi and W. Geerts, pp. 60–72, Springer-Verlag, London/Berlin.

Bruner, J. (1986) *Actual Minds, Possible Worlds*, Harvard University Press, Cambridge, MA.

Bruner, J. (1990) *Acts of Meaning*, Harvard University Press, Cambridge, MA.

Castells, M. (1996) *The Information Age: Economy, society and culture, volume I, The Rise of the Network Society*, Blackwell, Oxford.

de Castell, S., Bryson, M. and Jenson J. [accessed 23 March 2002] *Object Lessons: Towards an Educational Theory of Technology* [Online] http://firstmonday.org/issues/issue7_1/castell/index.htm.

De Kerckhove, D. (1997) *Connected Intelligence: The arrival of the Web society*, Somerville House Publishing, Toronto.

Egan, K. (1997) *The Educated Mind: How cognitive tools shape our understanding*, University of Chicago Press, Chicago.

Fairclough, N. (ed.) (1992a) *Critical Language Awareness*, Longman, London.

Fairclough, N. (1992b) *Discourse and Social Change*, Polity Press, Cambridge.

Gee, J. (1996) *Social Linguistics and Literacies*, Taylor & Francis, London.

Geertz, C. (1973) *The Interpretation of Cultures*, Basic Books, New York.

Giroux, H. A. (1999) Border youth, difference, and postmodern education, in *Critical Education in the Information Age*, eds M. Castells, R. Flecha, P. Freire et al., pp. 93–115, Rowman & Littlefield Publishers, Lanham.

Giroux, H. A. and Shannon, P. (1997) Cultural studies and pedagogy as performative practice, in *Education and Cultural Studies*, eds H. A. Giroux and P. Shannon, pp. 1–9, Routledge, London.

Heath, S. (1983) *Ways with Words: Language, life, and work in communities and classrooms*, Cambridge University Press, Cambridge.

Hirsch, E. (1987) *Cultural Literacy: What every American needs to know with an appendix what literate Americans know*, Vintage Books, New York.

Hoggart, R. (1958) *The Uses of Literacy*, Penguin, London.

Hutcheon, L. (1994) *Irony's Edge: The Theory and Politics of Irony*, Routledge, London.

Kaplan, R. B. (1966) Cultural Thought Patterns and Intercultural Education, *Language Learning*, 16, pp. 1–20.

Kern, R. and Warschauer, M. (1999) [accessed 11 November 2003] *Introduction: Theory and practice of network-based language teaching* [Online] http://www.gse.uci.edu/markw/nblt-intro.html.

Labov, W. (1972) *Language in the Inner City: Studies in the Black English Vernacular*, University of Pennsylvania Press, Philadelphia.

Lanham, R. A. (1986) The rhetorical paideia: the curriculum as a work of art, *College English*, 48, pp. 133–43.

Lanham, R. A. (1989) The electronic word: literary study and the digital revolution, *New Literary History*, 20 (2), pp. 266–90.

Lanham, R. A. (1993) *The Electronic Word*, The University of Chicago Press, Chicago.

Macedo, D. (1999) Our common culture: a poisonous pedagogy, in *Critical Education in the Information Age*, eds M. Castells, R. Flecha, P. Freire, H. A. Giroux, D. Macedo and P. Willis, pp. 117–37, Rowman & Littlefield Publishers, Lanham/Oxford.

Maddux, C. (1994) Editorial, *Journal of Information Technology for Teacher Education*, 3 (1), 133.

Maturana, H. R. and Varela, F. G. (1987) *The Tree of Knowledge*, New Science Library, Boston.

McCarthy, C. (1997) The problem with origins, race and the contrapuntal nature of the education experience, in *Education and Cultural Studies*, eds H. A. Giroux and P. Shannon, pp. 115–140, Routledge, London.

Morse, M. (1996) Nature morte: landscape and narrative in virtual environments, in *Immersed in Technology: Art and virtual environments*, eds M. A. Moser and D. MacLeod, pp. 195–232, The MIT Press, Cambridge, MA.

Negroponte, N. (1995) *Being Digital*, Alfred A. Knopf, New York.

New London Group (1996) A pedagogy of multiliteracies: designing social futures, *Harvard Educational Review*, 66 (1), pp. 60–92.

Phillips, R. B. and Steiner, C. B. (1999) Art, authenticity, and the baggage of cultural encounter, in *Unpacking Culture: Art and commodity in colonial and postcolonial worlds*, eds R. B. Philips and C. B. Steiner, pp. 3–19, University of California Press, Berkeley.

Pratt, M. L. (1991) Arts of the contact zone, *Profession 91*, pp. 33–40, MLA, New York.

Rorty, R. (1989) *Contingency, Irony, and Solidarity*, Cambridge University Press, Cambridge.

Scribner, S. and Cole, M. (1981) *The Psychology of Literacy*, Harvard University Press, Cambridge, MA.

Shank, R. (1990) Case-based teaching: four experiences in educational software design, *Interactive Learning Environments*, 1 (4), pp. 231–53.

Soetaert, R. and Bonamie, B. (1999) Reconstructing the teaching of language: a view formed by the problems of traditional literacy in a digital age, *Journal of Information Technology for Teacher Education*, 8 (2), pp. 123–47.

Soetaert R. and Van Kranenburg, R. (1998) Cultural studies in language teaching: culture and language in a network, in *CALL, Culture and the Language Curriculum*, eds L. Calvi and W. Geerts, pp. 23–36, Springer-Verlag, London/Berlin.

Soetaert, R., Top, L. and van Belle, G. (1995) Creating a new borderland on the screen, *Educational Media International*, 32 (2), pp. 62–6.

Soetaert, R. and Mottart, A. (1999) Communicating complexity: content, interaction & media in teaching literature, in *Fiction, Literature and Media* ed.. M. Kooy, T. Janssen and K. Watson, pp. 23–38, Amsterdam University Press, Amsterdam.

Villanueva, V. Jr (1999) Sophistry, Aristotle, contrastive rhetoric, and the student of color, in *Pathways to Success in School: Culturally responsive teaching*, eds E. R. Hollins and E. I. Oliver, pp. 107–23, Lawrence Erlbaum, London.

Vygotsky, L. S. (1978) *Mind in society*, Harvard University Press, Cambridge, MA.

Welch, K. E. (1999) *Electric Rhetoric: Classical rhetoric, oralism, and a new literacy*. The MIT Press, Cambridge, MA.

Williams, R. (1976) *Keywords: A Vocabulary of Culture and Society*, Fontana/Croom Helm, London.

Part II
Learners and teachers

7 Playing and learning with digital technologies – at home and at school

Toni Downes

Introduction

With an increasing presence in homes and communities, digital technologies have become part of the fabric of many children's lives. In communities where digital technologies are in abundance, they have changed the way the adults and children relate to and interact with each other and with institutions such as banks, businesses, governments, libraries and schools (Covell and Whyte, 1999; Negroponte, 1995). Within the family, patterns of social interactions, work and leisure are changing through technological innovations such as mobile phones, DVD and CD players, digital and pay television, computers and the Internet (Angus *et al.*, 2003; Covell and Whyte, 1999; Negroponte, 1995). In Australia, many adults now use the Internet and mobile phones daily to conduct both their business and personal transactions (Australian Bureau of Statistics, 2000b). The Australian Bureau of Statistics (ABS) estimates that in 2000, 50 per cent of children (5–14 year olds) used the Internet either at home, school or another location (Australian Bureau of Statistics, 2003). In the United States of America, the Department of Commerce estimates that 90 per cent of children between the ages of 5 and 17 now use computers, and 60 per cent now access the Internet either at home, school or another location (US Department of Commerce, 2002).

Despite rapid increases in access, there exists a digital divide between 'technology rich' and 'technology poor' between and within developed and developing nations. Recent data from the Organization for Economic Cooperation and Development indicate that within the European Union the percentage of individuals using the Internet from any location varies from almost 60 per cent in Sweden to 10 per cent in Greece (cited in US Department of Commerce, 2002, Figure 1–3). Significant differences also exist across communities within nations, with key factors being social, cultural and financial capital and geographical location (Australian Bureau of Statistics, 2003; US Department of Commerce, 2000). Within communities there are also adults, families and children who have no desire to own or use a computer or who wish to avoid using them altogether (Australian Bureau of Statistics, 2000a; Furlong *et al.*, 2000). The complexities of the digital divide go beyond access to include the quality and nature of use and the social and cultural context of use. The significance of the digital divide, however, can only be fully appreciated through an understanding of how children make use of these technologies, and how their interactions shape their activities, their engagement in learning and schooling and their developing under-standings of themselves and their social and physical worlds.

This chapter focuses on children's use of computers and the Internet and reports recent research findings and current thinking around the key issues of access and equity, the social and cultural contexts of chil-dren's use, the nature of computer-based activities and children's perceptions of the differences between home and school 'computing'. It ends with a brief discussion about the implications for education. In the main, it draws on national demographic data from Australia and the US and from a major Australian study of children's use of computers in homes (Downes, 1998, 2000, 2002a, 2002b, 2002c) and the later UK Screen Play research (Furlong *et al.*, 2000, Facer *et al.*, 2001a, 2001b, 2001c; Facer and Furlong, 2001; Sutherland *et al.*, 2000, 2001).

Access and equity

Issues of access and equity stem from the differences children experi-ence in relation to physical access of computers and the Internet in their homes, schools or communities, to the nature of use afforded by the physical resources and to the social and cultural context of use. Many studies have clearly linked children's access to computers in their homes to the general demographics of their families. These studies have found that the key demographics are: socio-economic status, geograph-ical location, household type (that is number of adults), nature of parental employment and ethnicity (Downes, 1997; Becker, 2000; Australian Bureau of Statistics, 2000a, 2000b, 2003; US Department of Commerce, 2000, 2002).

National statistics in Australia and the US indicate that household ownership has increased significantly over the last five years. In partic-ular, there is evidence that ownership has increased most dramatically in households with lower socio-economic status (SES), households outside capital cities and in single parent households with children. Regardless of these increases, the overall relationship with demographics still holds (Australian Bureau of Statistics, 2003; US Department of Commerce, 2002). The differences now extend beyond the simple absence or presence of a broadly functional computer to the absence or presence of multiple computers and a reasonable range of digital devices that connect to computers. This includes black and white printers, colour printers, scanners, digital cameras, modems, CD burners, DVD players and access to the Internet. Difference in regard to access to this broader range of resources compounds the divide. For example, the US Department of Commerce (2002) found that overall Internet use among children has a wider differential by income and ethnicities than just computer use. The Screen Play study found that even within families that owned some of these devices, access was restricted because of the cost. For example, some children were limited to the amount of colour printing they could do or time they could spend on the Internet because of the associated costs.

Another dimension of the digital divide relates to the differences children and their families experience in regard to the cost and quality of network services, that is, reliability, bandwidth and the nature of the online content. Lazarus and Mora (2000) found that the issues around online content were lack of localized information and lack of cultural and linguistic diversity as well as high literacy demands. Each of these created further barriers for low income and non-English speaking background communities who used or tried to use the Internet.

These equity issues around access and beneficial use of computers and the Internet in homes is further compounded by the fact that children who are least likely to have access at home live in communities where they are less likely to have access through neighbourhood centres, such as libraries, Internet cafés or friends, and attend schools where they are less likely to have access to the best computing resources and expertise (Becker, 2000). The Real Time study in Australia (Meredyth *et al.*, 1999) and statistics from the National Center for Education Statistics (2000) in the US indicate that there are differences across communities and locations in resource provision within schools, particularly with regard to Internet access. Notwithstanding this, many schools do play a role in providing access to computers and the Internet for children who do not have access at home. Local libraries also play an important role. In the US Department of Commerce study (2002) local libraries were the most common point of access for students who used the Internet at school but not at home.

Whether it is the case or not, both parents and children feel that access to computers and the Internet at home makes a difference. Many parents view children without a computer in their home as being at a disadvantage with regard to school (Downes, 1998; Kraut *et al.*, 1996). Children feel that they are left behind their peers if they have older model computers (Furlong *et al.*, 2000) or if they have no access to computers at home (Cappella, 2000) or that they are at an advantage if they do and their peers do not (Groundwater-Smith *et al.*, 2000). These views are not surprising given the amount of commercial, government and educational 'hype' around the links between ICTs, the knowledge economy and improved educational outcomes (Dede, 2000).

The social and cultural context of children's use at home

The social and cultural contexts of children's use of computers in their homes are shaped by social constructions, structures, discourses and practices both within and outside of the home (Caren *et al.*, 1989; Downes, 1999; Facer *et al.*, 2001 a, b, c; Silverstone *et al.*, 1992; Sutherland *et al.*, 2000; Wheelock, 1992). Generally computers arrive in homes in response to parental need to use them for work or to provide an educational benefit for children (Downes, 1998; Sutherland *et al.*, 2000). Downes (1998) found that children whose parents use computers in their workplace are also able to provide technical and user support and provide a greater range of equipment in the home. This support was gendered, in that male adults were most likely to bring expertise and experience into the home, though complexities related to class and gendered family roles were found. For example, in a number of working class families in the study, where fathers worked in trades and mothers in offices, mothers were the computer users and provided support based on their experiences with office applications. In most families mothers were the facilitators of homework so these mothers also became involved with children's computing activities as they related to homework, whether they did or did not have expertise with computers.

The Downes and Screen Play studies both identified family discourses and described how they shape computer use in the home (Downes, 1998, 1999; Facer *et al.*, 2001 a, b, c; Sutherland *et al.*, 2000). Both found that these discourses were embedded in complex constructions of childhood as well as technology. Downes (1998) identified two sets of discourses that played a key role in positioning children's home computing. The first of these sets involved the contradictory pairing of children as vulnerable, lacking power and as needing protection (Engelbert, 1994), and society as needing protection from children who are seen by some as inadequately socialized beings with darker forces beneath a thin layer of civilization (Barker, 1989, cited in Buckingham, 1994). These constructions underpin moral panic around the content of what children watch on television or videos, play in computer games, and deliberately or inadvertently come across on the World Wide Web (Downes, 1998). The second set of constructions that plays a significant role was the contrasting discourses of 'the child as learner' and 'the adult as worker'. These lead to points of agreement and conflict between parents and children about computer use (Downes, 1999) as they interacted with the different constructions of the technology: computer as future, computers for education, computers as tools and computers as entertainment.

Both parents and children engaged in discourses around 'computer as future' and 'computers for education'. Points of agreement included the following: children had to learn about computers now to prepare them for their role as adult workers; homes and schools were legitimate sites for children to learn about computers; and using computers at home and at school was mainly about learning to use them. Points of conflict were generally related to the constructions of 'computers as tools' and 'computers as entertainment', which were the dominant discourses of children.

With regard to 'computers as tools', children viewed themselves 'as workers', workers who could benefit from using the computer as a tool to do their 'work'. They found it was easier to write, easier to find information and easier to present written work well when they used a computer. They used computers to create artefacts: stories, cards, web pages, multimedia presentations and assignments. They conceived of the computer as an essential tool for their present role of worker. While parents agreed that computers played a legitimate role in helping their children undertake traditional school-related tasks, such as accessing and presenting information, they did not see this as an essential role. In contrast, parents viewed their children as 'learners', not 'workers'. In fact some parents expressed concerns that children might forget how to do things 'by hand' or the 'hard way' that, as learners, they were vulnerable to forgetting.

'Computers as entertainment' was by far the dominant discourse of the children. They spoke about the importance of computers as a source of entertainment. In the Downes study, which focused on children between the ages of 5 and 12, game playing was the major entertainment activity while on the computer (Downes, 1998). In a later study with older children, Downes found it was a broader mix of Internet use and game playing (Groundwater-Smith *et al.*, 2000). Both studies found that children who played games saw game playing as an active form of leisure activity where the process of trying to win or of winning was pleasurable. In general, parents in the study were comfortable about children using the computer to play games provided there was some educational or recreational value in them and they were not used excessively or inappropriately or in preference to homework. Parents and children agreed that game playing could develop useful skills. Points of conflict between parents and children were more around practices and were managed through rules: rules about when, for how long and what type of games could be played. The Screen Play and other studies have found that generally parents are also comfortable with children accessing the Internet for leisure, as long as there are appropriate limits on the amount of time spent and the nature of the activity (Angus *et al.*, 2003; Furlong *et al.*, 2000).

Downes (2002b) and Furlong *et al.* (2000) found that family rules were used to manage points of conflict. Rules generally reflected a 'hierarchy' of legitimate use, defining who was allowed to use the computer, for how long and for what purposes. Priority access was generally given to those wanting to 'work' over those wanting to 'play' and older family members had priority over younger ones. Downes (1998) found that the most common family rule was limited time for game playing on the computer because of the time consuming nature of this activity. Family rules delivered a strong message to children that computers were for 'work' as well as 'play'. In some families, they also interacted in particular ways with family discourses and children's patterns of use to produce important outcomes for girls. In the study, Downes found that girls' preferred activities were more closely aligned with parents' priorities; these preferred uses were accorded higher status than game playing was and this facilitated girls' access to the family computer.

Children's use of computers in their homes

Children's use of computers in their homes, while clearly situated within the social and cultural contexts created by the discourses and functionality of the available resources, vary through children's choice and pattern of activity. Types of activities chosen by children vary by age and gender (Downes, 1997, 2002a; Land, 1999; Mumtaz, 2001; Shields and Behrman, 2000; Subrahmanyam *et al.*, 2000). For example, games are the most common activity with younger children; boys are more likely to play games and use the Internet; and girls are more likely to use the computer with friends or siblings. Children undertake a wide range of activities using computers in their homes, but only a limited range of very common tasks: game playing, word processing and looking up information for schoolwork (Ba *et al.*, 2002; Downes, 2000), and for older children, also using the Internet for interacting with popular culture sites (Angus *et al.*, 2003).

Table 7.1 lists all types of use as found in recent studies of children's use at home (Angus *et al.*, 2003; Ba *et al.*, 2002; Becker, 2000; Downes, 1998, 2000, 2002a; Downes *et al.*, 1999; Groundwater-Smith *et al.*, 2000; Land, 1999; Stanger and Gridina, 1999; Subrahmanyam *et al.*, 2000; US Department of Commerce, 2002; Woodward and Girdina, 2000). In the table, the term 'text' is used in the generic sense of cultural artefact or in the children's words 'things', as in typing 'things' up, making 'things', looking 'things' up (Downes, 1998). It includes written, aural (music, sounds, speech), visual (clip art, photographs, animation, video, 3D images) or multimedia digital artefacts. The activities have been grouped in this way to reflect the way children talk about their activities (Downes, 2000). In particular it highlights the range of creative activities where children are the producers of artefacts that will, on many occasions, be used by others.

The system of categorization does not differentiate whether children are using a local or Internet resource. For example, children can browse Internet or CD-ROM sources of information and they can create cards or play games locally or online. In the table, the third column provides some examples of the different types of software and system environments within which children undertake their tasks. The table also distinguishes between more common and less common tasks that children undertake. This classification is based on an analysis of activities described in the recent studies mentioned above. The table uses normal and italic fonts to make the distinction.

While it would be rare to find any one child engaged in all of these activities, the range is indicative of the potential use of any computer (connected to the Internet). Importantly, it juxtaposes the activity of game playing with the more generic use as a tool to create and use texts and as a medium for communication. When viewed in this way, it is not surprising that for many children the 'tool' function of the computer is so important. Using a framework developed by Downes (1998) the four types of activities can be further classified by nature and purpose. Activities can be leisure-related or work-related; and leisure-related activities can be either playful or purposeful tasks. Figure 7.1 shows the relationship between the nature and purpose of the tasks.

Using this framework to describe children's use of computers in their homes provides insights into interrelationships between children's playing, learning and working when using computers. For example, when children played games they often moved between episodes of game playing that were playful, in the sense of 'fiddling around', to find out more about a particular place or event within the game, and espisodes that were purposeful, in terms of 'beating my dad' or improving their score. In a similar way, they used information texts in a playful way, when 'surfing' CD-ROMs or the World Wide Web. In this case, the pleasure is in the process and there is no particular endpoint in mind. They also used texts in purposeful ways, in terms of looking up a favourite pop group or searching for a particular item in a shop. Work-related activities were always purposeful tasks in that there was an 'end product' in mind. Usually these were connected with schoolwork. Within these purposeful tasks, however, children often engaged in playful episodes. These episodes involved taking time out to 'check out' or 'figure out' something or merely to 'enjoy' or 'play' along the way. This ability to shift backwards and forwards from work and play as needed basically allowed them to complete purposeful tasks through playful means, that is, to learn while working.

Many children highlighted this through their simple comments: 'I can play Paintbrush', 'I played typing stories' and 'I played Encarta' (Downes, 1998). The use of the word play not only refers to the 'playful episodes' but also to the purposeful tasks. In the latter case, the word applies to the skilful use of the features of the computing software to produce an artefact, a bit like 'playing an instrument' or 'playing sport'. Importantly, the integration of playful episodes into purposeful leisure-related and work-related activities leads these experiences to become

Table 7.1 Classification of children's use of computers

Activity	Tasks	Using
Game playing	Exploring the game environment Competing against self Competing against computer Competing against local players Competing against remote players	System provided games Installed games Downloaded games Internet games
Creating texts	Composing writing Editing writing Decorating writing Constructing images Manipulating images Designing texts with words and images Making texts with words and images *Creating sounds* *Manipulating sounds* *Creating Web pages* *Composing music* *Designing and constructing objects* *Integrating writing, images and/or sounds* *Building MUDs and MOOs*	Word processors Email software Bulletin boards Draw, paint and photo packages Music writing software Media players Multimedia authoring packages Web page authoring packages
Using texts	Locating Browsing Searching Viewing, listening and/or reading Downloading Scanning Recording Using Organizing *Transacting purchases, sales and exchanges*	Installed packages CD-ROMs WWW Bulletin boards

'playful' for the children. In the minds and words of the children, the computer becomes a 'playable tool'.

Playing, working and learning at home

The affordance of the computer as a 'playable tool' facilitates the blending of play, practice and performance. At different times and for different purposes any one of these processes may come to the foreground as children move freely them as their need or mood dictates. This ability to blend play, practice and performance when using a computer as a tool in the home

Table 7.1 (continued)

Activity	Tasks	Using
	Transacting funds transfers	
	Visiting MUDs and MOOs	
Communicating	*Phoning*	Internet
	Emailing	Digital phones
	Chatting in chat room	Bulletin boards
	Chatting one to one	Chat rooms
	Desktop video conferencing	
	Text messaging	
	Role playing	
	Joining an interest group	
	Searching for people with particular characteristics	
	Sending greeting cards etc.	
	Interacting with others in MUDs and MOOs	
Using technical processes	Booting the computer	Operating systems
	Shutting down the computer	Installed software
	Running software	Internet
	Loading files	
	Saving files	
	Printing files	
	Managing files	
	Customizing software	
	Fixing problems	
	Recording sounds	
	Scanning/digitizing images	
	Dialling and connecting to network service	
	Downloading from network	
	Altering desktop features	
	Installing software	
	Altering system configuration	

Source: adapted from Downes (2002a)
Note: tasks in italic are less common tasks.

provides children with a powerful degree of control over their ways of interacting with purposeful tasks that they do not normally have. Opportunities for playful learning and working are often confined to traditional areas of play or early childhood learning. Through computer use in the home children now have a greater degree of power not only over what and when they engage with learning, but importantly 'how', even with work that relates to school. In the Downes study (1998) children as young as 7 and 8 years old talked positively about their sense of control over their interactions with the technology and the learning opportunities

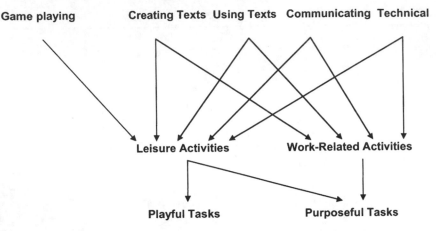

Figure 7.1 A framework of children's use of computers

afforded by the new technologies. Possibly it is in this area that the technology has most power to transform children's lives. The technology affords them a greater degree of control over how they work; it affords work-based learning through playful means.

There is also evidence of other learning benefits. In the Downes study many children asserted that many of the games they played also provided them with real world skills, such as handling money, driving safely, problem solving, decision making and manipulation. The young people described in Tapscott's (1998) *Growing up Digital*, who were regular users of interactive online environments, such as email, bulletin boards, chat rooms, MUDs and MOOs (MUDs, Object-Oriented), spoke of learning, among other things, about identities, relationships, representations, reactions and decision making. Turkle's work in the early 1980s (Turkle, 1984) provided detailed insights into how identities and relationships develop in technology rich environments and how the technologies afford different ways of interacting with the world. A recent Australian study (Angus *et al.*, 2003) also provides rich description of how the within-the-home lives of all three members of a family changed as a result of their use of the Internet.

While much of the learning associated with using a computer is consistent with, and even critical for, success in a knowledge-based, global, networked society, there are many cautionary tales that need to be told before we can assert that regular interaction with computers and complex learning environments in the home transforms the lives of children beyond the home. There is no doubt that children who regularly use computers in their homes engage with new forms of learning, develop new understandings and learn new skills (Heppell, 1996). But whether these collectively create 'a new kid in the kitchen' (Smith *et al.*, 1995) or whether this 'new kid' has been empowered to better navigate the global world is a more difficult question to tackle. Angus *et al.* (2003) provide a cautionary tale about over-emphasizing the impact through their detailed images of children who have engaged with such high-powered learnings, but are not necessarily empowered beyond the home. They argue that the social networks and cultural capital that children have access to through their family context mediates the relationship between children and technology and between 'child at home' and 'child at school' let alone 'child in the globalised digital world'. What has emerged from the literature, however, is evidence of a significant 'disjunction' between the learning opportunities in the home and in the school.

Differences between home and school computing

The main differences that children experience between home and school computing relate to a sense of control over how, when and why they use computers and a lack of recognition of the skills and abilities that children bring with them from their home computing. Children in the Downes study reported that they rarely used computers at school; when they did so, they were told what to do and how to do it and they rarely had a chance to finish what they did. In particular, the very learning processes that ensured success and pleasure at home were discouraged or discounted. According to Mumtaz (2001), children found school use of computers 'tame' in comparison to home use. Word processing, a common activity in school, was also found to be time consuming and boring by children (Buckingham, 1994). The young people in the Screen Play study focused their dissatisfaction on the prescriptive nature of the activities, the quality (particularly speed) of the technology at school compared to home, the lack of time for playful discovery, and limited access to the computers and the range of social and technical resources (Screen Play, 2000). Essentially, the tensions relate to time, control and the nature of learning. At home, they were in control, they were able to manage time to complete tasks they wanted to complete and they moved between play, learning and work to suit. At school they did not.

When talking to teachers Downes (1998) found that their beliefs and practices were situated within the same discourses as parents and children, but that conceptions of learning and schooling interacted with these to create a different stance about use of computers in schools. The dominant discourses for teachers were computers for the future: the child as learner, the school as a place to learn and learning as practice (not play or performance). Hence it was important for children to learn about computers at school ready for their role as adult workers. This led to a skills agenda where children learn pre-defined skills (Furlong *et al.*, 2000) and in Australia, testing regimes (NSW Board of Studies, 2003). Furthermore, because children were learners and not workers, access and time to use 'computers as tools' were not only unimportant, such use was viewed to a certain extent as problematic. School was seen as a place where children practise skills; if use of computers bypasses some of these skills/processes then a debate occurs in the same way that the debate around the use of calculators in schools still occurs.

Educating the digital generation

If schools were conceived of as places where children do intellectual work, and in the process of doing such work, learn skills and understandings that enhance their work and their understanding of the world in which they live, then it would be almost impossible to argue against the notion that children need the full range of intellectual tools and technologies, both traditional and new, at their disposal to best achieve the outcomes of such schooling. But such conceptions of schooling are rare.

The notion of the separation of learning from doing permeates schooling. Students are dominantly positioned as learners, not workers, not even apprentice knowledge workers. This is not new to education, nor applied only in relation to the newer computer-based technologies. Previous historical positionings of reading and writing also separated learning from doing. It has only been in the last decade that the discourses, curriculum and classroom practices have placed learning to read in the context of reading a range of texts, and learning to write in the context of writing a wide range of texts. This issue of the separation of learning and doing is also played out in the commentaries surrounding many of the current theories of learning (McInerney and McInerney, 2002). Relatively recent terms such as situated cognition, learning through apprenticeship, scaffolded learning and authentic assessment all imply the convergence of learning and doing, that is, of learning through performance.

The prevalent conception of parents and teachers that learning about computers and learning to use computers are separate from using computers for learning merely reflects one side of the community debate about learning. Until this debate is resolved or at least foregrounded in discussions about the use of traditional technologies and new technologies in schooling, the strong and commonly held conceptions of 'computers as the future' and of 'children as learners' will ensure that the new technologies continue to be marginalized. The import of this is that it is fundamental rethinking of the conceptions of learning and schooling and childhood that are critical to the reconceptualizing of the use of computers in schooling. Until this is accomplished it is hard to see how the complex learning that is afforded by digital technologies in the home can also be a reality in schools, and the new learning that children bring from home can find recognition and authenticity in school.

Conclusion

If there is any potential for digital technologies to be used in homes and schools to transform children's lives, it will require a significant and fundamental shift in how we conceive of childhood, learning and schooling. Within the current framework of discourses and practices in homes and schools, complex learning and interactions afforded by computers in homes may well not translate to the empowerment of the 'child at school' and the 'child in the global world'. As Angus *et al.* (2003) warn, the cultural capital found in homes may ensure that this is differentially experienced by children from different social backgrounds and hence create a digital divide that goes well beyond access and use.

Even with these cautions about not overestimating the degree of transformation, in the home, let alone the school, the issues that relate to access and equity are still significant. Even if children do little more that play games, type 'things' up and look 'things' up in the home, they are becoming confident and competent with a set of skills that will be vital in their adult lives. They are becoming comfortable with a technology that underpins the control and transfer of global information and communication. The digital divide excludes too many children from these experiences and resulting competencies.

References

Angus, L., Snyder, I. and Sutherland-Smith, W. (2003) Families, cultural resources and the digital divide: ICTs and educational (dis)advantage, *Australian Journal of Education*, 47 (1), pp. 18–39.

Australian Bureau of Statistics (2000a) *Household Use of Information Technology,* Cat 8146.0, Commonwealth of Australia, Canberra.

Australian Bureau of Statistics (2000b) *Use of Internet by Householders, Australia,* Cat 8147.0, Commonwealth of Australia, Canberra.

Australian Bureau of Statistics (2003) *Year Book Australia 2003 Communications and Information Technology: Household use of information technology, Australia,* Commonwealth of Australia, Canberra.

Ba, H., Tally, W. and Tsikalas, K. (2002) [accessed 30 August 2003] Investigating children's emerging digital literacies, *The Journal of Technology, Learning and Assessment*, 1 (4) [Online] http://www.bc.edu/research/intasc/jtla/journal/v1n4.shtml.

Barker, M. (1989) *Comics: Ideology, Power and the Critics*, Manchester University Press, Manchester.

Becker, H. J. (2000) Who's wired and who's not: children's access to and use of computer technology, *The Future of Children*, 10 (2), pp. 44–75.

Buckingham, D. (1994) Television and the definition of childhood, in *Children's childhoods: Observed and experienced*, ed. B. Mayall, pp. 79–96, Falmer, London.

Cappella, E. (compiled) (2000) Appendix B: what children think about computers, *The Future of Children*, 10 (2), pp. 186–91.

Caren, A., Groux, L. and Douzou, S. (1989) Uses and impacts of home computers in Canada: a process of reappropriation, in *Media Use in the Information Age: emerging patterns of adoption and consumer use*, eds J. Salvaggio and J. Bryant, Lawrence Erlbaum, Hillsdale, NJ.

Covell, A. and Whyte, F. (1999) *Digital Convergence: How the merging of computers, communications and multimedia is transforming our lives*, Aegis Publishing Group, Rhode Island.

Dede, C. (2000) Emerging influences of information technology on school curriculum. *Journal of Curriculum Studies*, 32 (2), pp. 281303.

Downes, T. (1997) A matter of equity: computers in Australian homes, *Australian Educational Computing*, 12 (1), pp. 743.

Downes, T. (1998) *Children's use of computers in their homes*, PhD thesis, University of Western Sydney, Macarthur. Available from t.downes@ uws.edu.au.

Downes, T. (1999) Childrens and parents' discourses about computers in the home and the school, *Convergence*, 5 (4), pp. 10443.

Downes, T. (2000) Children talking about their use of computers at home and at school, in *Taking Children Seriously: Proceedings of the National Workshop, Childhood and Youth Policy Research Unit*, eds J. Mason and M. Wilkinson, pp. 23752, University of Western Sydney, Sydney.

Downes, T. (2002a) Blending play, practice and performance: childrens use of computer at home, *Journal of Educational Enquiry*, 3 (2), pp. 2134.

Downes, T. (2002b) Childrens and families' use of computers in Australian homes, *Contemporary Issues in Early Childhood*, 3 (2), pp. 18296.

Downes, T. (2002c) Perceptions of how ICT has the potential to inflence children beyond the curriculum: home/school/community links, in *ICT in the Primary School: Changes and challenges*, eds A. Loveless and B. Dore, pp. 2335, Open University Press, Buckingham.

Downes, T., Arthur, L., Beecher, B. and Kemp, L. (1999) [accessed 30 August 2003] Appropriate EdNA services for children eight years and younger: report commissioned by Education.Au for the EdNA Online Pathways Project [Online] http://www.edna.edu.au/edna/go/pid/337.

Engelbert, A. (1994) Worlds of childhood: differentiated but different –implications for social policy, in *Childhood Matters: Social theory, practice and politics, Volume 14*, eds J. Qvortrup, M. Bardy, G. Sgritta and H. Wintersberger, pp. 285298, Avebury, Aldershot.

Facer, K., Furlong, J., Furlong, R. and Sutherland, R. (2001a) Constructing the child computer user: from public policy to private practices, *British Journal of Sociology of Education*, 22 (1), pp. 91408.

Facer, K., Furlong, J., Furlong, R. and Sutherland, R. (2001b) Whats the point of using computers: the development of young peoples computer expertise in the home *New Media and Society*, 3 (2), 199219.

Facer, K., Furlong, J., Furlong, R. and Sutherland, R. (2001c) Home is where the hardware is: young people, the domestic environment and access' to new technologies, in *Children, Technology and Culture*, eds I. Hutchby and J. Moran-Ellis, Falmer, London.

Facer, K. and Furlong, R. (2002) Beyond the myth of the cyberkid: young people at the margins of the information revolution, *Journal of Youth Studies*, 4 (4), pp. 45169.

Furlong, J., Furlong, R., Facer, K. and Sutherland, R. (2000) The National Grid for learning: a curriculum without walls? *Cambridge Journal of Education*, 30 (1), pp. 91–110.

Groundwater-Smith, S., Downes, T. and Gibbons, P. (2000) *Information Technology in Teaching and Learning*, unpublished evaluation report for SCEGGS Darlinghurst, University of Western Sydney, Sydney.

Heppell, S. (1996) [accessed 31 August 2003] Multimedia and learning: normal children, normal lives; that's the revolution [Online] http://www.ultralab. anglia.ac.uk/pages/ultralab/A_Good_Read/Normalchildren.html.

Kraut, R., Scherlis, W., and Mukhopadhyay, T., (1996) The HomeNet field trial of residential Internet services, *Communications of the ACM* 39, pp. 55–63.

Land, M. J. (1999) Evidence of Gender Disparity in Children's Computer Use and Activities, paper presented at the Annual Meeting of the Association for Education in Journalism and Mass Communication, New Orleans, LA.

Lazarus, W. and Mora, F. (2000) [accessed 31 August 2003] *Online Content for Low-income and Underserved Americans: The digital divide's new frontier*, The Children's Partnership [Online] http://www.childrenspartnership.org/pub/ low_income/index.html.

McInerney, D. and McInerney, V. (2002) *Educational Psychology: Constructing learning*, 3rd edn, Prentice Hall, Sydney.

Meredyth, D., Russell, N., Blackwood, L., Thomas, J. and Wise, P. (1999) *Real Time: Computers, change and schooling – national sample study of the information technology skills of Australian school students*, Australian Key Centre for Cultural and Media Policy, Brisbane.

Mumtaz, S. (2001) Children's enjoyment and perception of computer use in the home and the school, *Computers and Education*, 36, pp. 347–62.

National Center for Education Statistics (2000) *Stats in Brief: Teacher use of computers and the internet in public schools*, US Department of education, Office of Educational Research and Improvement, Washington, DC.

Negroponte, N. (1995) *Being Digital*, Knopf, New York.

NSW Board of Studies (2003) [accessed 10 June 2003] Computing Skills Assessment Updates – Board Bulletin Articles [Online] http://www.boardof studies.nsw.edu.au/syllabus_sc/vol11no6.

Screen Play (2000) [accessed 10 June 2003] *Screen Play: An exploratory study of children's techno-popular culture*, report submitted to Economic and Social Research Council [Online] http://www.bris.ac.uk/Depts/Education/final summary.doc.

Shields, M. K. and Behrman, R. E. (2000) Children and computer technology: analysis and recommendations, *The Future of Children*, 10 (2), pp. 4–30.

Silverstone, R., Hirsch, E. and Morley, D. (1992) Information and communication technologies and the moral economy of the household, in *Consuming Technologies: Media and information in domestic spaces*, eds R. Silverstone and E. Hirsch, pp. 15–31, Routledge, London.

Smith, R., Curtin, P. and Newman, L. (1995) Kids in the kitchen: the educational implications of computer and computer games use by children, paper presented at the Australian Association for Research in Education Annual Conference, Hobart.

Stanger, J. D. and Gridina, N. (1999) *Media in the Home 1999: The fourth annual survey of parents and children*, Annenberg Public Policy Center, University of Pennsylvania, Philadelphia.

Subrahmanyam, K., Kraut, R. E., Greenfield, P. M. and Gross, E. F. (2000) The impact of home computer use on children's activities and development, *The Future of Children*, 10 (2), pp. 123–44.

Sutherland, R., Facer, K., Furlong, J. and Furlong, R. (2000) A new environment for education? The computer in the home, *Computers and Education*, special edition, 34, pp. 195–212.

Sutherland, R., Facer, K., Furlong, R. and Furlong, J. (2001) A window on learning with computers in the home, in *Educational Technology and the Impact on Teaching and Learning*, Proceedings of an International Research Forum at BETT 2000, ed. M. Selinger and J. Wynn, Research Machines, Oxford.

Tapscott, D. (1998) *Growing Up Digital: The rise of the net generation*, McGraw-Hill, New York.

Turkle, S. (1984) *The Second Self: Computers and the human spirit*, Granada, London.

US Department of Commerce (2000) [accessed 2 October 2001] *Falling Through the Net: Toward digital inclusion*, US Department of Commerce, National Telecommunications and Information Administration (NTIA), Washington, DC [Online] http://www.ntia.doc.gove/ntiahome/fttn00/contents00.html.

US Department of Commerce (2002) [accessed 10 June 2003] *A Nation Online: How Americans are expanding their use of the Internet*, US Department of Commerce, National Telecommunications and Information Administration (NTIA), Washington, DC [Online] http://www.ntia.doc.gov/ntiahome/dn/.

Wheelock, J. (1992) Personal computers, gender and an institutional model of the household in *Consuming Technologies: Media and information in domestic spaces*, ed. R. Silverstone and E. Hirsch, pp. 97–112, Routledge, London.

Woodward, EH IV and Girdina, N. (2000) *Media in the Home 2000: The fifth annual survey of parents and children*, Annenberg Public Policy Center, University of Pennsylvania, Philadelphia.

8 Learning and teaching adult basic skills with digital technology

Research from the UK

Harvey Mellar and Maria Kambouri

Adult basic skills

Lack of basic skills has been seen as a key factor in disadvantage, high levels of unemployment and social exclusion. This linkage has been demonstrated across a number of Member States within the European Union (Basic Skills Agency, 1999) and also worldwide. The International Adult Literacy Survey (IALS), a 22-country international study of adult functional literacy conducted between 1994 and 1998 (OECD and Statistics Canada, 1995, 1997, 2000), showed that there was substantial variation in literacy and numeracy levels; Scandinavian countries showed small proportions of adults operating at the lowest levels (e.g. 7 per cent in Sweden) whilst a number of English speaking countries such as the UK, Australia, Canada and the US showed much higher proportions (over 20 per cent in some cases). Total illiteracy is rare within the UK, but one in sixteen adults if shown a poster advertising a concert being held at a specific place cannot identify where the concert is being held, and one in four adults cannot calculate the change they should get out of £2 when they buy three articles of value 45p, 45p and 68p.

Within the UK, it is estimated that maybe some 7 million adults are operating at low levels of literacy and numeracy. The impact on personal economic prospects and the national economy are estimated at billions of pounds per year (Bynner and Parsons, 1999). Despite the scale of the problem, relatively few take up relevant training. In 1998 the number involved in adult literacy and numeracy courses was estimated at about 250,000 (DfEE, 2001). As to how the UK got into this situation, the Pisa Report (OECD, 2001) may give some clues in its indication of the UK education system as a high-quality education system, but with relatively low equity; it produces some very well qualified pupils, but fails to meet the needs of large numbers of school students and so many reach the end of compulsory schooling with low levels of literacy and numeracy.

The publication of the IALS survey provoked international debate, and a flurry of policy initiatives in many countries to address the problem of poor basic skills. In the UK in 1999 a working group on adult basic skills chaired by Sir Claus Moser developed a strategy for addressing the perceived skills deficit and this led to the launch of a major national remediation programme, entitled 'Skills for Life', with some £1.5 billion of funding in the first three years. This programme was set the goal of reducing, within ten years, the numbers of people with poor basic skills to half the current levels.

One aspect of this strategy was the promise to deliver the benefits of digital technology to this group of learners. The Moser Report declared: 'At the heart of improved quality in delivery and materials must be increased use of Information and Communication Technologies (ICT) to improve basic skills' (DfEE, 1999: para. 9.26). As to how this was expected to happen, the Moser report made the following claims:

- ICT is a powerful tool to raise levels of literacy and numeracy.
- Computers and multimedia software provide attractive ways of learning.
- The Web enables access to the best materials and the most exciting learning opportunities.
- ICT offers a new start for adults returning to learning.
- The Internet and digital TV technology can reach into the home.
- Learners who use ICT for basic skills double the value of their study time acquiring two sets of skills at the same time.

The term ICT as used in this report refers to a wide range of digital technologies, including: desktop computers, interactive multimedia, laptop computers, interactive whiteboards, interactive digital television, mobile phones, personal digital assistants (PDAs), the Internet and the Web (whether accessed via interactive TV, a PC or a mobile phone).

These claims about the value of digital technologies for addressing the basic skills needs of the target group can be seen to have three strands. The first three claims assert that digital technologies provide exciting and effective educational possibilities. The next two claims are about using digital technologies as ways of connecting with communities of learners who are seen as having been excluded by traditional education provision. In the last claim we see a link to a third theme, that is, that digital technologies involve a new set of skills. These three themes will structure much of what we have to say in this chapter.

Within the UK the use of digital technologies within the Skills for Life strategy is implemented largely (though by no means exclusively) through two major organizational structures. One is within adult learning centres, and further education colleges and the other is through Ufi/learndirect. Further education colleges in the UK are colleges open to learners over 16, which offer a wide range of courses, and in particular a wide range of vocational courses. Skills for Life courses within this context have to compete with other courses for access to digital technology resources within the college. Ufi/learndirect (http://www.ufiltd. co.uk/) is a public–private partnership set up in 2000 to provide online training across a number of areas, including computer skills, business skills and Skills for Life. In 2002–3 learndirect had 2,000 franchised local centres, some 850,000 learners, with over 100,000 of these taking Skills for Life courses. It is funded by the government to provide free Skills for Life training. The learning materials used are chiefly interactive electronic teaching materials delivered either online or on CD-ROM that can be accessed via computers at local centres, at home or in the workplace. The materials vary in type from straightforward interactive exercises to sophisticated gaming environments.

Research studies

At the time these claims about the effectiveness of using digital technologies to teach adult learners with basic skill needs were made in the Moser report, there was very little research in the area. The research that did exist was not particularly supportive of the claims. For example, a UK national study carried out in 2000 (Brooks *et al.*, 2001) with a sample of some 2,000 learners found that 54 per cent of tutors reported that their learners had access to computers in every session with a further 29 per cent reporting that there was access on some occasions, but the study found no significant correlation between frequency of access to computers and reading gains. Alongside this, there was a range of reports of innovative work using digital technologies with basic skills learners in the UK (e.g. Kelly, 1999; Horsburgh and Simanowitz, 1999a, 1999b; Harris and Shelswell, 2001) and internationally, particularly in the US, Canada and Australia (see for example TECH21 at http://www.tech21. org/).

Over the last five years we have carried out, with a team of researchers at the Institute of Education, University of London, a range of studies looking at the role of digital technologies in supporting adult basic skills. These have included evaluations of the uses of interactive multimedia materials, of the potential of interactive digital television, of educational games and of the use of PDAs. We have looked at provision in colleges and through learndirect centres (Mellar *et al.*, 2001), at the use of computers to tackle basic skills needs in prisons (Kambouri and Kett, 2001), and at the use of laptops to reach communities who would not otherwise access basic skills provision.

Learning

First we report on two projects that directly addressed the theme of the effectiveness of learning through computers and interactive multimedia for people with basic skills needs but which also have something to say about the two themes of accessing excluded communities of learners, and the emergence of new forms of technological literacy. The first project was carried out in 2000–1, before the present learndirect model was established, and set out to investigate the role of digital technologies within learning centres teaching adults with basic skills needs and to make recommendations to Ufi/learndirect. The second project, two years later in 2002–3, set out to evaluate the effectiveness of the specific delivery approach adopted by learndirect both in terms of the materials produced and the support structures put in place to Skills for Life needs.

Our first study of computer use in learning centres showed that using interactive multimedia did indeed appeal to a wide range of adult learners, and was particularly successful with young male learners who were not otherwise interested in learning, and that there was some evidence of impact on literacy skills, in particular reading. Important pedagogic factors were found to be: assessment of learning needs, consideration of learning styles, careful integration of computers into teaching and intensity of use of digital technology. Important organizational factors were found to be: availability and training of tutors, accessibility of ICT resources to basic skills learners, level of technical support, and prevailing institutional culture with respect to basic skills, ICT and learning.

The study was based on visits to 11 centres with a good track record of the use of computers in adult basic skills provision, including further education colleges, community centres, outreach centres, learning shops, a prison and a refugee organization. Within these centres we interviewed 71 managers and tutors and 124 learners. The majority of the learners interviewed were also tested on their literacy and/or numeracy skills and 70 of these were post-tested some two-and-a-half months later.

The use of digital technologies for basic skills provision in most centres was at an early stage of development. There were a small number of tutors who were highly experienced in the use of computers to teach basic skills learners, but on the whole, tutors described themselves as relatively new to computers. The chief applications in use were found to be a small range of basic skills software, office software (principally word-processing, and presentation software, and the Internet (both for email and for accessing the Web).

We were particularly concerned to examine the role of the tutor, and found that both tutors and learners saw the role of the tutor as crucial, but that there was also some support for the idea that computer use might increase learner autonomy for certain learners and that about 20 per cent of learners interviewed saw the greater autonomy in learning offered by computers as important.

The use of digital technologies was succeeding in attracting new learners, and the great majority (92 per cent) found the use of computers motivating. The learners who were being attracted were often young men, and the majority had levels of numeracy roughly equivalent to what the UK National Curriculum would expect of an average 11 year old. More formally, they were at Entry 3/Level 1 with respect to the Adult Literacy and Numeracy National Qualifications framework (see QCA, 2000).

We found significant improvement between pre- and post-tests in reading for learners at Entry 2/3, but no statistically significant differences for learners at other levels, or for numeracy or for learners who spoke English as an additional language (though the numbers in these groups tested were small and so it would be harder to show statistically significant changes). Yet the retention rate between pre- and post-tests was 64 per cent, which is high when compared with other studies in the area of basic skills, giving another indication of the motivating effect of the use of digital technologies. Case studies supported the argument that digital technologies could have a significant overall impact on some learners. In interviews with learners two-thirds said that computers had helped them to learn, and most felt that their literacy goals were being met; however, many felt that their numeracy goals were not being met and many felt that their expectations about preparation for specific vocational areas were not being met.

The impact of the changing nature of skills was indicated by the fact that many learners said that they had made gains in computer skills though this had not been one of their initial learning goals, and over a quarter indicated that their work aspirations had altered to include a desire for a greater involvement with computers in their future work.

Two years on from this study, in the period October 2002 to March 2003, we carried out an in-depth study of learndirect centres. The earlier study had taken place before the establishment of the learndirect model and there was evidence that there had been some stabilization of computer provision in the area of basic skills provision, that there was now a significant group of tutors with some degree of experience both in computer skills and basic skills teaching, as well as an established body of online materials. We were able to clearly identify a group of learners who preferred to work more autonomously though they often needed strong support at the start of their learning. The positioning of many learndirect centres in non-traditional sites (for example in converted railway stations, pubs and shops) had also gone some way towards opening access to communities of learners excluded by traditional sites of learning. Materials had been developed to appeal to specific groups of learners, in particular a small range of games aimed specifically at young male learners who are difficult to attract into learning.

In this second study, we identified nine centres and carried out 24 staff interviews and 61 interviews with learners as well as observations of them working with learndirect materials. We visited the centres and the learners on two occasions with a gap of between four and eight weeks.

The learners were all using learndirect Skills for Life materials and were attending between one and four hours a week (two on average). Whilst many learners had computers at home, none reported use of learndirect Skills for Life materials at home; by contrast learndirect reports an overall figure of around 25 per cent of users using materials at home across the full range of its courses. This difference reflects the fact that the Skills for Life model is much more support dependent, and so visits to learning centres are more important than for other learndirect courses. The centres were being successful in attracting new learners, often those with low self-confidence and memories of school failure. Many were motivated by a desire to acquire computer skills, but equally important was the wish to improve literacy skills. Other motives included improving numeracy skills, expanding work opportunities, preparing for further educational opportunities, helping children, and developing self-esteem and confidence.

Most learners (79 per cent) had deliberately chosen flexible, technology based learning and 58 per cent said that they preferred this as their main method of learning. However, class based tuition was preferred by the majority of ESOL (English for Speakers of Other Languages) learners, with technology based learning seen as a supplement mainly for practice. The great majority of learners felt that they had made progress in terms of literacy, numeracy, computer skills and confidence between our two visits, and this was confirmed by assessments as well as by observations of the visiting research officers and by centre staff.

The Skills for Life model adopted by learndirect incorporates a significant element of tutor support, and there was evidence that learners responded best to learndirect courses that had a significant element of inbuilt support and came with supplementary materials, and to courses that allowed support staff to track and assess progression, and thus to be alerted to problem areas for the learner. Learners asked for more feedback from the materials for 'where, when and how' they were going wrong. There was evidence, therefore, of a push for the materials to provide more support for the learner to act autonomously and to develop their abilities to learn on their own. Learners with a wide range of abilities were attracted to learndirect, however, because the materials are targeting a middle level of ability (Entry 3/Level 1); learners with lower levels of skills can not be catered for and are being referred to other forms of provision.

Most learners appreciated the support they received from staff, though some felt they were not receiving the specialized support needed to address their needs. These perceptions corresponded with our own observations, which indicated a great degree of care and support given by staff in most cases, but that staff were sometimes overstretched, and were not always adequately trained for the demands being made on them in terms of pedagogical support in basic skills. Staff who had familiarized themselves with the full range of learndirect Skills for Life materials were able to make most effective use of them. The biggest problem that was raised by tutors, however, was the burdensome nature of the administrative system.

As a specific element of this study we looked at educational software based on games formats. These formats had been specifically designed in order recruit young adults (mainly male) who might otherwise be reluctant learners into some learning through the intrinsic interest of the games. Two games have been launched: *Max Trax*, which is an arcade-style driving game in which the learner negotiates a racing circuit whilst answering mathematics problems; and *Runner*, which is a three-dimensional online game that aims to teach language and communication skills. *Runner* is set in London 40 years from now. Players are 'runners' and, when a simple drop-off goes wrong, they are plunged into an online adventure that includes kidnapping, foiling an assassination plot and saving the city. Players engage in dialogue with game characters and use information they gain to progress through the game.

Learners perceived *Max Trax* as both a game and a learning activity, and the great majority described it as an enjoyable activity. Most identified the learning goals as developing their mathematics skills. *Runner* was clearly recognized as a game by young adults, though they often could not identify what was being learnt; those few who could identify what was being learnt said that *Runner* gave meaning and purpose to reading. Mature second language learners found it to be a means for application and consolidation of existing learning, but the majority of mature learners were not motivated to play games and perceived *Runner* as obstructing learning and engaging the learner in too many irrelevant tasks. Tutors were unaccustomed to using games as part of their teaching, and observations by the research team point to the importance of the tutor's mediation to stress key literacy goals during game-play. There is little doubt of the popularity of the games with young adults and with a section of more mature learners for whom they were not originally intended.

These two studies relied to a large degree on interviews with learners and tutors, and they left unanswered some important questions about how tutors actually work with computers in the classroom. In an ongoing study, this time for the National Research and Development Centre for Adult Literacy and Numeracy, we have carried out a series of classroom observations in order to get a more accurate picture of everyday practice. Working closely with tutor-researchers in East London colleges, we drew up procedures for carrying out classroom observations and then carried out detailed observations in 11 classrooms using computers in adult literacy, numeracy or ESOL. Each class was observed three times by the research team, and on at least one other occasion by one of the other tutor-researchers. We have now drawn up detailed descriptions of the teaching in these classrooms based on these observations and we are in the process of analysing this data in order to draw out general conclusions. Close working with the tutor-researchers has been valuable in gaining insights into present practice. Early findings point to a variety of styles of computer use closely related to the teaching styles and philosophies of the tutors, and it would seem that the classes were all strongly tutor led, with comparatively little movement towards the more collaborative styles of teaching and learning sometimes associated with computer use in schools and higher education.

Reaching excluded communities of learners

We have already discussed some of the ways in which the design of learning materials and of learning support systems has been targeted at attracting groups conceived of as excluded from basic skills provision. We have also carried out some specific investigations of more directly focused initiatives in this area, first, in the area of education for young offenders, and second, in the use of laptop computers in order to enable provision in more community oriented settings – pubs, local centres, people's homes etc.

A number of studies have pointed to a connection between prisoners and low levels of basic skills, and we have worked with a number of projects examining the possible role of digital technologies in providing basic skills learning within prisons. In one European Commission (EC) funded project, teaching staff and students from prisons in England, Ireland, France and Belgium participated in creating video and sound recordings of young offenders taking part in discussion forums around themes that they had selected. These clips were translated into the three project languages (English, French and Flemish) and included in a final CD-ROM. The materials produced were developed using the authoring tools embedded in an existing product – New Reading Disc – produced by Cambridge Training and Development Ltd (CTAD). The creation of new learning activities based around learners' needs and interests was intended to make the experience more fulfilling and to centre the learning on the learners themselves. The process was found to be motivating for prisoners, enabling them to use technology to communicate (and exchange information through their teachers about prison systems in other countries) and also to improve a wide range of literacy skills. This work is presently being extended through another EC funded project which has developed simple multimedia authoring tools – simplified Web authoring and animation tools – with which users can create animations and presentations around themes related to issues in health education that relate to their own lives.

Computers have been employed as one method of taking provision out of education centres into local communities through so called 'outreach' schemes. In one such scheme 1,500 laptop computers and associated equipment were allocated to about 300 local authorities and voluntary and community organizations. Evaluations showed clear evidence of widening participation and increased confidence in using the technology (Wood, 2000; Clarke *et al.*, 2000; Kambouri *et al.*, 2002). Our own evaluation found that the scheme had been effective in promoting new basic skills provision particularly in voluntary organizations. The portable nature of laptops contributed to a widening of participation in the community, and this provided a route for new learners. Providers often enhanced the centrally provided computer resources by financing other digital technologies such as digital video cameras, web cams, text-to-speech software, and so on. The use of laptops also empowered learners with basic skills needs: laptops were seen by learners and tutors as friendly, personal, on a par with mobile phones and certainly less threatening than stand-alone PCs. Access to the state of the art laptops contributed to enhancing learner self-image and hence had an impact on learning participation and retention in learning.

Much of our discussion has centred on the use of computers and interactive multimedia, but there are other digital technologies that are likely to have a significant impact in the area of basic skills. The two major candidates are interactive digital TV and mobile computing (mobile phones, including video-phones and PDAs). A range of projects are beginning to look at how these technologies might be used to provide greater access to presently excluded communities. These particular technologies may have specific implications for the way we organize learning. They tend to be associated with much smaller units of learning, bite sized, on-demand learning, initially at least in order to increase the learners' self-confidence in their own ability to learn.

The potential for television to have an impact in the basic skills area has been well illustrated by the experience of the National Association of Legal Assistants (http://www.nala.org/), the since it managed to reach 25 per cent of the total viewing audience in Eire for some of its basic skills programmes. There is a hope that interactive digital TV can access the audiences that TV reaches, groups who would not have access to computers, or be interested in attending courses, for it can deliver a degree of interactive learning than TV alone cannot do. We carried out an evaluation of some early work in the area of interactive digital TV for basic skills, the EU funded Upgrade project (1998–2000), which was based on learning activities built into TV programmes; other more recent approaches have tried to build on the increasing popular use of games on interactive digital TV.

Another approach to attracting learners is through highly mobile devices, such as mobile phones and PDAs. Some ongoing projects are exploring the more creative side of the use of these technologies for communication and writing. Others are looking at the incorporation of games, and even of some of learndirect's teaching products, onto PDAs. Research in these areas is at an early stage, and we are still struggling with how we investigate and measure learners' casual mobile use of such technologies, before we can begin to address its effectiveness in supporting learning.

Conclusions

At the start of this paper we identified three themes within the claims made for digital technologies in the area of adult basic skills, and which we restate here as questions:

- In what ways can digital technologies be used with this group of learners to enhance their learning?
- Can digital technologies be used in such a way as to include presently excluded communities of learners with basic skills needs?
- What *are* the new basic skills of the twenty-first century?

We do not yet know enough about really effective ways of using digital technologies with this group of learners. In our own work thus far we have attempted to explore and describe present practice; in the next stage of our research within the National Research and Development Centre for Adult Literacy and Numeracy we wish to explore systematically a range of intervention approaches in order to develop further the use of digital technologies within this area. One of the biggest issues for learning support in this area is to what extent the technology can help this particular group of learners in becoming more autonomous, for whilst many basic skills learners wish to work with a tutor, there is a significant number of learners who are strongly attracted by more autonomous ways of working, but do not know how to make it work for themselves. On the other hand, we are as yet seeing little use of collaborative learning techniques with basic skills learners, despite the fact that in schools and in higher education the use of digital technologies has been strongly associated with more collaborative forms of learning.

Perhaps the single biggest issue for digital technologies within the area of basic skills at the moment remains the issue of access and motivation. Computers and interactive multimedia have been seen to be powerful incentives for learners to get involved. Often learners come into provision looking for computer skills but then find that they have literacy and numeracy problems that get in their way, and so are helped to begin to focus on these. Others are motivated to stay within a course because of the computer skills element. For some, computers and inter-active multimedia provide an alternative route into education, where traditional classroom approaches have failed them in the past. The flex-ibility of access promised by digital technologies is a major attraction. However, while learndirect centres remain open access and students can more or less pop in when they want, there is as yet little indication of this group of learners accessing such materials from home. Some 25 per cent of all learndirect learners (that is those taking computer courses, business courses, etc.) are accessing courses from home, but we found very little evidence of Skills for Life learners doing this. Can digital tech-nologies genuinely help to widen provision? Are they enabling us to address the learning divide, or is the digital divide simply replicating the learning divide? Gorard, in an analysis of survey data on adult educa-tion, came to the conclusion that:

> access to ICT does not, in itself, make people anymore likely to participate in education and (re)engage with learning. Access to ICT continues to be largely patterned according to long-term pre-existing social, economic and educational factors. Thus, like educational qual-ifications, access to ICT is a proxy for the other, more complex, social and economic factors that pre-date it rather than as a direct contrib-utory factor in itself.

> (2002: 11)

He goes on to question the value of the available materials:

> Much of this so-called 'new' ICT-based educational provision is either repackaged 'old' educational provision and courses or a narrow provision of new courses. ... The majority of learndirect's 800 specialist courses have been in basic and advanced IT skills and tied into existing learning providers such as further education colleges – hardly the cornucopia of diverse learning opportunities (anything) being made available 'anytime' and 'anywhere'.

> (2002: 12)

The first of these comments finds strong echoes in work being carried out in East London by one of our doctoral students (Bariso, 2003). The second comment is a common lament amongst anyone who has looked through learndirect's course offerings. But the story does not exactly stop there. We have seen learndirect centres offering genuine access to technological resources that would not have been available otherwise, and we have seen a range of projects in which digital technologies have been specifically targeted to address social exclusion issues with some success. Of course access to ICT, in itself, will not achieve any of these things. E-learning products generally do not live up to their promises, but there are some very good examples, and the challenge in the immediate future for learndirect is to further develop innovative approaches such as those they have begun based around games.

Many authors have argued that digital technologies have implications for our ideas about literacy more generally (see, for example, Chapter 1 and Chapter 6 in this collection) and these debates have to some extent been reflected within the discussions around basic skills. So, for example, ICT is coming to be seen as a basic skill in its own right, as the report of the Post-16 E-learning Strategy Task Force advising the Department for Education and Skills concludes:

> Reading and writing are universally accepted as basic entry requirements for social inclusion. However, it is clear that a lack of ICT skills, including not having the skills to learn through ICT, is potentially now as great a barrier to employability and social inclusion as a lack of achievement in literacy and numeracy have been to date ... We recommend that by 2010 everyone should have access to ICT as a basic skill as an entitlement. The ICT entitlement should include an e-learning skills component.
> (Post-16 E-learning Strategy Task Force, 2002: 4)

Adding that:

> ICT user skills include those most frequently required in employment, for example, those associated with the Internet, email, word processing and other commonly used business packages. We also include an element of e-learning skills in the definition of ICT user skills; no individual who has undertaken ICT basic user skills programmes should struggle to engage with the basic principles of e-learning.
> (2002: 7)

Others within the basic skills area have argued for a much wider view of technological literacy, for example humanITy writes:

> Traditionally we have emphasised traditional, autonomous, discrete literacy which says: the more complex the set of skills to complete a task the fewer those who can perform them all. ICT, inclusive, collaborative literacy says: The more complex the set of skills to complete a task, the greater the number who can become involved. We need to think much more of the second and much less of the first.
> (humanITy2003: para. 7)

Carvin (2000) developing from a definition of basic literacies distinguishes a number of elements of relevant new literacies, including:

- Technological Literacy: the ability to utilize common ICT tools, including hardware, software and Internet tools like search engines.
- Information Literacy: the skills to ascertain the veracity, reliability, bias, timeliness and context of information.
- Adaptive Literacy: the willingness to learn new tools and to apply previous ICT learning to new situations.

How we define these new literacies will be extremely important in determining whether we genuinely manage to address the issue of basic skills needs, or whether we only succeed in solving the last century's problems but fail to solve those of the present century. A range of empirical work is necessary in order to clarify the demands actually made by new technologies for the range of audiences presently being addressed by the Skills for Life programme.

Note

These research projects were supported by Ufi Limited, the organization that, together with its partners, has established an e-learning network of over 2,000 learning centres and set up learndirect's national learning advice service.

References

Bariso, E. (2003) The computer revolution: friend or foe to FE college staff, *British Journal of Educational Technology*, 34 (1), pp. 84–8.

Basic Skills Agency (BSA) (1999) *European Social Exclusion Project*, Basic Skills Agency, London.

Brooks, G., Hewitt, R., Hutchinson, D., Kendall, S. and Wilkin, A. (2001) *Progress in Adult Literacy: Do learners learn?* Basic Skills Agency, London.

Bynner, J. and Parsons, S. (1999) *Literacy, Leaving School and Jobs*, Basic Skills Agency, London.

Carvin, A. (2000) More than just access, *EDUCAUSE Review*, November/ December.

Clarke, A., Reeve, A., Essom, J., Scott, J. *et al.* (2000) *Adult and Community Learning Laptop Initiative Evaluation*, National Institute of Adult Continuing Education (NIACE), Leicester.

DfEE (Department for Education and Employment) (1999) [accessed 12 June 2003] *A Fresh Start: Improving literacy and numeracy (The report of the working group chaired by Sir Claus Moser)*, DfEE, London [Online] http://www.lifelonglearning.co.uk/mosergroup/index.htm.

DfEE (2001) [accessed 12 June 2003] *ICT Access and Use: Report on the benchmark survey*, DfEE, London [Online] http://www.dfes.gov.uk/research/data/uploadfiles/RR252.doc.

Gorard, S. (2002) [accessed 12 June 2003] *Lifelong Learning Trajectories in Wales: Results of the NIACE Adult Learners' Survey 2002* [Online] http://www.cf.ac.uk/socsi/ICT/niacewales.doc.

Harris, S. R. and Shelswell, N. (2001) [accessed 12 June 2003] Building bridges across the digital divide: supporting the development of technological fluency in adult basic education learners, in *Proceedings FACE Annual Conference 2001*, ed. A Mason, pp. 42–53, FACE, Bristol [Online] http://www.comp.glam.ac.uk/pages/staff/srharris/pdfs/Building%20Bridges%20Final%20Draft.pdf.

Horsburgh, D. and Simanowitz, D. (1999a) Basic skills and ICT: a marriage made in heaven? *Active Learning*, (10), pp. 44–50.

Horsburgh, D. and Simanowitz, D. (1999b) Write and ROM – best practice for multimedia use in basic skills, *Basic Skills*, September, pp. 7–9.

humanITy (2003) [accessed 12 June 2003] Briefing paper no 1: ICT development and basic skills strategy, humanITy: inclusion in the information age [Online] http://www.humanity.org.uk/articles/pub_ictdevelopment.shtml.

Kambouri, M. and Kett, M. (2001) [accessed 12 June 2003] *New Technologies for Young Offenders: Evaluation report* [Online] http://www.connectproject.org/evaluation/default.asp.

Kambouri, M., Mellar, H., Goodwin, T. and Windsor, V. (2002) *Evaluation of the Impact of Laptop Computers and Basic Skills Software to Support the Teaching and Learning of Basic Skills; Report to the Basic Skills Agency*, unpublished report.

Kelly, H. (1999) New approaches to adult basic education, *Basic Skills*, September: 23–26.

Mellar, H., Kambouri, M., Wolf, A. and Goodwin, T. (2001) [accessed 12 June 2003] *Research into the Effectiveness of Learning through ICT for People with Basic Skills Needs: Report submitted to Ufi June 2001* [Online] http://www.ufiltd.co.uk/press/papers/literacyguide.pdf.

OECD (2001) *Knowledge and Skills for Life – First Results from PISA 2000*, OECD, Paris.

OECD (Organization for Economic Cooperation and Development) and Statistics Canada (1995) *Literacy, Economy and Society: Results from the International Adult Literacy Survey*, OECD and Statistics Canada, Paris and Ottawa.

OECD and Statistics Canada (1997) *Literacy Skills for the Knowledge Society: Further results from the International Adult Literacy Survey*, OECD and Statistics Canada, Paris and Ottawa.

OECD and Statistics Canada (2000) *Literacy in the Information Age: Final Report of the International Adult Literacy Survey*, OECD and Statistics Canada, Paris and Ottawa.

Post-16 E-learning Strategy Task Force (2002) [accessed 12 June 2003] *Get on with IT: The Post-16 E-learning Strategy*, Task force report [Online] http://www.dfes.gov.uk/elearningstrategy/news/uploads/GetOnwithIT_Doc.pdf.

QCA (Qualifications and Curriculum Authority) (2000) [accessed 12 June 2003] *Adult Literacy and Numeracy National Qualifications* [Online] http://www.qca.org.uk/nq/bs/.

Wood, A. (2000) *A guide to Outreach with Laptops*, NIACE and DfEE, Leicester.

9   Teachers and teaching innovations in a connected world

Nancy Law

Introduction

Schools face multiple pressures in the twenty-first century, including engagement with more ways of employing information and communication technology (ICT) in learning and teaching, and changing curriculum and teaching practices to foster the development of the life-long learning abilities of students. Many countries announced their ICT in education plans at the turn of the millennium, often in conjunction with or as part of nationwide education reforms. These policy initiatives were often coupled with major investments to equip schools with the necessary ICT infrastructure and to provide staff development opportunities to teachers. It is important now to consider the impact these changes have had on teachers and teaching. This can provide the basis for identification of trends in the development of learning and teaching practices and the associated changes in teachers' roles and competences over the first ten to fifteen years of the new millennium, and consideration of the extent to which these trends are similar across different countries. This chapter addresses these issues through the analysis of case study data from 28 countries, collected as part of an international comparative study of innovative pedagogical practices using ICT.

The role of the teacher in facilitating learning in schools continues to be central in the determination of curriculum goals and learning processes and, increasingly, in deciding how ICT is used in learning and teaching. Many forms of ICT-related staff development have been introduced throughout the world, varying from external in-service courses to informal exchanges of experiences within schools, from obliging teachers to acquire a digital driver's licence (e.g. in the United States (NCATE, 1997; ISTE, 1998) and in Europe (EURYDICE, 2000)) to laissez-faire approaches that capitalize on the intrinsic motivation of teachers. Despite all these efforts, surveys have shown that teachers still lack confidence in using ICT in their teaching practices (e.g. BECTA, 2001). The difficulties encountered relate in particular to identification of pedagogically sound uses of ICT that add value to the learning process. There is a growing expectation that the introduction of computers in schools should be more than introducing new educational technologies; it should be linked to or in support of wider educational renewal and reform aimed to prepare students for lifelong learning (Law and Plomp, 2003). Lifelong learning ability is increasingly seen as a requirement for twenty-first century citizenship. ICT is seen as making a vital contribution to education for lifelong learning (e.g. ERT, 1997) and this is reflected in general education policy documents (e.g. in Hong Kong, see Education Commission, 2000) or embedded within plans for information technology in education (e.g. in Singapore, see Singapore Ministry of Education, 1997).

In order to achieve such education reform goals, teachers need to engage in a transition to achieve new goals and develop new approaches to learning and teaching. Successful efforts to integrate the use of ICT necessarily involve considerable changes in the roles and competencies of the teachers concerned. Are we to see a fundamental change in education and an accompanying 'reinvention' of the teaching professional as a consequence of the introduction of ICT in schools?

Possibly motivated by a desire to better anticipate what effective schools and classrooms of the future would be like, and the accompanying contextual factors that contribute to their emergence, there has been considerable interest in recent years in studying ICT-supported educational innovations. Two well-known international comparative studies of this nature are the OECD case studies on 'ICT and the Quality of Learning' (Venezky and Davis, 2002) and the Second Information Technology in Education Study Module 2 (SITES M2) case studies of 'Innovative Pedagogical Practices Using Technology' (Kozma, 2003). These yielded important insights for understanding innovations beyond the available literature, which mainly drew on action or experimental research. The latter study in particular provided detailed reports of the nature of the pedagogical practices and the teachers' roles, activities and institutional support and contexts through case studies that were selected as exemplars of the most innovative ICT-supported pedagogical practices in their respective education systems. This chapter reports on a detailed analysis of the case reports collected in the SITES M2 study, 'examines the communality and differences across the case studies reported and discusses implications for teachers and teaching in the twenty-first century.

An international comparative study of innovative pedagogical practices

An earlier phase of the SITES study (Pelgrum and Anderson, 1999) found evidence of a worldwide shift towards more collaborative student-directed inquiry-based learning with associated changes in the teacher's role and the form of classroom practice. A national panel of experts in each country selected cases where there was evidence of four factors: (1) technology playing a substantial role; (2) significant changes in the roles of teachers and students, the goals of the curriculum, assessment practices, and/or the educational materials or infrastructure; (3) measurable positive student outcomes; (4) sustainability and transferability. In addition, the pedagogical practice had to be innovative – as locally defined – and should prepare students for lifelong learning in the information society so as to accommodate the circumstances and cultural differences in each country. Details of the design of the study are described in the Study Prospectus (available from http://www.sitesm2.org/).

The pedagogical practices found in these 130 cases could be roughly grouped into six types. Three of the pedagogic types engaged students in productive learning tasks, namely project work, scientific investigations and media production. The other three pedagogic types were more closed and prescriptive, and therefore the demand on students was lower because they were only required to follow instructions. These were task-based learning, virtual schools and online courses, and expository learning.

Project work

There were 56 cases of project work. This label was often used to describe learning activities that were extended in time, with well defined aims and intended products. Often it demanded students to work in groups and to go through the different stages of project task progression. However, a careful examination of the project descriptions revealed that these could be further distinguished into five types of projects. The most demanding of these were *research projects*, which generally started with a relatively weakly structured question. A key part of the learning experience for the students was to engage in the process of refining the research question and then going through an inquiry process to arrive at an answer.

Example of a research project

The HIV/AIDS and Population Project was carried out with Grade 7 (lower secondary) students in South Africa. Four teachers designed a seven week long curriculum programme that engaged students in research on HIV/AIDS related issues, focusing on epidemiology, as well as the values and life skills of HIV/AIDS prevention. In addition to the content goals, the intent was to help students to develop collaboration, problem solving, computer literacy and presentation skills. The teachers engaged in different activities according to the phase of the project:

introducing the innovation and its goals, setting up groups and initiating the research process, facilitating the use of Excel for information processing and helping with project review. Students worked in small groups on one sub-topic, and discussed their activities and work plan in relation to the guiding document prepared by the teachers. They conducted the research using the Internet as the main source of information and other software applications as tools to organize findings and to make presentations.

The other forms of project work were much less inquiry focused. By far the most popular form was the *thematic project*. In these, students were assigned a theme, such as the El Nino climate phenomenon, as a context for gathering information and developing a product that illustrated the understanding gained by the students in the process. In some cases, the different groups of students were all required to work on the same set of tasks, and in other cases, the different teams worked on different tasks related to the same theme to contribute to a large, coordinated product.

A third variation of project work was the *study trip*. This might be a thematic or research project culminating in a study trip that formed the focal point of the learning experience.

The *online discussion project* was another variation of project work where the production of a tangible outcome was not important. The focus was on getting students to express and explore ideas through a web forum. Such projects might involve only students from the same school, but in some cases they involved collaboration with other schools or sometimes even with people outside the education community, such as graduates or outside experts.

The last form of project work found was the *aggregated-task project*, which in terms of the nature of the learning task was more like task-based learning. These consisted of a number of short, well-structured tasks (each to be completed in one to two lessons) related to the same theme such that the aggregate would deliver a product referred to as a 'project'.

Scientific investigations

Scientific investigations, of which there were just seven cases, differed from the other five types of practice in that they had a clear subject matter focus on science and often involved scientific experimentation or simulations using technology. They were inquiry-focused, but differed from more general kinds of research project in that the research questions tended to be more well defined and focused. The technology used and the facilitation required were often specific to the scientific area concerned. This might also be one of the reasons why there were only seven scientific investigations among the 130 case studies analysed.

Example of a scientific investigation

This problem-based learning, computer-assisted scientific investigation involved the collaborative efforts of three senior science teachers, who were the heads of biology, chemistry and physics in a well-established girls' school in Hong Kong. Science students in Grades 10–13 (upper secondary) in this school participated in this innovation. The teachers wanted to introduce scientific investigations into the curriculum so that students could generate the problem to be investigated as well as formulate the method of inquiry, conduct experiments and interpret the results to arrive at a conclusion. Students were organized into 30 small groups. Each group had to identify a problem that the members considered to be interesting and/or important to investigate. Each group then designed and conducted an investigation using a data-logging system and associated software for the data collection and analysis. The students then had to determine whether the results so obtained were able to address their problem. Often, difficulties were encountered and the students had to modify or improve their design until they were able to find an answer. As the students themselves identified the problems, the teachers had to facilitate the inquiry process while engaging in a similar learning process to the students. Each group had to produce, as a final product, a laboratory guide for the investigation so that other students could follow the instructions and conduct the experiment accordingly.

Media production

The 29 cases of media production had many of the pedagogic features of project work and were sometimes referred to as projects in the case reports. The key distinguishing feature of this type of pedagogical practice was the central focus on the production of a specific media product, for example visual images, animation, music or video productions. The quality of the product, including its technical sophistication, was often an important learning focus.

Example of a media production

This digital art project was carried out with a group of upper primary students, aged between 9 and 11, in a government primary school in Singapore. It was conducted as a two-hour weekly co-curriculum activity, known as the Digital Art Programme, for children who had basic Chinese brush painting skills. The programme involved one art teacher. The use of ICT enabled students to broaden their knowledge of art, allowing them to explore art pieces of similar genre to develop a better understanding of the characteristics of specific art forms. It also enabled the students to create different art forms with one just one medium, for example Chinese brush painting and water-colour. They were also able to edit and refine their work much more easily. ICT also allowed teachers to share and discuss the work of different students with the whole class. This promoted the exchange of ideas among students and the development of their communication skills.

Task-based learning

In the three approaches discussed so far, students were engaged in productive open-ended learning tasks involving a creative learning process, often resulting in a tangible product. In contrast, the activities in the 21 cases of task-based learning were close-ended and tightly defined. Whilst these cases were often referred to as 'student-centred', as during much of the learning time students were engaged in learning activities, the demands on the students were much lower than in the previous three pedagogic types as they were required only to closely follow instructions.

Virtual schools and online courses

Virtual schools refer to educational organizations that offer a variety of subjects using structured online materials, including a comprehensive web site, a detailed curriculum and timetable on a year-round basis. Many of the subjects offered were multi-disciplinary in nature and most schools would not have sufficient enrolment and/or teaching expertise to offer these by themselves. Some of the virtual schools were administered by a central provider such that interested schools just subscribed to their services. In other instances, the virtual school might be a coordinated effort of a number of schools to form a virtual school network.

Other than virtual schools, which were relatively formal establishments of some scale, there were also online courses organized by schools as a supplement to the general school curriculum. An online course might be used to deliver a complete course, or just cover a few learning units in a particular subject. Online courses were generally organized as enrichment rather than as a central component of the existing school curriculum. Altogether there were 14 cases of virtual schools or online courses.

Expository teaching

This was the least popular amongst the innovative pedagogical practices nominated, accounting only for three out of the 130 cases analysed. Here the technology was used to enrich the teacher's' exposition that formed the core of the learning activity.

Roles of the teacher in pedagogical practices using ICT

If the case studies collected are to be interpreted as providing an indication of what future classrooms could be like, the above analysis has provided some evidence that there is a shift, in the countries studied, towards more collaborative, student-directed, enquiry-based and productive modes of learning. It is also possible to explore the potential impact of these shifts on the roles and competencies required of teachers and consider whether the changes in pedagogical practice bring about fundamental changes in the roles played by teachers as well.

Altogether 13 roles were identified from the descriptions of the teachers' activities within the 130 cases studies. It is apparent from this list of roles, presented in Table 9.1, that many of these are long-standing and familiar approaches in traditional schooling, especially those that are listed at the top of the table, roles T1–T4. These involve teachers explaining or presenting information, giving task instructions, monitoring students' progress and assessing students' learning outcomes. However, new roles did emerge; the roles lower down the list are less often found in traditional classrooms.

All of the listed roles from T5 onwards were in some ways associated with the use of ICT and/or the introduction of more enquiry-based or productive modes of learning. Role T8 was the only one that was explicitly ICT related. However, many of the roles in fact require some levels of technical competence and fluency. The kind of learning support provided in T5 was mostly technical in nature, though it might sometimes include other pedagogical advice such as conceptual or problem solving support when the students were working on their learning tasks. The teaching materials developed by the teachers (as coded in T6) were

Table 9.1 The pedagogical roles played by teachers

Code	Teacher's pedagogical role	% of cases found
T1	Explain or present information	42
T2	Give task instruction	51
T3	Monitor students' task progression	74
T4	Assess students	59
T5	Provide learning support (incl. technical support) to students	70
T6	Develop teaching materials	41
T7	Design curriculum and learning activities	41
T8	Select ICT tools	6
T9	Support/model students' enquiry process	29
T10	Co-teaching	29
T11	Support team building and collaboration of students	18
T12	Mediate communication between students and experts	4
T13	Liaise with parties outside school	22

generally in digital format, implying that the teachers needed to possess some level of media production expertise. The teaching materials produced were either used by the teachers to support their own explanation or presentation of information, or used by students as self-access learning materials. On the other hand, the design of curriculum and learning activities (T7), whether these relate to the use of digital materials or not, would not require technical expertise beyond understanding the nature and use of those materials. T9 is specifically related to supporting the enquiry process when students were engaged in open-ended enquiries. Such support was often provided through working as co-learners with students, thus modelling for them the enquiry process, rather than through direct instruction.

The roles T10–T13 were all associated with the fact that many of the classrooms in the case studies were much more "open" or "connected" to the outside world. Traditionally, teachers work as individuals in classrooms isolated from each other. Learning was also very much a form of activity that students take responsibility for on an individual basis. In 29 per cent of the case studies, the teachers were collaborating with other fellow teachers within or outside their own schools in organizing the teaching and learning activities. There was also a much stronger tendency for learning to be organized as a collaborative activity, since students working collaboratively in teams were a central feature in nearly all of the practices categorized as project work, scientific investigations or media production. It was thus not surprising that supporting the team building and collaboration of students was one of the teachers' roles found in the case studies. In fact, the relatively low percentage of cases (18 per cent) showing evidence of the teachers playing the role T11 may be indicative of the lack of teachers' awareness and/or expertise in supporting team learning in students. T12 and T13 were roles that teachers played when parties outside the school sector were involved in the teaching and learning process. Such instances may include the organization of field trips and other learning activities where liaison with parties outside the school sector may be necessary (T13). In some instances, the learning issues went beyond the normal school curriculum and the expertise of the school teachers and outside experts were involved in contributing to students' learning. The teachers mediated the communication between the students and the experts (T12). Much of the mediation work of teachers in these cases was facilitated by the use of ICT.

As discussed earlier, T5–T7 are roles that teachers have been playing in traditional classrooms, with the additional requirement of technical competence when technology is employed. Thus, there might not be any fundamental change in the pedagogical roles played by the teacher if they were not played in tandem with roles T9–T13. If more open, collaborative, student-directed, enquiry-based modes of learning are to be the dominant form of school-based learning of the future, then the roles T9–T13 will be more prevalent as the innovative practices become the mainstream peda-gogical practices of the future. In this sense, we may refer to the roles from T9 onwards as the key *'emerging'* roles, while the roles T1–T4 are the more traditional ones. Further, it can be seen from the percentage frequency of occurrence of the various roles in the cases presented in Table 9.1 that the traditional roles still dominate even within this set of innovative peda-gogical practices collected from around the world.

Five broad categories of pedagogical roles associated with ICT-supported innovations

It is apparent from the above discussion that the various roles played by the teachers were not mutually independent, and that they should be connected with the specific features of the innovative practices. A K-means cluster analysis, which is an exploratory multivariate proce-dure for identifying meaningful groupings in a dataset by clustering the cases into different assigned numbers of groups (SPSS Inc, 1999), was conducted on the set of teachers' roles in the 130 case studies. In this procedure, the cluster-solution that provides the most meaningful inter-pretation of the different cluster characteristics as reflected in the weighting of the cluster centres corresponding to each variable is then taken as the optimal solution. In this study, the analysis results for five clusters yielded the most meaningful results and the resulting cluster centres are presented in Table 9.2.

It can be seen from Table 9.2 that the 130 case studies can be grouped into five clusters, each having a combination of teachers' roles that can be identified with a holistic set of pedagogical functions. The roles played by teachers in the case studies identified in Cluster 5 were in fact very similar to that traditionally expected of teachers. It is apparent that in engaging in innovations in this cluster, the main change that the teachers faced was a technical one, as technical expertise would be required in fulfilling roles T5 and T6. It is also noteworthy that even though only 3 of the 130 case studies belonged to the category of expository learning according to the description given of the type of practice, the actual role played by the teachers in 30 of the cases was essentially the same as those in traditional classrooms.

The most prominent roles played by teachers in the 59 cases in Clusters 3 and 4 were arguably just subsets of the roles played by teachers in traditional settings, as exemplified in the Cluster 5 cases. While teachers involved in Cluster 5 were presenting information, giving instructions and assessing students' performance, the most common roles played by the teachers in the Cluster 3 cases were those related to administration of learning tasks: giving task instructions, monitoring progression and providing learning support to student. The most common roles played

Table 9.2 K-means cluster analysis of teachers' roles

Traditional ↑ / ↓ Emerging

Cluster number (number of cases in cluster)	1 (26)	2 (15)	3 (36)	4 (23)	5 (30)
Interpretation of cluster — Teachers' role	Facilitating exploratory learning	Guiding collaborative inquiry	Administer learning tasks	Provide learning resources	Present, instruct and assess
T1 Explain or present information	0.08	0.73	0.03	0.57	0.90
T2 Give task instruction	0.00	0.40	0.83	0.26	0.80
T3 Monitor students' task progression	0.77	0.80	0.89	0.17	0.93
T4 Assess students	0.85	0.93	0.28	0.26	0.83
T5 Provide learning support to students	0.81	0.93	0.72	0.17	0.87
T6 Develop teaching materials	0.12	0.20	0.19	0.78	0.73
T7 Design curriculum and learning activities	0.15	0.73	0.14	0.26	0.90
T8 Select ICT tools	0.00	0.13	0.03	0.09	0.10
T9 Support students' enquiry process	0.73	0.80	0.00	0.22	0.07
T10 Co-teaching	0.23	0.80	0.25	0.35	0.10
T11 Support team building of students	0.19	0.80	0.06	0.13	0.03
T12 Mediate between students and experts	0.00	0.13	0.03	0.09	0.00
T13 Liaise with parties outside school	0.15	0.33	0.28	0.17	0.20

Note: a shaded cell indicates that the weighting for the particular role in a specific cluster was >50%.

by teachers in Cluster 4 cases were presenting information and developing teaching materials. It was as if one needed to innovate just in order to give up some of the roles teachers traditionally played.

The key emerging roles were present more strongly in the practices of teachers involved in Clusters 1 and 2. In particular, most of the teachers in these two clusters were engaged in supporting students in their enquiry process. It appeared that most of the teachers in Cluster 1 were giving up some of the traditional roles to focus on supporting students' enquiry. Teachers in Cluster 2 seemed to have taken on not only most of the traditional pedagogical roles, but had also engaged in collaborative teaching with fellow teachers and exerted tremendous efforts in all of the emerging roles ranging from supporting enquiry to supporting and mediating collaborations. This was certainly not a simple accomplishment on the part of these teachers, and may also explain why this was the smallest of the five clusters, having only 15 cases.

Innovative ICT-supported pedagogical practices

The earlier analysis of the 130 cases into six pedagogic types revealed that at the organization and activities level, expository teaching and task-based learning appeared to be more traditional while project work and scientific investigations seemed to be the most intellectually demanding practices as these required students to engage in collaborative enquiry. It is now possible to analyse how the roles played by the teachers in the cases correlate with the pedagogic type of the practices. Table 9.3 provides the distribution of teachers' role types across the different types of pedagogic practices.

Table 9.3 Cross-tabulation of teachers' role clusters and innovative practices

	Emerging ←					→ Traditional	
Type of practice *Teachers' role cluster*	*Scientific investigation*	*Project work*	*Media production*	*Virtual schools/ online courses*	*Task- based learning*	*Expository teaching*	*Total*
Fascinating exploratory learning	4	14	7	1	–	–	26
Guiding collaborative enquiry	–	10	5	–	–	–	15
Administer learning tasks	1	16	8	4	7	–	36
Provide learning resources	1	8	4	4	5	1	23
Present, instruct and assess	1	8	5	5	9	2	30
Total	7	56	29	14	21	3	130

(left margin: Emerging ↑ / Traditional ↓)

A very prominent observation, as revealed in Table 9.3, is that the roles played by the teachers in each of the six pedagogical practices were very diverse, even though the descriptions provided of the classroom teaching and learning activities for those cases were similar. The most consistent pedagogical practices were expository teaching (where the most prominent 'roles were to provide learning resources and to present, instruct and assess students) and task-based learning (where the most prominent roles included the role cluster 'administer learning tasks' in addition to the two role clusters found in expository teaching). Virtual schools and online courses appeared to be rather traditional in their pedagogical approach, even though the technology used in the delivery was comparatively sophisticated.

For practices where the prominent roles played by the teachers were related to supporting enquiry, nearly all of them were organized in the form of project work, media production or scientific investigation. This indicates that these three forms of pedagogical practice probably provide the kind of learning context more conducive to facilitating student enquiry, and will be referred to as the *emerging pedagogical practices*. On the other hand, even for the seven cases of scientific investigations reported, the prominent roles played by teachers in three of these cases were rather didactic and not related to the facilitation of exploratory learning. It is also noteworthy that the distributions of cases across the five teachers' role clusters for project work and media production were almost identical, indicating that teachers might not perceive any peda-gogical differences in the roles demanded of them in these two types of practices. Further, teachers' facilitation of enquiry was only prominent in 42 per cent of the cases in these two types of practices. This is strong evidence that the format and curriculum organization of pedagogical practices per se would not be sufficient to bring about changes in teachers' roles in the classroom, which is arguably the key to changing the roles played by students in the classroom, and hence the kind of learning outcome that can be achieved (Law *et al.*, 2002).

There is clear evidence in the results listed in Table 9.3 that the format and curriculum organization of the pedagogical practices implemented in classrooms alone would not determine the actual pedagogical roles of the teachers. Even within the set of 130 innovative pedagogical practices carefully selected and collected around the world, teachers' roles were found to be predominantly facilitative of enquiry in only 32 per cent of these cases. Clearly, there is a long way to go in bringing about deep changes in pedagogy in schools and classrooms even in the most innovative pedagogical endeavours. Further, it is important to recognize on the basis of the present results that there cannot be a simple 'transfer' of innovative practices within or across institutions by just replicating curriculum materials and/or curriculum activities. Staff development that promotes deep changes in teachers' roles and practices is of paramount importance.

Multiple dimensions of innovation and the teacher's role

While the discussion so far has centred on the pedagogic type and teachers' roles in the innovative case studies using technology, these are not the only aspects of change and innovation that were evident from the study. In fact, in addition to the teacher's role, there are five other dimensions (or aspects) of innovation that could be identified from the case studies: the intended learning objectives of the classroom practice, the role(s) of the learner, the nature and sophistication of the ICT used, the connectedness of the classroom, and the kinds of learning outcomes exhibited by the learner during the process. These six dimensions of innovation are in fact the six key elements in any curriculum implementation involving ICT use. When the features of each case study are examined along each of these six dimensions, it becomes apparent that there is a marked diversity across cases for the other five dimensions as well. If we take the 'traditional' classroom to be typically one that is knowledge-focused, teacher-centred, does not use ICT, is isolated from the outside world, where teachers only assesses students on cognitive learning outcomes, and where students only follow instructions and learn from the teacher, then theoretically the most innovative classroom would be one that uses appropriate technology to support the development of collaborative enquiry abilities through the provision of authentic learning contexts, where the students undertake self-directed collaborative inquiry supported by the teacher who facilitates team building and reflection, guides the exploratory process as well as mediates communication between students and various outside parties such as co-learners, and assessment is primarily based on authentic evidence generated during the learning process such that it can reflect not only the cognitive outcomes but also much of the process outcomes targeted. However, it was also found that while many cases reflect innovative characteristics along one or several of the six dimensions, it was very rare to find one that was very innovative along all six dimensions. Details of the scale of innovativeness used in this analysis are reported in Law (2003). For instance, in the case study example of scientific investigation presented earlier in the chapter, it was rated very innovative in terms of the roles undertaken by the teachers and students as well as in the sophistication of ICT used. However, the classrooms in this practice were essentially isolated from outside communities, and the goals of learning targeted by the teachers and the methods used for assessment were still rather cognitively focussed. Figure 9.1 displays in diagrammatic format

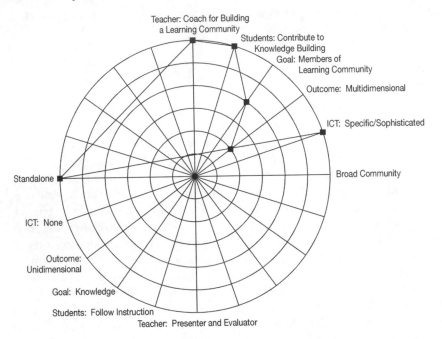

Figure 9.1 Innovativeness diagram for scientific investigation case study

the extent of innovativeness for this case study along each of the six dimensions. A score furthest away from the centre in the lower left quadrant would be most traditional while a score furthest away from the centre in the upper right quadrant would be most innovative.

Among the six dimensions of innovation, the teacher's role is arguably the most important one as it is the teacher who orchestrates the various elements within a classroom practice. However, Figure 9.1 highlights the fact that even when the teachers have paid due attention to their changing roles, there is still room to improve the practice and this multi-dimensional view of innovation would help teachers to pay attention to all of the six dimensions of innovation in their curriculum planning and implementation.

A comparison of teachers' roles in innovative practices around the world

The 130 case studies of innovation collected from 28 countries revealed a range of pedagogical practices as well as different clusters of teachers' pedagogical roles, providing evidence that some pedagogical practices had features that were more conducive to supporting students' collaborative inquiry, even though the practice characteristics alone were insufficient to determine the pedagogical roles played by the teachers. Results from an earlier survey study, the SITES Module 1, found cross-national differences in terms of the reported pedagogical approaches employed in integrating the use of ICT in schools (Pelgrum and Anderson, 1999). These differences appeared to be linked to the prevalent school and classroom culture in the different countries. It is possible to consider here whether a similar relationship is evident in the current study of innovative practices. As the average number of case studies analysed per participating country was less than five and the number of cases from each country varied enormously from one to eleven, it was not possible to examine cross-national differences. However, as countries within a region tended to have greater cultural and curriculum similarities, it is worthwhile to explore tentatively whether there were regional differences around the world.

Table 9.4 presents the number of cases belonging to each type of pedagogical practice and each teachers' role cluster for the case studies analysed from that region. Based on the analysis presented in the previous sections of this chapter, it is possible to group broadly the practice types scientific investigations, project work and media production as the emerging practices and group the teachers' role clusters facilitating exploratory learning and guiding collaborative enquiry as emerging pedagogies. The proportion of cases in each region belonging to these two broad categories are presented in Table 9.5.

While the number of cases in each category for each region is too small to claim any statistical significance, the results in Table 9.5 provide very interesting and noteworthy patterns that could be explored in further studies. First of all, in terms of the type of pedagogical practice employed in the pedagogical innovations, the proportion belonging to the emerging practices was approximately 80 per cent for all regions except Asia, and more than 50 per cent even for Asia. On the other hand, with the exception of Southern Africa, which was only one region with five practices, even for the country with the highest proportion of cases employing emerging pedagogies, Western Europe, the proportion was only 35 per cent. Furthermore, Eastern Europe had 79 per cent of its innovative practices belonging to the emerging practices while only 14 per cent indicated that the teachers employed emerging pedagogies. On the other hand, 25 per cent of the innovative practices in Asia reflected emerging pedagogies though it had the lowest proportion of emerging practices, 53 per cent. These figures indicate that it is much more difficult to change pedagogy than to change practice worldwide. Furthermore, it was much easier to 'transfer' practices, giving rise to very similar proportions of emerging practices around the world, than to adopt new pedagogies, resulting in a much wider diversity in the proportions of emerging pedagogies in the different regions.

Table 9.4 Innovative practices and teachers' role clusters by world regions

Region (participating countries in region)	Americas (3)	Western Europe (12)	Eastern Europe (5)	Asia (7)	Southern Africa (1)	Total (28)
Type of practice						
Scientific investigations	0	2	1	4	0	7
Project work	3	35	5	9	4	56
Media production	3	17	5	4	0	29
Virtual school/online course	2	9	0	3	0	14
Task-based learning	0	7	3	10	1	21
Expository teaching	0	1	0	2	0	3
Total	8	71	14	32	5	130
Teachers' role cluster						
Facilitating exploratory learning	0	17	0	6	3	26
Guiding collaborative enquiry	2	8	2	2	1	15
Administer learning tasks	0	26	5	5	0	36
Provide learning resources	3	10	2	8	0	23
Present, instruct and assess	3	10	5	11	1	30
Total	8	71	14	32	5	130

Table 9.5 Emerging practices and emerging pedagogies by world region (%)

Region (participating countries in region)	Americas (3)	Western Europe (12)	Eastern Europe (5)	Asia (7)	Southern Africa (1)	Overall (28)
Emerging practices	75	76	79	53	80	71
Emerging pedagogies	25	35	14	25	80	32

Teachers' roles and teacher professional development in a connected world

Since the 1950s, the advent of computers brought high hopes of the power of technology to revolutionize and improve education. With the invention of the personal computer and the consequent increase in the accessibility of computers to schools since the 1980s, such optimism has been seriously challenged. In reviewing the use of ICT in education worldwide, Blurton (2000) found consistent evidence that ICT-mediated instruction using conventional teaching methods was not any more effective than traditional face-to-face instruction. The case studies of innovative pedagogical practices using technology collected in the SITES M2 study makes an important contribution to our understanding of how the power of ICT could best be harnessed. The analysis presented in this paper provides indications that in many countries around the world ICT is beginning to play a significant role in bringing about fundamental changes in curriculum goals and pedagogical practices when accompanied by significant changes in the pedagogical roles played by the teachers.

The findings also indicate that teachers as professionals have become more connected, working collaboratively with colleagues and members of the broader community to bring about more challenging and more fruitful learning experiences for their students. In relation to this greater connectedness, it is interesting to note the tendency towards a preference for particular pedagogical approaches. There is, however, a long way to go in terms of changing the pedagogical roles of the teacher from the more didactic towards the more facilitative. An encouraging observation from the case reports was that teachers taking part in the innovations were enthusiastic about their experiences and the learning they gained in the process, relating the latter to their engagement in the innovation process, and the collaboration they had with colleagues and students. Hence, it seems that there are indications that this form of learning in authentic situations is not only a model for the education of students in the future, but that it could be considered as an ideal model for continuous staff development.

It is very heartening to note that some of the teachers who engaged in the innovations have in fact not only created new practices, but also contributed to a re-invention of the teaching profession through the new pedagogical roles they creatively developed and adopted. Case studies of innovative practices should be further explored to develop new models of professional development for teachers as actual engagements in curriculum and pedagogical innovations probably provide the best authentic learning contexts to prepare teachers for the challenges of the twenty-first century.

References

BECTA (2001) *Emerging Findings from the Evaluation of the Impact of Information and Communication Technologies on Pupil Attainment*, British Educational Communications and Technology Agency, Coventry.

Blurton, C. (2000) *New Directions in Education*, UNESCO, Paris.

Education Commission (2000) *Learning for Life Learning through Life*, Education Commission, HKSAR, Hong Kong.

ERT (1997) *Investing in Knowledge: The integration of technology in European education*, European Round Table of Industrialists, Brussels.

EURYDICE (2000) *Information and Communication Technology in the Education Systems in Europe*, EURYDICE, the Information Network on Education in Europe, Brussels.

ISTE (1998) *National Educational Technology Standards for Students*, International Society for Technology in Education, Eugene, OR.

Kozma, R. (2003) (ed.) *Technology, Innovation, and Educational Change: A global perspective*, International Society for Technology in Education, Eugene, OR.

Law, N. (2003) Innovative classroom practices and the teacher of the future, in *Information and Communication Technology and the Teacher of the Future*, eds C. Dowling and K. W. Lai, Kluwer Academic Publishers, Dordrecht.

Law, N., Lee., Y. and Chow, A. (2002) Practice characteristics that lead to '21st Century learning outcomes', *Journal of Computer Assisted Learning*, 18 (4), pp. 415–26.

Law, N. and Plomp, T. (2003) Curriculum and staff development, in *Cross-national Policies and Practices on Information and Communication Technology in Education*, eds T. Plomp, R. Anderson, N. Law and A. Quale, Information Age Publishing Inc, Greenwich, CT.

NCATE (1997) *Standards, Procedures, and Policies for the Accreditation of Professional Education Units*, National Council for Accreditation of Teacher Education, Washington, DC.

Pelgrum, H. and Anderson, R. (1999) (eds) *ICT and the Emerging Paradigm for Life Long Learning*, IEA, Amsterdam.

Singapore Ministry of Education (1997) [accessed 5 October 2002] *Masterplan for IT in Education*, Ministry of Education, Singapore [Online] http://www1.moe.edu.sg/iteducation/masterplan/summary.htm.

SPSS Inc (1999) *SPSS Base 10.0 applications guide*, Chicago, IL.

Venezky, R. L. and Davis, C. (2002) *Quo Vademus? The Transformation of Schooling in a Networked World*, OECD/CERI, Paris.

10 Teaching with video cases on the Web

Lessons learned from the Reading Classroom Explorer

*Richard E. Ferdig, Laura R. Roehler,
Erica C. Boling, Suzanne Knezek,
P. David Pearson and Aman Yadav*

Online learning represents an important new turn for education, and particularly for teacher education and teacher professional development. Researchers have argued the need for emerging technologies for active and interactive learning in the field of teacher professional development (Beavers, 2001; Sparks and Hirsh, 1997). Although there are some limiting factors and potential problems (e.g. having a good Internet connection), there are a number of benefits that even face-to-face workshops fail to provide. Those advantages include extensive resources, opportunities for achieving specific goals, convenience, flexibility, a larger learning community and the ability to interact with emerging technologies (Yoder, 2002). Additional benefits, such as convenience of location or the reduction of time constraints, make educational opportunities more affordable and practical (Sujo de Montes and Gonzales, 2000). Teachers are also becoming increasingly engaged with online learning, suggesting that new technologies may fundamentally change their own professional development (RAND, 1995).

Literacy researchers and instructors have also noticed possibilities in web-based learning (Ferdig *et al.*, 2002; Teale *et al.*, 2002). Although much of the software produced has been aimed at student emergent literacy acquisition, there has been an important shift towards online professional development in both pre-service and in-service professional development. These new systems, becoming more ubiquitous in the United States with state, local and national literacy mandates (such as President Bush's 'No Child Left Behind' Act of 2001), combine video, graphics and text to present exciting and interactive learning environments in which teachers can explore exemplary literacy practices.

The Reading Classroom Explorer (RCE) is one such literacy pre-service tool that utilizes video cases video clips, and databases to showcase exemplary literacy instruction. The project began in 1997, and project members have been researching the use of the tool since 1998. In this chapter, we summarize and highlight the longitudinal RCE work, with the goal of answering two important questions. First, what does a successful Web-based learning environment, specifically one that utilizes video to instruct pre-service literacy instructors, look like? Second, what happens when we implement a video and Web-based learning environment into pre-service literacy classrooms?

The Reading Classroom Explorer (RCE)

Current research has offered evidence that student teachers experience tension between their field experiences in elementary classrooms and the usually reform-oriented instructional techniques that they learn about in their methods courses (Hughes *et al.*, 1998). This tension is mixed with concern over the conventional pedagogy of their reading and writing methods classes, where instruction is limited to books and lectures about the teaching methodology (Ferdig *et al.*, 2002). They express the need to see models of challenging, reform-oriented teaching in action (Ferdig *et al.*, 2002; Hughes *et al.*, 1998).

Even classroom observations and internship experiences can fail to provide teacher candidates with desirable teaching and learning experiences. Some candidates do not have opportunities to observe their subject matter of interest, others work in field sites that do not offer teaching examples that align with the pedagogical and theoretical focus of the university preparation programmes, and still others are so busy 'helping' (e.g. grading papers) that they have few opportunities to 'watch' expert pedagogy when it is offered.

Furthermore, even when the models are strong, teacher candidates do not necessarily possess the tools to transform observations and practice into instances of deep reflection and ways of acting (see Dunkin *et al.*, 1993; Feiman-Nemser and Buchman, 1986; Goodman and Fish, 1997; Hughes *et al.*, 1998). Securing admission into a practicum or apprenticeship type of experience does not guarantee access to 'truly meaningful experiences' (Kinzer and Risko, 1998), nor does it guarantee access to diverse approaches to language and literacy instruction or diverse student perspectives (intellectually, ethnically or culturally). Even if a university instructor is blessed or gifted enough to secure rich field experiences, many teacher candidates do not know how to take advantage of such situations.

RCE has begun to build a bridge between the university classroom and K-12 classrooms for pre-service teachers in their literacy instruction. RCE users can explore a variety of literacy practices in elementary classrooms through video cases with 24-hour access to vivid, concrete images of desirable instruction. RCE has over 300 video clips of exemplary teaching practices from 10 different schools, with each clip ranging from 30 seconds to 5 minutes in length. The video clips demonstrate teachers using a variety of instructional groupings and formats (e.g. small group, large group, discussions, partner reading, etc.) while working with students in preschool and grades K-5. Some of these clips include children with English as an additional language and children with special educational needs. In teacher education settings, hypermedia systems like RCE can bring the 'real' classroom into the university classrooms and labs, while also providing important scaffolding to help learners make sense of what they are viewing.

Specific features of RCE

Hughes *et al.* (1998) describe RCE as a new form of educational instruction for pre-service teachers. They note that it differs from conventional forms of instruction by providing: user control of information; on-demand access to multimedia, including video clips, transcripts (text), audio clips, supplemental reading topics and applicable research articles (citations); the ability to juxtapose media from several school sites; the ability to search for information using school location, theme, key words or even words appearing in the transcript of the video; and areas for individual journal entries, collaborative notes, and bulletin board discussions.

RCE provides footage of schools nationwide spanning socio-economic levels and geographic regions. RCE video images provide teachers with access to many models of teaching-in-action. The many different types of media from various classrooms combine in an environment in which the user has a significant amount of control over the delivery of these video images. There are five ways to select movie clips. These varied search mechanisms allow users to review clips from multiple perspectives, a feature supported by cognitive flexibility theory (Spiro *et al.*, 1992). First, a user can select a movie by school location. Using the format of a case, they can follow a specific teacher or set of children through a literacy curriculum. The second way to search for clips is to click on a 'major' theme. In doing so, a user is presented with all of the titles of clips associated with that topic such as 'teacher goals and objectives' or 'literature-based instruction'. Third, each clip also has a number of keywords related to it. These keywords are more specific than themes; they include words such as 'assessment' or 'book clubs', or they might represent something specifically dealt with in that clip such as reference to children's authors and illustrators such as 'Mercer Mayer' or 'Ann Grifalconi'. It is helpful to think of the 'themes' as the table of contents, and the 'keywords' as RCE's index. The fourth way to find specific clips is to search for words in the transcripts that accompany all clips. This is not only helpful for users with very specific searches, but it is also a powerful mechanism if a user previously viewed a clip and remembered the content of the clip but not necessarily the title. Finally, users have the option of selecting movies from a list of clips they have not yet seen.

Once a movie clip or case is selected, the system utilizes video streaming technology, thus offering users minimal (a few seconds) download time after which the video plays on their screen, buffering the rest as the video proceeds. The video is accompanied by a transcript, as well as guiding questions that support user understanding and reflection of the practices viewed in that clip. These features allow the users to visit, revisit, analyse, critique, compare and contrast a set of diverse classrooms in the rich, flexible and idiosyncratic manner that hypermedia provides. Once they have viewed a clip and thought about the associated questions, they can store their responses and/or questions in a personal notepad included on the page. The notepad is a space within the RCE web site where users can write and save notes to keep track of their reactions to video clips or draft answers to discussion questions. This allows the users to reflect on the video clip as they are watching it and save their notes. This notepad can be recalled at anytime, allowing users to reflect on their reactions or add further comments during later viewing sessions. If users want to view a varying perspective, they can click on a button to view anonymously other users' notes about that particular clip. A final feature in viewing the RCE video clip is the opportunity to see archived copies of students' work. Thus, if the teacher and student in a video are discussing a specific paper, the RCE user could see a copy of that paper.

After viewing a clip, RCE users can also choose to interact with both their peers and their instructors in online discussion forums. Online forums are considered beneficial for several reasons. Student teachers can access them whenever they wish, using appropriate technology. Forums provide opportunities for collaboration and interaction, and though the university students may participate in collaborative talk concerning video cases in class, online forums are available at any time. Even when students view strong cases of literacy instruction, they may not transform their observations into instances of deep thinking about practice if they are not given multiple opportunities to discuss what they have seen. Most students require the give and take of debate and discussions with their peers in order to develop their ideas (Coser, 1970; Weedman, 1999). Online forums allow teacher candidates to discuss the cases they have seen, while still giving them plenty of time for thoughtful planning and composing of their shared responses. From a sociocultural perspective (Vygotsky, 1978), they also provide multiple ways for the pre-service teachers to mediate the transformation of information into knowledge.

In addition to posting in the discussion forums, RCE users can also create and share more formal writing. In the writing space, users are provided with the tools necessary to write papers and then submit them to their instructors. The users can also make their work public by choosing to share their papers with their classmates or peers who are not part of their own classes. As with the discussion forum, users can link movies to their papers, thus using RCE video clips as evidence to support their arguments.

A final feature of RCE to be highlighted is the database of research articles. The article database stores various pieces related to the different video clips, which can be searched according to keywords. These can be keywords generated by the users themselves, as well as keywords related to the video clips viewed. The users can, therefore, look for research articles that detail research conceptually related to the instruction viewed in the clips. Some of the database titles are linked to full-text online versions, while others are simply listings of references users gather themselves.

Implementation of a web-based literacy technology

The second major question explores the implementation of a Web-based literacy technology. We based our work on the studies that have shown technology has the potential to transform the structures of interactions between students in classrooms (Beach and Lundell, 1998) and to transform the role of the teacher from that of 'direct deliverer of instruction' to a facilitator of learning (Askov and Bixler, 1998: 179). We understand that the orientation of the teacher or predisposition of their students can limit how technology is integrated into classrooms and university courses (Tierney and Damarin, 1998). We also understand that when college instructors use computers in their classrooms, the computers are often used like overhead projectors and are not 'integrally woven into pre-service curricula in ways that make college instruction more effective' (Kinzer and Risko, 1998:185).

We have used these studies as we have implemented RCE in teacher education courses. Our investigations reveal that RCE can support instructors' teaching and enhance student learning in literacy teacher education courses. Instructors who teach these courses have discovered various ways to implement RCE so that it meets the needs of individual learners (Boling, 2003). They use RCE to support the content and goals of their courses and to solve individual teaching dilemmas. Instructors have used RCE to challenge students' assumptions about teaching and learning and to introduce them to strategies for building inclusive learning communities. Interviews with instructors and students have revealed that RCE can serve as a bridge between students' coursework and their field experiences (Boling, 2002). Teacher education students have also benefited from RCE because it can assist them in acquiring new knowledge about literacy instruction (Boling, 2001; Ferdig *et al.*, 2002; Hughes *et al.*, 2000; Knezek, 2002).

Instructor use and impact on instructors

Instructors engaged students in a variety of RCE-based activities in their classes to support the content and goals of their courses (Boling, 2003; Ferdig *et al.*, 2002; Knezek, 2002). For example, some instructors asked groups of students to view video cases or clips for different purposes and then complete a jigsaw activity that allowed students to converse and share their different interpretations of what they saw. In other instances, instructors had groups of three to five students sitting at a single computer selecting clips for examples of 'best practice'. Once students reached a consensus on their favourite clips, they then posted messages on the discussion forum, describing their clips and their rationale for choosing them (Boling and Roehler, 2002).

In addition to using RCE to provide images of instructional practices, instructors also used RCE to solve various teaching dilemmas that they encountered while teaching their courses (Boling, 2003). One instructor described frustration with her class because students were not using each other as resources for learning. So she created an RCE assignment where students viewed clips and investigated different aspects of literacy instruction. Students then taught one another by showing and discussing these clips to their classmates in a class presentation. By using RCE in this way, instruction in this teacher education class moved from a teacher-centred to a student-centred approach. Other instructors described similar changes in their instruction and explained how using RCE allowed students to take more control and responsibility for their learning.

Student use and impact on students

Even though contemporary cognitive theories 'view learning as an active, constructive process that is heavily influenced by an individual's existing knowledge and beliefs and is situated in particular contexts' (Borko and Putnam, 1996: 674), many pre-service teachers begin their professional training with more traditional views of teaching as telling and learning as remembering (Calderhead, 1988). One of the challenges that teacher educators face is trying to find ways that challenge the traditional views of teaching and learning that many pre-service teachers bring with them to their teacher education courses. Some of the pre-service teachers who used RCE stated that the kind of innovative literacy instruction that they saw in RCE clips was very different from the kind of instruction they received when they were elementary students (Boling, 2002). The RCE research team investigated how these different approaches and views of literacy instruction impacted on teacher education students when they used the program.

Findings reveal that viewing and discussing RCE clips challenged many pre-service teachers' prior assumptions about teaching and learning (Boling, 2001, 2002; Boling and Roehler, 2002). Using RCE also supported novices in acquiring the knowledge and skills that are needed to provide literacy instruction that is based on students' needs. Observations of classes, analyses of student work, interviews with teacher education students and students' responses to surveys and questionnaires have revealed that instructors' various uses of RCE allowed students to view and better understand the kind of literacy instruction that was being discussed in their courses (Boling, 2003, 2002; Siebenthal *et al.*, 2002). RCE allowed students to see that the kind of literacy instruction they were studying was actually occurring in classrooms, even if they themselves had never experienced such instruction as a student. One pre-service teacher commented, 'We are inundated with a series of new concepts, and to see them being put into practice gave them validity' (Boling, 2003). Some students who were previously sceptical of certain types of innovative literacy instruction stated that viewing RCE clips enabled them to see that such teaching 'was possible' and did indeed occur.

Using RCE also allowed students multiple opportunities to compare and analyse different types of instructional practices. Students who used RCE stated that it was helpful to be able to go back and revisit clips so that they could compare, contrast and better understand the various types of teaching practices that they were viewing (Boling, 2002; Boling and Roehler, 2002; Hughes *et al.*, 2000). Some of these students even revisited clips on their own at home. After viewing and discussing clips, students were able to give specific examples of how RCE supported their understanding of teaching reading and writing to elementary students. In some instances, students actually took instructional ideas from RCE clips and incorporated them into lesson plans that were being developed and taught in the field (Boling, 2002).

Three instructors who used RCE taught literacy methods courses that specifically focused on how teachers create inclusive literacy learning communities (Boling, 2001, 2002; Boling and Roehler, 2002). The 'inclusive learning communities' theme was integrated throughout the entire course, and RCE was used to support this theme. For example, in one class when students were asked to view RCE clips that represented comprehension strategies instruction, they later revisited these clips and discussed whether or not the instruction in the clips promoted an inclusive learning community. As they discussed issues of inclusion with the clips, students began to develop an increased awareness of the topic. Students broadened their definitions of 'inclusion' and 'diversity' and became more knowledgeable of various literacy pedagogical approaches that can be used when working with diverse learners.

In addition to supporting learning in coursework, pre-service teachers also described how RCE supported and complemented the field

component of their classes. Some students described how RCE clips reinforced the kind of instruction that they were seeing in their field
placements (Boling *et al.*, 2002). This reinforced the instruction that they
were learning about in their methods courses. One student explained
how her first visits to her field classroom were not very helpful because
she wasn't sure what she should be observing. She then explained how,
after viewing and discussing RCE clips in her methods course, she began
to see similar instruction used in her field placement. This enabled her
to her make more focused observations in the field and allowed her to
think about variations and adaptations that might be made to the instruction that she was observing. Other students described how RCE
supported the field component of their course because it allowed them
to see instruction that was *not* being modelled in the field.

Strategies for implementing Web-based learning environments

The implementation of RCE in literacy education courses reveals that it
can have a positive impact on both the instructors and students who
use it (Boling, 2003; Hughes *et al.*, 2000; Siebenthal *et al.*, 2002). Through
our studies we have learned that technology support and assistance are
extremely important for those instructors who are integrating technology
into their courses for the first time (Boling, 2003, 2002). Instructors benefit
when classes have access to computer labs, and instructors are more
motivated to use new programs when technology problems can be
quickly resolved. Instructors who have limited knowledge of computers
greatly benefit when they receive technology assistance.

Instructors who are not familiar with the program they are using are
more likely to meaningfully integrate it into their courses when they
receive support and suggestions from experienced users (Boling *et al.*,
2002). We suggest that support can be provided in a number of ways.
For example, users can form online support groups and share instructional ideas through discussion forums. Experienced users can offer
workshops or serve as mentors for those who are integrating technology
for the first time. Novice instructors, in particular, would also benefit
from having instructional support as they face the challenges of teaching
a student population with which they are unfamiliar. More experienced
instructors, even those without knowledge of technology, could still offer
support and guidance for those who are relatively new to teaching
university courses.

RCE has proven to be an adaptable program and has been used in a
variety of ways to support the needs of individual instructors and
students. Instructors have used it as both a key component of their course
and as a separate, out of class, extra-credit assignment for students.
Programs like RCE can be integrated with actual instruction so that

instructors can provide models of the concepts and strategies that are being introduced in their courses. These programs can also be used to support individual or group enquiry projects where students investigate questions about teaching practice. The program allows instructors and students the flexibility to view clips in class, in separate computer labs or at home. It also allows them to present and discuss clips during class presentations.

RCE supported instructors as they faced the challenge of introducing progressive, student-centred teaching approaches to students who had experienced more traditional, teacher-centred instruction when they were in elementary, middle or high school. Our studies reveal that instructors can scaffold learning when novices view clips by providing prompts for viewing and offering multiple opportunities for discussion. Instructors can use the program in ways that help students recognize and challenge their prior assumptions and beliefs.

Conclusion and future research

In a time when students and others are criticizing teacher education programs and methods courses for being 'too theoretical' and of little use (Feiman-Nemser, 1983; Lampert and Ball, 1999), we have found that hypermedia programs like RCE can serve as a link between theory and practice and between coursework and fieldwork. Our studies show that RCE provides pre-service teachers with opportunities to learn what literacy instruction is, what it looks like and how it is done. University students in literacy methods courses gain significantly more knowledge about literacy instruction than students in control classrooms. RCE is an example of the impact of a marriage between online videos and pre-service education. Instructors who used RCE state that the depth and breadth of their instruction has increased. They also indicate that the gulf between current levels of access to high-level technology for all students lessens the value of RCE.

Our next steps as researchers are to understand how we can best provide scaffolding for learners who use RCE so that these connections and links between theory and practice become common practice in communities of learning. Future studies will also investigate how support systems can be put in place for instructors who are teaching in a new digital era and who are just beginning to learn the impact that technology can have on teaching and learning.

Note

RCE is available online at: http://www.eliteracy.org/rce. This research was completed with the support of the Center for the Improvement of Early Reading Achievement (CIERA) and the Office of Educational Research Improvement (OERI).

References

Askov, E. and Bixler, B. (1998) Transforming adult literacy instruction through computer-assisted instruction, in *Handbook of Literacy and Technology*, eds D. Reinking, M. McKenna, L. Labbo and R. Kiefer, pp. 167–84, Lawrence Erlbaum, Mahwah, NJ.

Beach, R. and Lundell, D. (1998) Early adolescents' use of computer-mediated communication in writing and reading, in *Handbook of Literacy and Technology*, eds D. Reinking, M. McKenna, L. Labbo and R. Kieffer, pp. 93–112, Lawrence Erlbaum, Mahwah, NJ.

Beavers, D. (2001) Professional development: outside the workshop box, *Principal Leadership*, 1 (9), pp. 43–46.

Boling, E. C. (2001) Literacy instruction and pre service teacher understanding, paper presented at the 51st Annual Meeting of the National Reading Conference (NRC), San Antonio, TX.

Boling, E. C. (2002) Using narrative and case scenarios in a literacy teacher education course: a look at pre service teachers confronting issues of diversity, paper presented at the 52nd Annual Meeting of the National Reading Conference (NRC), Miami, FL.

Boling, E. C. (2003) The transformation of instruction through technology: promoting inclusive learning communities in teacher education courses, *Action in Teacher Education*, 24 (4), 64–73.

Boling, E. C., Knezeck, S. and Siebenthal, S. (2002) Using RCE within the university setting: potential pitfalls and future gold mines, paper presented at the symposium 'Literacy, Teaching, and Learning with Hypermedia: Using RCE in Pre service Education' at the 52nd Annual Meeting of the National Reading Conference (NRC), Miami, FL.

Boling, E. C. and Roehler, L. (2002) Preparing educators for diverse classrooms: teacher candidates investigate written and hypermedia cases, paper presented at the symposium 'Preparing Educators for Diverse Classrooms' at the Annual Meeting of the American Association of Colleges of Teacher Educators (AACTE), New York.

Borko, H. and Putnam, R. T. (1996) Learning to teach, in *Handbook of Educational Psychology*, eds D. C. Berliner and R. C. Calfee, pp. 673–708, Macmillan, New York.

Calderhead, J. (1988) *Teachers Professional Learning*, Falmer, London.

Coser, L. A. (1970) *Men of Ideas: A sociologist's view*, Free Press, New York.

Dunkin, M. J., Precians, R. P. and Nettle, E. B. (1993) Effects of formal teacher education upon student teachers' cognitions regarding teaching, *Teaching and Teacher Education*, 10 (4), pp. 395–408.

Feiman-Nemser, S. (1983), Learning to teach, in *Handbook of Teaching and Policy*, ed. L. Shulman and G. Sykes, pp. 150–70, Longman, New York.

Feiman-Nemser, S. and Buchman, M. (1986) Pitfalls of experience in teacher preparation, in *Advances in Teacher Education*, eds J. D. Raths and L. G. Katz, vol. 2, pp. 61–73, Ablex, Norwood, NJ.

Ferdig, R. E., Roehler, L. and Pearson, P. D. (2002) Scaffolding pre service teacher learning through Web-based discussion forums: an examination of online conversations in the Reading Classroom Explorer, *Journal of Computing in Teacher Education*, 18 (3), pp. 87–94.

Goodman, J. and Fish, D. R. (1997) Against-the-grain teacher education: a study of coursework, field experience, and perspectives, *Journal of Teacher Education*, 48 (2), pp. 96–107.

Hughes, J. E., Packard, B. W. and Pearson, P. D. (1998) [accessed 14 July 2003] Reading Classroom Explorer: navigating and conceptualizing a hypermedia learning environment, in *Reading Online* [Online] http://www.reading online.org/research/explorer.

Hughes, J. E., Packard, B. W. and Pearson, P. D. (2000) The role of hypermedia cases on pre service teachers' views of reading instruction, *Action in Teacher Education*, 22 (2A), pp. 24–38.

Kinzer, C. K. and Risko, V. K. (1998) Multimedia and enhanced learning: transforming pre service education, in *Handbook of Literacy and Technology*, eds D. Reinking, M. McKenna, L. Labbo and R. Kieffer, pp. 185–202, Lawrence Erlbaum, Mahwah, NJ.

Knezek, S. (2002) Making connections in on-line discourse: challenging education students' beliefs about literacy teaching and learning, paper presented at the 52nd Annual Meeting of the National Reading Conference (NRC), Miami, FL.

Lampert, M. and Ball, D. L. (1999) Aligning teacher education with contemporary K-12 reform visions, in *Teaching as the Learning Profession: Handbook of policy and practice*, eds L. Darling-Hammond and G. Sykes, pp. 33–53, Jossey-Bass, San Francisco.

RAND (1995) [accessed 14 July 2003] *Technology and Teacher Professional Development* [Online] http://www.ed.gov/Technology/Plan/RAND/Teacher. html.

Siebenthal, S., Roehler, L. R. and Pearson, P. D. (2002) Exploring the use of reading classroom explorer in multiple university pre service classrooms, paper presented at the 52nd Annual Meeting of the National Reading Conference (NRC), Miami, FL.

Sparks, D. and Hirsh, S. (1997) A New Vision for Staff Development, Association for Supervision and Curriculum Development, Alexandria, VA and the National Staff Development Council, Oxford, OH.

Spiro, R. J., Feltovich, R. J., Jacobson, M. J. and Coulson, R. L. (1992) Cognitive flexibility, constructivism, and hypertext: random access instruction for advanced knowledge acquisition in ill-structured domains, in *Constructivism and the Technology of Instruction*, T. M. Duffy and D. H. Jonassen, pp. 57–75, Erlbaum, Hillsdale, NJ.

Sujo de Montes, L. and Gonzales, C. (2000) Been there, done that: reaching teachers through distance education, *Journal of Technology and Teacher Education*, 8 (4), pp. 351–71.

Teale, W. H., Leu, D. J., Labbo, L. D. and Kinzer, C. (2002) CTELL: a case-based approach to pre service education for teaching reading in grades K-3, invited paper presented at the Harvard Literacy Institute, Cambridge, MA.

Tierney, R. and Damarin, S. (1998) Technology as enfranchisement and cultural development: crisscrossing symbol systems, paradigm shifts, and social-cultural considerations, in *Handbook of Literacy and Technology*, eds D. Reinking, M. McKenna, L. Labbo and R. Kieffer, pp. 93–112, Lawrence Erlbaum, Mahwah, NJ.

Vygotsky, L. S. (1978) *Mind in society*, Harvard University Press, Cambridge, MA.
Weedman, J. (1999) Conversation and community: the potential of electronic conferences for creating intellectual proximity in distributed learning environments, *Journal of the American Society for Information Science*, 50 (10), pp. 907–28.
Yoder, M. B. (2002) Is online professional development for you? *Learning and Leading with Technology*, 29 (4), 6–9 and 557–9.

Part III

Intercultural interactions

11 Digital technology to empower indigenous culture and education

Paul Resta, Mark Christal and Loriene Roy

Introduction

Digital information and communication technologies afford a dual potential for indigenous communities. Throughout this chapter the phrases American Indian, Indian, Native and indigenous peoples refer to the descendants of the indigenous peoples of what is now referred to as the United States. New technologies have the potential to support and sustain Native culture and the potential to accelerate its erosion. In education, the new digital technologies may empower and support the creation of new culturally responsive learning resources and environments for Native children. They may also be used to accelerate the dominance of Western-based modes of thought, culture and learning strategies into the educational environments of Native children and provide non-tribal members with access to cultural knowledge without the knowledge or sanction of tribal communities. This chapter will discuss both the ways that information and communication technologies have contributed to the loss of Native culture, language, history and traditional knowledge and the ways that digital technologies may be used in culturally responsive ways as a tool to empower Native culture and education.

The indigenous peoples of North America represent over 500 tribes, each of which is a separate sovereign nation with its own unique language, traditional knowledge, cultural values and worldviews. Many of these communities are situated in remote rural areas. Native communities experience the highest levels of poverty of any demographic group in the United States with 85 per cent of students in federally supported Indian schools eligible for reduced price or free lunches (Pavel *et al.*, 1997). In addition, the Native communities on reservations are on the farthest side of the digital divide in access to technology and information resources (Solomon *et al.*, 2003).

Information problems confronting Native American communities

As noted by May (1991), Native American communities have two major information problems. The first problem is that others have little accurate information about past or current Native American culture and history from a Native perspective. Little material about Native tribes is recorded in a form that is easily available to tribal members and others. There are comparatively few books containing the histories, medical and technological knowledge and other important contributions made by Native Americans:

> When books are found they typically are written by non-Native authors who are able to only convey Native arts in general ways. While such publications may be useful, they are only limited indicators of the richness of Native culture. The great bulk of oral traditions of native peoples have not been captured and may be lost for posterity. Without recording this in some fashion we will lose it.
>
> (May, 1991: 2)

A second problem is that most Native communities and schools have had limited access to information resources that may be of benefit to their communities and schools. Most Indian communities are poorly served by public library systems despite a critical need for information to enhance learning, economic development, planning and decision-making within the community.

Information and communication technologies and loss of Native culture

Media such as television, radio, films, audio CDs and computer games have resulted in massive and continuous exposure of Native youth to Western cultural values and information with few opportunities for reinforcement of their own cultural heritage. Many aspects of culture including language, traditional diet, oral histories and cultural knowledge are lost in the flood of Western culture embedded in the media (Resta, 1992). For example, at the end of the nineteenth century, there were over 600 Native American languages. Today, approximately 200 languages remain in current use, and about 50 of those languages have ten or fewer elderly speakers (Skinner, 1999). The Indian Nations at Risk Task Force notes that:

> American Indian and Alaska Natives, with languages and cultures found in no other place in the world, are in danger of losing their distinctive identities. Many members of the younger generation

know little or nothing about their Native languages, cultures, rich histories, fine arts, and other unique features of their cultural identities. Elders, once important teachers in transmitting the historical, cultural, and practical knowledge to the young, are no longer a part of the educational systems.

(1991: 31)

Mander (1991) described powerful examples of the ways that television can homogenize perspectives, knowledge, tastes and desires to make them resemble the tastes and interests of the people who transmit the imagery and sound. He chronicles the dramatic changes that took place in a Dene community near the remote northern Canadian village Yellowknife when television was first introduced. The bulk of the programming came from mainstream commercial fare such as *Dallas*, a 'soap opera' that represented a powerful assault upon the cultural sensibilities of the Native community. There was only one hour a week of local programming, which only occasionally included Native people. Very soon young people lost their traditional respect for elders and their interest in language and storytelling, and the relationships between men and women deteriorated.

The content and imagery delivered by information and communication technologies reflect the worldviews of the majority culture that can have a profound impact on Native youth. In addition, the technologies themselves are not value-neutral with respect to cultures. Science and technology of the Western world also have embedded beliefs and worldviews, such as those expressed by Charles Darwin. Arguments to the contrary are increasingly 'untenable in today's world, when science and technology have become cognitively inseparable and the amalgam has been incorporated into the economic system' (Shiva, 1990: 237). Shiva asserts that to accept technology is to accept a particular view of reality. This view of reality may not be congruent with the worldviews of Native cultures that resist Western assumptions of change and progress. Reynar indicates that resistance of indigenous knowledge to change is one of its most enduring strengths. Although modern culture has emphasized the value of change as a virtue and necessary feature of modern society, indigenous cultures have, on the other hand, 'established their ways of life in balance with a living and dynamic ecology, by cautiously engaging in change. Change is not undertaken for change's sake, as is the case, all too often, in *modern* cultures' (1999: 298).

For many years the formal educational systems serving Native children have been based on the Western European paradigm of education, learning and worldviews rather than traditional Native modes of learning. The initial efforts toward educating Native children were directed toward the goal of removing the children from their communities and indoctrinating them into the values, culture and modes of thought of Western European culture. Although this goal has changed over the years and Native communities have been successful in assuming greater control over the educational experiences of their children, there remain continuing challenges resulting from the lack of culturally responsive learning resources and activities in many schools serving Native students. Textbooks and educational software that are used in schools serving Native children have been developed for adoption by large states such as California, Texas, Florida and New York. Typically, these materials provide few references to support or reinforce Native cultural values, history or knowledge (Resta, 1992). Native students reading their history texts may feel that they have no history as evidenced by the lack of representation of their people in the historical narratives. This is a problem confronting many indigenous peoples:

> The Native people . . . are not allowed a valid interpretation of their history, because the conquered do not write their own history. They must endure a history that shames them, destroys their confidence, and causes them to reject their heritage. Those in power command the present and shape the future by controlling the past, particularly for the Natives. A fact of imperialism is that it systematically denies Native people a dignified history.
>
> (Adams, quoted in Deloria, 1971: 28)

There are many other examples that could be cited of the role that media has played in the loss of Native cultures and language. At its worst, technology has been a reflection of cultural imperialism:

> A form of oppression exerted by a dominant society upon other cultures, and typically a source of economic profit, cultural imperialism secures and deepens the subordinated status of those cultures. In the case of indigenous cultures, it undermines their integrity and distinctiveness, assimilating them to the dominant culture by seizing and processing vital cultural resources, then remaking them in the image and marketplaces of the dominant cultures.
>
> (Whitt, 1998: 141–2)

Native adaptation of technology

It is hoped that the emerging digital technologies may serve a different role and purpose for Native peoples in the future. Throughout history, tribes have adopted and adapted non-indigenous technologies. Europeans first introduced the horse in North America as a tool for conquest. Plains tribes recognized the value of the horse as both a means of defence and a useful resource for supporting traditional life through hunting and transportation. The plains peoples carefully adopted the horse into their culture and became among the world's finest horsemen. Native women used European glass trade beads to decorate clothing and everyday items, transforming a Western commodity into a new art form. The success of Western technology has also been dependent on indigenous collaboration. During World War II, approximately four hundred Navajo men combined knowledge of their unique language with technology to create a code that was used during every battle in the Pacific theatre. Not only did the Codetalkers provide an unbreakable line of defence, but also they did not divulge their contributions until the United States federal government declassified the code in 1969.

Perhaps technology may play similar roles in empowering Native peoples to not only support economic development but to make their voices heard globally, to share what is sharable about their culture, and to create their own culturally responsive learning resources for the education of their children.

Digital technologies to revitalize culture and provide more culturally responsive learning environments

The new information and communication technologies offer the potential and new tools to empower Native communities to develop digital curriculum resources that reflect and honour their culture, history and resident knowledge of the community. As noted by Delgado this potential can only be realized:

> if Native people are central to the development and dissemination of such materials. Rapidly, we are engaging in a whole new world of digital knowing; this path, like others in our lives, must not be taken lightly or without thought. We must speak to its energy, ensure that the route that it takes is visible to our eyes, and reflect on the time and space that it demands and the good that can come of it.
>
> (2003: 297)

For technology to be a tool for empowerment, a number of conditions must be met: Native peoples must have access to quality computers, connectivity to the Internet, teachers who are skilled in using the new technologies, technical support, ongoing professional development and high quality, culturally relevant digital content. Under these conditions, the digital technologies offer the potential for Native peoples to create their own cultural content and curriculum resources 'at their own speed, in their time, under their own conditions, using their own knowledge and judgment that defines equity/equality' (Delgado, 2003: 98).

Protocols for information and communication technology use in tribal communities

Tribal communities have long been organized for efficient communication and equitable sharing of the responsibilities for leadership, defence, sustenance, learning and medicine (Roy and Cherian, 2002). Information and communication technology efforts, though, must be developed in agreement with cultural protocols, etiquette and procedures of behaviour. In addition to the intra-tribal cultural protocols, the concept of protocol provides a framework for information and communications technology in tribal communities when the introduction of new technologies represents a negotiation across sovereign and cultural boundaries. One definition of protocol given in the Webster College Dictionary, 'the customs and regulations dealing with diplomatic formality, precedence, and etiquette', suggests the need for special concern and guidelines for the cross-cultural communication that technology development often requires. Other senses of protocol are 'an agreement between states' and 'an annex to a treaty giving data relating to it' and they stress the nature of negotiations between sovereign entities that technology development may represent. There is a technical sense of protocol that refers to 'a set of rules governing the format of messages that are exchanged between computers'. Cultures are not computers, but this sense of protocol may provide a metaphor for the need for guidelines for the balanced and equitable exchange of information between different worldviews.

The need for protocol becomes especially relevant with respect to Native culture that is shared with the non-Native communities. While non-Native America commodifies Native culture and places indigenous peoples in the past, Indian country is establishing new economies, rediscovering and revitalizing indigenous expressions, and participating in political and social issues affecting contemporary life such as natural resource management and protection of treaty rights. As tribal communities are engaging in grass-roots initiatives, they are also starting to take control over physical and intellectual access to their cultural past and contemporary expressions. Use of information and technology in tribal communities must shift from the paradigm of non-indigenous technologists creating new avenues for opening access to Native material culture to one where Native communities direct use of technologies that balance access to cultural knowledge with tribal community rights to control delivery of content. This Native-directed philosophy of access is seen in recent publications as well as in the development of recent documents and policies that address intellectual and cultural property rights concerns.

Fixico, a Native historian, warns that 'the sensitivity of tribal knowledge, especially that of ceremonials, should compel scholars to publicly acknowledge a code of ethics and responsibilities to avoid exploiting American Indians' (1998: 84). In a report for the United Nation's Commission on Human Rights, Daes describes this different world view: 'Indigenous peoples do not view their heritage in terms of property at all – that is, something which has an owner and is used for the purpose of extracting economic benefits – but in terms of community and individual responsibility' (1993: 8–9). She adds that when indigenous people do share intellectual and cultural property 'consent is always temporary and revocable'. Native people are starting to understand that the protection afforded by the legal mechanisms of trade marks, patents and copyright may not provide the protection needed to safeguard communal rights to knowledge across generations. Native sentiments may be better expressed in discussions of intellectual and cultural property rights, concepts that Jojola (1998) notes are still evolving.

Several existing policy documents can be used to initiate conversations on use of and access to cultural property, providing a starting point for a protocol for working with and within Native communities. Some policies guide decision-making with a given Native community. The Hopi Cultural Preservation Office (2003) outlines its 'Protocol for Research, Publications and Recordings' on its Web page. These guidelines describe the elements that should appear in a research proposal. Such a proposal should describe the proposed intent of a given project or its benefit to the tribe. It should outline any associated risks, how the researcher aims to obtain informed consent, how Native people's privacy will be protected, and how individuals will be compensated. The protocol clearly specifies the scope of tribal ownership of cultural content.

A number of international documents address concerns about intellectual property. The Mataatua Declaration passed by the First International Conference on the Cultural & Intellectual Property Rights of Indigenous Peoples (1993) expresses the views of this congress of 150 indigenous delegates from 14 countries. It lists recommendations to indigenous peoples worldwide, to states, national and international agencies, and to the United Nations. The people themselves must identify intellectual and cultural property and then design ethical guidelines for those outside the Native community to follow. Local communities should also establish advisory groups to guide protection, access, and/or use of material culture. It calls on state, national and international agencies to recognize indigenous rights and work with indigenous peoples to develop new means for acknowledging community ownership across generations, ownership not only for new cultural material but for historical material as well. They call on international agencies to help fund initiatives as well as enforce the recommendations that communities develop.

Daes notes that 'Accelerating the rate of Western research on indigenous knowledge is, at this point in time, more of a threat to indigenous peoples than a benefit to them' (1993: 28). Paula Gunn Allen's (1998: 62) viewpoint is that 'telling the old stories, revealing the old ways, can only lead to disaster'. Swisher wrote: 'If non-Indian educators have been involved in Indian education because they believe in Indian people and want them to be empowered, they must now demonstrate that belief by stepping aside' (1998: 192). This statement can be extended to non-Native researchers in other fields. Daes (1993) explains that the key issue is one of control.

A Native approach to technology

One goal of an appropriate protocol for the development of information and communication technology is to bring the Native worldview into an equitable or ascendant position with respect to the dominant Western worldview, leading to a Native approach to technology. Roy and Cherian (2002) have shown how indigenous information professionals are using technology to serve their communities. They have organized their discussion in a format inspired by the Anishinabe clan system:

> Traditional Anishinabe culture recognized that a healthy community was dependent upon individuals contributing varying and supportive skills and abilities. ... [T]he Anishinabe clan system created a balance to satisfy the five communal needs for Leadership, Defense, Sustenance, Learning and Medicine. People were born into social units that were symbolized by dodaim or totem or guardian animals that manifest the attributes needed in a healthy society.
>
> (Roy and Cherian, 2002: 7)

Other Native people may find other culturally responsive ways of thinking about how technology may serve their communities, but the Anishinabe clan system illustrates one Native way of seeing the world where all actions are interconnected in a natural and spiritual ecology that is reflected in the tribal social structure. The following discussion of Native technology makes use of the structure in Figure 11.1 that is discussed by Roy and Cherian. The roles shown in Figure 11.1 should be seen as interacting and overlapping in a social ecology. Because a given technology initiative might address several social functions at once, the placement of the technological initiatives shown here is suggestive and changeable. Protocol is presented here as an element that suffuses the whole enterprise of information and communication technology development.

Leadership

Leadership is critical to the successful functioning of the other social roles of technology development that support sustenance, medicine and

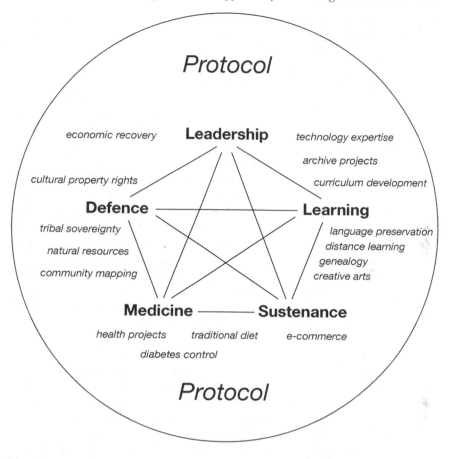

Figure 11.1 Technology use with respect to the social functions described by the Anishinabe clan system

learning. Leadership involves developing a shared vision, planning, building capacity and infrastructure to support tribal initiatives, creating local expertise and knowledge in relevant technologies, and developing partnerships with supporting agencies. Funding alone will not lead to successful technology adoption. Kamira (2002) maintains that 'Such technology programs take more than money. They take perseverance, a unified agenda, and cooperation among diverse organizations and programmes. Moreover, they take getting together in real time and space.'

Leadership qualities emerge within the context of communities of practice that provide a variety of forums where people who share common interests, concerns and expertise can exchange knowledge and ideas, create vision, develop partnerships and design programmes that meet the needs of Native people.

The American Indian Higher Education Consortium (AIHEC) is one example of a community of practice that is providing leadership in the development of Native technology. Davis and Trebian (2001), members of key AIHEC planning committees, indicate that overcoming the digital divide in tribal communities requires the development of Native leadership in technology so that Native people become the 'engine' of technology innovation rather than 'ride the caboose' of the technology train. Tribal colleges and universities (TCUs) can take a leadership role in accomplishing that goal by improving their 'human, software, and hardware technology' to 'develop tribally and culturally centred applications of information technology' (Davis and Trebian, 2001: 44). Building these capacities involves coordinated efforts to improve the technology infrastructures of TCUs, strengthening science and technology education programmes, improving the distance education skills of TCU staff, and 'developing partnerships with private industry, the federal government, research alliances, mainstream colleges and private foundations' (Davis and Trebian, 2001: 45). AIHEC technology committees maintain a consistent and sustained vision of developing Native technological expertise and infrastructure across a number of funded initiatives in order to permanently end the social and economic disparity across the digital divide.

Other communities of practice in Native technology have grown out of organizations, conferences, online communities and funded projects. For instance, the National Indian Telecommunications Institute (2003) promotes the use of the Internet in Native communities for language and cultural preservation, education, economic development and self-governance. The Bureau of Indian Affairs Office of Indian Education Programs (2003) supports numerous educational computing projects in federal and tribally controlled K-12 schools, including the annual Access Native America conference where American Indian educators share their best practices using educational technology.

Learning

Educational technology holds a tremendous potential for the creation of culturally responsive curriculum and learning environments for Native students. Native people maintain a great interest in technology to revitalize their cultures and languages through education. Natives have benefited from a wide array of educational applications and projects, including archive projects, virtual libraries and virtual museums, curriculum development, Native language education, distance learning, genealogy programmes and digital applications in the creative arts.

The Alaskan Native Knowledge Network (2003) is a project of the Alaska Federation of Natives and the University of Alaska that provides online resources for educators, including guidelines for the development of culturally responsive curriculum, Alaskan Native clip-art, and a searchable database of culturally based curriculum materials. It has a vast collection of links to web sites worldwide that are dedicated to sharing and preserving indigenous knowledge.

The Four Directions project, a consortium of 19 tribally controlled K-12 schools and university, public and private sector partners, operated between 1996 and 2002 to develop educational technology capacities (Allen *et al.*, 1999). One of the legacies of the project is an online database of culturally responsive curriculum materials developed by project participants (Four Directions, 2003). Another is a number of virtual museum projects created by students and teachers in the project (Christal *et al.*, 2001; Christal *et al.*, 2002; Christal, 2003).

Many tribal communities have been involved in language revitalization efforts involving technology. The San Juan Pueblo community (New Mexico) collaborated with linguists at the University of Washington to create a Tewa Language CD-ROM, featuring interactive exercises as well as cultural stories, songs and images (Jacobs *et al.*, 1998). Hannahville Indian School in Michigan (2003) is developing an online picture dictionary of Potawatomi words for students and a teacher vocabulary that will support teachers to give common classroom instructions in Potawatomi.

Distance education has proven to be a boon to Native communities. Salish Kootenai College on the Flathead Reservation in Montana offers a catalogue of low-cost, high-quality courses using state-of-the-art distance education technologies including email, web services, video conferencing, video production, public television broadcasts and satellite uplink (O'Donnell, 2000). Bay Mills Community College provides online courses, including an online two-year degree in child development (Bay Mills, 1997–8). Dull Knife Memorial College in Lame Deer, Montana provides special education courses via interactive television ('Interactive special ed.', 2000).

Tribal community libraries have also employed technology in collecting, preserving and providing access to information. For example, the Chickasaw Nation and Sealaska Corporation have digitized archival materials. Many tribal community libraries provide technology training and public access computing. The Haskell Cultural Center (2003) in Lawrence, Kansas, has created a searchable database of the 800 images in the Reinhart Collection of photographic portraits taken of Native people from 1898 to 1900.

Sustenance

Over millennia tribal people have been sustained by the land through hunting, gathering, fishing and traditional agriculture. Today, gaining sustenance usually involves economic activity. The remoteness of many reservations often makes economic enterprise problematical. Native entrepreneurs are finding technological solutions to the lack of economic opportunity by implementing e-commerce projects and promoting tribal businesses on the Web.

As Juneau (1998) has documented, Oneida Indian Nation pioneered Native e-commerce by creating the first tribal web site on the Internet that remains in operation today (Oneida Nation, 2003). Another example is the non-profit e-commerce web site called American Indian Art from the Pacific Northwest (2003) supported by the Northwest Indian College on the Lummi Reservation in Washington State. The site features artists and their biographies, and offers their work for sale.

The traditional sources of Native sustenance have not been completely abandoned, and there is a renewed interest in revitalizing the old practices. The Alaska Traditional Diet Project (2003) mixes Western science and Native wisdom to survey the dietary practices of Alaskan Natives and the dangers of contaminants in the environment on traditional food sources. Tohono O'odham Community Action has produced video and print guides that promote the traditional Native diet as a key component for wellness (Scientific American Frontiers, 2003). The dietary link to health in the Native population reinforces the medicinal role of indigenous foods.

Medicine

In the United States, Native people die from diabetes, alcoholism, tuberculosis, accidents and suicide at much higher rates than non-Natives. In Arizona, life expectancy for Whites is 72, but for Natives it is 55 (Nichols, 2002).

The special health needs in Native communities have largely grown out of historical conditions. Removed from their traditional lands, they were forced to adopt new lifestyles that eroded their well-being. For instance, when indigenous people were concentrated onto reservations, the traditional Native diet was replaced by government 'commodities', consisting of non-traditional foods like white flour, oil and sugar. Native people still heavily rely on 'imported' commodities for sustenance. The pan-Indian staple of fry bread is one Native adaptation to the new food sources. One outcome of this change of diet has been epidemic levels of diabetes in many Native communities.

There are several Native technology initiatives designed to address the diabetes problem. DreamCatchers and Navajo Health Promotions (2003) have produced two aerobic exercise and diabetes education videos, *Rez Robics* and *Rez Robics for Couch Potato Skins* and promote the free distribution of the videos on the Web. The Native American Diabetes Initiative (2003) provides a strong educational web site that promotes diabetes education and information on traditional foods, which are seen as a way of returning to good health.

Another barrier to better Native health is the lack of heath services and affordable health insurance. The federal Indian Health Service receives less than half the budget it requires to serve its constituents adequately (Nichols, 2002). Consequently, Native people have sought to gain more control over their own health services and combine traditional healing practices with Western medicine. The Association of American Indian Physicians (2003) is dedicated to improving health in Native communities by promoting education in the medical disciplines and honouring the traditional practices for wellness. The association's web site provides information on conferences and programmes in Native health, databases of information regarding Native health issues and links to sites on traditional healing.

Defence

Indigenous people continue to be vigilant of assaults upon their population, culture and lands. Today these assaults can take the form of land disputes, pollution and cultural theft and expropriation. Digital warriors are finding ways to defend tribal interests. As noted above, establishing protocols for access to Native culture is one successful defence strategy. Native communities are also using technologies such as Global Positioning Systems (GPS) to document locations of natural resources, cultural sites and pollution on tribal lands. These data become important tools for the maintenance of tribal sovereignty, resources and security.

For instance, GPS and Geographic Information System (GIS) technology are employed by tribal college students, faculty and community members at Fort Belknap College, Montana, to document sites on their reservation that have cultural and ethnobiological significance (Fort Belknap, 1997). The Stockbridge-Munsee Band of Mohican Indians used ground-penetrating radar equipment to identify unmarked gravesites in a 150-year-old rural cemetery (Tribe finds unmarked graves, 2003). Students in Dine College's GIS programme study the impact of non-indigenous trees on river ecosystems and the origin of solid waste (Dine College, 2003). Students at Santa Fe Indian School have been using GPS technology for community based education projects, such as documenting pollution below the Cochiti Dam (Mehojah, 2003).

By using a structure that is based on a Native way of seeing the world – the Anishinabe clan system – the preceding sections have sketched a picture of the potential that information and communications technologies have in serving Native community needs. A few examples were given under each social role to present a richer picture of this potential.

Conclusion

This discussion of the protocol of ways in which Native people in the United States are re-developing their culture and heritage as well as their education may also be relevant elsewhere in the world. Since the first contact with Western civilizations, Native people have encountered unique challenges and opportunities in adapting to and adopting Western technology. Too often technology has proven to be an expression of cultural imperialism that imposes the Western worldview and dismisses or exploits Native culture and knowledge. Delgado (2003), as a Native scholar, acknowledges the potential of technology to improve the lives of indigenous people, but cautions that this should be done on Native terms in ways that are congruent with the indigenous worldview. This critical point has extremely important implications if technology is to be a tool for empowerment for Native people rather than a powerful expression of Western hegemony. Vision and leadership in technology development must come out of the Native community.

The concept of protocol has been posed as a context for the Native development of technological solutions to social needs. As presented here, protocol is not a single, precise guideline for proper and ethical conduct with and within Native communities, but rather finds much of its expression in policy statements, laws, declarations, guidelines and research protocols regarding interactions between Western and indigenous cultures. Much protocol will involve implicit understandings that emerge after cooperating parties have worked together toward common goals over time. The hallmark of a protocol's efficacy will be the extent to which the Native worldview is expressed in a given enterprise. It was in the spirit of protocol that the Anishinabe clan system was used as an organizing structure for a description of Native technology applications. This chapter also suggests that other native cultures and nations consider appropriate protocols and strategies.

References

Alaska Native Knowledge Network [accessed 1 June 2003] *Alaska Native Knowledge Network* [Online] http://www.ankn.uaf.edu/.

Alaska Traditional Diet Project [accessed 1 June 2003] Alaska Traditional Diet Project [Online] http://www.atsdr.cdc.gov/alaska/.

Allen, N., Christal, M., Perrot, D., Wilson, C. *et al.* (1999) Native American schools move into the new millennium, *Educational Leadership*, 56 (7), pp. 71–4.

Allen, P. (1998) Special problems in teaching Leslie Marmon Silko's Ceremony, in *Natives and Academics: Researching and Writing About American Indians*, ed. D. Mihesuah, pp. 55–64, University of Nebraska Press, Lincoln and London.

American Indian Art from the Pacific Northwest [accessed 31 May 2003] *American Indian Art from the Pacific Northwest* [Online] http://ebuynativeart.com/home. htm.

Association of American Indian Physicians [accessed 31 May 2003] Association of American Indian Physicians [Online] http://www.aaip.com/.

Bay Mills (1997/8) Creating virtual college, *Tribal College Journal of American Indian Higher Education*, 9 (3), pp. 34–5.

Bureau of Indian Affairs Office of Indian Education Programs [accessed 1 June 2003] Bureau of Indian Affairs Office of Indian Education Programs [Online] http://www.oiep.bia.edu.

Christal, M. (2003) Virtual museum projects for culturally responsive teaching in American Indian education, PhD dissertation, University of Texas at Austin.

Christal, M., Roy, L., Resta, P., Cherian, A. and Kreipe de Montaño, M. (2001) [accessed 1 June 2003] Virtual museum collaborations for cultural revitalization: the four directions model, paper presented at the Museums & the Web Conference in Los Angles, CA, March [Online] http://www.archimuse.com/ mw2001/papers/christal/christal.html.

Christal, M., Resta, P., and Roy, L. (2002) [accessed 1 June 2003] Virtual museum projects in Native America, *ERIC Update*, 23 (2) [Online] http://ericit.org/ newsletter/Volume23–2/articles.shtml.

Daes, E. (1993) *Study on the Protection of the Cultural and Intellectual Property of Indigenous Peoples,* United Nations, Geneva, Switzerland.

Davis, T. and Trebian, M. (2001) [accessed 1 June 2003] Shaping the destiny of Native American people by ending the digital divide, *Educause Review*, 36 (1), pp. 38–46 [Online] http://www.educause.edu/ir/library/pdf/erm0112.pdf.

Deloria, V. Jr (1971) *Of Utmost Good Faith,* Straight Arrow Books, San Francisco, CA.

Dine College [accessed 31 May 2003] Geographical Information System Program [Online] http://shiprock.dinecollege.edu/Dept/MathNatSci/gis1.htm.

Delgado, V. (2003) Technology and Native America: a double-edged sword, in *Toward Digital Equity: Bridging the divide in education,* eds G. Solomon, N. Allen, and P. Resta, Allyn and Bacon, Boston, MA.

DreamCatchers and Navajo Health Promotions [accessed 29 May 2003] What is Rez Robics? [Online] http://www.dreamcatchers.org/rezrobics/index.html.

First International Conference on the Cultural & Intellectual Property Rights of Indigenous Peoples (1993) [accessed 17 February 2003] The Mataatua declaration on cultural and intellectual property rights of indigenous peoples, a declaration drafted and passed in Whakatana, Aotearoa, New Zealand, June [Online] http://www.tebtebba.org/tebtebba_files/susdev/ik/mataatua.html, also at http://aotearoa.wellington.net.nz/imp/mata.htm.

Fixico, D. (1998) Ethics and responsibilities in writing American Indian history, in *Natives and Academics: Researching and Writing About American Indians,* ed. D. Mihesuah, pp. 84–99, University of Nebraska Press, Lincoln and London.

Fort Belkap (1997) Researches culture sites, *Tribal College Journal of American Indian Higher Education,* 9 (2), p. 32.

Four Directions [accessed 1 June 2003] Four Directions [Online] http:// www.4directions.org/.

Haskell Cultural Center [accessed 1 June 2003] Reinhart photography collection [Online] http://www.haskell.edu/archive/Reinhart.htm.

Hannahville Indian School [accessed 1 June 2003] Nah Tah Wahsh [Online] http://www.hvl.bia.edu/.

Hopi Cultural Preservation Office [accessed 31 May 2003] Protocol for research, publications and recordings: Motion, visual, sound, multimedia and other mechanical devices [Online] http://www.nau.edu/~hcpo-p/hcpo/index. html.

Indian Nations At Risk Task Force (1991) *Indian Nations at Risk: An educational strategy for action,* US Department of Education, Washington, DC.

Interactive special ed. classes offered at DKMC (2000), *Tribal College Journal of American Indian Higher Education,* 11 (4), p. 36.

Jacobs, S. Tuttle, G. and Martinez, E. (1998) Multimedia technology in language and culture restoration efforts at San Juan Pueblo: a brief history of the development of the Tewa Language Project, *Wicazo sa Review,* 13 (2), pp. 45–57.

Jojola, T. (1998) A revision on revisionism: American Indian representations in New Mexico, in *Natives and Academics: Researching and Writing About American Indians,* ed. D. Mihesuah, pp. 172–80, University of Nebraska Press, Lincoln and London.

Juneau, D. (1998) Oneida tribal web site: http://one-web.org/oneida, *Wicazo Sa Review,* 13 (2), pp. 149–51.

Kamira, R. (2002) [accessed 31 May 2003] Te Mata o te Tai – the edge of the tide: rising capacity in information technology of Maori in Aotearoa, paper presented at the Conference on Information Technology in Regional Areas, Rockhampton, New Zealand, August [Online] http://www.pauainterface. com/TeMataOTeTai-ITiRA.pdf.

Mander, J. (1991) *In the Absence of the Sacred,* Sierra Club Books, San Francisco.

May, J. (1991) *Technological Needs: Joining the information age,* Office of Vice Provost for Information Resources California State University, Chico, CA.

Mehojah, W. (2003) Technology and Native American education, keynote address presented at the Society for Information Technology & Teacher Education conference, Albuquerque, NM, March.

National Indian Telecommunications Institute [accessed 1 June 2003] NITI: National Indian Telecommunications Institute [Online] http://www.niti.org/.

Native American Diabetes Initiative [accessed 28 August 2003] Native American Diabetes Initiative [Online] http://www.nativeheritage.net/index.htm.

Nichols, J. (14 April 2002) [accessed 30 May 2003] Indian health care: Separate, unequal, The Arizona Republic [Online] http://www.azcentral.com/news/ specials/indianhealth/0414healthmain.html.

O'Donnell, M. (2000) [accessed 31 May 2003] Salish Kootenai College distance education [Online] http://www.aihec.org/salish.pdf.

Oneida Nation [accessed 31 May 2003] Welcome to the Oneida Indian Nation [Online] http://oneida-nation.net/.

Pavel, D., Curtin, T. and Whitener, S. (1997) *Characteristics of American and Alaska Native Education: Results from the 1990–91 and 1993–94 schools and staffing survey,* National Center for Education Statistics, US Department of Education, Washington, DC.

Resta, P. (1992) Minorities and the new information technologies in higher education: barriers and opportunities, in *Minorities in higher education,* McGraw-Hill American Council of Higher Education Series, New York.

Reynar, R. (1999) Indigenous people's knowledge and education: a tool for development, in *What is indigenous knowledge?* ed. M. Justiz, pp. 285–304, Palmer Press, New York.

Roy, L. and Cherian, A. (2002) [accessed 31 May 2003] Information technology and educational achievement for indigenous peoples, paper presented at the Library & Information Association of New Zealand Aotearoa in Wellington, New Zealand, 17–20 November 2002) [Online] http://www.confer.co.nz/lianza2002/Roy.pdf.

Scientific American Frontiers [accessed 1 June 2003] *Fat and happy?* [Online] http://www.pbs.org/saf/1110/hotline/hlopez.htm.

Skinner, L. (1999) Teaching through traditions: incorporating languages and culture into curricula, in *Next Steps: Research and practice to advance Indian education,* eds K. Swisher and J. Tippeconnnic III, pp. 107–134, ERIC, Charleston, WV.

Shiva, V. (1990) Reductionism science as epistemological violence, in *Science, Hegemony and Violence,* ed. A. Nancy, pp. 232–3, Oxford University Press, Delhi, India.

Solomon, G., Allen, N. and Resta, P. (2003) *Toward Digital Equity: Bridging the education divide,* Allyn and Bacon, Boston, MA.

Swisher, K. (1998) Why Indian people should be the ones who write about Indian education, in *Natives and Academics: Researching and writing about American Indians,* ed. D. Mihesuah, pp. 190–200, University of Nebraska Press, Lincoln and London.

Tribe finds unmarked graves (27 April 2003) [accessed 1 June 2003] *Duluth News Tribune* [Online] http://www.duluthsuperior.com/mld/duluthtribune/news/ local/5728164.htm.

Whitt, L. (1998) Cultural Imperialism and the Marketing of Native America, in *Natives and Academics: Researching and writing about American Indians,* ed. D. Mihesuah, pp. 141–2, University of Nebraska Press, Lincoln and London.

12 Refugee children in a virtual world

Intercultural online communication and community

Liesbeth de Block and Julian Sefton-Green

Introduction

CHICAM (Children in Communication about Migration) is a European wide three-year action research project (2002–5) funded by the European Commission. CHICAM aims to explore the ways in which media production and communication might allow refugee and migrant children to share, compare and express their experiences of migration. The more political objective is to explore how the content and processes of this communication could inform policy initiatives in the areas of migration and children. Indeed, three of the specific research themes are closely connected to relevant policy areas in the social arena: friendship and peer relations, school or work and family. The fourth theme is designed to examine how audio-visual language is used by the children in the project in intercultural communication and could be used to promote intercultural communication. This theme is particularly important considering the number of different languages represented in the project – encompassing the European languages of the partnership and also the languages of origin for the children.

The idea for CHICAM grew out of a small-scale research programme with refugee and migrant children in one primary school in London (de Block, 2002). As part of the data collection, the researcher decided to involve the children in making videos about their lives. The children filmed their local area, at home and at school, and made cut-out animations of their journeys to the UK. This approach of using media in participatory research is being increasingly used with children (Gauntlett, 1996; Bloustein, 1998; Goldman-Segal, 1998). It offers another level to the data gathering and in this case allowed the children to talk about potentially difficult subjects at a distance.

Another research project, which was running concurrently at the Centre for the Study of Children Youth and Media, was studying an exchange of youth video productions between Germany, the UK and the Czech Republic (Buckingham, 2001). The interest here was to examine what forms of visual symbolism and representation the young people would draw on in their productions and how these would be received and understood by other youth audiences. These ideas of the uses and possibilities of visually based intercultural communication informed the thinking behind CHICAM.

A significant new element in CHICAM, however, was the use of the Internet to facilitate a greater sharing of experiences beyond the immediate new local communities and to make the videos and communication more immediately available. An awareness associated with this development was that many of these children were becoming increasingly familiar with global communications through family email connections, satellite, television, chat rooms, etc. (Livingstone, 2002).

CHICAM hoped to be able to build on the children's existing knowledge of new communications and on their interest in media and media production. It aimed to draw these together to explore their everyday experiences of migration and settlement in different European contexts. From the research side, this demanded a cross disciplinary approach, drawing on the areas of migration and refugee studies, media and cultural studies, sociology and policy studies. On the media production side, we needed to involve media educators and media artists with experience of working with children as well as people with an interest in and knowledge of communication and the arts. The practical media work and empirical research work are based in six clubs, which meet weekly. Most of the clubs are after-school clubs based in schools and community centres; in Greece, for example, the club meets in the offices of the Council for Refugees. All the children attending the clubs are recently arrived refugees or migrants between the ages of 10 and 14 years. In some cases the children already know each other; in others it is the first time they have met. They come from a wide range of countries. The club in the UK for example comprises children from Angola, Kenya, Somalia, Sierra Leone/Guinea, Sri Lanka, Pakistan, Lithuania, Russia and Colombia. The children all have very different experiences of migration (Brah, 1996). Each club is run by the researcher and media educator in that centre. In several cases a community worker or teacher who knows many of the children outside the club also participates.

The clubs are linked through a project web site (http://www.chicam.net), which is designed on three levels. A public site holds the project details and finished research papers. Towards the end of the project it will also host compilations of the media productions from the clubs on thematic lines. A second level, entered by password, is for the children in the clubs to view the productions from the clubs and to post and exchange comments about them. There is also a general bulletin board for topics not directly related to the media work. A third level is for the researchers. Here the same media productions are on view as well as a space to discuss research concerns and ideas as they arise and to enter brief weekly notes on the club work and issues that arise (based on the field diaries of the researcher and observations by the media educator).

At the time of writing, CHICAM is almost halfway through the three years funded by the European Community. The clubs have been up and running for six months and have around four more months to run depending on the local summer holiday arrangements. We hope that many of the clubs will continue in some form beyond this and several partners are putting such plans in place. This chapter attempts to take a step back and to examine one aspect of the project: CHICAM assumptions, expectations and realities in the context of current debates about children and 'new' digital technologies. We aim here to discuss some issues that the research so far is raising for us.

Children and new digital technologies – the rhetoric

The aspirations for the CHICAM project crystallized a number of assumptions relating to the alleged potential of 'new' digital technologies. These roughly divide into three categories relating to social exclusion, creativity and communicativity. We will detail these first before moving on to a description of some of the issues raised by the project's activities in practice.

Key arguments about the Internet relate to the question of universal access. Livingstone and Bovill (1999) show how connection to the Internet across Europe varies but is likely to be higher in households with children. At its best, household access to the Internet is more than 60 per cent, which compares unfavourably with the growth of mobile telephony. The formal education sector aspires to 100 per cent connectivity but this figure obscures the actual capacity of children in schools to be online at any given point of time. Most European governments use a rhetoric that promotes the role of the State in ameliorating the kind of social inequalities that govern household access to the Internet (Bangemann *et al.*, 1994). For example, in the UK, initiatives such as UKOnline aspire to place computers in low-income communities, particularly emphasizing inhabitants of deprived districts and explicitly targeting socially excluded categories of people, including refugees. However, accounts of such programmes (Hellawell, 2001) show that such intentions, although well meaning, can often fail to connect with an individual's motivation or with real uses. In some ways, CHICAM belongs to the same category of initiatives since it aims to provide purposeful interventions for disenfranchised social groups.

A second kind of rhetoric surrounding new technologies relates to their supposed capacity to enhance forms of creative expression (Buckingham *et al.*, 1999). Like the rhetoric around social inclusion that blurs arguments around access with assumptions about uses, this discourse confuses the potential of digital technology with assumptions about its actual uses in real social contexts. Thus the relative ease and simplicity of production offer the possibility of making digital artists out of all of us, especially when compared to the previously arcane and complex world of film, digital video, design and audio recording. Studies of what people actually do with digital technologies in the home or other more formally organized social settings are few (Harvey *et al.*, 2002; O'Hear and Sefton-Green, 2003). They show that despite some changes to the processes of creative production, access to digital technology has not fundamentally altered the key conceptual practices of making media. CHICAM offers young refugees the opportunity to make films (digital video) about their experiences of migration and exile and in this respect it drew on a tradition of 'personal writing' and individual creative expression familiar to a particular tradition within the school English curriculum.

The use of video in particular as the prime creative product for the young refugees was intended to build upon notions of video as an international medium that is to some extent non-verbal. Community and educational uses of video stress its capacity for developing shared group authoring processes (Goodman, 2003) as well as the individual expression mentioned above, and this feature seemed appropriate to explore common experiences. There is a tension between community uses of video and the more individual authoring associated with filmmaking. However, that debate has yet to be articulated, especially in the new and possibly different context of digital video production.

The capacity to make video in digital formats is intricately related to our third theme: communicativity. The possibilities offered by the Internet as a new and simple means of distribution that can carry digital films begin to be part of the same argument regarding the differences making digital films might actually offer prospective film-makers. The Internet appears to offer a new and simple means of distribution allowing individuals and groups the capacity for relatively unfettered direct communication, both synchronously and asynchronously. The use of the Internet as a distribution medium and its capacity to provide direct communication both underpinned CHICAM. Whilst dominant media have tended to use the Internet as a complementary medium, working in harness with mainstream broadcasting media, there have been a number of initiatives to exploit the unique nature of the Web as a distribution medium. However, moving images do not travel well over the Internet due to bandwidth issues and the architecture. Davis *et al.* (1997) discussed case studies that demonstrated the challenges that remain with an increased bandwidth. This means that commonly held expectations about moving image languages that have developed for the cinema screen, the mass audience, and modified for television need further modification to communicate successfully over the Internet. The small computer screen and even smaller video clip often found online means that a new language of film needs to be developed to make this a feasible means of distribution. Additionally, the expectation that the moving image is likely to be consumed by a group, as occurs in the cinema or the family home, needs rethinking, given the personalized nature of interaction with the computer screen.

The video communication developed online in CHICAM also offered the additional possibility of sharing and communicating in text, audio or with non-moving images. In many ways this model of communication builds on the 'pen-pal' ideas familiar from schooling. Other practices within English language education also suggest that writing for real audiences develops communicative competencies (Britton *et al.*, 1975). These principles underpinning the development of writing abilities have yet to be fully researched in respect of the Internet (Selfe, 1999). However, for CHICAM the process was complicated by the fact that, except in the cases where children shared the same language, the children participating had to work in the project language – English – as a second or additional foreign language. This point draws attention to the mediating roles that the teacher, artists and researchers played in the context of this project. One of the key claims for digital technologies in all of the aspects discussed above is that it is universally accessible, i.e. that the conventional raft of mediators required for making video or for less complex kinds of communication appear not to be required. Therefore, the young refugee groups we wished to work with would be enabled, to some extent, to have direct control over these processes.

In summary, we can see that the rhetoric of empowerment surrounding digital technologies in respect of their putative capacity to develop social inclusion, creativity and communication are undercut by two common tensions: that between individual and groups; and the mediation needed for communication to take place. The CHICAM project aimed to find ways to work with the technology within these constraints.

Mediation

Over the year to date, as the media productions have progressed and the web site has started to be used we can see how many layers of mediation are operating in each interaction between the clubs and indeed within the clubs. While these are usually unavoidable they can inhibit the social interaction or change it to such an extent that it can lose immediacy and affect motivation. The exchanges between clubs are taking place within the continually changing constraints of equipment, media expectations, social relations, Internet and research ethics, technical expertise, language and literacy and research expectations.

Probably the first thing that interested all the children was the possibility of 'making films'. However, this also became the first point at which the adults became significant players in the children's communication. Most of the children had no experience with cameras and none had any experience of editing. Building a visual narrative rather than a home video document was new territory. It demanded not only new skills but also new ways of thinking. Some of the children tended at first to lose patience with learning how to load the cassette, set up the tripod, decide angles and shots, prepare storyboards and plan the filming. They wanted the adults to do these things for them. There was a familiar tension between gaining the knowledge that would facilitate greater autonomy in the longer term and doing something immediately for now. In order to put videos on the Web and begin the communication between the clubs, the children had to master the technology and become more independent users.

In the clubs and in this chapter we refer to the 'productions' the children are making as if they are finished polished pieces. The term 'production' brings with it both adult and child expectation and has in many ways set the parameters of what is deemed acceptable to show to the other clubs. Digital equipment makes 'production' more accessible in one sense but it also demands new approaches and expectations. We are still exploring how the children view what they are making in relation to their other media experiences, but already it is clear that there are many fairly set notions for both adult and child. For example, in the UK club, a refugee stated that the piece he was editing was not finished because it was 'too short'. Here length defines gravitas. When the UK club was viewing a group production aimed at introducing themselves to the other clubs, one child stated that it could not be sent because it did not give enough 'information'. Having to edit out some information made the rest of it invalid. From another angle another child became very frustrated when his 'spy movie' did not look slick enough and did not match the speed of the films he watches on TV or the games he plays on the computer.

The club members were constantly negotiating their individual and group social relations and identities, as well as negotiating their relationship with the different media and equipment. Many of the clubs have built on the existing friendships of the children either in a special language class (as in Germany) or an existing media club (as in Sweden). Others brought children together who did not know each other at all or only vaguely. The Greek club drew children together whose families had clear, shared links to the Greek Council for Refugees. The children in the UK were mostly strangers although they attended the same school. This had social consequences that affected the interactions within the club as children began to negotiate with each other as well as the new adults. At first some children were reticent about participating.

Others focused entirely on sorting out and confronting the hierarchies and gender relations. In this situation the focus was on what was happening in the here and now rather than on building contacts with other clubs.

In the UK club, for example, David's progression and developing confidence in his media productions and himself illustrates the complex nature of the relationship between the technology, the social relations and his own personal motivation. Looking at three productions he was involved in, it is clear that from the first he was maintaining a distance. He was not interested in using the camera or editing the final result. He preferred to act. This way he could be 'cool' and not be seen to make mistakes or to be fumbling in front of the new group. He did not want to be 'taught'. In the second production he began to play with sound, using objects in the room and some voice work, creating a sound track to go with visuals other club members had selected and edited. In order to do this he had to involve other voices, other club members, but he was in charge and he was only using simple sound equipment. He edited in the sound takes and began to get a feel for editing on a production in which he was not visible. He accepted the help of the media educator because he was clear about what he wanted to do and he had taken the initiative.

Then David stopped any production work and spent some time using the Internet, exploring Tupac sites. In the third production he was again the performer, performing a rap he had written himself. This time he edited it largely on his own and played a little with effects, yet he was still reluctant at first for it to be seen outside the club. He then took a break from the club. When he was told that there were some responses to the rap, he was interested but not eager to reply. Sports and going out with immediate friends have taken his interest. At every point he had been reluctant to talk about his life, his home and his identity as 'refugee'. Although he had only been in the country for a relatively short time he had styled himself and wished to be seen in every way as a London youth. It was only in one-to-one interviews and after some time that he was willing to talk to the researcher about his life.

Negotiating social membership of the club took on an additional edge because several of the children were reluctant to identify themselves as refugees or migrants. By doing so they would label themselves as 'other' in their own eyes and in the eyes of their new community. For example, after one of the sessions Fatima had a long discussion with her mother about what a refugee was and why people needed to move from one country to another, which she reported to me as having nothing to do with her. Gabriella's friend was shocked to learn that children, including her friend, could be refugees at all. These discussions must also be understood in the context of ongoing highly negative media and a public debate about refugees and asylum seekers.

A third aspect of the social relations that affected the work in the clubs was the fact that as refugees, many of the children had very difficult emotional histories. Many were making stressful social adjustments and often had important family responsibilities (Richman, 1998; Rutter, 2001). In the UK club there were several children in this position. For example, Ruqiya had lost her father who was a doctor in Somalia. Her house in the UK had recently burned down and the family had been moved into temporary accommodation. They were forced to start rebuilding their lives for the second or third time. David, from Angola, travelled on his own and was living with his uncle. No one knew where his parents were. One club member was suddenly absent from the club and it was later learned the family had been returned to Russia. Many of the children collected younger siblings from school, making club attendance difficult, and most took a lot of responsibility for helping with domestic chores and supporting the family. All these factors affected attendance and continuity as well as raising issues fundamental to making videos about their lives, including trust, vulnerability and privacy.

This brings us to our responsibilities as adults working with children (who are refugees) and the Internet. All project members agreed a broad ethical framework regarding privacy and child and guardian agreements about the use and dissemination of research data and visual material made in the clubs. This was absolutely necessary to protect the children and families and meet ethical research guidelines. Thus the web site was managed and monitored centrally and was only accessible through a password. However, these controls worked against speed and openness and especially slowed down the 'instant' communication promised by the Web. There was a time delay before new 'productions' were uploaded and viewable. The children were not freely able to show their friends and family what they had been doing and what the other clubs had said about it. The cycle of production, distribution and reception became privatized, mediated and controlled.

These protective delays were exacerbated by both expected and unexpected technical difficulties, which added a fourth form of barrier. Some of the children and adults were disappointed by the small size of the screen and the resultant loss of detail. Many were also having problems gaining regular access to the Internet at all. Often the low bandwidth resulted in delay and slowly playing videos. In other cases media educators were not sure how to proceed and there were some elaborate instructions flying to and fro amongst the research team.

One of the complexities of the project was that not only were we working with the different European languages of the countries in which the clubs are located and different levels of fluency in those languages, but we were also working with the many languages spoken by the children in the clubs (approximately 20). The project language was English. The plan had always been that as many of the media productions as possible would rely on visuals rather than spoken language. Two problems arose. First, the children themselves were very focused on language because language acquisition is a priority for children arriving in a new country. It is their route to making friends and thus to acceptance and security. Second, it is a sophisticated and somewhat alien idea to have to examine the complex world of non-verbal communication and be able to translate this into media form. Indeed the children in the UK club were frustrated by the lack of concrete verbal information when they watched a video from Germany that had tried to do this.

Once the children had viewed a video the idea was that they would respond either with a comment or question that would begin or continue a discussion across the clubs. Again language, and this time also literacy skills, were necessary. Except in the UK club and in individual cases where a child might be independent in English (or able to write in their own language to other children literate in that language) the children were again dependent on adult assistance and therefore supervision.

In summary, these different levels of mediation interact and make the picture a complex one of overlapping needs and negotiation between the social and the technical, the individual and the group and between adult and child.

Community

In the previous section we outlined some of the social negotiations that needed to take place alongside the development of technical expertise in the clubs. Here we want to explore how the children in the UK club appeared to construct community and how this related to constructions of audience.

One of the themes of the research was to look at the children's ideas about friendship, particularly their experiences of making friends in their new locations and maintaining former friendships. What emerged was a wide and highly differentiated range of categories of friendship: school, home, religious, chat room, faraway, email, club, girl, boy, etc. Many of these would apply to all children not just refugees. However the range of categories for children living in different cultures and who have moved long distances physically and culturally multiplies accordingly. The discussion then also ranged over what self-images they wished to portray in different situations and to different people and how their identities shifted and changed.

Within the UK club we observed the children getting to know each other, negotiating their contacts and maintaining their boundaries. Gender, age, language, religion and economic circumstance were major factors in who spoke to who, who would work with who, who was worth annoying to the point of open conflict, who was tolerated and who was 'rated'. They protected their privacy but also were able, especially, in the discussions about friendship (after some real disagreements and a lot of talk about gossip and backstabbing), to agree on what made a good friend and how to be a good friend.

As these alliances developed, individuals became more interested in each other's media work. We began to have regular viewings within the club of work in progress. However, the main factor here was that we moved away from concentrating on group work and encouraged more individually authored pieces. With the video work, the web site or the computer game acting as an intermediary, the children felt safer showing an interest in each other or moving across the room to initiate contact. This reinforces the drive to community identified above, where it may be that video as a means of communication works in this context through a process of display to a known audience; this is the opposite of impersonal narrow or broad casting. The next key stage is whether it is possible to expand this to the other clubs and to develop an interest and sense of belonging in the network of clubs.

At first they watched the videos from the other clubs almost warily. David could hardly get himself to sit and watch at all. Sometimes there were remarks about the very different contexts of the clubs or the fact that there were children in Germany who wore the hijab; but this fact only raised suspicion about whether the video was indeed from Germany at all. These exchanges were important in gaining an understanding of the European contexts and migration patterns but contained no real personal connection. So far, the children in the UK club, at least, considered most of the videos as irrelevant and of no consequence to what they themselves were doing, but we are aware that such connections take time to develop. What they appeared to be doing was judging the other children to assess whether they were cool enough to consider at all. Members of several clubs were clearly impressed by the style and looks of particular children. Interestingly the children in clubs in more 'stylish' countries such as Italy were deemed more 'attractive', fulfilling another form of national stereotyping.

We had anticipated some crossovers of interest and cross-fertilization of ideas during the exchanges of videos. The area in which this began to happen was in music (rap) and the styles of dress and body gesture that accompany this. This began when the Italian club chose to put Eminem on the soundtrack of their introductory video. Interestingly some of the adults were not happy with this choice and expressed a concern that this was somehow detracting from the children's creativity, whereas others argued that it opened up an obvious point of contact through popular culture. This strand of exchange developed with David's rap (mentioned above) and some reply raps and voice box moves from the Netherlands. In children's day-to-day peer relations this is how initial contacts are made and developed.

During the exchanges of the first videos several of the children in different clubs requested photos and wished to exchange gifts. They wanted to study what these other children looked like, to examine who they were as we would when we meet people face to face. We put group photos up on the web site but these also appeared unsatisfactory. What they wanted were portraits, and preferably in hard copy, to get to know the individuals (a process they were going through in their own clubs) before they could commit themselves to any interest in the other clubs. Somehow we needed to find ways of personalizing the exchange, of creating a known audience, as they were in the process of doing in their own clubs.

The children's media interests and uses outside the club reflected their 'multiple identities', the ways in which they wished to play with these identities (as themselves and anonymously) and the ways in which they constructed community and audience. Most of the girls were avid chat room users and, although chat is technically an anonymous medium, we observed children passing each other in the corridor and laughing about the fact that they had met each other on chat lines the night before. Many of these children did not meet outside school and, we found out, they hardly met in school as they were often in different classes that did not share the same half-hour lunch break. At other times there was much giggling at the computer and we would discover that they were exploring more 'anonymous' chat. Although much of this play had clearly sexual overtones, it also performed crucial social functions, creating, confirming and maintaining community connections.

In many locations refugees end up living in poverty. This creates a challenging environment and, in the UK at least, there was a real fear of going out and about in the local area. Children and parents were nervous of going home alone and staying late for club sessions even though the club finished at 5 pm. The school catchment area was very wide and children lived difficult journeys apart; there were few places where they felt they could meet and hang out and using the Internet enabled them to play together in leisure time. In addition their choices of web sites and chat rooms, such as Bangladeshi chat, were often culturally defined, confirming other community connections. The children felt these were safer and more appropriate for them to use as they maintained religious and cultural connections (Blunt, 2000). More personal uses also complemented these. Fatima, for example, used the Internet to keep in touch with friends she missed in Kenya, maintaining another community to which she hoped to return one day.

However, some of the children did not have these possibilities. Saieed laughed when I asked if he kept in contact with friends in Guinea. Neither he nor his friends there had access to the technology or the money to email or telephone. He had left without telling his friends that he was going or where he was going, and this was the case for many refugee children. He was no expert on the Web and was shy to expose his lack of knowledge. David relied on school access and was always keen to be on the Internet as much as possible, exploring '2Pak' and other music sites. He maintained that the sexual explorations of the girls were shocking but in fact was caught out when the girls discovered he was well acquainted with one of the more explicit sites. Claudio spent part of one session typing in his name to see who his namesakes were. He was thrilled to find a Spanish dancer and later in the session began to dance himself.

Although the CHICAM structure of the technology allowed children to submit audio, drawings, text or indeed virtually any kind of communication, it may be that the clubs emphasis on video as the prime activity and means of expression worked against the communicativity of the project. The children were motivated to make video on a number of different levels: to gain experience of the medium; to learn technical skills; to use it as a group activity; but only gradually, the more they learned about it, to use it as a vehicle for personal expression. Video's primary function as a perceived recorder of reality means that the children were more likely to see their films as local, immediate and context-specific expressions rather than as authored constructs. It therefore did not make sense for them to pose the videos online for hypothetical peer audiences. If this is true, it tells us quite a lot about how children of this age and experience invest in video. It appears that they may make videos in ways that are quite different from the expectations of adult film-makers. Again this emphasizes a clash in culture because video and the Web have developed out of seemingly similar technical approaches, but actually quite distinct communicative processes.

Developing the clubs and the exchanges was a process of developing a set of new social connections, local and virtual, and an attempt to create a community based on shared migration experiences. However, many migration experiences were still private and painful and the children's main current interest was 'the here and now'. At this age, their main interest was the current popular culture that allowed them to participate as part of an active audience and thus have access to current social connections.

Conclusion

Our interest in this chapter has been to examine the often contradictory discussions about children, the public and private spheres and the potential of new digital technologies in the light of the work of the CHICAM project so far. Our analysis of the children's motivation in their work goes to the heart of some of the political aspirations implicit in the project – to place children's voices within the policy making arena.

The aim was for the children to become partners in making visible their experiences of migration to different European countries. By facilitating the production of visual presentations that would then be circulated and discussed and replied to by others who have had similar experiences, our aim was that the children would gain some agency in how they are perceived and interpreted in policy and in research. The formal research themes of the project address policy concerns directly, but the project was always open for other forms of connection and discussion. We had thought that the luxury of a research project that allowed a full year of sustained work with small groups of children making media productions would be long enough both to develop the technical and social skills needed locally and to allow for the development of a committed dialogue between groups of children living at a distance, but connected through the Internet.

However, while the work in the individual clubs has progressed and many interesting and relevant productions have been completed, there have been many more built-in technical, social and motivational barriers to developing the Internet exchanges in the time allowed than we had hoped. The thrust of our argument is that in this project it appears that the day-to-day interactions of the children's lives focused primarily on constructing an immediate social world. This was the case even when there were the possibilities of developing 'other' virtual worlds. The virtual was more acceptable when it related to the here and now and current face-to-face social contacts and so became an extension of these existing relationships. To build new virtual contacts that were distanced was more daunting, even where these might relate to important personal shared experiences. Where the virtual contacts appeared to have potential they related to current shared popular culture rather than past experiences.

Writing this chapter has also been an interesting process. It has demanded that we step back from the day-to-day practical and technical concerns of the club and the coordination of the different research centres and examine the project's fundamental assumptions as they relate to children and new digital technologies. As we had hoped, it has brought several underlying concerns to the surface. It has begun an exploration into why some of the processes are working differently from expected and highlighted several important research concerns and potential findings. Already we can see how the role of new technologies in affecting social or educational policy working with refugees, or by implication other excluded groups, needs extraordinary care, awareness of the power relations involved and 'on the ground' localized facilitation if initiatives like this are to make a real and quantifiable difference to children's lives.

Note

The research partnership is made up of seven complementary centres bringing different expertise and experience and interests to the project: The Centre for the Study of Children, Youth and Media, Institute of Education, London, UK; WAC Performing Arts and Media College, London, UK; Fondazione Centro Studi Investimenti Sociali, Rome, Italy; Centre for Research in International Migration and Ethnic Relations, Stockholm University, Sweden; Department of Media Education and Media Centre, University of Ludwigsburg, Germany; Institute of Multicultural Development, Utrecht, The Netherlands; The Greek Council for Refugees, Athens, Greece.

References

Bangemann, M., Cabral da Fonseca, E., Davis, P., de Benedetti, C. *et al.* (1994) *Europe and the Global Information Society: Bangemann Report Recommendations to the European Council*, European Council, Strasbourg.

de Block, L. (2002) *Television as a Shared Space in the Intercultural Lives of Primary Aged Children*, PhD thesis, Institute of Education, University of London, London.

Bloustein, G. (1998) 'It's different to a mirror 'cos it talks to you': teenage girls, video cameras and identity, in *Wired-Up: Young people and the electronic media*, ed. S. Howard, University College London Press, London.

Blunt, G. (2000) *Virtually Islamic: Computer-mediated communications and cyber Islamic environments*, University of Wales Press, Cardiff.

Brah, A. (1996) *Cartographies of Diaspora: Contesting identities*, Routledge, London.

Britton, J., Burgess, T. and Martin, N. (1975) *The Development of Writing Abilities*, Macmillan, London.

Buckingham, D. (ed.) (2001) Special issue on video culture, *Journal of Educational Media*, 26 (3).

Buckingham, D., Harvey, I. and Sefton-Green, J. (1999) The difference is digital? Digital technology and student media production, *Convergence: The Journal of Research into New Media Technologies*, 5 (4), pp. 10–21.

Davis, N. E., Wright, B., Still, M. and Thornton, P. (1997) Pedagogy and protocols for collaborative teaching and research through SuperJANET and ISDN in Higher Education, *Innovations in Education and Training International*, 34 (4), pp. 299–306.

Gauntlett, D. (1996) *Video Critical; Children, the environment and media power*, John Libby Press, Luton.

Goldman-Segal, R. (1998) *Points of Viewing Children's Thinking: A digital ethnographer's journey*, Lawrence Erlbaum Associates, Mahwah, NJ.

Goodman, S. (2003) *Teaching Youth Media: A critical guide to literacy, video production and social change*, Teachers College Press, New York.

Harvey, I., Skinner, M. and Parker, D. (2002) *Being Seen, Being Heard: Young people and moving image production*, British Film Institute, London.

Hellawell, S. (2001) *Beyond Access: ICT and social inclusion*, The Fabian Society, London.

Livingstone, S. (2002) *Young People and New Media*, Sage, London.

Livingstone, S. and Bovill, M. (1999) *Young People, New Media*, report of the research project 'Children, Young People and the Changing Media Environment', London School of Economics, London.

O'Hear, S. and Sefton-Green, J. (2003) Style, genre and technology: the strange case of youth culture online, in *Doing Literacy Online*, eds I. Snyder and C. Beavis, Hampton Press, New York.

Richman, N. (1998) *In the Midst of the Whirlwind: A manual for helping refugee children*, Save the Children and Trentham Books, Stoke on Trent.

Rutter, J. (2001) *Supporting Refugee Children in 21st Century Britain: A compendium of essential information*, Trentham Books, Stoke on Trent.

Selfe, C. (1999) *Technology and Literacy: The importance of paying attention*, University Press, Carbondale, IL.

13 The role of local instructors in making global e-learning programmes culturally and pedagogically relevant

Michelle Selinger

Introduction

Is pedagogy in different cultures around the world substantially different or has globalization resulted in a blending of beliefs about what is best in teaching and learning and can this educational practice become universal? There are numerous concerns about the globalization of education through e-learning and programmes taught at a distance. Although there are very few programmes that have the extensive global reach of the subject of this chapter, the Cisco Networking Academy Program, there are many other programmes in the education and training arena that are developed in one country and taught in others. The Academy Program has become a meeting point for an international community of teachers to collaborate on teaching the same vocational programme effectively in their own cultures. From a recent internal evaluation in Europe, the Middle East and Africa it has become clear that the responsibility for making this programme culturally and pedagogically relevant lies in the hands of local instructors and in the support mechanisms available to them to share good practice from around the world. This chapter indicates the ways in which local instructors have supported students' studying the programme, describing good and not so good practices with digital media. It examines the factors that support or inhibit students' learning and the assumptions that are made. It then draws conclusions about the necessity for, and nature of, local support for an education programme that is developed in one country and delivered in another.

Research on e-learning is international but how it is viewed in terms of teaching varies between countries since norms in the relationship between student and teachers vary across cultures. There are also issues about language of instruction and support. I have discussed in an earlier paper the cultural and pedagogical implications of a global e-learning programme (Selinger, 2004). Bates (1999) explains his concerns about distance education and e-learning:

The problem is that providing distance education courses in a foreign language is not just a technical issue. As well as the actual language, such courses come with alien social and cultural contexts. Examples are drawn from another culture, idioms often do not transfer between cultures, and even the style of writing may be alien.

(Bates, 1999: 8)

He also describes cultural differences in the approach to teaching:

There is a tendency in 'Western' courses from the United States, Britain, Canada and Australia to encourage critical thinking skills, debate and discussion, where students' views are considered important, and where the views of teachers can be legitimately challenged and where student dissent is even encouraged. In other cultures, there is great respect shown by students for the teacher, and it is culturally alien to challenge the teacher or even express an opinion on a topic.

(Bates, 1999: 8)

It is for this reason that locally based tutors are vital to the success of any global education programme. These tutors are familiar with the prevailing pedagogical approaches in their region or country, so they intuitively understand ways in which they can support students' adaptation to teaching styles and resources developed elsewhere.

The Australian National Training Authority Strategy for 2001 (accessible at http://flexiblelearning.net.au/policies/year2001/finrep.htm) quotes Rumble (2000) in pointing to the importance of local instruction. It also cites Mason: 'the big issue in global education is the cultural one ... Much of the promise of the globalisation movement in education depends on how successfully cultural differences are addressed' (1998: ix–x).

Much criticism of global education is levied at Western ideals. Aikenhead (1996) conceptualized culture according to the norms, values, beliefs, expectations and conventional actions of a group. In the literature on science education Cobern and Aikenhead (1998) perceive science as a subculture of Western or Euro-American culture. They argue that:

because science tends to be a Western cultural icon of prestige, power and progress (Adas 1989), Western science often can permeate the culture of those who engageit with ease. Assimilation or acculturation can threaten non-Western cultures, thereby causing Western science to be seen as a dominating power (Battiste and Barman 1995; Simonelli, 1994).

(Cobern and Aikenhead, 1998: 41)

Is this true of technical education too or is training in networking international? The fact that the Internet has become globally accepted and that the standards of Internet protocol, although inherently Western and invented through Western scientific methods, have to be global in order for networks to communicate, suggest that training in this area might be different. In the research discussed below, there was never any indication of Western imperialism. This may be because local instructors are empowered to teach students in their own context and through familiar pedagogical approaches.

The Cisco Networking Academy Program

The Cisco Networking Academy Program is a suite of web-based and instructor led vocational courses in IT skills designed in the United States. The first Cisco programme to be developed was the Cisco Certified Network Associate Program (CCNA). CCNA was designed to train students to instal, maintain and troubleshoot computer networks through public–private partnerships between Cisco, governments, educational institutions and non-governmental organizations. The course was originally conceived to be taught in high schools to students aged 16 and over, but it is now taught to students from the age of 16 to 60. In all courses offered through the Academy programme the underlying teaching and learning model is based on a cognitive constructivist view of learning. Hands-on labs are included and are perceived as the pivotal element of the Academy programme with considerable emphasis given to the labs by the development team. The web-based materials were written to help students make sense of the labs and to provide a theoretical perspective. These web resources make extensive use of flash animation, graphics and, more recently, video extracts, e-simulations and remote labs. The CCNA is taught in 151 countries worldwide to nearly half a million students, over half of whom are outside the United States. The CCNA is based on four 70 hour semesters of study, each accompanied by a series of chapters and associated online and practical assessments at the end of each chapter and each semester. The online assessment system was originally based on multiple choice questions, and since this research took place there have been considerable developments. For example, more procedural assessment tasks have been introduced using 'drag and drop' technologies and e-simulations. There is extensive instructor training supported by a global online facility to support the sharing of information and teaching ideas.

Many institutions, particularly those in higher education, have introduced the Academy programme as an adjunct to an introductory networking course or as a replacement because it introduces a strong, hands-on, practical element into the course. This is an aspect often missing in traditional courses because the cost of equipment is high or because the institution does not understand the significance of combining the theoretical component with a practical element to foster student understanding. In other institutions the programme was used to provide the first foray into e-learning and it has encouraged the developments of other courses. Otherwise the course is no different to any other. Instructors are key to its delivery and success and students are taught in timetabled classes.

Role of the private sector in education

Cisco has invested over US$200 million in the development of the curriculum, the learning environment and assessment tools. The curriculum is updated regularly and the online assessment has been regarded as leading edge as it moves way from multiple choice testing to more procedural types of assessment. No individual academic institution can afford to invest in such developments and therefore such corporate initiatives are welcome in the IT market, where there are constant advances in technology and it is essential that students are given up to date information to be able to compete for jobs without further training. The scalability of such a programme can only be achieved by a robust management system, quality assurance and an infrastructure that ensures training and support for instructors.

The Academy programme fits into Cisco's corporate social responsibility agenda (Chambers, 2003) and this is confirmed by Porter and Kramer (2002) in a paper exploring the advantages of corporate philanthropy. They cite Cisco as a company that has 'used its unique assets and expertise, along with its worldwide presence, to create a programme that no other educational institution, government agency, foundation, or corporate donor could have designed as well or expanded as rapidly' (2002: 12–13) and that has focused on 'social needs that affect its corporate context and utilizing its unique attributes as a corporation to address them' and 'to demonstrate the unrealized potential of corporate philanthropy' (2002: 7).

Evaluation of the Cisco Networking Academy Program

The research that is presented in this chapter is derived from the author's visits to 57 Academies in eleven countries within Europe, the Middle East and Africa (EMEA). This EMEA region is one of Cisco's six 'theatres'. Around 100 instructors were individually interviewed, and interviews were also conducted with over 300 students, usually in groups of three, in order to triangulate the data gathered from instructors. Some classes were observed. In addition 1,700 web-based questionnaires were collected from students and instructors across the region. The countries visited represented the range of economies and cultures within the region. The study investigated and quantified the factors that affect the ways in which instructors taught the CCNA course, including how a United States model of pedagogy had been accepted or adapted into different cultures with varying pedagogical paradigms. It also focused on the constraints and effects that web based teaching can have on pedagogy when Internet access is limited and/or expensive. Additionally, the model used to train instructors was evaluated in the light of the findings.

Generally the programme was very well received by both students and instructors. They particularly liked its direct relevance to work opportunities and web-based learning gave students the opportunity to pace themselves, to revisit concepts, and to go beyond the curriculum through the hotlinks embedded in the course materials. The hands-on labs and other practical activities made the programme particularly appealing, and students liked working together on the threaded case study, which is a project that goes across the third and fourth semesters of the CCNA course. The online multiple choice assessment was often supplemented with written tests and practical assignments by many Academies because many instructors did not believe multiple choice assessment was sufficiently rigorous, especially where the course was taught in higher education, which was often the case in EMEA.

Pedagogy

Magnusson and Svensson suggest that:

> Every teacher, tutor or instructional designer has his or her individual view on learning, expressed as a 'pedagogy-in-use'. Such a personal theory of learning can be aligned with one, or influenced by many pedagogical theories from literature, but are to a large extent dependent on personal experiences and preferences of learning.
>
> (2001: 3)

The research described here confirms the results of these and other studies in this area and indicates that cultural beliefs about teaching and learning have some impact on the way the CNAA programme is taught. More revealing was the apparent impact of the lack of experience and knowledge of how traditional instruction interfaces with web-based teaching materials for teaching and learning. The pedagogical principles of the Cisco Academy are based on a spiral curriculum model in which students are introduced to and work with new concepts. These concepts are then set in the context of earlier concepts that were previously taught in the programme before the students go on to the next stage. This is perceived as unnecessary repetition in some countries because students are expected to work on assimilating new knowledge into existing knowledge by themselves. In other countries it is also thought as unnecessary, because the instructors perceive it as their job to do this. These differences are subtle and do not cause much cognitive conflict, but nevertheless instructors are relied upon to help students make sense of the underlying teaching styles within their own cultural context.

As stated earlier, the CCNA is taken by students whose ages range from 16 (the age group for which the programme was originally designed) to university age and mature students who may be taking the Academy programme part time. The entry levels of understanding of the subject and the maturity of the students' approach to learning is not catered for, and indeed would be difficult to do so, in such a large programme. This is another reason for instructor input to mediate between student and curriculum approach. A number of key features have recently been added which can partially address this. Using content delivery technology, the Academy programme now has a personalization feature whereby students can do pre-assessments and then be directed to those areas of the curriculum they need to study. If students need to retake an assessment, they can be offered alternative pages to study rather than re-reading pages already visited.

Where students' Internet access was limited, or where students had difficulty studying the web-based curriculum outside class for reasons of cost or lack of access, then it was not always possible for instructors to work with their students in the way they wanted. Instructors felt that they had to give much of the time allocated to theory for students to read the curriculum rather than engaging in discussion and collaborative activities. In a few instances, regardless of how much Internet access students had, there were concerns as to the extent to which some instructors thought the web-based materials could do the teaching alone without instructor intervention. In these classes instructors completely changed their normal teaching approach and made the resources the focus of the class rather than introducing students to concepts through instruction and discussion, and using the curriculum as a sophisticated textbook to support students' learning.

Constructivism in different countries

The constructivist philosophy was therefore not always borne out in practice by some Academies, except perhaps in the hands-on activities. In other Academies, activities were described or observed in which students collaborated on all aspects of their course. There were examples of constructivist activities in which instructors encouraged students to teach the principles of chapters to others; concept mapping was used in some cases; and in labs there were extra problem solving tasks set in which instructors helped to scaffold students' understanding through the use of questions designed to focus students' attention on troubleshooting techniques. Certainly in Academies where instructors had a sound grounding in pedagogical theory, practices were more likely to include a range of teaching styles aimed at engaging students and maximizing their learning. However, not all instructors came from a teaching background. Some were network or other IT specialists working in the field. Although they often made excellent instructors and were valued by students for their expertise and knowledge, they were less likely to be well versed in teaching techniques. The best instructors observed were those who had both sets of skills.

Observed teaching styles

Most instructors spent some time planning their lessons, but one or two let the curriculum do the teaching and only prepared the lab kit. The Instructor Tool Box (tips and ideas for teaching the Academy programme) was used in some countries but not in all. It was used more frequently in countries with similar pedagogical principles, like the UK, and in the United Arab Emirates (UAE), where many instructors were recruited from the United States, the UK or Canada. However one instructor based in the UAE said that his students perceived PowerPoint presentations as extra work so he rarely used them. 'It's a very oral culture,' he explained, 'and the students explain ideas to each other that they have read.' In many of the countries visited, instructors used the animations and graphics from the web-based curriculum materials. They projected these images onto a large screen when teaching students about difficult concepts. Most instructors reported looking at the Instructor Tool Box at some stage, taking away some ideas (often timings for each chapter) and then developing them to their own style.

In Sweden, for example, instructors said they made little use of the Instructor Tool Box as the presentation style did not match their approach to teaching and learning, and they did not like PowerPoint as a teaching tool. One instructor explained, 'Here we use the board more, talking more and perhaps some small work groups.' In other countries the language barrier was a problem. A Hungarian instructor explicitly stated that he wanted the instructor support materials to be made available in Hungarian. The presentations and other teaching resources all tend to be in English, which means that instructors either have to translate them, which is time consuming, or talk to the English slides in their own language. Some non-English speaking Academies, including the Italians, did translate the resources but rarely shared them by submitting them to the Instructor Tool Box although they did sometimes email them to other Academies in the locality. In Italy the Cisco Academy Training Center had made digital recordings of lessons that were then made available on a web site to help instructors understand how to teach aspects of the Academy programme. Lesson ideas were also shared, but again none of these were posted on the Instructor Tool Box in the instructor community. An instructor in South Africa in a regional Academy said he had used some of the materials in the Instructor Tool Box. He had found that the lesson plans were good for guidance, ideas and ensuring nothing important was omitted. He is developing his own set of lesson plans so that his teaching is adapted to the environment in which he works.

Many excellent ideas like these for teaching the Academy programme rarely go outside the individual Academy. Instructors seem reluctant to post their ideas on the worldwide instructor community web site. Sometimes there is some sharing of ideas and practice within institutions. From interviews with instructors it appears that a more formalized way of sharing practice within each country would be well received. This has now been recognized and country-based communities are being developed with instructors. It is hoped that these will encourage ideas, worksheets and presentations in home languages to be posted online and shared.

Group work

On the whole, group work took place only in labs. There were a few occasions when instructors encouraged students to work together on an aspect of the web-based curriculum. If students did not understand something, they might ask a peer or an instructor, but otherwise they studied alone. However, in one class in Germany, students were given responsibility to teach aspects of the curriculum to their peers, while in another German Academy a group of students were allowed to go ahead provided that they gave support to others in the class. These 'fast track' students spent considerable amounts of time at home going through the curriculum and made use of instant messaging to discuss the curriculum with each other. In several Academies, students were asked to select a chapter and take turns to summarize it for the rest of the group. In the UAE, a group of three females described how they learnt the content of a chapter together: 'Each student takes a section and reads and explains to us. The next student takes the next section and explains to us. So you think [you are] helping each other. Yeah, and we are' (UAE student).

Some instructors did encourage students to help each other to understand a concept, as one instructor explained:

> What is interesting it's not always the same people that are helping the others, and they can often translate what I said into not quite the right answer, but it's the answer that is understood, and from further up – question and answer, practical observation, whatever – one can see that the one that has had difficulty has actually grasped the concept that was being presented.
>
> (UK instructor)

In one class in the UK, some students had not understood sub-netting and the instructor had asked one of the stronger students to spend some time with that group to help them to understand the concept while she worked with another group on labs.

How instructors support students

In class, students reported that they had no preferences as to whether they wanted their instructors to present prior to or after reading a chapter, but they were unanimous in their desire to have some instructor-led teaching. Instructors who did not do this were criticized by students. Instruction also changed as instructors gained more experience of the course and students' reactions to it. As instructors became more familiar with students' responses to the curriculum they gave more direct teaching by providing additional examples and explanation, or setting up group activities for the more difficult aspects of the course.

Students who were reading the curriculum in English as a second language said they preferred it when their instructor explained the content of a chapter in preference to them reading it first. Two females from UAE explained this as follows:

> It became very difficult the facts I read and didn't actually understand, and she came and explain it, it sticks then I understand. She asks us to read it again after the explaining.
>
> (One student)

> Maybe we spend lots of time reading, reading the lots of things and memorise and they are not important. But they show us what is the important points. It makes for us clear ... After understanding it we read it again. The first impression was that if I didn't understand chapter 4 and 5, I read it first and then understand and [it] stick with me. You see I read the sentence and correct and its [. . .] meaning. So when I read it again, I will stick with this one.
>
> (Another student)

Making meaning is an issue, particularly when English is the students' second language. Instructors may need to provide some introduction to the online resources so that when students read it on their own there is less likelihood of misunderstanding.

The Instructor Guide suggests that students should be encouraged to take notes and use logbooks. Generally mature students did take notes, but younger students did not. Many students wanted printed notes from the Web so they could highlight important parts, and where curriculum access was limited, instructors had printed out the materials for students. Some instructors provide handouts to students, often with blank spaces to complete and these served as notes that students could use for revision purposes prior to tests. Other instructors developed a set of handouts for students on the main points for the chapter they were studying. This type of support was greatly appreciated and is a strategy that could model and encourage good note taking.

A South African instructor clearly summed up the instructor's role in the web-supported Academy programme: 'It's a major component for us because it fits in so nicely with our strategies. It's constantly being updated. It's being updated by the networking leader in the world. It uses modern teaching methods.' But he added, 'We do have to supplement; we can't just rely on online teaching, that's not going to do the trick.'

Electronic communications

Students in some Academies who were in part-time courses could email their instructors with queries, although there were rarely any community forums where students could answer each other's queries. Exceptions included the only distance-learning version of the Academy programme that was run in Spain and in a German vocational school where students spend several weeks away from school on work placements. In these situations the students still had to complete the practical activities and in Spain it was arranged for them to go to a centre to complete these. In these cases email is used to communicate the topics to be studied for the next class and to discuss problems the students might have in understanding aspects of the curriculum. The Spanish Academy has set up a discussion forum so that students can also respond to these questions. The instructor moderates the discussion and intervenes where necessary, but the students tend to support themselves. The instructor explained:

> I get a daily report from the community that's made up of everything, so I can see what questions are there, what responses are made there, so I can intervene if they're making a mistake. If they're going to do wrong directions, [I can] say 'Stop' at this point.
>
> (Spanish instructor)

The new facility to support local communities should support the sharing of practices familiar to the culture and in the language of instruction, as well as enabling students to communicate with students from within their class, their country and across the world.

Structure of lessons

Lessons varied widely, both within countries and across countries, from e-reading being the norm in some classes with very little instructor input, to no students spending time alone on the web-based curriculum during a lesson. One group of instructors in a German school do not like to keep stopping students during lab work or when students are using the e-simulations. They tell the students that if they have any questions or problems they must write them on the board. Later the instructors bring the class together to try to solve the problems as a whole group. In another school in Germany, the students are asked to make mind maps as they work through the curriculum, an idea developed from the Instructor Tool Box. In contrast, observation in Italy showed that at least one instructor spent most of the lesson giving students sub-netting problems to solve. He engaged students in discussion, encouraged them to work collaboratively on a set of problems and then invited a student to present his or her solutions to the rest of the group.

On the whole instructors kept their classes on the same chapter rather than allowing students to go at their own pace. This made it easier to set lab exercises and to hold whole-class lessons. When students worked at their own pace they tended to do labs on their own and there was no collaborative spirit in the class. The atmosphere appeared lifeless. Instructors who permitted self-paced learning tended to have no teaching background and therefore little understanding of the need for differentiation strategies or for peer support and collaboration.

In an attempt to understand the range of teaching practices and the nature and quality of instructor input, both instructors and students were asked to describe their lessons. The following are some examples:

> The students read the Curriculum before they come to the lesson and then there are several ways [to proceed]. One way is to give students the task to talk about the chapter to the other students. And the other way is that we talk altogether in the classroom, so that the teacher leads the discussion and the students have to answer several questions, or to explain several topics of this chapter they've prepared.
>
> (German instructor)

> Our teacher comes in and explains what the lesson's gonna be about, not the whole lesson. But before that we have to – he tells us to read the Curriculum, [and to] understand as much as we can, and then he'll explain everything. And then we can read it again. Gives us exercises to do so that we understand – prepares us for the exam. Exercises – filling in blanks, questions about the chapters. Sometimes notes, he writes notes that can help us, and then we have time to write our notes or read the chapter. It depends on, like, how many times we have to read it to understand it.
>
> (UAE student)

[There is no online curriculum in classes] but we always discuss the problems we had before and after the exams. So after the exams, every time, we [discuss] every question. Whoever made a mistake we ask him what was the problem, and we discuss why was it a problem, and the student can tell why he made that mistake – what was mixing up in his head.

(Hungarian student)

Experience of teaching the course shows instructors where they might need to customise the Academy programme to suit their own students' needs. In a South African Academy the instructor modified aspects of the programme after receiving feedback from about 400 students. Depending on where they were in their studies, he discovered that not only did some students have little or no background in information technology, most were unfamiliar with online learning and as a result the instructors had to develop some extra written materials to support students' learning.

The accompanying text books were also added in this Academy as students were using 'cut and paste' rather than making their own summary notes: 'They don't feel they have the confidence or maybe it's just too much of a mind shift for them.' This Academy now gives the students fairly lengthy lectures on around 95 per cent of a chapter, but encourages students to interrupt and ask questions. 'I don't want to do 100 per cent because then they are going to feel that they don't have to go through the online curriculum. So we always leave some stuff out and we will tell them that there is more on this but they need to go and find out.' The instructor 'grabs some information out of the online curriculum' or uses presentations from the instructor community. Additionally his team adds in other content they feel should be included but which is not currently in the online curriculum.

Some instructors liked to take the class away from the PCs and give lectures to the students in a different room. This was mainly with older students in universities and colleges where teaching was more classical. These lectures often went beyond the Academy curriculum as well, developing concepts in more detail and depth. Setting pre-reading varied from country to country and it was considered unnecessary in some cultures such as the Swedish and Danish cultures. Students were expected to have autonomy and to be self-motivated. It was up to them as to how much they read before or after a class. It also depended on whether they had access to the curriculum outside the classroom.

Summary and conclusions

The results of this study have indicated clearly the importance of local instructors in the global Cisco Networking Academy Program, and the design of the course is premised on a face-to-face teaching model. Indeed, half of the CCNA course is based on hands-on labs. However, the content and structure of the online materials are relied on heavily by the instructors and it is not always clear to them that use of these materials can be both similar and different to teaching with other forms of media, such as text books and video. These findings may be related to any global programmes designed in one country and taught in another whether using a face-to-face, distance or e-learning model.

One of the main and most important conclusions from the evaluation was that instructor training is required to give more focus and that instructors need to become aware that they are the most important element in the success of students following the Cisco Networking Academy Program. It is the instructor's role to make this global programme culturally and pedagogically relevant for their students. Although the programme is culturally neutral, in that Internet working relies on international terminology and standards, the ways in which the programme relates to an individual country's infrastructure will vary. Instructors have to ensure that students are prepared for work in their own country and also need to make any adaptations to the presentation of the curriculum to ensure that students are comfortable in their usual learning environment.

This research fits Bates' (1999) outline where he lists some of the benefits of working through local partners: 'cultural adaptation, assistance with student recruitment, tutoring, and assessment, local accreditation/ qualifications, and contributions to content and programme design to ensure local relevance' (Bates, 1999: 12). The Cisco Networking Academy Program certainly makes use of all these features and it has an international team of instructors who contribute to further development to ensure that many of the cultural issues that arise are addressed where possible. However, no generic programme can be truly localized and it is up to the local instructors to ensure that any anomalies and pedagogical differences in the web-based material are addressed to ensure the success of their students. The planned country-based communities are likely to add a further dimension to such localization. In summary, these are the ways in which the local instructors can make global e-learning programmes culturally and pedagogically relevant.

References

Adas, M. (1989) *Machines as the Measure of Man: Science, technology, and ideologies of western dominance*, Cornell University Press, Ithaca, NY.

Aikenhead, G. S. (1996) Science education: border crossing into the subculture of science, *Studies in Science Education*, 26, pp. 1–52.

Bates, T. (1999) Cultural and ethical issues in international distance education, paper presented at Engaging Partnerships Collaboration and Partnership in

Distance Education UBC/CREAD conference, 21–23 September, Vancouver, Canada.

Battiste, M. and Barman, J. (eds) (1995) *First Nations in Canada: The circle unfolds*, UBC Press, Vancouver.

Chambers, J. (2003) [accessed 24 August 2003] John Chambers discusses social responsibility and citizenship at the World Economic Forum [Online] http://newsroom.cisco.com/dlls/ts_012703.html.

Cobern, W. W. and Aikenhead, G. S. (1998) Cultural aspects of learning science, in *International Handbook of Science Education*, eds B. J. Fraser and K. G. Tobin, pp. 39–52, Kluwer Academic Publishers, Dordrecht.

Magnusson, M. and Svensson, L. (2001) Technology and pedagogy in e-learning: a case study of attitudes among content experts, in Proceedings of IRIS24, August, Ulvik, Norway.

Mason, R. (1998) *Globalising Education: Trends and applications*, Routledge, London.

Porter, M. J. and Kramer, M. E. (2002) [accessed 24 August 2003] The competitive advantage of corporate philanthropy, *Harvard Business Review*, R0212D [Online] http://www.netacad.it/upload/pdf/HBRarticleCN.pdf.

Rumble, G. (2000) [accessed 24 August 2003] The globalisation of open and flexible learning: considerations for planners and managers, *Journal of Distance Learning Administration*, 3 (3) [Online] http://www.westga.edu/~distance/ojdla/fall33/rumble33.html.

Selinger, M. (2004) Cultural and pedagogical implications of a global e-learning programme, *Cambridge Journal of Education*, 33 (1) (in press).

Simonelli, R. (1994) Sustainable science: a look at science through historic eyes and through the eyes of indigenous peoples, *Bulletin of Science, Technology & Society*, 14 (1), pp. 1–12.

14 Case method and intercultural education in the digital age

Marsha A. Gartland, Robert F. McNergney,
Scott R. Imig and Marla L. Muntner

Our challenge

Teaching and learning by the case method on the Internet can help us learn about others and also learn about ourselves. This chapter provides an introduction to the ways online cases and case methods work. That is followed by an example of teaching teachers by means of a case study. Lastly, the potential for using international online exchanges in teaching and teacher education is explored.

Cases and opportunities

Imagine the following scenario. A college sophomore comes to her foundations of education class prepared to discuss the previous night's reading on educating a multicultural student population. Instead, she and her classmates watch as their professor enters a web address (http://www.casenex.com) on the classroom computer and the CaseNEX web site appears. The professor navigates the site and the multimedia case 'Project Cape Town' begins to play.

As she watches, the young woman notes inconsistencies between her textbook's best-practice theories and the teaching methods employed in the Model C schools in Cape Town, South Africa, where recently integrated students and teachers begin to experience their similarities and differences. The teachers, she believes, should be doing more to guide the students through this process.

When the video ends, the young woman is quick to share her observations with her classmates. To her surprise, many disagree with her and a lively discussion ensues. The professor guides the conversation by having class members identify the major issues in the case. Their teacher, a professor, also encourages the class to consider explicitly the values of people depicted in the video. Students share knowledge they possess that might be relevant to the issues. Finally, the professor challenges the class to devise actions or opportunities to mitigate the identified issues and identify possible consequences for those actions.

In the days that follow, the young woman and her classmates will log onto the Internet to perform many operations, including: viewing Project Cape Town again; reading expert perspectives on the case; participating in discussions on the Project Cape Town discussion site; sharing their opinions with their professor via private electronic journals; consulting a virtual reference library and searching the Internet for related readings; and, through videoconferencing or chat, discussing the case with another culturally diverse group of educators geographically distant from themselves. Throughout this process, the participants in this class will become familiar with the technological tools they use, as well as with the issues in the case.

Case methods are typically used in professions in which complex interactions require professionals to exercise judgment rather than to apply rules and principles in prescriptive ways. The use of cases in the training of professionals in the United States began at Harvard Law School in 1870 and now has a well-documented history in law, medicine and business. Case studies have also recently begun to take root in teacher education.

Real-life scenarios lie at the heart of case studies. In education, these problem-centred stories can focus on issues of teaching and learning in classroom situations, education policy conflicts and challenges related to colleagues, parents or administrators. Often expert analyses from different perspectives accompany cases and suggest that there are no right answers; instead different perspectives are presented for exploration to help educators practise making decisions about teaching and learning. Case studies encourage a vibrant connection between theory and practice – one that is often missing in lecture and textbook learning. Because cases are based in practical reality, they offer credibility and relevance to contemporary education issues and problem solving skills (Shulman, 1992).

The theoretical basis for this learning can be found in the work of practical theorists such as George Herbert Mead (1934), Lev Vygotsky (1978) and John Dewey (1938). Mead stressed the importance of role-taking as a catalyst for growth and maintained that active participation in 'real-world' activities offered conditions appropriate for development. Vygotsky stressed the role of discourse and social interaction in development, presenting learners with a variety of perspectives and problems to solve. The key to Vygotsky's theory is his postulation of the 'zone of proximal development', which is described as a person's range of potential for learning and development. Dewey elaborated on the important interplay between action and reflection, highlighting the importance of integrating theory and practice. All developmental theorists agree that learning begins with a knowledge disturbance. This perturbation has been a major focus of enquiry, prompting numerous studies seeking to identify elements and conditions necessary for such growth (Firth and Pajak, 1998).

The stories represented in cases are as varied as the teaching methods used to enhance them. Instructional techniques range from use of quasi-Socratic discussions led by skilled instructors to student-oriented reading, reflection and reaction (Shulman, 1992). Through case studies, educators learn not only about theory and practice but also about morals and ethics, thereby becoming more capable and multiculturally aware problem solvers. Like professionals in law, business and medicine, educators typically engage in advanced research, writing and presentation skills when analysing cases. As participants confront different values, they develop an enquiry-oriented teaching approach and a strong foundation on which to build consistent teaching behaviour.

The resulting recognition of different values and actions are what make cases rich and successful teaching tools (McNergney *et al.*, 1999). A case's many layers allow for this and encourage participants to experience real-world teaching and learning situations as they are, not necessarily as they should be. As participants gather different ways to view the case issues, they work reflectively on their own dialogue and analyses, treating these as a form of second-order text (Shulman, 1992). In Piagetian terms, the balance between discomfort and safety then allows participants to engage in critical reflection and confront established beliefs, biases and stereotypes (Houser and Chevalier, 1996) rather than to avoid confrontation. As a result, educators can become more adequately prepared for the challenges facing today's schools. Combining these methods with multimedia technologies creates even more powerful and immediate results.

CaseNEX was founded at the University of Virginia with this combination of strategies in mind. CaseNEX case studies in teacher education programmes support increased professional knowledge, heightened problem solving skills, and the purposeful use of technology. Instructors encourage educators to study teaching and learning using situations that are familiar and distant, both physically and philosophically. The collection of over sixty cases in the CaseNEX library concern educational life in elementary, middle and high schools across the United States, plus cases about education in Australia, Cuba, India, South Africa, the Netherlands and France. Parenthetically, the distant cases represent an important addition to standard teacher education curricula to stretch the knowledge base of teacher candidates and encourage a global perspective.

This set of case-based curricula delivered online uses multimedia technologies to allow geographically disparate teachers to come together to consider educational problems. The first web-enabled case, Project Cape Town, was delivered via the Internet in 1995. The CaseNEX model is not distance learning in the traditional sense; the approach is more accurately described as 'distributed education' supported by the World Wide Web. Students attend weekly class sessions at their site and an on-site instructor, who has completed a training session sponsored by CaseNEX, guides student work. With the diversity of participants and the introduction of multimedia web technologies, the practice of 'making the strange familiar' (McNergney, 1994) has taken case-based instruction to a new level of intercultural and interactive teaching and learning.

Working from the scenarios that are slices of real classroom life, student and other teachers learn to apply a case-study method during their courses. The method consists of five steps for making judgments in teaching and learning situations (McNergney *et al.*, 1994; McNergney and Medley, 1984):

1   identifying issues, problems, dilemmas, and opportunities;
2   recognizing multiple perspectives;
3   calling up available knowledge;
4   proposing actions; and
5   forecasting consequences of such actions.

These processes should help to summon participants' intellectual responsibility, encouraging them to be cognizant of the issues and knowledge that guide their thinking and actions rather than uncritically accepting ideas. In exploring other perspectives and considering the possible consequences of proposed actions, participants also increase their understanding of the complex moral decision making and the complicated realities inherent in teaching. In doing so, they become better equipped to face similar issues in their professional lives.

Studies have demonstrated that teachers who participate in CaseNEX are better at identifying problems, designing educational interventions to address them, and evaluating the effects of their teaching (Bronack, 1998; Imig, 2003; Kilbane, 2000). A recent study of online and face-to-face offerings of CaseNEX courses also suggests that live and virtual treatments were equally as effective for promoting the moral development of teachers who entered the programme with relatively low moral reasoning skills (Gartland, 2003).

Cases in an online community

The majority of educational problems cannot be solved procedurally by applying a formula; similarly, case methodology invites solutions that must be found by an interactive consideration of means and ends. While methods of teaching cases vary, reflection and analysis are consistent components. 'Dilemma discussion' is the technique most often recommended for facilitating the development of moral reasoning and reflection (Rest, 1993). 'Case-method learning' or ' case discussions' are dilemma discussions, which provide a vehicle to investigate the multi-focal dilemmas of education that link theory and practice and explore morals and ethics while enhancing problem-solving skills.

Unlike strictly video-based or text-based cases, multimedia cases provide the benefits of technology along with the complexity of case content. The Internet enables the delivery of multiple media that, when combined, can create and enhance the verisimilitude of cases and the interaction in teacher education. The cases available on the World Wide Web utilize various forms of hypermedia that allow participants the flex-ibility to choose their own pathways through case materials (Merseth and Lacey, 1993). Working online also enables synchronous and asyn-chronous conversations that contribute to the participants' construction of knowledge by bringing various perspectives to bear on case analyses and discussions.

Network-based learning environments that provide opportunities to discuss educational issues with one another are fairly new. In the more advanced models for online courses using the World Wide Web, partic-ipants have access to a variety of global library resources, online publications and journal articles, audio and video files, and desktop videoconferencing. In such environments, learners take more responsi-bility for their own learning processes as they collect, record, and analyse data and reflect on previous understandings within an environment that gives the opportunity for students to interact together to build a community of learners (Jonassen *et al.*, 1995). CaseNEX is the first web-based environment to offer cases and interactions in such a manner.

A case in point

Project Cape Town, the international case from the CaseNEX library introduced earlier, illustrates some of the ways multimedia cases enhance intercultural connections and the ways these connections can deepen understanding of issues closer to home.

Project Cape Town was created using raw video footage from two Model C schools in Cape Town (Kent, 1997). These schools were among the first to pioneer racial integration in South Africa. By happenstance, the Cape Town video footage was taken during the same week that South Africa ratified the constitution which eventually led to the elec-tion of Nelson Mandela as President. (This event marked the historical transformation of the country's government and culture.)

The first video segment of the case focuses on a music class. The teacher of the class is white, and all the students in the class are black. The teacher encourages the students to sing songs from their tribal culture, yet the spontaneity and loose structure of the tribal songs appear to be at odds with her European notions of performance. This tension can be inferred by observing the interaction between the teacher and the students in the video. The meeting of the two previously segregated cultures in a music class offers a rich event for exploration.

The second segment shows a videotaped interview of an Afrikaans and an English teacher at one of the schools. The teacher discusses two interesting dimensions related to the recent integration of the school: language differences and discipline problems. The language issues involve the tendency of some black students to speak loudly in public places. The teacher says this was a cultural artefact rooted in past practice when the belief was that if one spoke loudly in public, others would know the speaker was not gossiping. She continues by describing the white students' reactions to this behavior. The discipline dilemma concerns the frequent tardiness of many of the black students who use unreliable public transportation to travel an hour or more to school (unlike their white counterparts). The teacher raises the questions of whether it is correct to punish such tardiness and whether no punishment would be perceived as fair by the white students. This interview clearly describes some of the daily issues that arise from integration.

The third video segment draws from a speech given by a senior black student to her peers at a high school. She describes her own thoughts regarding the fact that even though black and white students share the same physical space, they still remain segregated socially. Her reflections are compelling. The inclusion of a student's perspective enriches the case and case discussion tremendously.

The fourth video segment comes from a lesson on perceptions taught by an English teacher. The teacher uses a demonstration with hats to illustrate how people's perceptions can be changed easily by relatively minor factors. The lesson is engaging and addresses issues of how people get along with one another. Because this video footage contains actual teaching, viewers can focus directly on classroom events. These four selections (two classroom scenes, a teacher's perspective and a student's perspective) reflect a diversity of issues and perspectives.

Online multimedia case studies provide opportunities for the interaction, reflection and perturbation that are the foundation of effective education. CaseNEX instructors work with students using online journals and discussions to enhance these opportunities for learning by prompting further reflection and a deepening sensitivity to intercultural issues. Similarly, participants' growth in intercultural awareness and communications skills are encouraged through interactions with one another within this web-enabled community.

The Developmental Model of Intercultural Sensitivity is a useful model to guide participants' growth in intercultural differences (Bennett, 1986;

1993). Using concepts from cognitive psychology and constructivism, this model breaks responses to cultural difference into six stages. The first three stages are considered ethnocentric and when operating within them, a person's own culture is considered central to reality. The second three stages are considered ethno-relative in that the view of one's own culture is set within the context of others (Hammer and Bennett, 1998). Ideally, as a person gains exposure to and understanding of other cultures, their reactions progress along this continuum and they eventually gain the ability to accept, respect, adapt to and integrate cultural differences.

Instructors using case studies can encourage movement along this continuum by responding to participant journals and discussion responses. The following examples from Project Cape Town asynchronous discussion group on the Web illustrate this approach. The discussion revolves around the first case scene in which the white music teacher is at odds with the spontaneity and looseness of her students' tribal singing: 'I have found that it is hard to be good at two things at the same time. There is a limited resource of time, and the teacher would not be able to provide an in-depth study on both musical styles. As long as the students are enjoying music, I think whatever she does is ok.'

This discussion response falls within Bennett's ethnocentric-minimalization stage in that it diminishes cultural differences and considers them inconsequential. The challenge at this stage is to 'continue learning about one's own culture and to avoid projecting that culture onto the experience of others' (Hammer and Bennett, 1998). An appropriate instructor response might be: 'Aside from differences in musical styles, how else might the teacher's culture differ from that of her students'? In what ways might the two be alike? Similarly, reflect on a time you have interacted with someone outside your own culture. In what ways do your two cultures differ? In what ways are they similar?'

The next discussion response falls within Bennett's ethno-relative-acceptance stage in that it acknowledges and accepts cultural differences. The challenge at this stage is to view the 'world through the lens of a different world view while maintaining your own commitments to values' (Hammer and Bennett, 1998: 16):

> In this music class we find a group of black students and a white teacher. This event only recognizes the black students in the class, which makes me wonder if there are only these black students in this particular class. It makes this class sound almost as if it is segregated. If this is the case, then the school does not seem to be addressing its goal of being an integrated school. However, I feel this teacher has the right ideas. Even though she is partial to European traditions of performance, she encourages the students

to express the musical concepts embedded in their own culture, and to do so in their own ways. Her actions promote the culture of these students. She helps bring some meaning to the material the students are learning.

(Fieldwork notes)

An appropriate instructor response would encourage the participant to emphasize the importance of both cultures and make connections to her teaching strategies: 'How might you envision responding appropriately to the students' singing while also honouring your musical heritage? Think of an analogous situation in your own teaching experience. How might you respond to the unique cultural needs of your student while honouring your cultural norms?' These discussions permit participants and instructors to collaborate while exploring cases and their understanding of both global and local issues, opportunities, and perspectives grows.

The future is now

Cases are no substitute for real life. Teachers need rich, challenging experiences with real children in real situations to foster continued professional development. Yet these first-hand experiences are expensive and difficult to provide consistently. The objectivity provided by the case studies described in this chapter allows aspiring and experienced teachers opportunities to stand back, analyse, reflect, evaluate and collaborate in finding effective solutions to complex education challenges. Cases on the Web open pedagogical possibilities for teachers and teacher educators connected to the Internet to work in ethnically diverse and internationally varied contexts. Both case content and collaborative cross-culture study groups encourage educators to broaden their professional horizons in safe yet challenging ways that real life does not often afford.

References

Bennett, M. (1986) A developmental approach to training for intercultural sensitivity, *International Journal of Intercultural Relations*, 10 (2), pp. 179–95.

Bennett, M. (1993) Toward ethnorelativism: a developmental model of intercultural sensitivity, in *Education for the International Experience*, ed. R. Paige, pp. 21–71, Intercultural Press, Yarmouth, ME.

Bronack, S. C. (1998) *Analyzing Multimedia Cases: Teacher development in a Web based environment*, unpublished doctoral dissertation, University of Virginia, Charlottesville, VA.

Chevalier, M. and Houser, N. (1997) Pre-service leaders' multicultural self-development through adolescent fiction, *Journal of Adolescent and Adult Literacy*, 40 pp. 426–36.

Dewey, J. (1938) *Experience and Education*, Collier Books, New York.

Firth, G. R. and Pajak, E. F. (eds) (1998) *Handbook of Research on School Supervision*, Macmillan Library Reference, New York.

Gartland, M. A. (2003) *Case-Method Learning Online: Influencing Teachers' Moral Reasoning*, unpublished doctoral dissertation, University of Virginia, Charlottesville, VA.

Hammer, M. R. and Bennett, M. J. (1998) *The Intercultural Development Inventory (IDI) Manual*, Intercultural Communication Institute, Portland, OR.

Imig, S. R. (2003) *CaseNEX evaluation data*, Unpublished manuscript, University of Virginia, Charlottesville, VA.

Jonassen, D., Davidson, M., Collins, M., Campbell, J. and Haab, B. B. (1995) Constructivism and computer-mediated communication in distance education, *The American Journal of Distance Education*, 9 (2) pp. 7–21.

Kent, T. W. (1997) *Project Cape Town: A description of the use of a multimedia Web case*, unpublished doctoral dissertation, University of Virginia, Charlottesville.

Kilbane, C. R. (2000) *Preservice teachers' use of multimedia cases*, unpublished doctoral dissertation, University of Virginia, Charlottesville, VA.

McNergney, R. (1994) Videocases: a way to foster global perspective on multicultural education, *Phi Delta Kappan*, 76 (4).

McNergney, R. F., Ducharme, R. F. and Ducharme, M. K. ed., (1999) *Educating for democracy: Case method teaching and learning*, Lawrence Erlbaum Associates, Mahwah, NJ.

McNergney, R. F., Herbert, J. M. and Ford, R. E. (1994) Co-operation and competition in case-based teacher education, *Journal of Teacher Education*, 45 (5), pp. 339–45.

McNergney, R. F. and Medley, D. M. (1984) Teacher evaluation, in *Developing Skills for Instructional Supervision*, ed. J. M. Cooper, pp. 147–78, Longman, New York.

Mead, G. H. (1934) *Mind, Self, and Society*, ed. C. W. Morris, University of Chicago, Chicago.

Merseht, K. K. and Lacey, C. A. (1993) Weaving stronger fabric: the pedagogical promise of hypermedia and case methods in teacher education, *Teaching & Teacher Education*, 9 (3), pp. 283–99.

Rest, J. R. (1993) Research on moral judgment in college students, in *Approaches to Moral Development: New research and emerging themes*, ed. Andrew Garrod, pp. 201–11, Teachers College Press, New York.

Shulman, L. S. (1992) Toward a pedagogy of cases, in *Case Methods in Teacher Education*, ed. J. H. Shulman, pp. 1–30, Teachers College Press, New York.

Vygotsky, L. S. (1978) *Mind and Society: The development of higher mental processes*, Harvard University Press, Cambridge, MA.

15 Intercultural learning through digital media

The development of a transatlantic doctoral student community

Andrew Brown and Niki Davis

Digital technology is acting as a catalyst, accelerating change and opening up ever increasing opportunities for those with access to multimedia information and communication technologies. Those of us in this privileged position have increasing access to networks of resources and people, and enriched experience through contact with diverse cultures. At the same time, digital media offer tantalizing potential to increase access to education, and to intercultural experiences, more generally, that should enhance and broaden education for all. However, it is now recognized that such potential cannot be realized without the preparation of teachers to use digital media and communication technologies effectively (UNESCO, 2002). Related professional development is also essential for those who work with educational technology, including service providers and designers of multimedia. Central to such systemic development is the preparation of tomorrow's leaders of educational technology, such that they may adopt multi-level and intercultural perspectives on the complex educational systems within which they work (Davis, 2002). This chapter describes new perspectives on intercultural learning that have emerged from our research and development work with senior practitioners and research students. In particular, we will focus on a transatlantic project that is working to establish cross-institutional, and cross-cultural, doctoral communities using strategies that utilize digital technology in blending face-to-face and online collaborative work with the exchange of students, faculty and staff. Consideration of this project will help us to illustrate our emerging understandings, and will provide the basis for presentation of directions for further research. A central theme in our discussion will be culture shock in web-based communities.

The need for intercultural competence

There is growing awareness of the need to develop intercultural communication and global perspectives. Martin and Nakayama (2000) identify six motivating factors to improve intercultural communication:

- A *technology push* that directly links an ever increasing diversity of people and cultures, by minimizing the effects of spatial and temporal separation and through the provision of language support.
- An *economic imperative* as trade and commerce become increasingly global in scale and yet must continue to meet local needs and concerns. This also applies to trade in education and training (Mason, 1998).
- The *personal motivation* that comes with our inquisitive and exploratory nature as human beings developing self-awareness.
- An *imperative of peace* and hopefully its maintenance in the long term.
- A *demographic imperative,* as our societies become increasingly diverse.
- *Ethical imperatives* that arise from challenging ethical issues that arise with variations in beliefs and norms.

These imperatives have brought the authors of this paper, colleagues and students collaboratively to research and develop the potential of technologies to enhance the professional development of the next generation of leaders in educational technology. In addition to the general motivations listed above, our specific educational interests include the following: first, the educational enrichment that is made possible by making connections with authentic audiences, collaborators and resources beyond the everyday environment (see Davis, 1997, for a review of telecommunication activities in the curriculum); second, the benefits of reflection on professional practice when the familiar becomes strange and a comparative view of education is achieved; third, the potential of digital media as a means to disseminate good practice in intercultural communication, in particular through the modelling of good practice in education and training.

McLuhan (1967) coined the term 'global village' and highlighted the ways in which the medium and the message act synergistically. With the increasingly complex part played by communication technologies in education and training, we believe that it is now critical to improve the education of educators and the training of the trainers to include intercultural perspectives and to actively develop interculturally aware and sensitive practices in teaching.

Culture shock, digital media and communities

In parallel with the characterization of contemporary cosmopolitan life as marked by discontinuity and fragmentation, there is an increasing emphasis on the importance of a sense of common culture in providing a basis for the formation of identity and community. Whilst culture provides a set of shared interpretive resources with which individuals and groups within a community make sense of their personal and collective experiences, the understandings, values and beliefs on which common interpretation, and thus communication, rest remain largely invisible to members of the community. The principles of cultural recognition and realization are, to a large extent, acquired and deployed tacitly. This can lead to a tendency for us to read the practices of other cultures in terms of our own tacit understandings. Alternatively, in circumstances in which we have difficulty in making sense of the cultural practices of others, for instance in extended periods living in another country, it can lead to dissonance and discomfort as we struggle to comprehend the apparently incomprehensible and resolve the seemingly irresolvable. It is this confrontation of our own ingrained, and often unexamined, interpretive frameworks with the everyday practices and understandings of another culture that provides the foundation for the complex of feelings that has come to be known as 'culture shock'. If a successful cross-cultural experience involves moving from one set of beliefs, understandings and values to another through a process of cultural transition that enables us to better understand and interact with others in the 'global village', then it is essential to understand the processes of culture shock and to develop intercultural competence.

Culture shock can be experienced when people are immersed in settings that are unfamiliar to them. The phenomenon of culture shock is studied as part of many foundation social science courses (see, for example, Macionis, 2003) and is acknowledged as an important issue for projects involved with international education. Immersion in a new culture presents both learning opportunities and significant risks. Action is therefore taken wherever possible to mitigate the adverse effects of culture shock. International student centres in many host universities routinely brief incoming foreign students and others preparing to study there from abroad on the stages of culture shock that they will experience. The first stage includes aspects of euphoria at the novelty of new environments, and then moves though disorientation towards depression as the individual grieves for the loss of their 'normal' environment until the third stage of acceptance and, finally, healthy acclimatization. Students are also warned to expect a similar, less severe cycle of discomfort on their return home from studying abroad. Outgoing students preparing to study abroad are also briefed on the phenomenon of culture shock and occasionally work though exercises to increase the benefits of cross-cultural immersion. Cultural preparation includes familiarization before departure with foreign artefacts and coaching for problem-solving behaviours including communication appropriate for common situations. For example, learning to express common greetings and words with which to say thank you along with appropriate body language.

The use of computer mediated communication and other digital technologies in bringing together new communities of learners can also provide an experience that is akin to immersion in an unfamiliar, culturally strange environment. Distance education today includes strategies to encourage formation of collaborative study groups and learning communities (see Palloff and Pratt, 1999, for example). Students commonly find this way of learning very stimulating and engaging, and it is not unusual to find that some students wish to continue their virtual community beyond the end of the class schedule. However, on the way some students seem to experience elation in the early stage, followed by depression during which they complain about feelings of disorientation in the 'virtual classroom'. Niki Davis, for instance, recognized the characteristics of culture shock while researching distance learning and related teacher preparation. The authors' work to reduce culture shock for students studying abroad has suggested that this emotional reaction to web-based learning may be a form of culture shock. This realization is supported by the literature in computer-mediated communications that describes online environments in cultural terms, and is exemplified by the now common use of the term 'cyberculture' (see, for example, Bonk and King, 1998 and Preece, 2000). Increasingly, the cultural practices of web-based communities have themselves become the focus for anthropological and sociological research (see, for example, Baym, 2000; Hine, 2000; Miller and Slater, 2001; see also Chung, Dowling and Whiteman, Chapter 5, this volume).

These virtual communities offer the possibility of becoming culturally distinct contexts in their own right, and they also provide a means by which geographically, socially and/or economically distant cultural groups can meet and interact. Students or researchers meeting in these contexts thus face the triple challenge of working in an unfamiliar virtual environment, engaging with the established or emerging culture of the virtual environment and attempting to negotiate and gain an appreciation of cultural differences between participants. In our experience, it is easy for the extent of these challenges to be underestimated.

In attempting to develop an online, cross-cultural community (as we have with our doctoral students, see discussion below), decisions have to be made about the particular environment to be used. Possibilities range from publicly available, open registration, discussion list style facilities – such as Yahoo! Groups and environments designed specifically for particular professional or other groups such as Think.com and Mirandanet – to commercially produced closed facilities designed specifically for online teaching – such as WebCT and closed bespoke environments designed by or for institutions for particular groups or specific functions. Each environment will have its own affordances, offering a different range of functions and facilities to the users and also different socio-cultural possibilities, for instance, social relationships represented by who has control of what, and culture implicit within the navigation and how messages are presented in relation to each other.

These 'environmental' conditions present challenges to users, in that they both enable and limit what can be achieved in terms of the development of an online community. It is often not immediately apparent to the users what the effects of the environment are, or how they are achieved. The web-based learning environment thus presents a first level of cultural challenge.

The culture of an online community begins to develop as interaction takes place within the chosen environment. For instance, particular modes of address become the norm, specific forms of agency are ascribed to or acquired by particular participants, and certain types of messages receive a favourable reception, whilst others receive a hostile reaction. Negotiation of the complexity of the emerging culture of an online community presents a second level of cultural challenge. Again, the characteristics and consequences of this may not be immediately apparent to participants.

The third level of challenge relates to the cultural understandings, experiences and expectations that participants bring to the online environment, and differences between these. At the simplest level, terms can have different meanings for different participants. Figuring this out can itself take time and lead to misunderstanding. At a more complex level, the interpretive frameworks brought to the interactions by participants from different backgrounds can lead to very different understandings and experiences of the content and the form of online discussion and interaction. Once again, it may not be immediately obvious to participants that experiences and interpretations differ within a group. If it is, it may not be clear to them what the causes or consequences are.

Each level of challenge presents the possibility of a form of culture shock. Whilst the feelings associated with this may be, at least initially, disturbing, we do not want to view this in wholly negative terms. With an awareness of the possibility of culture shock, participants are better prepared to appreciate and reflect constructively on differences within the group. Given that our own cultural frameworks are largely tacit, this is an important step in the establishment of more productive intercultural communication and interaction, and places us is a stronger position to realize the creative potential of cultural diversity and intercultural collaboration within and between groups.

Our discussion thus far has identified a need to incorporate intercultural perspectives in education, and to model good practice in the preparation of future leaders in educational technology, including teacher educators. It has also identified two broad challenges for educators today: first, how we develop our intercultural competencies for today's 'global village'; second, how we engage constructively with the experience of culture shock from immersion in an unfamiliar culture, in person or through digital media.

We accept these two challenges and plan to use them synergistically to enhance education and training. It is our belief that we may use culture shock to enhance learning, because we recognize that the shock of new culture often stimulates cognitive and emotional dissonance, which in turn brings us to a better understanding of others and ourselves. When managed appropriately, the individual can be enabled to reflect on personal behaviour and perceptions that had become routine and thus invisible from an early age. With appropriate strategies we aim to use the experience of culture shock experienced when studying abroad and/or through digital media to speed the development of intercultural competence in such a way as to model good practice for tomorrow's educators and for leaders of educational technology. The next section will describe our emerging understanding of relevant practice through a project at the highest level of education – the doctoral degree.

A transatlantic community for doctoral education

The International Leadership in Educational Technology (ILET) project sets out to bring together doctoral students and faculty in six universities, three in Europe and three in the US. We are developing and researching the production of an intercultural doctoral community with a focus on educational technology. A primary motivation for this project is the recognition that, whilst researchers and leaders in the use of educational technology are working in contexts that are increasingly culturally diverse, we have done little to prepare them for this. The idea of membership of and immersion in a community of researchers that is central to both the European and North American notions of doctoral level study provided, from our viewpoint, an ideal starting point for such a preparation. With the use of synchronous and asynchronous communication technologies, such as email, news groups, video and text conferencing and virtual learning environments, and the dissemination of research via the Web, the extent of a doctoral research community is potentially huge. Our engagement in such a globally connected but spatially and temporally distanced community, with none of the immediate existential communicative imperatives of physical immersion, can too often be from a culturally fixed and non-reflexive position. Thus the challenge facing the six participating universities is how to create contexts for intercultural interchange and interaction in which reflection on the very processes of this engagement is facilitated, and the implications critically considered. Our aim is for all involved to be able to engage in intercultural interactions in academic and professional contexts with greater understanding, and to relate this to the development of knowledge and practice in the areas of our expertise.

One major objective of the project is to enable doctoral students from the US to work and research as interns at one of the European partner universities and vice versa. The experience of studying and/or working in another country for an extended period time will clearly have a profound effect on the individuals involved. It will also act to consolidate links between the partner institutions. This learning thus extends beyond individual students and begins to have an effect on the institutions on both sides of the Atlantic. Much time and effort clearly has to be given to the preparation of students to make the most of this kind of experience. To this end we have created online and other digital resources for cultural preparation. To extend the benefits of the developing partnership between universities to students who are not intending or unable to travel, we have also developed a range of online seminars and reading groups. Our intention is to develop from this a clearer understanding of how to facilitate advanced learning and knowledge production in intercultural contexts, both face-to-face and virtual. Working with commercial partners and professional associations we have started to build on this to develop culturally appropriate online environments.

The first step in this process involved the development of mutual understanding between the faculty involved in the project. Although the project involves linking individuals and departments with expertise in educational technology, specific interests and approaches were diverse. Furthermore, the manner in which educational technology is used in schooling and higher education differs between the partner countries. Having to develop a common understanding of educational technology and having to create the conditions for research students to cross the Atlantic involved an exchange of perspectives and a growing understanding of the differences in our programmes and their underlying assumptions. The expectations we have of doctoral students are very different both within Europe and between Europe and the United States (Cowen, 1997). If we are to facilitate mobility and productive interchange, we have to find ways to understand and handle these differences. Fostering interchange between our doctoral students both helps us to do this and produces a generation of leaders in educational technology with a better understanding of their own and other cultures, making them more able to operate at both local and global levels.

Formal organizational agreements to facilitate collaborative teaching and research are essential and were also required by those funding this innovative project. The outcome of our initial collaboration was the production of a six-way Memorandum on Understanding between the partner universities. The process of gaining signatures for the six-way Memorandum on Understanding uncovered the first of many cultural challenges and increased the leaders' intercultural awareness as they learned who to approach to achieve acceptable equivalence and avoid slighting any of the partner universities. Was the Rector of the University of Barcelona equivalent to the President of a US university or the Director of the Institute of Education within the federal structure of the University of London, and who should sign first? The solution was to identify an underlying principle, namely the leader of the institution in this case, and to use the weight of previously appended signatures to swing those who might feel risk in endorsing such a document.

This memorandum has laid the foundations for both movement of faculty and doctoral students between the universities and the creation of a range of experiences that incorporate intercultural communication on the Web. We have, for example, run a series of transatlantic reading groups and created opportunities for people to join web-based courses that run at other universities and collaboratively between universities. The principle in the agreement is that every university will permit students, faculty and staff to use their facilities at no cost, while enjoying the same benefits for their own students, faculty and staff. This is accompanied by careful quality assurance and shared research in and development of innovative practice.

Whilst these collaborative activities provide potentially rich intercultural experiences, they also present, as we have indicated above, the possibility of culture shock. Their strength is that they provide a legitimate opportunity to reflect upon issues relating to cultural diversity in computer-mediated contexts. Thus these courses and seminars both take communication technology as a focus and use it to enable intercultural interaction. This interaction in turn becomes a legitimate focus for discussion, which facilitates critical reflection on the relationship between cultural, and linguistic diversity and the characteristics and consequences of different forms of computer-mediated interaction. Online academic and professional discussions can, for instance, be every bit as socially and culturally differentiating and excluding as face-to-face encounters. The web-based component of the project enables us to explore the relationship between culture and factors such as the content of the curriculum, forms of pedagogy and the structuring and characteristics of the online environment. We have found, for instance, that within the group there are strong commitments to particular educational ideologies, which relate to the cultural background of participants, and this affects the form of online environment in which people feel most comfortable. Virtual study abroad raises many of the same issues as physical study abroad. Given the increasing ease of access to opportunities to 'study abroad' online and the degree to which interaction on the Web is increasingly intercultural, these issues become ever more pressing.

In recognition of the value of these experiences both for individuals and institutions, we have extended our proposed Certificate in Intercultural Educational Technology, endorsed by all six partner universities, to include doctoral students who participate in the web-based activities and who provide mentoring and support for those who are able to take up the opportunity to travel. All participants will have the opportunity to develop reflective accounts of their intercultural experiences and develop these into an electronic portfolio that can be submitted for the award of the ILET certificate.

Since the initiation of the ILET project in autumn 2001, we have been building a rich collection of publicly available resources on the Web to support faculty and participating doctoral students (http://www.public. iastate.edu/ilet). We intend to add edited material from the electronic portfolio to the ILET web site, thus supplementing our developing collection of learning resources with student material. In autumn 2002 the web site provided the home for the project's first international reading group, during which online discussions moved across professional and university web-based discussion groups on both sides of the Atlantic. The disorientation of virtual transatlantic travel across virtual university platforms was clearly evident.

Both faculty and students provided resources for the reading group. For example, students in Barcelona linked the reading group to a project developing intercultural awareness with undergraduates (the LARA project, and the Cultura project – see Furstenberg *et al.*, 2001). The first virtual exchanges and team teaching took place in this way. A second reading group, in which readings were discussed in Spanish in order to establish the two main languages of the project, quickly followed the first reading group. This reading group remained in one web environment, Spanish Yahoo! Groups. More activities are planned for the coming year.

The English language continues to dominate the Internet, so the project is keen to support students in gaining an appreciation of minority languages. Danish and Catalan partners, at Aalborg University and the University of Barcelona, have been working to support study abroad by developing flexible learning materials for use on the Web. These materials cover both culture and language. For example, in autumn 2002, two Danish interns at Iowa State University led the development of Danish materials. Kristine Ellis laid the foundation for the development of intercultural studies materials in digital media while Eva Jansen initiated similar development of Danish language materials with support from students studying distance education and teaching in Iowa State University. The innovative approach of the latter distance education course is described in Davis and Nilakanta (2003). Subsequently these materials have been further developed and trialled online.

The first study abroad experiences involving physical travel started with an intensive course in June 2003 at the Institute of Education, University of London. This summer course focused on international issues in educational technology. It became a formal, accredited course in the University of Florida doctoral programme. It was less formally incorporated into programmes for partner universities with the participation of students and faculty from all universities. The course provided an opportunity to establish on-site collaboration and links that we hope will develop into internships and longer-term partnerships for European and US faculty and doctoral students. The next strategically important development is in autumn 2003 when the first doctoral transatlantic internships take place. These students will become the first ILET future leaders to become interns and teachers in higher education abroad, while continuing their doctoral research. Together with faculty, they will pave the way for further exchanges with improved cultural and language preparation and other scaffolding to turn culture shock into a less threatening and a more effective means of developing intercultural competence and good practice in education and training with educational technology.

The emergence of good practice in intercultural communication through digital media

At the time of writing, the ILET project is two-thirds of the way through its three-year span. There are promising indications of the development of good practice that will provide a model for future leaders of educational technology. Through them, these approaches and experiences can be passed on to future generations of teachers and learners. We can review progress against the recommendations of the UNESCO (2002) holistic framework for curriculum planning and institutional development for information and communication technologies in education. Four clusters of competencies are proposed, surrounded by four overarching themes defining the essential conditions for sustaining change. The four clusters of competencies are: technical issues; pedagogical issues; social issues; and competencies associated with collaboration and the networking of people. The four overarching themes are: vision and leadership; lifelong learning; context and culture; and planning and management of change. Many of these competencies and themes have been long recognized in developments in the UK and the US and elsewhere. What is of interest here is the recognition of competencies relating to collaboration and networking and of a clear relationship between the competencies and the overarching themes in order to maximize sustainability. At the heart of this are two questions. First, are we achieving the development of competencies in and through collaboration between and networking of people? Second, are we doing this in a way that is relevant to and realizable in diverse contexts in a cultural appropriate manner?

The reading groups run in collaboration with all universities have proved feasible. The first group moved across institutional and national learning environments and this proved to be most challenging for participants. From the accounts of participants, it also provided the most stimulating intercultural experiences. With the idea of culture shock online in mind, it is now possible for us to redesign the activity so that it becomes a better educational experience for all students and faculty. Our objective will be to use the expected cognitive dissonance created by engagement with a diversity of cultural practices, and the subsequent possible disorientation, to identify and learn from these experiences. The face-to-face intensive course in London has provided many ideas and resources for such development.

Over time the web-based learning will become blended with the physical movement of the few students who will travel across the Atlantic as part of the project. These people will act as ambassadors for their home cultures and so are witnesses to the shock experienced in a new environment. It should be noted that many of our doctoral students do not come to their doctoral studies from either Europe or the US and they therefore have already experienced culture shock in their 'home' university context. The lived experience of these ambassadors and the digital artefacts that are added to the web site will support our understanding of diverse cultures and contexts for students who are unable to travel. For example, a recent London Academy visit to a 'beacon' primary school with wonderful art and curriculum displays in the east end of London, where the children are roughly one-third European, one-third Asian and one-third African Caribbean in background, demonstrated graphically and viscerally to project participants that London is an ethnically diverse city, and one in which the diversity enjoyed can be both local and global. We observed digital technologies in use in the school classrooms, a video-conference with a class in the US and discussed plans to introduce wireless mobile technologies in the following school year. In discussion of the experience, while waiting for the train back to central London, participants from Florida expressed both culture shock and delight in this cultural diversity and unexpectedly rich use of digital technologies. This was noted in the reflections of a Jamaican student studying in Iowa who had been particularly keen to visit London where she knew that she could meet friends from Jamaica while 'abroad'. Digital stories created by the London Academy participants will further elaborate these experiences and contrasts. These will help future students engage and identify with the challenges and opportunities provided by such cultural diversity. These experiences and artefacts can be used to support discussions in the online reading groups and other courses. Encounters such as this in the university and in local communities will also encourage doctoral students to return to London to support curriculum and teacher development and develop their own research, with increased depth of understanding of themselves, of their part in a transatlantic doctoral community and of the relationship between the local and the global with respect to learning, teaching and research.

During the intensive programme in London, the obstacles to inter-cultural communication identified by Barna (in Samovar and Porter, 1994) were clearer than they had been in the online reading groups and courses. Barna notes that non-verbal misinterpretations are more difficult to overcome when living intensively in a specific visceral context. Linguistic differences in vocabulary, idioms, syntax and dialects caused few difficulties in the academic context of the Academy because we were moving frequently between our different US forms of English, and assistance with the translation and clarification of ideas was at hand. The US visiting participants did, though, find the experience tiring and hard to navigate in many ways, both academic and in relation to life skills. The effects of culture shock were attenuated by frequent interpretation of activities and ideas into more familiar terms, thus reducing anxiety caused by ambiguity, which both underlies and compounds the mis-interpretations noted above.

Similar anxiety was observed in the online reading groups, where students appeared to be easily disoriented, despite the guidelines and maps provided to help navigate time differences and locate online discussions, readings and other activities. We have learnt, though, that we can plan to reduce the disorientation in future reading groups and explicitly support participants in grasping subtle connotations in language use and to recognize different contexts in new environments, as suggested by Barna. Reflection on experiences of culture shock will also be a key strategy in the development of intercultural competence. Such reflective discussion has already been found to be a successful in an online course environment designed to prepare teachers for distance education (Davis and Nilakanta, 2003).

In conclusion, we believe that good practice in intercultural interaction through digital media is emerging and we will be able to develop a strong transatlantic doctoral community that expands the breadth of expertise available in the preparation of future leaders of educational technology. It should also be possible to understand our own diverse practices in doctoral education more deeply from a comparative view-point in education after some years during which we will be interpreting our cultural practices for each other and creating digital artefacts to illustrate contrasts and underlying principles that inform good practice. Our aim to better prepare future leaders of educational technology with inter-cultural competence and lived strategies to adopt and develop in their work appears achievable, through creation of our transatlantic community extended through a blend of digital media into our differing cultures. The imperative of peace and other motivations noted by Martin and Nakayma (2000) appear to have technology pushing us in an effective direction that may have important implications for education worldwide.

Acknowledgements

This chapter was informed by the ILET project supported by a grant from the Fund for the improvement of Postsecondary Education, US Department of Education. However, those contents do not necessarily represent the policy of the Department of Education, and you should not assume endorsement by the Federal Government. The DGEAC in the European Commission provided matching funds. ISU Council of International Programs also supported both projects.

References

Barna, L. M. (1994) Stumbling blocks in intercultural communication, in *Intercultural Communication: A reader*, eds L. A. Samovar and R. E. Porter, Wadsworth, Belmont, CA.

Baym, N. (2000) *Tune In, Log On: Soaps, fandom, and online community*, Sage, Thousand Oaks, CA.

Bonk, C. J. and King, K. S. (eds) (1998) *Electronic Collaborators: Learner-centered technologies for literacy, apprenticeship, and discourse.* Lawrence Erlbaum Associates, Maywah, NJ.

Cowen, R. (1997) Comparative perspectives on the British PhD, in *Working for a doctorate*, eds N. Graves and V. Varma, Routledge, London.

Davis, N. E. (1997) Do electronic communications offer a new learning opportunity in education? in *Using Information Technology Effectively in Teaching and Learning: Studies in pre-service and in-service teacher education*, eds B. Somekh and N. Davis, Routledge, London.

Davis, N. E. (2002) Leadership of information technology for teacher education: a discussion of complex systems with dynamic models to inform shared leadership, *Journal of Information Technology for Teacher Education*, 11, pp. 253–71.

Davis, N. E. and Nilakanta, R. (2003) Quality @ a distance includes preservice teachers: one case- and project-based approach, in *Quality Education @ a Distance*, ed. E. Stacey and G. Davies, Kluwer Academic Publishers, Dordrecht.

Furstenberg, G., Levet, S., English, K. and Maillet, K. (2001) [accessed 1 September 2003] Giving a virtual voice to the silent language of culture: the Cultra project, *Language Learning and Technology*, 5 (1), pp. 55–101 [Online] http://llt.msu.edu/vol5num1/furstenberg/default.html.

Hine, C. (2000) *Virtual Ethnography*, Sage, London.

LARA [Online, accessed 1 September 2003] European project learning and residence abroad, http://lara.fdtl.ac.uk/lara.

Macionis, J. J. (2003) *Sociology*, ninth edn, Prentice Hall, New Jersey.

Martin, J. N. and Nakayama, T. K. (2000) *Intercultural Communication in Contexts*, second edn, Mayfield Publishing Company, Mountain View, CA.

Mason, R. (1998) *Globalising Education: Trends and applications*, Routledge, London.

McLuhan, M. (1967) *The Medium is the Message*, Bantam, New York.

Miller, D. and Slater, D. (2001) *The Internet: An ethnographic approach*, Berg, Oxford.

Palloff, R. M. and Pratt, K. (1999) *Building Learning Communities in Cyberspace: Effective strategies for the on-line classroom*, Jossey Bass, San Francisco.

Preece, J. (2000) *Online Communities: Designing usability, supporting scalability*, John Wiley, New York.

UNESCO (2002) *ICT in Teacher Education: A planning guide*, UNESCO, Paris, France.

Part IV
Building communities

16 A cross-cultural cadence in E

Knowledge building with networked communities across disciplines and cultures

Elsebeth K. Sorensen and Eugene S. Takle

Introduction

Transcendence of constraints is at many levels a key element in the tapestry of expectations to the implementation of information and communication technologies (ICT) in processes of collaborative learning: transcendence of the limitations imposed on collaboration through the parameter of time; transcendence of distances enabling global access to learning resources hitherto unknown; transcendence of cultures connecting people across national borders, and transcendence of disciplines allowing for the design of more holistic, problem-oriented processes of learning in virtual environments. 'Learning together apart' (Kaye, 1992: 1) could be a suitable slogan for the expectation to learn through ICT now and in the future.

Distributed collaborative learning in virtual environments generally takes place through the learner's manipulation of symbols, including text, graphics, pictures and video (Sorensen, 1993). To establish a dimension of practice in virtual learning processes may be a complex task, which perhaps either requires the integration of computer supported collaborative learning (CSCL) tools, including shared whiteboard, shared document tools or the use of online simulation, which provide virtual practice. But there is also the possibility of achieving a dimension of practice through cross-disciplinary collaboration between courses.

This paper reports on the outcome of a cross-disciplinary and international collaboration between two web-based courses. Each in their own way, as well as together, mirror an attempt (through the use of two types of ICT) to transcend not only disciplines but also national borders, and to deal with the establishment of a dimension of practice in their learning processes. The two courses were: a Danish distributed CSCL course from the humanities on how to design teaching and learning in pedagogically appropriate ways using ICT technology (i.e. the whole research area of CSCL); and an American mixed-mode CSCL course (on-campus and web-delivered) from the sciences on global environmental issues. The collaboration has implied a transcendence of both geographical and conceptual borders. First, it transcends geographical borders, enabling knowledge dissemination and access to learning resources in a global sense. Second, the collaboration has implied a cross-disciplinary dimension. Finally, the collaboration has crossed the strong and traditional borders between the sciences and the humanities. The following sections describe the collaboration and its outcome.

The collaborating courses

The Danish course

The Danish course – at Aalborg University – was one of three courses in a one year distributed CSCL university education programme (within the humanities) for high school teachers and for people from the educational system of organizations, on how to implement, in pedagogically reflected ways, ICT in different types of learning processes. The one year education programme was offered as continuing education on a half-time basis.

- *Goals*: to be able to integrate ICT in teaching and processes of development in appropriate ways, and – at a high level – to be able to guide and implement the use of ICT in teaching and learning as well as in other organizational contexts.
- *Content*: the course dealt with the whole area of CSCL in the light of learning theory. In this way the course not only identified with the whole area of CSCL, but was also itself an example of what it was trying to teach.
- *Structure*: the course – as well as the whole education programme – was implemented on the Web, using the virtual environment 'Virtual-U' (developed at the Simon Fraser University in Vancouver) under the auspices of the asynchronous learning environment. Each of the two semesters contained two physical weekend seminars at the university.
- *Pedagogical model*: the pedagogical approach of the whole education programme has been 'Project-oriented Project Pedagogy' (POPP) (Dirckinck-Holmfeld, 1990; Fjuk and Dirckinck-Holmfeld, 1997). POPP has in fact been applied as the overall pedagogical approach of the entire university, across sciences in all teaching and learning activities. Within this pedagogical model the majority of activities take place as group activities, including the exam, and it has similarities with North-American 'problem solving' or 'project-based

learning' (Koschmann *et al.*, 1994), in the sense that students work on projects and try to address the problem in a scientific (empirical) manner rooted in practice. There is one essential point, however, where POPP differs from problem-based learning: the group 'owns' the problem, so to speak. In other words, the group itself has to find or construct the problem. POPP has its roots and ideology in the 'critical emancipatory thinking' established in the 1970s. A very important element in this approach to learning is a dimension of practice.

The US course

The US course – at Iowa State University – was a conventional course, within the sciences, for senior undergraduates or beginning graduate students at a US university. It has gradually migrated to a web base over the last five years, with new features being added as ancillary software has become available. We also have introduced learner-centred activities in place of or supplemental to conventional lectures.

- *Goals*: to help students come to an understanding of the interconnectedness of the global environment and the role of humans in charting its future trajectory, by design or default; to instil an appreciation for and recognition of authoritative literature on global-change issues; and to engage students within the course and across national and cultural boundaries in dialogue on global-change issues, including ethical issues.
- *Content*: the course encourages dialogue on the human role in the change in our global environment by putting students in the role of policy makers having to address the scientific, societal, political and ethical issues surrounding such issues as climate change, ozone depletion, deforestation, desertification, biodiversity, water degradation and global human population.
- *Structure*: the global change course consists of a sequence of learning modules on different global-change topics, each having evolved from a conventional university class time period. Each unit has a set of objectives, summary information on the topic, student-submitted collaborative (two or three students) summary of class time discussion, 'problems to ponder' as discussion starters for the electronic dialogue, and extensive lists of web and other information on the learning module topic. Each unit has its own electronic dialogue for student discussion among themselves and with outside experts or representatives of selected groups.
- *Pedagogical model*: students manage their interaction with the course and instructor through their personal electronic portfolios with

password protection (Taber *et al.*, 1997). Pre-class time electronic quizzes (available and automatically graded through the portfolio) require students to synthesize background material in preparation for class time discussion. Student 'ownership' of the course is encouraged through posting of student class time summary discussion. Electronic dialogue on individual learning unit topics is graded on the basis of both participation and quality of comments toward achieving unit learning objectives. An authentic research-quality climate model allows students to learn by experimentation about physical processes occurring at the plant–soil–atmosphere interface. Over the Internet, students pose questions, test hypotheses, execute numerical experiments, acquire tabular and graphical experimental results, and summarize results in either personal or group portfolios. The course is viewed by the designers as a laboratory for experimenting with a variety of pedagogical techniques and initiatives (Taber *et al.*, 1997).

The design of the collaboration

The whole collaboration was bridged on two learning technologies: the Web and video-conferencing. As an initial focal point for the collaboration, we designed an exercise for the Danish students, working within the context of their course on ICT and pedagogical methods, to work also within the context of the global change course as a basis for evaluating its functionality and pedagogical methods. These evaluations were done by use of technologies used in both courses: portfolio from global change and video-conference from the Danish sequence course. Each student was issued with a password-protected electronic portfolio as a launching point for exploring three features of the course, namely the use of quizzes and class summaries for encouraging integrative thinking, use of simulations as a means of allowing open-ended hypothesis testing, and use of the electronic portfolio as a personal space ('room' or 'office') for managing interaction with the course. Students used their portfolios to post their evaluations through both private comments to the instructors and through public postings by which they engaged in dialogue with other students and instructors.

A meeting between pedagogical traditions

The collaboration between the Aalborg University course and the Iowa State University course has brought together two different pedagogical traditions. It is interesting to note that the virtual software environment used in the Danish course was developed in North America. Academic and pedagogical tradition and didactic approaches in North America, within the area of open learning, differ from the Danish approaches in at least two ways.

First, it is part of the American pedagogical tradition that the role of the designer and the role of the teacher are often distributed between two people. This division is thus more easily applied and maintained, with an accompanying stronger emphasis on learning as 'instruction' with clearly defined tasks, techniques and didactics (Fjuk, 1998; Sorensen, 1997). This also counts for the US interpretation of 'collaborative learning'. The pedagogical tradition in Denmark does not prescribe a division of roles in terms of educational design and educational delivery. Consequently, the designer and the teacher are usually the same person. Also, partly as a result of this, educational didactics have not been standardized, but left to the individual academic to decide upon. In this respect, the global change course was an exception. Both design and delivery were carried out by the same team of people. This made the dynamic process of integrating learning processes in the virtual environment very smooth and fast.

Second, at Aalborg University all teaching and learning activities are based on the specific pedagogical theory and understanding of POPP (see also the section above on the Danish course). This means, among other things, that the problem or task for study cannot be part of any prior implemented direct instruction or formalized instructional technique. At a general level, the global change course was based on the pedagogical approach, which in North America is named 'cooperative learning'. It shares many features and techniques with 'collaborative learning', but at the same time it also differs in the degree of 'sharedness' of the activities and sub-tasks involved in the collaboration (Dillenbourg *et al.*, 1995). Put in mathematical terms we could say that the pedagogical approach of collaborative learning is a true subset of cooperative learning.

Principled discussion of joint outcome

Transcending geographical and conceptual borders in collaboration and learning is not a simple task (Martin and Nakayama, 2000). Nevertheless, even with fundamental differences in pedagogical understanding and approach, the collaboration has spawned new and valuable insights into the development and use of general instructional principles, methods, techniques and applied technologies in design of collaborative learning in virtual environments. The following discussion and evaluation of outcome of our collaboration will be approached mainly from the perspective of distributed CSCL. Consequently, although the mixed-mode global change course in principle covers two methodological sides in terms of design and delivery, it will be viewed and treated primarily from a distributed CSCL perspective.

Formalized techniques in the design of asynchronous distributed CSCL

Some of the techniques used on the American course are given below.

Quizzes

Extensive use of quizzes in learning was one of the reservations of the Danish side towards North American instructional tradition. For many years quizzes had been eliminated from Danish pedagogical thinking, but the collaboration brought them back into the light to be reviewed anew, and it was realized that an important pedagogical potential had been overlooked, and that learning could be supported in several ways using quizzes in reflective ways. Quizzes that simply lead to recall of facts are of little value in long-term learning; by contrast, quizzes that require reflective thinking and synthesis of ideas spanning different topics can stimulate deeper thinking. As implemented in the global change course, the student chooses the one correct answer but also has an online dialogue box to enter supporting (or challenging) information. Quiz results can assist the instructor in identifying issues that need additional attention. It should be pointed out, though, that constructing quiz questions that require synthesis is a complex task that requires discipline-specific and pedagogical knowledge.

Simulations

The global change course used simulations as ways for students to experiment with parts of the course content. Put in different terms, we may view this as a way of incorporating a dimension of symbolic practice into asynchronous distributed CSCL processes. If we assume a theoretical view of learning that recognizes the specific value of the dimension of practice as an important parameter in learning, then 'simulated practice' has a value comparable to physical practice. In addition, simulation techniques have value because they are consistent with the virtual, symbolic world. The value of simulation is well recognized with types of areas that imply physical training and skills, such as the training of pilots. However, it has not yet had the same status within areas that employ a high degree of reflection in learning, such as when students explore an infinite range of possible outcomes to test hypotheses. In sum, simulations provide students with access to computer-based models that can be used both in the theoretical realm of hypothesis testing and in the practical realm of the decision-making process.

Collaborative action and interaction (dialogue)

The pedagogical value of the collaborative learning activities in the global change course, such as class summaries, appeared beyond any doubt. Posting of class summaries by teams of two or three students, as in the case of global change, has great learning value in that it is a learner-driven activity, which requires some degree of 'understanding'. It also engages the students and supports the creation of (a learner-driven) electronic dialogue. However, the collaborative activity could be enhanced by asking students to formulate questions that will bridge the class time discussion on the face-to-face meeting in the global change course and the follow-on electronic dialogue on the same topic.

It frequently happens in the face-to-face discussion that questions come up for which no one has the answer or there is a need to do a calculation or gather together critically needed information to move the discussion thread forward. So, on this topic, the face-to-face discussion cannot move forward and is suspended. Such dilemmas can, however, more easily be handled in the asynchronous online environment. There is need to summarize online the face-to-face discussion so that the thread can be picked up and seamlessly be migrated to the Web and completed online.

Online portfolios

In the Danish course the idea of a personal space to provide 'home' and overview was provided through an individual homepage, as an external add-on to the Virtual-U environment, which the students themselves were able to tailor and 'furnish' as their skills for using the software tools for this developed gradually throughout the course. The forum intended to hold the personal dialogue with the teacher was not used. Being rooted deeply in the pedagogical idea of collaboration, only collaborative dialogue was encouraged. The learning process in a virtual world is lonely for some students and devoid of personal interaction. The evaluation of the electronic portfolios in the global change course indicated that a personal portfolio seem to offer a personal space to which the student could retreat for some security and control throughout the learning process.

When existing and acting in the virtual world, we often cannot directly use the knowledge of relation and navigation we are (bodily) familiar with from the real world (Lakoff and Johnson, 1980; Sorensen, 1991). This causes us to feel less in control, and this again produces insecurity, which does not promote motivation to stay and learn. A personal 'office' where the student feels pretty much in control (also with respect to the ability to 'furnish', etc.) could potentially be a tool, through which they can nourish their identity. In sum, merging the American use of electronic portfolios and the Danish idea of 'personal furnishing' seems the optimum choice.

Quantity and quality in the design of asynchronous distributed CSCL

Quantity as a means of stimulating interaction

The problem of stimulating interaction in online learning is very frequently experienced and is a problem reported in the literature concerning distributed CSCL. Much research generally sees this as a problem related to course design and facilitation (Feenberg, 1989; Fjuk, 1998; Sorensen, 1999). A certain apprehension has been formed by the position that in a free and truly student-owned dialogue one cannot 'force' student comments, the thinking being that 'force' is not a true learner-driven motivation for engaging in a dialogue. The problem of creating interaction remains a very complex problem, especially from a constructivist and collaborative theoretical position, in which interaction is viewed as a central key to learning. The problem of getting students to talk is a recurring problem, treated as 'lurking' (Feenberg, 1989) in the literature. We know that it may be rooted in socio-psychological issues, such as the fear of having a comment electronically stored for everyone to return to and be viewed by others as stupid, or perhaps inhibition with respect to expressing oneself in writing.

Requiring a minimum number of comments from students was not part of the Danish course, but it was part of the American one. The collaboration and evaluation done by the Danish students have caused the Danish side to acknowledge that 'forcing comments' may not be of much value in itself, but nevertheless is a very functional means of ensuring two types of learning processes occur: first, the student's formulation in writing of their thoughts, as writing is in some ways thinking made tangible; second, the stimulation of interaction and the communication of the ideas of 'presence' and 'shared space', a feeling conducive to learning. It is clear that the lack of shared physical implantation in *time* and *space* (the parameters usually providing consensus around communicative structure and status) is lacking in the online environment (Sorensen, 1999). Put in different terms, the symbolic character of the shared virtual environment (where the only sign of presence is 'a comment') causes a need for distributed learners to have part of their communicative actions functioning as expressions of 'presence'. Correspondingly, the 'presence' of others is a high motivating factor for expressing thoughts (only a few people engage in a verbal dialogue when they are all by themselves). 'Silence' in electronic dialogues communicates 'there is nobody here' (Feenberg, 1989). In sum, requiring numerous comments as a means of ensuring the development of a dynamic interactive dialogue should be viewed as a fruitful approach.

Use of quality and quantity for evaluation

The challenge of evaluation of online learning is also a recognized problem in distributed CSCL research. A challenging issue explored on the global change course has been the use of quantity and quality for evaluating/marking student performance in relation to the electronic dialogue. Quantity is, of course, easy to measure. Evaluating quality consists of looking for evidence of independent concept analysis, reflective thinking, going beyond material presented in the learning units, reporting a real-world observation that exemplifies a concept, or carrying out a calculation relating to a class item (e.g. one student calculated how much global sea level rose as a result of a break-off of a large chunk of ice from Antarctica). Examples of low quality include requesting factual information without stating a conceptual basis for needing such, stating an opinion with no logical basis, straying from the discussion topic without logical reason to do so, and lack of precision and brevity in discussion.

The metaphor of a committee meeting is used for the discussion, because it is the kind of experience that most students will face in employment situations. The metaphor implies processes like 'bringing information' or 'bringing some skill' that a committee needs to complete its task. The metaphor also denotes that participation by everyone is desirable and so, in the global change course, at least five electronic comments are required for full credit. The committee functions well when each member responds, when appropriate, to another committee member and so, in the global change course, each student must respond to at least two other students. The committee also functions well when each participant offers relevant information that contributes to the task; good information usually elicits response from others and irrelevant information usually leads to a change of topic. Committee participants should come to the meeting prepared, so they should not ask questions for which information was provided in advance unless it was unclear. Therefore, in the global change course, online discussion should not ask for a repeat of class material, but should include requests for clarification or implications that provide high-quality discourse, thereby advancing the dialogue at an authoritative level.

Using this evaluation model, the following discussion characteristics are rewarded as being high quality because they help the committee move toward achieving its task: questions requesting clarification of ambiguous points; new and relevant authoritative information; opinions substantiated with logical arguments from accepted facts; synthesis of given information; hypotheses whose testing would lead to new insight; or a calculation that reveals new insights e.g. a calculation of rise of sea level. On the other hand, the following characteristics do not lead to a productive committee process but may contribute to a loss of credibility to the author: sweeping generalizations; impractical solutions; unsubstantiated claims; questions raised that are broad and reverse the progress of the discussion; and degrading or impolite comments.

The instructor's portfolio view allows the instructor to distil an individual student's discussion messages in a single document. This allows scanning of responses over all topics for a single student to look for patterns of the characteristics listed above. The instructor is helped somewhat by a form of peer evaluation in that interesting topics usually generate many comments, and irrelevant dialogue often goes unanswered.

Structure and meta-communication in the design of asynchronous distributed CSCL

Research shows evidence of an enlarged need for structure and structuring at all levels in online learning processes. The global change course has indicated that employment of structure should not only be concerned with the overall learning design and with communication, including a consistent structuring of the electronic fora, but it should also be employed in the detailed structuring, contextualizing and meta-communication of each little building stone of content in building the learning process. In the global change course, for example, the learning overview unit 1–1 with the NASA picture was judged by the Danish students as an excellent example of careful and thorough content-process building. Although first and second generation distance learning materials have demonstrated a clear focus on structuring content, this seems to be a part of the past in many cases of third or fourth generation distance education. The move to third generation was a very radical move to a qualitatively new organization or paradigm for distance education (Nipper, 1989; Sorensen 1997), which left the focus on content behind and changed the role of the teacher (Davis and Nilakanta, 2003). Reflections on the 'content' of a course based on the Internet have mostly been concerned with trying to employ the potential of 'new multimedial ways to communicate the content'; in other words, a perspective aiming at enhancing – through the use of pictures, graphics, sound, etc. – the quality of the material by employing other 'senses' of the learners, having different preferences in relation to learning styles and perception.

The use of video-conferencing in the design of asynchronous distributed CSCL

In the Danish course the use of video-conferencing was implemented in the design as a way of getting practical experience with a technique treated theoretically as part of the content. Therefore reflection on own experience in relation to both form and event was part of their challenge. Overall the video-conference of one an a half hours was perceived as a good experience and considered a valuable tool for distributed collaborative learning situations, in which synchrony in time usually is an exception. There were comments which suggested that the 'scene' on the Danish side could be improved, that it was too much like watching TV because of the setting. However, the very interactive way the session was composed on the American side in small thematic units was perfect and allowed for a very interactive experience, so much so that at times it totally eliminated the feeling of TV watching. A way of improving the setting could be for the Danish side to have teams of four students, each clustered around individual small tables, with each team having responsibility for a particular theme. This would emulate news analysis TV programmes where a team of four news analysts or subject experts enter into a dialogue with a remote person. However, it would make more work for the camera person, who would have to move from one table to another. The recording of the video-conference was implemented on the Web in the virtual environment of the Danish course, so that the remote students who were not able to participate could access the resource from home.

In sum, the video-conference worked as a very creative and interactive tool. There are some important key points that are likely to be important for a good learning experience. Prior preparation through dialogue in portfolio between the parties to the videoconference promotes acquaintance and security to talk. In addition, composing the session in small interactive units also allows for mutual dialogue.

Conclusions and future perspectives

This paper has described the outcome of a process of 'mutual learning' achieved through a diversity established across national borders. By use of a cross-disciplinary and cross-cultural collaboration between two web-based courses, we have explored issues like pedagogical approaches to collaborative learning and evaluation of learning in asynchronous, distributed virtual environments on the Web. A variety of online pedagogical problems and techniques have been treated and considered, and two important tools for collaboration in distributed CSCL have been evaluated. The next phase of our cross-cultural and cross-disciplinary collaboration will be to build on this initial experiment to explore ways of infusing project elements indigenous to the Danish system into the global change course and to deploy some web-based functionality developed in the global change course into the Danish sequence of courses.

The overall intention behind the collaboration has been mutual learning and knowledge building across both disciplines and national borders. In very broad terms, the Danish course is an example of what it teaches, and the collaboration has brought a dimension of virtually based 'practice' and of 'reflection in practice' into the distributed CSCL situation of the Danish students. As for the American course, some pedagogical aspects of the global change course were evaluated using the pedagogical tools within the course itself, and the designers enjoyed the benefit of feedback from the Danish students on design, delivery and pedagogical techniques. The synergy of web-based learning and videoconferencing were also explored within the cross-disciplinary context for collaborative learning.

Acknowledgments

Contributors to the design and implementation of the global change course include Doug Fils, Michael Taber, Jennifer Hodson and David Flory. The course was implemented under the auspices of the International Institute of Theoretical and Applied Physics. Contributors to the design and implementation of the Danish course include Thue Ørberg at the Institute of Communication, Aalborg University, and the Danish students participating in the evaluation of the global change course.

References

Davis, N. E. and Nilakanta, R. (2003) Quality @ a distance includes preservice teachers: one case- and project-based approach, in *Quality Education @ a Distance*, eds E. Stacey and G. Davies, Kluwer Press, Amsterdam.

Dillenbourg, P., Baker, M., Blaye, A. and O'Malley, C. (1995) The evolution of research on collaborative learning, in *Learning in Human and Machines: Towards an interdisciplinary learning science*, eds P. Reimann and H. Spada, pp. 189–211, Pergamon, London.

Dirckinck-Holmfeld, L. (1990) *Kommunikation på trods og på tværs, Projektpædagogik og datakonferencer i fjernundervisning*, Aalborg University: Picnic-Nyt (9), Aalborg.

Feenberg, A. (1989) The written world, in *Mindweave: Communication, computers, and distance education*, eds R. Mason and A. R. Kaye, pp. 22–40, Pergamon Press, Oxford.

Fjuk, A. and Dirckinck-Holmfeld, L. (1997) [accessed 2nd September 2003] Articulation of actions in distributed collaborative learning, *Scandinavian Journal of Information Systems*, 9 (2) [Online] http://www.intermedia.uio.no/cool/docs/F&D-97.pdf.

Fjuk, A. (1998) *Computer Support for Distributed Collaborative Learning: Exploring a complex problem area*, Dr Scient Thesis, Department of Informatics, University of Oslo.

Kaye, A. R. (1992) Learning together apart, in *Collaborative Learning Through Computer Conferencing*, ed. A. R. Kaye, pp. 1–24, Springer-Verlag, The NATO ASI series, Heidelberg.

Koschman, T. D., Myers, A. C., Feltovich, P. J. and Barrows, H. S. (1994) Using technology to assist in realizing effective learning and instruction:

a principled approach to the use of computers in collaborative learning, *Journal of the Learning Sciences*, 3 (3), pp. 227–64.

Lakoff, G. and Johnson, M. (1980) *Metaphors We Live By*, The University of Chicago Press, Chicago.

Martin, J. N. and Nakayama, T. K. (2000) *Intercultural Communication in Contexts*, second edition, Mayfield Publishing Company, Mountain View, CA.

Nipper, S. (1989) Third generation distance learning and computer conferencing, in *Mindweave: Communication, computers, and distance education*, eds R. Mason and A. R. Kaye, pp. 63–73, Pergamon Press, Oxford.

Sorensen, E. K. (1991) Metaphors and the design of the human interface, in *Collaborative Learning through Computer Conferencing: The Najaden papers*, eds A. R. Kaye, pp. 189–99, Springer-Verlag, The NATO ASI series, Heidelberg.

Sorensen, E. K. (1993) Dialogues in networks, in *The Computer as Medium*, eds P. B. Andersen, B. Holmqvist and J. F. Jensen, pp. 389–421, Cambridge University Press, Cambridge.

Sorensen, E. K. (1997) Learning in virtual contexts, in *Navigation, Interaction, and Collaboration*, PhD-afhandling, Aalborg Universitet, Denmark.

Sorensen, E. K. (1999) Collaborative learning in virtual contexts: representation, reflection and didactic change, presented at the ICTE99 conference, Edinburgh, March.

Taber, M. R., Takle, E. S. and Fils, D. (1997) Use of the internet for student self-managed learning, in preprints Sixth Symposium on Education, American Meteorological Society, Long Beach, California, February.

17 Telecollaborative communities of practice in education within and beyond Canada

Thérèse Laferrière, Alain Breuleux and Gaalen Erickson

Introduction

Lifelong learning is on the rise. All forms of learning contribute to fill the educational needs created by the social expectations of a knowledge society: formal learning in institutional settings; non-formal learning in workplace settings; and informal learning that may happen in any setting. Communities of practice are primarily hubs of informal learning, as demonstrated by Lave and Wenger (1991). For many centuries, they were the place for apprenticeship, but they faded into the background during the twentieth century as formal educational structures developed. Today, there is renewed interest in communities of practice and informal learning. For instance, Human Resources Development Canada is increasingly using the terminology of communities of practice, and a variety of organizations throughout our large country have begun to promote this form of learning using communities of practice in a strategic way. Digital technologies are not immune to these trends of informal learning and collaborative practice. An example of the use of these digital technologies in an informal educational setting is the SchoolNet Canada Initiative (http://www.schoolnet.ca), which has provided a unique context for the promotion of collaboration within and between learning communities. Teachers at all levels of the professional development continuum may potentially benefit from social participation in such a community. Participation in a community of practice is a powerful form of learning (Lave and Wenger, 1991). When expertise is de-localized or distributed, we have found that communities that combine face-to-face and online activities provide more learning opportunities to their members. To enhance teacher learning is important because it 'reaps learning gains for students, especially in the kinds of more challenging learning that new standards demand' (Darling-Hammond, 1998).

Not surprisingly, the Internet has been supporting communities of interest and diverse forms of online sharing. Web site addresses for resources and lesson plans were first to evolve. Then educational organizations adopted email and developed web sites to portray their school, professional organization or department. Now there is an emerging use of knowledge management tactics and online tools such as discussion forums in order to enhance participatory activities and even structure modes of telecollaboration within and between educational organizations. This chapter focuses on the latter. We will describe a project that enhances education and teacher education both locally and across organizations. We present an account of what is possible when it comes to accessing knowledge situated in educational organizations, be it a school or a university, and to mobilizing knowledge gained on-site and online. We have organized this chapter as follows: a brief description of our conceptual framework; the process of co-designing telecollaborative communities of practice in educational settings along with examples; an illustration of the development of one of these communities; and finally the lessons that we have learned from our work.

Conceptual framework

Learning and knowledge work are the result of cognitive and social activity. Studies on cognition, often called cognitivism or constructivism, have offered evolving conceptions of knowledge to educators, moving progressively from behaviourism to more cognitive and socio-cultural models of learning. Today, the professional knowledge base is inclusive of both individual and social approaches to knowledge. The approaches cohabit; knowledge is no longer conceived as just a product of the individual mind, but as the result of a collective endeavour and includes both cultural-historical and socio-cultural perspectives.

Socio-constructivism is an important foundation for the professional educator who fosters social interaction for purposes of learning (Vygotsky, 1978) and of knowledge-building (Bereiter and Scardamalia, 1989). Student engagement is understood to be the key and the learner-centred principles put forward by the American Psychological Association (1993) are illustrative of this position. Pre-service and in-service teacher education is no exception. The authors of this chapter are working in traditional universities in Quebec (Laval University, McGill University) and British Columbia (University of British Columbia), and we apply constructivist perspectives in both our teaching and research with teachers-to-be and practising teachers.

Our use of digital technologies, especially discussion forums, has been guided by socio-constructivist and socio-cultural perspectives. While conducting various learning activities, we have applied participatory design features and turned our classrooms into network-enabled communities of practice. The two key socio-cultural concepts that are central to understanding the dynamics of learning in communities of practice are legitimate peripheral participation and situatedness of activity:

- *Legitimate peripheral participation*: Lave and Wenger (1991) reformulated the more traditional conceptions of learning by locating it in a participation framework rather than describing it as a body of knowledge located in the head of the individual. That is, in a community of practice, the individual is not learning a discrete body of abstract knowledge meant to be applied in later contexts, but is being inducted in a set of social practices through a process they call 'legitimate peripheral participation'. For instance, a pre-service teacher who is doing a practicum with an experienced teacher is learning to teach by performing under attenuated conditions and with limited responsibilities.With time, the pre-service student teachers become more competent at learning to teach and they gain increased access to the exercise of more complex roles in the practice of teaching.
- *Situatedness of activity*: Situated learning, as defined by Lave and Wenger, is the kind of social engagement that provides the context for one's learning. This concept expresses Lave and Wenger's view that 'agent, activity and the world mutually constitute each other' (1991: 33). The authors see it as a transitory concept 'between a view according to which cognitive processes (and thus learning) are primary and a view according to which social practice is the primary, generative phenomenon and learning is one of its characteristics' (1991: 34). In their view, learning is not simply 'some reifiable process that just happened to be located somewhere; learning is an integral part of generative social practice in the lived-in world' (1991: 35).

Communities of practice are 'nodes for the dissemination, interpretation and use of information. They are nodes of communication' (Wenger, 1998: 252). Wenger (1998) presented a community of practice as being a composite of the three following characteristic elements: mutual engagement to do things together and to act as a collective; a negotiated joint enterprise towards which members feel a responsibility; and a shared repertoire of resources including tools, experiences and stories. 'Mutual engagement' describes the way that the members of a community of practice interact with one another in order to improve what they do. What gives coherence to this interaction is the mutual engagement of participants within the community as they negotiate how something is to be done. Practice does not exist in the abstract. It exists because people clarify and define how actions should be done under specific circumstances and how their actions could be improved. 'Joint enterprise' describes the way the members of a community of practice are engaged in the same kind of work. Their practices are the property of the community that they form over time by the sustained pursuit of the same large purpose. Finally, 'shared repertoire' of the members of a community of practice is the work that they do, plus methods, techniques, tools, routines, concepts, stories and gestures that the community has produced or adopted in the course of its existence and which have become part of its practice. It also includes the language that members use to describe their work, as well as the styles by which they express their forms of membership and their identities as members.

Telecollaborative communities of practice in education are an existing community of practice that may use electronic networks for information sharing or online social interaction, within and beyond its primary unit or organization, or its very existence may be the result of the advent and use of digital technologies. Where there is a broad diversity of expertise in a telecollaborative community (such as researchers, teacher educators, teachers and students), the possibilities for increased learning by all of the participants is extended. Learning and knowledge building digital artefacts are evidence of how members create meaningful statements about the world and of how the gap between theory and practice may be reduced. Two socio-cultural concepts that are key to this understanding of telecollaborative communities will now be described: reification and regime of competence (Wenger, 1998):

- *Reification*: Digital technologies play a fundamental role in allowing one to enter a telecollaborative community of practice and see the manifestations or reifications of the community. The community's web site becomes an artefact of this learning: mission statement, participation forums, online productions and, in some cases, data-collection tools and research results. In other words, what used to be in files or on the walls is digitalized. Virtual participation in the social practice emerges as a new kind of learning: for instance, in the LeTUS Community, devoted to project-based science in the Detroit urban schools (http://www.letus.org), teachers write and illustrate projects they have conducted with their students.
- *Regime of competence*: These forms of memory provide the basis for the evolution of the practice of the community; participants draw on their tacit and reified knowledge and a locally negotiated regime of competence unfolds (Wenger, 1998: 86). Earlier, Brown and Duguid (1991) had pointed out that learning and knowledge building within communities of practice is visible through: (1) narratives, used for diagnosing problems and as repositories of existing knowledge; (2) collaboration, as members engage in and share a common practice; (3) common understanding of the community's practice and common understanding of how to solve problems – knowing is validated and evolves through the negotiation of meaning (socio-constructivism).

For Wenger, knowledge, including new knowledge, is fundamentally related to practice: 'Knowing is defined only in the context of specific practices, where it arises out of the combination of a regime of competence and an experience of meaning' (1998: 141).

Participatory design of the TeleLearning PDS in Canada

Participatory design (co-design) of telecollaborative communities of practice is a new practice in and of itself. It was the first principle applied in the design of the TeleLearning Professional Development School (PDS) (http://www.telelearning-pds.org). The co-design of the TeleLearning Professional Development School Project, distributed across four universities in three provinces resulted in thousands of Canadian teachers, pre-service teachers and teacher educators (21 university-based teacher educators, 680 pre-service teachers and 2,350 school teachers) participating in telecollaborative communities of practice in order to gain insight into thoughtful and effective uses of digital technologies for learning and knowledge building purposes.

Leading teacher educators shared an interest in renewing university and school practices by enhancing community and using telelearning tools to this end. They cultivated local university–school partnerships. In Montreal, for instance, the McGill Network of TeleLearning Professional Development Schools (http://www.education.mcgill.ca/olit/institute/) was a telecollaborative community of practice first grounded in a well-established tradition at McGill University, the Summer Institute for in-service teachers. Pre-service teachers, graduate students and teacher educators interested in the use of digital technologies in classrooms as well as in collaborative inquiry were part of the joint enterprise locally and beyond (Breuleux *et al.*, 1999).

On the national scene, telelearning teacher educators and leading educators shared a vision, interconnected learning communities, with the SchoolNet Advisory Board of Canada (Henchey *et al.*, 1996). SchoolNet Canada's GrassRoots Program provided funding to thousands of teachers who participated in a telecollaborative community and reported on over 26,000 collaborative learning projects. TeleLearning PDS participants were provided with this funding opportunity and also more advanced opportunities to learn from one another in both synchronous and asynchronous ways, on-site and online.

Each of the three primary local sites – University of British Columbia's Community of Inquiry in Teacher Education (Vancouver), McGill's TeleLearning Network of Professional Development Schools (Montreal) and Laval University's TACT Community (Quebec City) – developed and co-designed virtual environments for support and communication (1995 to the present). Over time these projects have inducted new members on an ongoing basis through a process of legitimate peripheral participation. Pre-service teachers, in-service teachers and teacher educators all contributed to the creation of online resources and tools to support the integration of digital technologies to learning and teaching. During the 1998–2002 period, these communities put the focus on learning-to-teach in network-enabled classrooms through collaborative enquiry. This focus on enquiry is exceptionally exemplified by the Center for Learning Technologies in Urban Schools (http://www.letus.org), which unites teachers and researchers from the Chicago Public Schools, the Evanston Public Schools, the Detroit Public Schools, Northwestern University and the University of Michigan to design curricula for middle school science classes (Blumemfeld *et al.*, 2000). Participants engaged in site-based enquiries. The social practice became that of learning to teach with digital technologies through collaborative enquiry (situatedness of activity), one that has led to a number of socio-technical designs (Breuleux *et al.*, 2002). For example, The Community of Inquiry for Teacher Education is a pre-service teacher education cohort based at the University of British Columbia (CITE, http://www.educ.ubc.ca/courses/cite/) and it was designed to promote enquiry among all of the participants in three inter-connected communities of practice (Erickson *et al.*, in press). It uses a variety of digital tools including an online course, discussion forums, web-based assignments and electronic portfolios as a means of promoting enquiry among all three communities. CITE students have engaged in telecollaboration with other groups of students, teachers and researchers from other institutions across Canada and in Australia as they explored educational issues from a variety of perspectives and educational contexts.

Some participants have seen the responsibilities of and possibilities for their work expand, and conceived of themselves as network-enabled teachers (see Wenger's concept of identity, 1998). As pointed out by Lieberman (2003), 'professional networks can be construed as social practices that bind people together and provide a place and space for them to learn from one another – face to face and across great distances'.

Development of the TACT community

TACT (Technology for Advanced Collaboration among Teachers/ TéléApprentissage Communautaire et Transformatif; http://www.tact.fse.ulaval.ca) is a telecollaborative community of practice that began in 1995. With other TeleLearning-NCE researchers, its designers shared the view that collaboration was a very promising avenue for taking advantage of digital technologies for learning. A network of associated schools was being established at Laval University. The designers' idea was to create a telelearning professional development school by adding a fourth dimension, telelearning, to the professional development school model (Holmes Group, 1990), which already combined pre- and in-service teacher education as well as collaborative research. The TeleLearning-PDS was the first to be a virtual community of support and communication within the Research Network (Laferrière *et al.*, 1997).

Although participants were early adopters of digital technologies, they were primarily teacher educators and in-service teachers engaged in face-to-face professional development activities. Learning about digital technologies was their joint enterprise. Participants with basic technology skills focused on the integration of digital technologies to curricula. The more access to digital technology, the more they could explore possibilities of its use. Expertise developed in a number of schools, but most strikingly in a school-within-a-school programme where every student owned a laptop connected to the Internet in their classroom and at home (PROTIC Program, http://www.protic.net).

Beginning in 1998, pre-service teachers doing their student teaching on-site began to actively participate in online, collaborative, reflective practice using Virtual-U VGroups or Knowledge Forum and so gain legitimate peripheral participation in the PROTIC Community of Practice. They tackled authentic problems of practice through the use of digital technologies for learning purposes. Using Wenger's analytical framework, the analysis of one electronic forum by an outside researcher (Benoit, 2000) led to the following observations:

- *Mutual engagement*: Participants (Fall 1999) wrote a total of 301 messages over a six-month period. They posted concerns, descriptions and interpretations and critical comments.
- *Joint enterprise*: Participants defined a specific shared goal: learning to conduct collaborative project-based learning with school learners. They discussed means, elaborated strategies and consulted with one another.
- *Shared repertoire*: They used specific resources of the TACT repertoire and coordinated their actions. Negotiation, ownership and evaluation were features of their work.
- *Reification*: Cultural objects included the technological tools used to fulfil their mandate. Laval University's 'student-teaching red book' was reinterpreted so as to align with both the actions of the PROTIC Community of Practice and the general aims of the teacher education programme. Graduating student teachers left learning artefacts to the community (Laferrière, 2002).
- *Regime of competence*: Pre-service teachers doing their student teaching in student-owned laptop classrooms (in the PROTIC Program) were in a unique position to enquire into the effective uses of digital technologies due to easy access to technology, reflective time built into their training programme and mentorship from more expert participants. Their contribution to the advancement of practical knowledge through collaborative inquiry, within TACT, was

significant. For instance, three student teachers created carefully designed simulations for math and science learning using Cabri-Géomètre, a French software similar to Geometers SketchPad. Their simulations have been used within and beyond the PROTIC Community of Practice.

Every year their learning artefacts become more impressive. This can be partly explained by incoming participants' better acquaintance with basic digital technologies and partly by the telecollaborative community of practice's shared repertoire. Student teachers' learning artefacts, in-service teachers' and graduate students' online discussions and web pages, school-based and university-based teacher educators' research results are made available to incoming participants. All of these artefacts are devoted to the effective use of digital technologies in network-enabled classrooms and schools and relate to the study of authentic problems. Virtual practica for newcomers are now also part of the shared repertoire for pre- and in-service teachers as well as teacher educators. For instance, one virtual tour has been designed, mostly by graduating student teachers, to illustrate the learning and knowledge-building artefacts of six pre-service teachers involved in telecollaboration and knowledge building using the Knowledge Forum suite of tools. For instance, this activity contributed to the understanding of network-enabled learning communities and to the clarification of the role of the teacher as a guide in PROTIC classrooms. Although each semester of student teachers form a distinct network-enabled community of learners engaged in onsite and online activities with school learners as a part of their coursework, cooperative teachers and university-based teacher educators are connected to the TACT Community. The increasing quality of the learning artefacts is what gives meaning and value to the development of the TACT Community. The value added is an acceleration of the learning experience for incoming participants: they demonstrate better performance than their predecessors in terms of advanced reflection and complex practice. Moreover, contrary to regular courses or practica, more of the instructor's time can be devoted to creative work because he or she has less repetitive information to give out from year to year. Part of the teacher/supervisor's responsibilities are taken on by participants as they interact with one another face-to-face and online, within and across cohorts. This includes orientation, training and demonstration of practice.

The added value of collaboration across organizations lies in the critical mass of innovative practices that exist in one specific domain and towards which participants feel some sense of relatedness. The critical mass of innovative practices is distributed among sites. Although these are culturally based, they add up to provide an important form of support for participants' own local leading-edge practice. That is to say that, in spite of the cultural differences of Francophone Laval and Anglophone McGill participants, they contribute to becoming part of one another's telecollaborative communities when engaging in collaborative teaching or inquiry. For instance, they have explored problems such as the multidimensionality of discourse in discussion forums. Currently, participants from both institutions are investigating the role of the teacher in an action-research project conducted in remote small rural schools that have become network-enabled.

The TACT Community also collaborates with the Institute for Knowledge Innovation and Technology, Ontario Institute for Studies in Education in the University of Toronto (IKIT). The IKIT community extends online to Canadian and international members. Members of TACT are now joining local and distant practising teachers and researchers engaged in IKIT, employing asynchronous and synchronous online activities, using Knowledge Forum, the telephone and iVisit for teleconferences and video-conferences. Members of both communities have connected with the Center for Innovative Learning Technologies, based at four different locations in the United States (Doubler *et al.*, 2000). Furthermore, socio-technical issues were discussed with the designers of TAPPED-IN, an online community for teacher professional development fostered by a single organization (Schlager *et al.*, 2002). Now that TeleLearning-NCE funding is over, new funding sources have been secured for the TACT Community to continue to evolve and bridge teaching and research practices for enhancing teacher education and professional development.

Lessons learned

Telecollaboration is social innovation. It is well known in group psychology that collaboration is difficult to achieve. Group processes need to be attended to: for instance, the development of trust, openness, self-realization and interdependence (see Gibb and Gibb, 1967). The leadership of the person or team initiating a telecollaborative community is most important at first, but leaders must nurture other members to play an increasingly important role in the community. Access to technology is necessary, but there would not be telecollaborative communities of practice without participants seeing the opportunity to mutually engage in a joint enterprise likely to lead to satisfactory results. By design, the TeleLearning-PDS could only grow out of on-site successes at using digital technologies for learning and knowledge building purposes. Together, telecollaborative communities of practice created a shared repertoire characterized by a critical mass of reified objects, tools, learning and knowledge-building artefacts.

Telecollaborative communities of practice need to focus. Not only do communities of practice need a purpose, but they must have focus. In

Phase I (1995–97), forms of telecollaboration included posting a document online, sharing an experience, inviting newcomers into one's discussion forum, enquiring into a significant question and building knowledge. In Phase II (1998–2002), the designers of the TeleLearning-PDS chose deep understanding of the use of digital tools for learning as its focus of collaborative enquiry. Teaching for understanding in schools was the theme for undergraduate and graduate learners, teachers and teacher educators as learners and knowledge builders. Understanding one's own practice in network-enabled classrooms and that of others became the task at hand.

Substantive online discourse is the key. Common to all local telecollaborative communities of practice was the production of web pages, but it is online discourse that allowed for negotiation of meaning regarding a particular object of study or problem solving. Participation in online discourse was supported by electronic forums that were easily accessible (WebCT or eGroups) or by other forums that had special features such as multiple message classification and scaffolding devices. Participants need support but also need challenges to their opinions and ideas for collaborative reflective practice to advance.

The cultivation of telecollaborative communities of practice is a long-term process. Telecollaborative communities of practice emerge because early adopters of digital technologies see the possibility for fruitful human interaction dedicated to professional development. They also demonstrate sustained engagement in developing authentic online activities and meaningful productions that reify on-site activity and contribute to the negotiation of the regime of competence of the emerging telecollaborative community of practice. Schools and universities and their annual cohorts of students bring continuity and resources to telecollaborative communities of practice.

Telecollaborative communities of practice can develop bridges between university-based participants and school-based participants in ways that were hardly conceivable a decade ago. TeleLearning-PDS telecollaborative communities of practice are a clear manifestation of the claim that the division between formal and informal educational settings is eroding. The division between research and practice is also blurred. For instance, TACT is described in French as a 'communauté d'apprentissage, de recherche et de pratique' because formal and informal learning through practice and research are all key characteristics. As pointed out by Daele and Charlier, it is 'the capacity of a community of practice to conceptualize, reify and disseminate shared knowledge and knowledge building results that often contribute to the professional recognition of learning communities and communities of practice' (2002: 123).

Telecollaborative communities of practice have to be strong locally in order to reach out and have a significant impact on a broader basis.

In order to tap the emancipatory potential of technology for communities of practice, participants begin by conducting significant activity at a local level and then reach out to others working in other contexts. This is reflected, for instance, in the telecollaborative community of practice designed by Judi Harris. In Canada, she has influenced the McGill Network of TeleLearning-PDSs as well as teachers from the Province of Alberta (http://www.2learn.ca/Projects/Together/judi.html). Meanwhile, the TeleLearning-PDS has been a partner in the development of SchoolNet Canada (http://www.schoolnet.ca/home/e/research.asp). Lieberman (2003) has observed the same phenomenon in her study of teacher networks and notes that 'school reform networks suggest a different means of spreading reform – by scaling down (building local networks) in order to scale up (the more locals, the larger the network)'.

Summary

This chapter articulates a view of learning that is based on social participation and community membership and presents new forms of collaboration to enhance teacher education and professional development that make effective use of digital technologies to create telecollaborative communities of practice. Through participation in several research and development projects, thousands of Canadian teachers, student teachers and teacher educators have engaged in telecollaborative communities of practice that enhanced individuals' learning and supported the development of their professional development programmes over a six-year period. Participants' engagement in authentic tasks at local sites supported with digital media was essential for the virtual community's evolution. Design principles, conceptual and technical tools resulted in a rich discourse and the sharing of many learning artefacts with the ongoing community of practice. Research showed that telecollaboration is a social innovation, rather than technological and that telecollaborative communities of practice need to have a focus; to engage in substantive discourse online; to commit to a long-term process of cultivation; and to be strong locally in order to reach out and have a significant impact on the broader educational community. Finally, and most importantly, telecollaborative communities of practice can develop bridges between university-based participants and school-based participants that were hardly conceivable a decade ago.

This different view of learning, based on social participation and community membership, presented new forms of collaboration that enhance teacher education and professional development enabled by digital technologies. A shared vision, a capacity to connect and a desire for innovation in teaching (process and content) are, however, essential to the co-design and cultivation of telecollaborative communities of practice. Pre-service teachers need to be attuned to the constraints and resources, the limits and possibilities, involved in the practices of local communities investigating how to use digital technologies in thoughtful and effective ways. In-service teachers need not be afraid of publishing their results online (semi-public collaborative spaces) for the sake of their own professional development and that of other teachers. Teacher educators need to find creative ways of combining teaching and research in ways that not only enhance their own learning but also the collective knowledge of teacher professional communities. We submit that the perspective on learning and the models of telecollaborative communities that we have described above have both promise and potential for educators around the world who are seeking to bring about changes in their own practices and programmes. They should provide concrete exemplars and a common repertoire of objects and practices for others wishing to participate in similar endeavours. Finally, we are reminded of Fullan's (2000) claim that sustained educational change requires internal change, active connection to the outside community and a challenging, but nurturing external infrastructure. Telecollaborative communities of practice offer some promise in this regard.

Acknowledgements

The TeleLearning Professional Development School (TeLeLearning-PDS) Project was part of the activities of the Educating Educators Research Team and partners funded by the TeleLearning Network of Centres of Excellence (TeleLearning-NCE), Canada.

References

American Psychological Association (1993) *Learner-centered Psychological Principles: Guidelines for school redesign and reform,* Presidential Task Force on Psychology in Education, Washington, DC.

Benoit, J. (2000) Une communauté de pratique en émergence: Les stagiaires de l'École secondaire des Compagnons-de-Cartier, Étude de cas.

Bereiter, C. and Scardamalia, M. (1989) Intentional learning as a goal of instruction, in *Knowing, Learning, and Instruction: Essays in honor of Robert Glaser,* ed. L. B. Resnick, *pp.* 361–92, Earlbaum, Hillsdale, NJ.

Blumenfeld, P., Fishman, B. J., Kraicik, J., Marx, R. W. and Soloway, E. (2000) Creating usable innovations in systemic reform: Scaling-up technology-embedded project-based science in urban schools, *Educational Psychologist,* 35 (3), pp. 149–64.

Breuleux, A., Laferrière, T., Owston, R., Resta, P. and Hunter, B. (1999) [accessed 15 April 2003] *CollabU: A design for reflective, collaborative university teaching and learning,* Computer Supported Collaborative Learning Conference at Stanford Proceedings, Menlo Park, CA [Online] http://kn.cilt.org/cscl99/A07/A07.HTM.

Breuleux A., Erickson, G., Laferrière, T. and Lamon, M. (2002) Devis sociotechniques pour l'établissement de communautés d'apprentissage en réseau: Principes de conception et conditions de réussite résultant de plusieurs cycles d'intégration pédagogique des TIC, *Revue des sciences de l'éducation*, 28 (2), pp. 411–34.

Brown, J. S. and Duguid, P. (1991) Organizational learning and communities of practice: toward a unified view of working, learning and innovation, *Organization Science*, 1 (1), pp. 40–47.

Daele, A. and Charlier, B. (eds) (2002) Les communautés délocalisées d'enseignants, European Commission, Programme Numérisation pour l'Enseignement et la Recherche: Observation des usages et des pratiques dans le domaine de l'enseignement scolaire, Volet Usages et Normes, Usages et pratiques de ressources numérisées dans le domaine de l'enseignement.

Darling-Hammond, L. (1998) Teacher learning that supports student learning, *Educational Leadership*, 55 (5), pp. 6–11.

Doubler, S., Laferrière, T., Lamon, M., Rose, R. *et al.* (2000) [accessed 26 March 2003] The next generation of teacher online learning: a developmental continuum, a white paper, Centre for Innovation in Knowledge Technology [Online] http://www.cilt.org/resources/online_Learning.html.

Erickson, G., Darling, L., Clarke, A., Mitchell, J. *et al.* (in press) Creating a community of inquiry in a teacher education programme, in *Paradigmes Socioconstructivistes et Formation des Intervenants*, eds N. Bednarz and P. Jonnaert, Editions de Boeck, Brussels.

Fullan, M. (2000) The three stories of education reform, *Phi Delta Kappan*, 81 (8), pp. 581–4.

Gibb, J. and Gibb, L. (1967) Humanistic elements in group growth, in *Challenges of humanistic psychology*, ed. J. Bugental, pp. 161–70, McGraw-Hill, New York.

Henchey, N., Breuleux, A., Laferrière, T., Moll, M. *et al.* (1996) [accessed 15 April 2003] Vision of learners in the 21st century: vision statement, SchoolNet Canada [Online] http://www.schoolnet.ca/general/visions/e/vision.html.

Holmes Group (1990) *Tomorrow's Schools: A report of the Holmes Group*, Holmes Group, East Lansing, MI.

Laferrière, T. (2002) Telelearning: distance and telos, *Journal of Distance Education*, 17 (3), pp. 29–45.

Laferrière, T., and Willinsky, J. (1997) Patterns of connection, paper presented at the Annual Meeting of the American Educational Research Association, April, Chicago.

Lave, J. and Wenger, E. (1991) *Situated Learning: Legitimate peripheral participation*, Cambridge University Press, Cambridge.

Lieberman, A. (2003) Network geographies of educational change: the case of the national writing project, communication presented at the annual meeting of the American Educational Research Association, April.

Schlager, M. S., Fusco, J. and Schank, P. (2002) Evolution of an on-line education community of practice, in *Building Virtual Communities: Learning and change in cyberspace*, eds K. A. Renninger and W. Shumar, pp. 129–58, Cambridge University Press, New York.

Vygotsky, L. S. (1978) *Mind in Society: The development of higher psychological processes*, Harvard University Press, Cambridge, MA.

Wenger, E. (1998) *Communities of Practice: Learning, meaning, and identity*, Cambridge University Press, New York.

18 Informatics teacher training in Hungary

Building community and capacity with tele-houses

Márta Turcsányi-Szabó

Introduction

This chapter describes a pilot project involving children from tele-houses. Tele-houses are learning communities in Hungary using two sets of web-based learning (WBL) materials developed by TEAM Lab (described later) and mentored by future informatics teachers. The materials are based on a constructivist approach that allows different learning styles to emerge. The pilot project has been in progress for two sessions with an 'action research' process that aims to build a suitable model extendable to the whole network of tele-houses in order to contribute to the introduction of capacity building through distance education for such regions. This model includes a pedagogic framework with theoretical background that will build capacity in underdeveloped regions. It could be further extended to build a network for capacity building in general through tele-houses, schools and homes. At the same time it also provides a possible solution for informatics teachers to remain in the profession by providing mentoring services at a distance, while also working in industry.

Information and communication technologies (ICT) in education in Hungary has its roots in computer studies in secondary schools. Currently there is a strong tendency to shift from computer science topics towards the application of ICT in all fields, aiming to encompass teachers in all subject areas with the application of innovative methods and resources to benefit learning. There are increasing numbers of computers in schools, but the teachers themselves are conservative about their use in education. Those who had the chance to learn innovative methods of using ICT in education have often moved into industry to make a better living. More and more informatics teachers graduate each year from our universities, but fewer and fewer of these teachers remain in educational settings due to the low pay in comparison to industry.

Thus informatics teacher training requires a lot of investment and yet does not provide enough expertise for education, particularly in remote underdeveloped regions where the infrastructure does not facilitate new economies, and where there are no educational possibilities beyond the elementary school level. In some under developed parts of Hungary unemployment has soared to over 70 per cent, so the only realistic dream of young and old is to find a 'way out', often by moving away.

The Internet may support a way to develop these regions. However, promoting the use of computers with young children is an issue for some people. Although most people could agree that the Internet could serve adult education well, there is some opposition to virtual environments within children's learning (Colleen and Miller, 2003). There are successful projects, such as that led by Cohen (1987), where small children were better able to overcome their disabilities and attained enhanced learning more quickly by mastering the essence of written language and communication with others. Children can learn through the Internet without the help of adults about topics of their own interest, and this develops autonomy and self-esteem. In some situations, when the younger generation is the first to be fluent with technology, knowledge is actually transferred by the children themselves to their parents and family in a natural and effective way.

There are also concerns that Internet overuse or misuse might amplify problems, and that radical changes are needed in pedagogy in order to benefit from use. Rather than just gathering information, the Internet should be used to construct knowledge by learning to learn and developing problem solving skills, plus helping learners appreciate other cultures and enrich their lives. Furthermore, the impact of the Internet on different societies and on people with disabilities is significant. There is also potential to diminish disadvantage. Distance, local and individual challenges may be bypassed with access to a range of tele-learning and tele-mentoring facilities. Minorities and isolated groups can be provided with insights into differences and cultures around the world to encourage a sense of self-respect and individual value to help preserve and inspire self-identity, views and culture – stepping forward from being just a consumer to being a provider of information (see also Chapter 11). For disabled people, virtual travel experiences of many kinds can facilitate communication and participation in social activities, learning, e-commerce, financial services and shopping. The Internet can be used to research places and facilities to make mobility easier. Internet access can thus improve opportunities for all and could make a difference to individuals and communities' views of the future and their role in society, including an internal need to override social rules or to flee from the community (Knierzinger and Turcsányi-Szabó, 2002: 925). This then is the context for the story of our project in Hungary, which was carefully designed to address these concerns using web-based learning (WBL) to promote synergistic development of underdeveloped regions and to improve informatics teacher education and practice.

The tele-house and teacher training project

The Computer Clubhouse project (Resnick *et al.*, 1998) provided a model for our project, inspiring us to set up clubhouses to provide meaningful activities for children and young people to develop technological fluency, to support learning through design, to allow communities to emerge over time and produce mentors to guide newcomers, and to develop an environment of respect and trust. Yet such clubhouses presume a concentrated infrastructure and the presence of all sorts of high tech tools as well as different expertise from the very start. Now this is what tele-houses in underdeveloped regions definitely cannot provide from the beginning! But certainly, as time goes by, the infrastructure and proficiency could develop, and should be sought. In fact, each community is developing an individual flavour by attracting the special talents and professions present in its area to become an active part of the community.

Our project is led by the Teaching with Multimedia (TEAM) Lab at Eotvos Lorand University, which was established in 1997 within the Informatics Methodology Group involved with informatics teacher training (http://www.team-lab.ini.hu). The lab's aim is the application, teaching, experimentation, evaluation, research and development of innovative multimedia tools and methodologies for the benefit of effective learning and developing skills. Research and development includes the ergonomics and content development of educational applications, authoring tools, Internet and ICT environments, and evaluation of their effects in the learning process. Our main aim is to provide access to our most recent developments through our web pages for practising teachers as well as learners and to provide online help for implementation in the learning process. We involve our students in the whole process through course activities where they develop educational materials, and we introduce them into practical learning situations while performing research on their impact. These aims infuse this project, which has established a bond between the tele-house movement and TEAM Lab to provide a suitable and extendable environment for learning in partly isolated regions.

A tele-house is a multifunction ICT service centre with an open profile design for small villages. In other words it is 'a community telecommunications service house'. Tele-houses in Hungary emerged from active civil initiatives related to mass movements. At present there are more than 400 tele-houses in operation (www.telehaz.hu). Tele-houses also aim to provide services in capacity building for education. A culture leading to distance education needs to be accepted and practised in order to progress in the right direction, possibly leading to distance working as well. This in itself could improve prospects for the younger generation and their elders in a direct or indirect way. Tele-houses could provide a virtual 'way out' for people while physically remaining in their home region. They could permit a 'virtual sight outside' to promote connections, seek information and find economic possibilities.

The project was sponsored by the United States Agency for International Development and the Hungarian Ministry of Informatics and Communication through the project coordinating institution called the Foundation for Development of Democratic Rights. The project has gone through two phases: the first (January to June 2001) with five tele-houses involving about 70 children; the second (September to December 2001) with 11 tele-houses involving about 150 children. The first phase covered the least developed eastern regions of Hungary to investigate its introduction under the least favourable circumstances. The second phase involved tele-houses from all over the country to investigate sustainability. Efforts were also made to involve tele-houses for Roma people but it was not possible to establish those at the start of the project, so a further session will be needed to fulfil this aim. Funds were used mainly to provide necessary equipment, software tools, maintenance and supervision within the existing infrastructure. The tele-houses had to apply for the funds to provide a fairly good infrastructure from the start. Each local tele-house environment was required to provide hardware, software and training support as follows: hardware included multimedia computers, scanner, digital camera, digital drawing-pad, colour printer, laser printer and CD writer that could be accessed at times to suit children's schedules. Software included an adequate amount of licences from necessary software tools (Microsoft Windows and Office, Internet Explorer, FrontPage, Flash, Cool Edit, Corel Print Office, and Comenius Logo) plus Internet and email facilities. Finally, children's activities were supervised by dedicated local helpers, who volunteered to prepare children for the project by introducing the basic uses of computers, emailing and saving files and software including writing with Hungarian characters and playing Logo games. Helpers had to coach children and learned collaboratively with them throughout.

The global environment for tele-houses was provided by the Tele-house Centre with e-Room (http://www.eroom.com) as common working space and emailing services. TEAM Lab set up rooms for group projects and individual rooms for each tele-house, with room for all children to upload their individual work for submission and selected mentors from the fourth year class of informatics student teachers who had experience with children's activities. By the fourth year, students have a broad knowledge base of different applications, design of educational materials and LOGO Microworlds, evaluation of ICT tools and their constructivist use. The mentors trained through a two-semester course called tele-mentoring that was created for this purpose. In the course, student teachers learned about the basics of mentoring and learning at a distance, and they also went through a semester of mentoring a project with a group of children at an assigned tele-house.

Mentors were required to visit their assigned tele-house as often as they could, possibly once a month, and to maintain good contact with all children and local helpers; they were also required to acquire a fairly good idea of the local situation, individual and group problems, and to find ways to improve motivation. They were to answer communications within 24 hours and to provide a fixed weekly slot when they were available for synchronous communication over the phone or network chat. They were also required to guide each child, or group of children, individually on a path that suited best their personal growth, commenting positively on work submitted so as to induce further progress, and finally, to provide continuous evaluation on each child or group's progress.

The visits of mentors to their assigned tele-house were crucial events that determined the overall relationship of the individuals and groups. These occasions were fully used by participants to get acquainted with each other, develop confidence, establish personal relationships, and evoke the natural motivation of learners. At the end of the project a final camping activity took place in one of the schools, where children spent four days, with one day for special group activities as extensions of the project. About 40 Roma children and their guides from different areas were invited to the final camp to give them an insight into the project with the aim of initiating their participation. These days were spent together with joy in games, swimming and sports. Activities with the computer and away from the computer merged participants into a coherent group. The group-based activities involved: visual representation, writing, concept maps (starting out from the word 'tele-house') and creating a logo to represent their newly emerged group (a small computer picture that was printed in colour, cut out and pressed into a badge). In the afternoon participants presented the last assignments of their project work. Children were rewarded with presents and certificates of participation and they enjoyed the work of others, as well as being proud of their own work. The day concluded with a bonfire and singing. These real-life events, games and real communication have been the basic adhesives of community cohesion and supported continuation through virtual ties.

Web-based learning resources

The two WBL materials key to this project were NETLogo and Creative Communications. They were developed through years of project work at TEAM Lab. Both materials suggest a constructivist approach allowing different learning styles to emerge: NETLogo provides self-paced discovery learning with individual guidance, while Creative Communications provides project-based group learning with collaboration and group mentoring. Topics tackled aimed to answer 'What, When, How, and Why'. Selected topics were to be learned and used, supporting modelling activities, exploration and self expression. Both WBL materials were introduced into several school settings and into the tele-house project described here.

The instructional design principles underlying the two sets of WBL resources NETLogo and Creative Communications followed the guidance of Jonassen and his colleagues: that initial knowledge acquisition is better served by instructional techniques, based on traditional instructional design, whereas constructivist learning environments are most effective for the more advanced knowledge acquisition stage of learning (Jonassen *et al.*, 1993). The link between learning theories and instructional design practices are also underlined in teacher training (Moallem, 2001).

NETLogo is a Logo course material that includes self-paced activities and Microworlds that can be used in different subject areas together with their pedagogy (Turcsányi-Szabó, 2000: 387). Diverse starting points and links allow different paths to be taken by learners. A unit can be selected from a range to provide guidance on how to handle problems and to give tasks and projects to fulfil and submit. The material is bundled with a CD containing the Hungarian Comenius Logo authoring tool (Kossuth Publishing Inc, 1997) and a beginner's book (Stuur and Turcsányi-Szabó, 1998). The basic aim for elementary school children is to be able to utilize modelling as a tool for investigations through problem solving, building structures, and debugging ideas and virtual environments. Work should start out by playing with games and educational Microworlds, which are understood through use of the course material provided and its later modification. The process is based on self-motivated, self-paced learning how to learn. The basic aim for teachers and other helpers is to be able to utilize and configure educational Microworlds for children's needs and to guide children through modelling practices, so as to be able to design simple Microworlds for multi-disciplinary use.

Creative Communications is a complex project-based material that integrates subject knowledge and ICT skills to promote creative thinking and expression on an interdisciplinary platform. Project assignments are grouped into themes: Writing, Narration, Typography; Visual representation, Montage, Motion and Concept Maps. Participants choose one or two themes plus Concept Maps. They supplement each other's knowledge while working in groups. Assignments within a theme build on each other to facilitate authoring, with an emphasis on creativity and self-expression, and some require collaboration between the real and the virtual participating communities. The basic aim is that elementary school children should be able to express themselves and communicate using ICT tools as well as being able to collaborate in real and virtual environments. The process is based on self-motivation with the aim of learning how to fulfil deadlines while doing projects. The basic aim for teachers and other helpers is to be able to explore ICT tools and their application in different tasks, where the emphasis is not on the tool, but on the process of creation itself. They should also be able to integrate assignments with activities both with and away from the computer that enhance the creative process.

Pedagogical strategies and the theoretical framework

The features of group work were designed using characteristics described by Strijbos (2000) and informed by wider theoretical perspectives including social constructivism. Community learning that is based on individual and group learning can be described as 'collaborative learning'. Strijbos (2000) distinguishes between 'co-operative learning' and 'collaborative learning,' based on the amount of pre-imposed structure, task-type, learning objective and group size. He develops a classification model to illustrate differences between both perspectives and also various types of computer support for group-based learning. Strijbos summarized the literature to conclude that 'collaborative learning' (as opposed to 'co-operative learning') can be characterized as a personal philosophy of intra-group interaction (and not a set of structures to facilitate group performance), imposed on a domain that is not too well structured, where each member equally contributes whilst problem solving (without any pre-imposed division of labour).

Therefore the group size was kept to a maximum of ten – this allowed for possible dropouts. Children visited tele-houses at one group time slot and several free slots available during the week. Thus children mainly worked in groups of two or three, or double that size. Pairs often arose from existing friendships or family ties. Therefore the age of children varied; the children were mainly 10–14 years old but the activities attracted all ages, including even a three and half year old child, and led to positive interdependence during work that emerges from the natural ties of everyday life. McCormick and Scrimshaw (2001) note that the implementation of ICT should go beyond the narrow focus on computer–student interaction to require a level of change in practice, making it more efficient or effective to extend or transform it. Emphasizing the social constructivist perspective, ICT can extend the reach of the teacher, the learner or both:

Rather than simply acquiring concepts (the process of 'internalization' to cognitive constructivists), from a situated perspective, learners are seen as creating identities by learning to participate in communities. Knowledge, as seen from this perspective, is not constructed as an object acquired by individual learners (in the way cognitive constructivists would argue) but is a social process of knowledge construction. Meaning is created through participating in social activity. From this perspective, there is not an individual notion of a concept, but a distributed one. The learning process is viewed not as the transmission of knowledge from a knowledgeable to a less knowledgeable, but as engagement in culturally authentic activity, participation in a community of practice.

(McCormick and Scrimshaw, 2001: 37)

Individual accountability was attained through the constant individual submission scheme included within the WBL material and the one-to-one communication with a mentor, who occasionally provided additional individual tasks, although peer or small group work was preferred at times. The final group task had to have the form of a presentation that included 'the fingerprints' of all participants. The Creative Communication WBL material emphasized this additive nature by the compulsory choice of disjunctive themes and requested a final group task that introduced the whole community through collaborative work. Local helpers mainly acted as coaches, being themselves natural co-learners, and so facilitated constructivist learning in a self-paced autonomous 'student-centred' manner based on individual motivation. Social inclusion became a natural factor with common goals and it was soon realized that the strength of the group relied on individual inputs developed for all. For example, in one of the tele-houses a boy with a wheelchair did the assigned activities so well that, together with his parents, he persuaded a secondary school situated in another town to enrol him for further studies. Since then he has progressed well.

The WBL material provided freedom of choice and supported progress, because the child chose the topic and was guided to attempt all assignments. In all tele-houses children could choose which WBL material they wanted and then had to progress through its stages. This progression was an individual path in the case of NETLogo or through predetermined project work in the case of Creative Communications. Work initiated from the starting point advised by the mentor. NETLogo activities started with some games and then progressed to either the first course level or for advanced children a level assigned by the mentor. Creative Communications has an introductory project. Further assistance and coaching was provided by the mentor: individual coaching in the case of NETLogo, and group coaching in the case of Creative Communications. This implementation was a constructivist approach aligned with Logo philosophy, which is based on Piaget's theories (Logo is a programming language plus a philosophy of education often categorized as constructivism or discovery learning):

A crucial aspect of Logo spirit is fostering situations which the teacher has never seen before and so has to join the students as an authentic co-learner. This is the common constructivist practice of setting up situations in which students are expected to make their own discoveries, but where what they 'discover' is something that the teacher already knows and either pretends not to know or exercises self-restraint in not sharing with the students. Neither deception nor restraint is necessary when teachers and students are faced with real problems that arise naturally in the course of a project. The problem challenges both. Both can give their all.

(LCSI, 1999)

When children are the authors, designers and creators themselves, they research the topic, identify the relevant data, select supporting visuals, design the layout of text and graphics, determine how the information should be linked, debug problems, consider the nature of the intended audience, solicit feedback about their work in progress and share their final compositions with others. In this way they learn more about the topic than the one who ultimately uses the finished product (Druin and Solomon, 1996).

When problems occurred, children first consulted with peers, then with local helpers if consultations did not result in an effective solution. When a problem could not be solved locally, the children then consulted with the mentors. The first mentors were informatics student teachers, but it is hoped to build more capacity. Helpers who have already mastered the WBL materials and mentoring methods might be ready to become mentors for their own community or for a new learning community at a distance. This is a progressive approach to help the propagation of this movement and also to expand WBL materials for learning. The project has been further enhanced by the professional and personal ambitions of local helpers and staff in tele-houses. On one occasion a painter became a helper and supported an additional emphasis on visual expression. In another tele-house, a radio technician added an emphasis on the expression of sounds and in another situation a schoolteacher has connected the projects with school assignments.

The research process

The project has so far passed through two 'action research' cycles and has set up a model for education that could be extended with further research to provide a solution for the whole network of tele-houses and other underdeveloped regions. An overview of the processes used action research to support successful leadership of the project and it was common practice to make immediate note of important experiences. The project coordinator (the author and the head of TEAM Lab) provided overall leadership, while the administrative organizer from the Telehouse Centre arranged the events.

The project used an inductive research strategy that included separate descriptions by both local helpers and distant mentors of the local situation, the process used and problems encountered. The progress of each child was recorded with achievements and/or the challenges encountered with explanations of possible reasons plus experiences connected to the project. Data were collected from 70 children in five tele-houses who took part in the first phase and 150 children in 11 tele-houses who took part in the second phase. Four were common to both phases, plus one elementary and secondary school where teachers were allowed to use the materials freely. Structured questionnaires were completed in writing before and after activities. Items surveyed the individual situation and interest, subject knowledge in ICT, attitudes towards using computers, attitudes towards the role of ICT in society, and the attitudes, behaviour and the motivation of children towards computer games. The last, on computer games, was a separate research issue. In addition, a 30-minute IQ test measured logical, visual and problem solving abilities. These are being analysed in conjunction with the portfolio of work submitted by each learner to give a comparison of individual situations, abilities, basic knowledge, progress, achievements, test results and degree of creativity.

Results and future plans

Early results have been published (Abonyi-Toth and Turcsányi-Szabó, 2001; Turcsányi-Szabó, 2001; Turcsányi-Szabó, 2002) and empirical data is to be published shortly. A gallery of work submitted can be accessed online (http://matchsz.inf.elte.hu/telehaz/). Local helpers, mentors and researchers all agreed that every child has profited in one way or another from project activities. Children living in remote underdeveloped areas succeeded in mastering basic ICT skills and fluency in personal expression with a range of tools, as well as ways to learn at a distance. Most children are confidently using email as a new form of social communication. They now realize that computer games can be fun and that a whole lot of opportunities await them through the use of ICT. A lot of children have continued their studies in the field of informatics. Student teachers who tele-mentored children's activities learned about the needs of children, different methods and tools to develop skills, ways to motivate and evaluate, and the different platforms of ICT use in everyday life and expression. This experience also led to their understanding of the values and drawbacks of living in small remote communities and ways that might improve underdeveloped regions. They are very eager to continue with their tele-mentoring activities. The most straightforward way to develop friendships with children emerged through playing games; these developed close relationships between child and mentor and also built bonds within the learning groups. Many games emerged and were propagated among tele-houses. There was also evidence of one of the mentors helping children with their homework and giving them extra assignments to help to practise the topics.

The whole community of tele-houses became interested in finding a way to continue the project. After project funding ended, we offered continuation of our mentoring to produce web pages that would introduce their local town and community over the Internet. This opportunity opened the eyes of the local people to the tools and the possibilities of attracting outsiders to their region. One of the communities established an art school with media studies as a form of continuation, where local artists could support the skills of talented children. Tele-houses in the most underdeveloped regions are more than grateful for these opportunities, since, as they say, 'it is not only our eyes that have been opened, but those of the world too, to see us'. We have high hopes that our pilot project can become a normal routine, combining pre-service teacher training with practical mentoring for underdeveloped regions, thus providing the missing key for capacity building in these areas. We are also extending our mentoring for schools to introduce innovative learning materials and methods for in-service teacher training. This pilot project has established a bond between the tele-house movement in Hungary and TEAM Lab in providing a suitable and extendable environment for capacity building in partly isolated regions in Hungary.

Acknowledgements

Thanks to all the participants, DemNet and the sponsors USAID and IKB. This chapter was first presented as a paper at the annual conference of the Society of Information Technology for Teacher Education in 2003 and nominated for the SITE Digital Equity Award for Teacher Education. Niki Davis has edited the paper presented in the proceedings with the permission of the author.

References

Abonyi-Toth, A. and Turcsányi-Szabó, M. (2001) Developing multidisciplinary skills through a web based learning environment implemented for tele-houses, in Proceedings of the ICL2000, ed. M. Auer, CD, ISBN: 3–933146–67–4.

Cohen, R. (1987) *Les jeunes enfants, la découverte de lécrit et l'ordinateur*, PUF, Paris.

Colleen, C. and Miller, E. (eds) [accessed 24 August 2003] Fool's gold: a critical look at computers in childhood, Alliance for Childhood [Online] www.allianceforchildhood.net/.

Druin, A. and Solomon, C. (1996) *Designing Multimedia Environments for Children*, John Wiley, London.

Jonassen, D. H., McAleese, T. M. R. and Duffy, T. M. (1993) [accessed 24 August 2003] A manifesto for a constructivist approach to technology in higher education, in *The Design of Constructivistic Learning Environments: Implications for instructional design and the use of technology*, eds T. M. Duffy, L. J. Lowyck and D. H. Jonassen, Heidelburg, FRG: Springer-Verlag [Online] http://cad017.gcal.ac.uk/clti/papers/TMPaper11.html.

Knierzinger, A. and Turcsányi-Szabó, M. (2002) Internet, education and culture: should we care? in *Networking the Learner: Computers in education*, ed. D. Watson and J. Andersen, pp. 925–32, Kluwer Academic Publishers, Dordrecht.

Kossuth Publishing (1997) Hungarian Comenius Logo: Localisation of Blaho, in *Comenius Logo*, eds I. Kalas and P. Tomcsanyi, University Bratislava, Hungary.

LCSI (1999) *Logo Philosophy and Implementation*, Logo Computer Systems, Vermont.

McCormick, R. and Scrimshaw, P. (2001) Information and communications technology, knowledge and pedagogy, in *Education, Communication and Information*, eds J. Leach and S. Wiske, pp. 37–57, Routledge, London.

Moallem, M. (2001) Applying constructivist and objectivist learning theories in the design of a web-based course: implications for practice, *in Educational Technology and Society*, 4 (3).

Resnick, M., Rusk, N. and Cooke, S. (1998) [accessed 24 August 2003] The Computer Clubhouse: technology fluency in the inner city, Massachusetts Institute of Technology [Online] http://llk.media.mit.edu/papers/1998/clubhouse/.

Strijbos, J. W. (2000) [accessed 24 August 2003] A classification model for group-based learning, *European Journal of Open and Distance Learning* [Online] http://www.eurodl.org/eurodlen/index.html/.

Stuur, A. and Turcsányi-Szabó, M. (1998) *Comenius Logo játék és programozás*, Kossuth Publishing, Hungary.

Turcsányi-Szabó, M. (2000) Subject oriented microworld extendible environment for learning and tailoring educational tools – a scope for teacher training, in *Proceedings of World Conference on Computers and Education 2000*, eds D. Benzie and D. Passey, pp. 387–94, Kluwer Academic Publishers, Dordrecht.

Turcsányi-Szabó, M. (2002) Capacity building in tele-houses: A model for tele-mentoring, in *Learning with Technology in School, Home and Community*, eds G. Marshall and Y. Katz, pp. 267–273, Kluwer Academic Publishers, Dordrecht.

19 Building communities of practice in 'New' Europe

Christina Preston and Laura Lengel

Communities of practice are emerging as important bases for creating, sharing and applying knowledge. These communities share ideas and innovations, collaborating across traditional hierarchical structures and geophysical boundaries. What brings members of a community of practice together is a shared vision and goals, and a passion for mutual dialogue (Wenger, 1998). Communities of practice are often focused around critical issues or professional functions and frequently linked through virtual learning environments, using information and communication technology (ICT) to stay in constant contact despite geophysical or temporal differences. Current research, such as that presented in this volume, attests to the importance of community building for best practices. Most of this research and most talk of communities in practice generally occurs in the US and Western Europe (see for example, Hildreth and Kimble, 2002; Johnson, 2001). This is the same for communities of practice in education and in online and distance learning (Fraser, 2002; Grisham *et al.*, 1999; Haythornthwaite *et al.*, 2000; LeBaron *et al.*, 2000; Lengel and Murphy, 2000; Nachmias *et al.*, 2000; Rogers, 2000; Squire and Johnson, 2000). However, very little research is emerging from the New Europe (Lengel, 2000), which is defined for purposes of this chapter as Central and Eastern Europe (CEE), South-eastern Europe, the Newly Independent States and the Russian Federation.

This chapter focuses on a community of practice that links the 'New' (formerly Eastern) Europe with what has been traditionally conceptualized as Western Europe: this Anglo–Czech cooperation called Czech Miranda is linked to MirandaNet, an international professional development organization that was founded in Britain in 1992 for teachers and teacher educators responsible for in-service information and communication technology (ICT) programmes. The MirandaNet Fellowship includes ICT policy makers, industrial partners, researchers, teacher educators and teachers, especially ICT leaders for primary and secondary schools. The community is engaged in defining the cultural, social and political challenges that confront the teaching profession, changing teaching practice and creating an effective online learning community.

For more details on the history and activities of MirandaNet in the UK and other nations, please see http://www.mirandanet.ac.uk/fellowship/about.htm.

Media, both 'old' and 'new', have played an increasingly important role in the New Europe. Lubecka (2000) suggests that in the New Europe:

> the newly empowered local governments show much interest in creating citizens who value and understand democracy, its privileges and duties, and who, because of participatory competencies, help bring reforms. Media provide significant support to create a new awareness of acting 'civics.'
>
> (Lubecka, 2000: 37)

Media and ICT also provide spaces for preserving cultural and pedagogical identity and diversity. Czech Miranda and its parent organization MirandaNet flourish in this area. The MirandaNet Fellowship strives to span national, cultural, commercial and political divides to provide an innovative and inclusive forum for professionals. Partnership with industry, and with local and national governments is at the heart of the research, development and evaluation processes that underpin and support good practice. Individual learning patterns are celebrated through action research strategies and peer e-mentoring. MirandaNet Fellows share their experience and expertise through publication and online exchange of ideas. Overall, the community is building a professional knowledge base about the use of advanced technologies in transforming teaching and learning.

Building on the goals and successes of MirandaNet in the UK, Czech colleagues established the Czech Miranda community of practice in 1995, aiming not only to preserve Czech identity and diversity but also to enhance existing pedagogical practices with those from the communities of practice in other nations. The Czech Miranda community has also developed a national presence, with community leaders appointed as advisers to the Czech government about their international and national experience and expertise.

Political and pedagogical catalysts for change in a Czech community of practice

Understanding the nature of the Anglo–Czech community in practice depends on a consideration of the political, industrial and professional contexts from which UK and Czech educators are emerging. In the Czech Republic, a history of Austrian, German and Russian rule since the seventeenth century has created a teaching profession fraught with a lack of confidence in individual approaches and strategies. Without doubt, before the Velvet Revolution, Czech educators were concerned about disagreeing with the state. Dissidents were exiled, not allowed to teach or to engage in professional development courses or activities. At the other end of the scale, widespread apathy resulted from a desire simply to survive. What has been most debilitating for this inventive and imaginative nation has been the cultural isolation and the sense of failure in securing their intellectual freedom.

Emerging from this past, the Czech government is still searching for stability. But since the millennium there is real hope that new strategies for learning underpinned by technology are possible. For the first time schools have been invited to present cohesive school development plans which, while taking account of national standards, reflect local conditions and needs and the new freedoms made available through the democratic rule and practices emerging since 1989. Czech Miranda Fellows, emerging from a totalitarian government, have been concerned that their teaching profession remains fixed in the use of authoritarian modes for teaching both pupils and teachers. They have valued international curriculum exchanges as an important aspect of teachers' learning. MirandaNet workshops, seminars and online continuity facilitate teachers in developing curriculum projects. One of the Czech Fellows, a teacher who was selected to attend MirandaNet workshops in London and Prague about the Internet in teaching when she designed a collaborative online project with a British counterpart, notes that after a long period of political isolation, Czech teachers can gain from seeing how other teachers work and by sharing their concerns and interests. Czech teachers are interested in learning about collaborative and constructive learning that includes understanding democratic procedures and processes. The Fellow suggested there was very little independent learning practice and little effort to give Czech students more autonomy as learners.

On their first contact with the West, the Czech Miranda Fellows were disposed to think that all democratic institutions were perfect. Several Fellows were surprised to find that the British teaching profession also had its problems. They discovered that since the 1980s, a disaffected teaching profession had came into conflict with central government policy. An increasing role for commercial sponsorship and opportunities for growing educational markets were being developed through public–private partnerships alongside a national curriculum for all schools. Fundamental conflicts centre on the purpose of education, the content and the means of assessment and the meaning of standards. Some teachers have been opposed to curriculum links with the economic pressure to 'improve' the work force.

Before the Velvet Revolution, Czech teachers had been offered poor computers that required proficiency with programming languages, and this increased resistance amongst the profession. After 1989 teachers were offered more appropriate equipment through initiatives sponsored by the European Commission, but they were not enthusiastic because of their previous experience. In contrast, in Slovakia, multimedia networked computers were introduced later and were immediately popular because they were easy to use and more appropriate for the curriculum. In 2002 the Czech Ministry of Education eventually took the first steps to prioritize school teachers' needs for ICT funding and a voice in redefining their role in lifelong learning.

Diversity in the community of practice

In these circumstances it was not surprising that the MirandaNet approach, based on sophisticated partnerships with government and industry in the UK, had not yet appeared in the Czech Republic. Consequently, when MirandaNet Fellowship embarked on this Anglo-Czech collaboration, they expected to encounter significant diversity between the professional approach to ICT in each country, as well as differences in access. Many common professional challenges have also emerged as access to ICT has improved in the Czech Republic.

The Czech Republic has greater challenges. Most ICT teachers in the Czech Republic are experts from computer science, mathematics and physics, specifically trained in teaching ICT as a subject. In some schools, teachers from other curriculum subjects become involved as leaders of ICT projects. Training in ICT for new teachers remains patchy and there is no agreed curriculum. Many teacher education programmes still focus on technical skills and software training rather than on classroom application and management. There are improvements: the role of ICT coordinators is being developed and defined more precisely, and UK teacher visitors found plenty to admire in the early Czech approach to ICT. MirandaNet visitors were struck by the problem solving conducted by seventeen year old programmers and wondered whether too much computer science has been dropped in the UK. The fatigue felt by British teachers contrasted with the energy generated by the Czechs' new political freedom and the desire to be an inclusive society. The Czech profession is keen to learn from the experience of the West, even when this means learning English. MirandaNet Fellows were also struck by the high standards in the pursuit of excellence and an engaging national pride.

The Czech teachers have also highlighted the strengths they saw in their British colleagues. UK teachers exhibited self-confidence in articulating their teaching methods, with knowledge about evaluation and assessment procedures. The Czechs admired the national system of inspection of education (OFSTED) and the many professional organizations, including the National Association for Advisors for Computers in Education, the National Association for Information Technology in Teacher Education and the Association for Computing and Information

Technology Teaching. Professionally organized events, conferences and seminars with opportunities to ask questions and voice opinions were highly valued experiences for the Czechs. Better industry – education partnership and more information about other educational cultures were also valued. Joint annual MirandaNet workshops have been a regular event since 1996, with equal roles for the Czech and UK educators and development of shared views on the importance of preserving cultural diversity. Both UK and Czech Fellows think that their perceptions of each other's cultures have been fundamentally altered by long-term contact.

Although the differences stimulated the first exchanges, similarities have proved more fruitful for continuing collaboration. Some of the factors, which are common to the profession in each country, include a lack of respect for the teaching profession in society. Although the number of enthusiasts for IT in the curriculum is increasing, teachers who are determinedly conservative and traditionalist hold them back. In ICT teaching, age, position and professional experience are considered to have less weight than the willingness to learn. The distribution of men and women in MirandaNet is approximately equal, and gender issues are not considered to be significant in this group, in contrast to other male-dominated ICT professional organizations in both countries. Both groups of teachers felt resistance to the North American cultural influence of some software, especially CDs available to schools. In specific ICT matters, teachers expressed the hope that ICT might improve literacy and numeracy skills.

The considerable investment in ICT UK government initiatives over the last thirty years has had relatively little impact on the profession so far. In the UK £230 million have been invested in ICT teacher training focused on pedagogy and where this has not worked it is likely to be linked to an unreceptive school context in which leadership has been lacking (Preston, 2003). According to UK school inspectors only 15 per cent of schools are using ICT effectively (OFSTED, 2002). Since 2000 the Czech government has also made a significant investment in ICT projects in education with relatively poor results. The main reason seems to be much the same as in the UK. The new technologies were introduced into the existing traditional educational system instead of changing the system itself. Teachers in the Czech Republic have often had to teach themselves to use ICT, occasionally supported by European funding.

Despite the above challenges, many successes have emerged as a result of the Anglo-Czech alliance. The leadership of Czech Miranda has been encouraging collaborative lifelong learning for teacher educators across cultural boundaries, distributing knowledge about ICT in-service programmes more widely in the Czech Republic and developing assessment and evaluation systems. Coordinated by the Czech Technical University in Prague, a Joint European Project Grant has defined key concepts for an ICT teacher professional development programme, which has provided a useful start for present and future government programmes and increased facilities where teachers can join in with the community.

The success of these collaborating communities of practice has been recognized by awards made to its founders: Bozena Mannova, the Chair of Czech Miranda, and Christina Preston, the founder of MirandaNet, jointly received a 1998 Humanitarian Award from the European Union of Women for the Anglo-Czech alliance they have fostered. The judges considered this leadership from women to be significant especially in the Czech Republic where computers tend to be a male preserve and women rarely feature in major posts. The judges noted that the MirandaNet and Czech Miranda learning policies reflected a strong bias towards cooperation, collaboration, co-construction and independence in teachers' learning. The European Union of Women also praised the cross-cultural development of teacher education programmes in which each participating country had an equal role. Since a large proportion of teachers are women in both countries the judges praised the MirandaNet web site that is designed to appeal to women.

Maintaining cultural identity

Another important outcome of these communities of practice is their care to protect indigenous cultures and languages. Restoring and preserving local languages has been successful due to the efforts of the international MirandaNet community. In his handbook on the programme *Hyperstudio,* Wagner (1994) argues that literacy involves the ability to communicate within the medium of one's culture. As discussed in the first section of this volume, multimodality goes beyond traditional forms of reading and writing. This is why MirandaNet's initiatives are important for supporting cultures new to the Internet to find their own ways of communicating. The MirandaNet community has been guiding Czech students to develop creative ways of articulating and preserving their culture(s) through information and communication technology. For example, Czech Miranda members at the University of Ostrava guided Czech youth in the Tajfun theatre project (Telnarová *et al.;* 2000). The 15–17 year old student members of the Tajfun Theatre Group have also connected with other youth theatre groups from Poland and Germany in the New Europe to participate in a project called 'Legends and Myths of Central Europe' to preserve the cultures and languages of East Central Europe. Other MirandaNet members have guided students to co-produce theatre written and directed by Czech and Japanese students, and performed through video-conferencing. The links between the nations made during these artistic practices have remained long after the performances.

These initiatives are important, because there is a tendency for such technology-based projects to develop as simple copies of 'Western' cultures and approaches, rather than aligned with local and regional cultures in the New Europe. Lecturers at Charles University in Prague discovered this important issue when studying thirty different CD-ROM titles that had been donated by Microsoft. The teachers had planned to evaluate and use these products as a basis for professional multimedia production, but abandoned that plan because the emphasis on content and language in Microsoft products conflicted with Czech and European approaches. Some European leaders have also recognized that the choice of Microsoft products brings the risk of locking schools into a single commercial system when developing online services. European SchoolNet, which aims to 'raise awareness in the educational community of the value of the Internet as a teaching and learning resource,' is also against using Microsoft products because the culture of the company is perceived as authoritarian in its approach (EUN, 2003) and presents a ready-made US corporate solution that does not take full account of the need for linguistic and cultural diversity in Europe. However, insufficient finance continues to be a problem for educational products for smaller markets, such as those in New Europe.

MirandaNet initiatives have uncovered important connections across very diverse communities as they sought to bypass pre-packaged products and to create their own products. For instance, through their connection with the MirandaNet community in practice, Czech Miranda Fellows connected with MirandaNet Fellows in Chile, and realized how similar their experiences were under authoritarian rule. For forty years, while East Central Europe, South-Eastern Europe and the former Soviet bloc was dominated by a left wing, atheist dictatorship, Chile had a right wing Christian dictator. Under each authoritarian system, the MirandaNet members lost their right and responsibility to make decisions at the grass roots level, which weakened the spirit and lowered self esteem. The two women Fellows who opposed the dictatorships in Chile and the Czech Republic used the same metaphor in describing their experience of the repressive regime they had endured. One said that it felt like 'a lid came down on her head'. An adolescent at the time, she felt she 'lost her youth and her young adulthood in a sea of powerlessness'. Now that what she calls the 'lid' has been lifted, she sees a light of optimism, but she does not know which way to turn to reap the benefits of this new lifestyle.

Through the MirandaNet community these women, and many other community members, have decided which way to turn – to each other. Through the MirandaNet listserv, and the chat room on the MirandaNet web site, community members share concerns, experiences and ideas. They realize that, while in the past they were alone and isolated they now have a group that provides support and encouragement. Now that many members are no longer isolated but are struggling financially in ways not known during authoritarian rule, new concerns can be shared. For instance, one member wrote in the chat room about how, during communist rule, the banning of meetings was easy to circumvent in Czechoslovakia. But, she wrote, authoritarian central control is insidious. Russian domination was the subject of covert protest meetings. Czechs were united against a common enemy and there was a heady companionship in those days, with time spent singing protest songs and telling anti-Russian jokes. She wrote, 'In the days when the Russian puppets pretended to pay us and we pretended to work, we had time for each other. But not now. We have to make money. We have to make decisions. There is no humour and no uplift. We are all in the rat race like you.'

Those belonging to the online community also discuss their own views of MirandaNet and their role in the community. 'MirandaNet is both a network and a community. The people who belong share common interests, but what I find stimulating is the range of diversity, rather than simply interests in common.' Another member comments that, through this online community, 'there are no boundaries'.

Conclusion

The range of factors that make up good professional development training have become clear through our work with both MirandaNet communities. These include: ownership of hardware and online access; training in management of change theory and practice; attention to professional and administrative practice; emphasis on multimedia presentation skills; senior management involvement in staff training and curriculum projects; a whole school approach to ICT teacher education; substantial budgets for whole staff resources and training; strategies to raise teachers self esteem; industry–education partnership; support in funding raising strategies; mentoring; working with international colleagues on common projects; sharing experience with peers; action research methodology; extended fellowship development; opportunities for marketing the school ICT achievements; and the development of community links. For Czech teachers, knowledge of English is also important.

It is important that teachers are treated as individual and independent learners. They need support not only in teaching in these new ways but also in learning to be learners. It is important to understand that teachers are all different in their learning patterns and interests, and that is a key issue to consider when conducting and designing courses for teachers. Our experience of these interconnected communities of practice has conclusively proved that the impact of advanced information and communication technologies on the culture of teaching and learning overwhelms boundary considerations. MirandaNet is both a network and a community, and this chapter has described how an existing community can support the development of a new community and also enlarge its community energy in the process.

Acknowledgements

The British Council and Toshiba provided support for the Czech Miranda Fellows' travel to Britain. Partnership with industry is a central MirandaNet policy. Since the establishment of MirandaNet in 1992 several technology firms, such as Apple, BT, ICL, Elsevier, Oracle, Xemplar and Sherston, have contributed to the ICT teacher education programmes by giving hardware and software, workshop facilities and expert training. Hewlett Packard and Microsoft, for example, sponsored the ICT training centre in the Arabska Secondary School in Prague.

References

EUN (2003) [accessed 13 April 2003] European SchoolNet [Online] http://www.en.eun.org.

Fraser, J. (2002) Challenges to design educators lie in negotiating multiple discourses, *Goldsmiths Journal of Education*, 5 (1), pp. 52–63.

Grisham, D., Bergeron, B. and Brink, B. (1999) Connecting communities of practice through professional development school activities, *Journal of Teacher Education*, 50 (3), pp. 182–91.

Haythornthwaite, C., Kazmer, M. and Robins, J. (2000) [accessed 10 April 2003] Community development among distance learners: temporal and technological dimensions, *Journal of Computer-Mediated Communication*, 6 (1) [Online] http://www.ascusc.org/jcmc/vol6/issue1/haythornthwaite.html.

Hildreth, P. and Kimble, C. (2000) Communities of practice in the distributed international environment, *Journal of Knowledge Management*, 4 (1), pp. 27–38.

Johnson, C. (2001) A survey of current research on online communities of practice, *The Internet and Higher Education*, 4 (1), pp. 45–60.

LeBaron, J., Pulkkinen, J. and Scollin, P. (2000) [accessed 2 September 2003] Promoting cross-border communication in an international Web-based graduate course, *Interactive Multimedia Electronic Journal of Computer-Enhanced Learning*, 2 (2) [Online] http://imej.wfu.edu/articles/2000/2/01/index.asp.

Lengel, L. (ed.) (2000) Culture and Technology in the New Europe, in *Culture and Technology in the New Europe: Civic Discourse in Transformation in Developing Nations*, ed. L. Lengel, pp. 1–20, Ablex, Stamford, CT.

Lengel, L. and Murphy, P. (2000) Cultural identity and cyberimperialism: computer mediated explorations of ethnicity, nation and citizenship, in *Cyberimperialism? Global relations in the new electronic frontier*, ed. B. Ebo, Greenwood, Westport, CT.

Lubecka, A. (2000) Economic, sociocultural and technological contexts in the New Europe, in *Culture and Technology in the New Europe: Civic discourse in transformation in developing nations*, L. Lengel ed., pp. 33–49, Ablex, Stamford, CT.

Nachmias, R., Mioduser, D., Oren, A. and Ram, J. (2000) Web-supported emerging collaboration in higher education courses, *Journal of Educational Technology and Society* [accessed 23 March 2003] Promoting cross-border communication in an international Web-based graduate course, *Interactive Electronic Multimedia Journal* 3 (3), 94–104.

OFSTED (2002) *ICT in Schools: Effect of Government Initiatives*, Progress Report, HMSO, London.

Preston, C. (2003) [accessed 24 August 2003] Building a continuing professional development (CPD) plan over three years for a school cluster or a school, interim presentation on the lessons from NOF [Online] http://www.mirandanet.ac.uk/tta/index.htm.

Rogers, J. (2000) Communities of practice: a framework for fostering coherence in virtual learning communities, *Educational Technology and Society*, 3 (3), pp. 384–92.

Squire, K. and Johnson, C. (2000) Supporting distributed communities of practice with interactive television, *Educational Technology Research and Development*, 48 (1), pp. 23–43.

Telnarová, Z., Burianová, E. and Lengel, L. (2000) Kultura/Technologie Mladych: Youth Culture and Technology in the Czech Republic, in *Culture and Technology in the New Europe: civic discourse in transformation in post-communist nations*, ed. L. Lengel, pp. 253–72, Ablex, Stamford, CT.

Wagner, R. (1994) *Hyperstudio*, Hyperstudio, New York.

Wenger, E. (1998) *Communities of Practice: Learning, meaning, and identity*, University Press Cambridge, Cambridge.

20 A systemic approach to educational renewal with new technologies

Empowering learning communities in Chile

Pedro Hepp, J. Enrique Hinostroza and Ernesto Laval

Introduction

While the developed world moves swiftly towards a knowledge society where the abilities to use and process information become ever more important (OECD, 2002) many developing countries are finding it hard to keep pace. They are struggling with their economies and human resources to bridge a digital and cultural gap that is threatening the future of their new generations, but which seems to be relentlessly widening as time passes. This chapter offers an overview of the Enlaces (Links) programme, which is the information and communication (ICT) in education programme of the Chilean Ministry of Education.

The history of Enlaces started in the early 1990s when educational software was still in its infancy, multimedia was a research subject, and computers were expensive machines with few communication options and operating systems that were even clumsier than those available today. Many developing countries like Chile were considering investing in ICT for their educational systems, under pressure from a growing market, and yet there was no evidence of the impact of ICT on improving students' learning on a large scale and few success stories. Enlaces has a history with people as the protagonists, not technology. The people are mostly teachers, but also engineers, technicians and policy makers. All of them have devoted their best efforts to make sense of ICT for education in a country with few resources but where education is the first priority to improve the living standards of all its inhabitants.

Chile, among many Latin American countries, is addressing the challenge to develop a knowledge society by investing in new technologies and human resources to modernize its economy and public services with the aid of information and communication technologies. Chile and other developing countries have decided to introduce these technologies in education. The following reasons explain why:

- ICT can enrich the learning environments by providing new inter-active resources and services for teachers and students, including material that is produced by many institutions worldwide. Today this represents an impressive wealth in educational content. There are already a large number of these resources available to Chile, which shares the same language and a similar culture with most Latin American countries.
- ICT can brighten the horizons of youngsters and teachers, because of the possibility of accessing lively online resources around the world and the opportunities to communicate and collaborate with peers from different cultures.
- ICT can help to prepare youngsters for new work demands and further studies. It provides the tools and supports for the develop-ment of skills necessary for lifelong learning in an information society and in a market that increases the economic value of people who can deal with information and transform it into knowledge.
- ICT includes information management tools that can make educa-tional management more effective at all levels, including classrooms.
- There is a need to provide equitable access to digital resources and services for all youngsters and teachers. This is especially relevant for schools in more deprived or isolated communities where the population has fewer opportunities than people in urban locations.

Enlaces and educational reform

During the last decade Chile has undergone a very comprehensive reform that aims to improve the quality and equity of its educational system. An improved infrastructure for all schools, new textbooks, a new curriculum and better teacher salaries are some examples of this compre-hensive effort, which also includes an ICT component called the Enlaces or Links programme.

Enlaces provides infrastructure (hardware), educational resources (software) and, most importantly, long-term training and support to teachers in every school. Today, more than 8,300 subsidized schools all over the country and over 90 per cent of the student population have access to the new digital technologies. Figure 20.1 shows the growth of schools participating in Enlaces over the years. By the year 2005, the Ministry of Education expects to reach all schools with Enlaces. This is a major challenge considering that many rural schools are very small and that some are located in isolated valleys near the Andes Mountains, on the southern islands or in small fishing villages. The only school in Antarctica (with eight students) is connected to Enlaces and so is the school on Easter Island.

About US $50 million was spent on the Enlaces project over a decade of work to meet its targets, partly funded by the World Bank. To reach

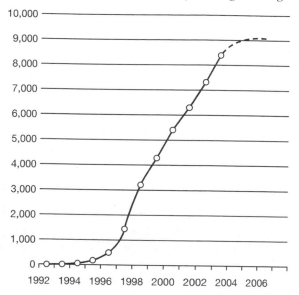

Figure 20.1 The Enlaces programme: yearly expansion 1992–2006

each school, Enlaces coordinates 24 universities that work with over 1,000 teacher trainers and 150 technicians throughout the country. To keep up to date, to try new technologies and to test new learning strategies with information and communication technologies, Enlaces relies mostly on the Institute for Information Technology in Education of the La Frontera University (http://www.iie.ufro.cl/) in southern Chile, which acts as the 'think tank' for Enlaces. Enlaces is therefore a very active and fruitful alliance between the teams from the Ministry of Education, the schools and the universities.

A growing programme for teachers in all locations

Enlaces started as an experimental project in 1990 in the Computer Science Department of the Catholic University in Santiago. In 1992 the Ministry of Education decided to test Enlaces' capacities in a contrasting scenario to the capital city. Therefore, in early 1993, the Enlaces team moved to the most deprived one in Chile, the southern Araucanía region. The team used this strategy to demonstrate that ICT could work in all kinds of schools including urban and rural, small and large, with and without indigenous students. In the mid 1990s Enlaces started to grow outside the Araucanía region and soon became a national programme with a presence in all regions.

The Enlaces team that started its design in the early 1990s benefited from international experience with computers in education, a new wave of educational software with lower hardware prices, and an intense international debate on the role of these new devices in education. One of the main lessons from this past experience was that computers would not have much educational impact on their own: it was realized that it is *the teachers* who are mainly responsible for change and improvements inside the classroom and also the ones who decide when and how to use the available resources, including computers. Therefore, Enlaces' strategy focused on the teachers from the very beginning and a scheme for long-term training and support scheme was the core strategy.

The teachers are the protagonists

A key dimension of Enlaces' work has been its staff development programme for building the capacities of school teachers, administrators and ICT coordinators. At the beginning, Enlaces dealt with fewer than 100 schools and the teacher trainers were mostly university employees. As more schools entered the programme a larger group of teacher trainers, mainly teachers from those schools experienced in Enlaces activities, had to be managed. In general these teachers were better trainers than the university academics, because they had classroom experience with first-hand knowledge of what works best in a school, and, as a consequence, their peers found it easier to believe their message.

Teacher training was organized around regular sessions conducted with teachers in their own schools for a period of two years. The first year was mainly one of familiarization with the technology, including electronic mail, word processors, electronic spreadsheets, and educational software. The second year focused on the pedagogical application of the technology, including classroom models, collaborative learning, and curricular projects (Laval and Hinostroza, 2002).

In general, most teachers found it easy to use computers for school and classroom management purposes and also rapidly learned how to navigate through the Internet and became regular email users. However, using the technology during classroom hours with their students proved to be a tough challenge. Teachers who were early adopters moved in a few months to classroom uses, but 'mainstream' teachers took more time and sometimes years before feeling comfortable with the technology in their classroom. Such teachers needed better arguments, good classroom models and examples that were closely related to their teaching models. They also needed appropriate student evaluation methods and technical support on hand ready to step forward. Enlaces has been addressing all these issues with varying results. The main lesson has been that the majority of teachers do not significantly modify their teaching practice because of the presence of computers; they merely adapt the technology to their practice (Cuban, 2001).

Powerful alliances to meet growing training demands

A critical moment for Enlaces and its teacher training strategy was in the mid 1990s when the project was scaled up from a small well controlled pilot project to a massive national programme with nearly 1,000 new schools every year (see Figure 20.1). This rapid expansion was the handled by the creation of the Enlaces National Support Network that currently involves a partnership between the Ministry of Education and 24 universities across the country. A Zone Center became responsible for the implementation of Enlaces in a large geographical zone managed by a group of six of these 24 universities. The six universities also became responsible for the design and development of training material and strategies that followed general guidelines but were fine tuned to the reality of the schools inside their zone. The Zone Center established agreements with other universities and institutions, in turn, in order to cover its entire zone with institutions that are as close as possible to the schools. This decentralized scheme has successfully trained teachers and established long-term relationships among institutions and schools that share a social, cultural and economical reality.

Along with the Enlaces National Support Network, the Ministry maintains a special partnership with the Institute for Information Technology in Education at the University of La Frontera (http://www.iie.ufro.cl/), which had conducted the pilot stage and had designed most of the training strategies and materials. It also developed some educational software and maintained a research group that explored new technologies and ways of using ICT with classroom teachers. This long-standing relationship between a research centre and the Ministry proved to be a fruitful approach to steer a policy that needs strong management capabilities at the Ministry level and also requires keeping up to date in a fast changing field such as ICT for education.

The technology

Enlaces provided, to each school that enters the programme, a number of computers connected to a local area network, Internet connection, furniture, productivity and educational software accompanied by training and technical assistance. The number of computers provided to each school was small because of the limited budget of the programme. It was based on the schools' student population: schools with less than 100 students received three computers and one printer; schools with 100 to 300 students received six computers and two printers; schools with more than 300 students received nine computers and two printers. These figures were improved later through further Enlaces investments, private donations and school purchases.

By 2002, subsidized schools in Chile had ICT laboratories with an average of 13 computers each, and a ratio of 45 students per computer

(51 in primary and 31 in secondary schools). These figures include more than 56,000 computers acquired for Enlaces through public international biddings and the equipment acquired by the school owners or donated by parents and other institutions.

The provision of educational software remains a key issue. Enlaces' approach has been to ensure a large variety of software in each school so that teachers can choose the ones that best suit their requirements. All the software purchased by Enlaces is carefully evaluated by specialists, ensuring its quality as well as its alignment with the Chilean curriculum. Additionally, Enlaces has developed guidelines and examples for the teachers on how to use some of the software in the classroom. Each year Enlaces conducts an international bidding process to buy educational software for the schools. In addition, the Institute for Information Technology of the Frontera University produces for Enlaces a CD that contains a collection of free-ware, donated software and also software developed in-house. By 2003, Enlaces had bought 16,704 copies of encyclopaedias, 60,469 sets of educational software and 140,000 licences of software, and had distributed 58,464 copies of CDs with software collections.

Although the use of the Internet in education is a widespread phenomena today (OECD, 2001), when Enlaces started in the early 1990s it was not (Hepp *et al.*, 1992; Hepp *et al.*, 1994). At that time, school networks were very new and simple, even in developed countries. Despite this, Enlaces built an educational network that has enabled teachers and students in hundreds of schools to communicate, collaborate and access resources around the world, thus reducing their isolation and enriching the available educational resources. Today, 85 per cent of Chilean students have access to the Internet in their schools.

Enlaces developed a user friendly software called La Plaza (The Town Square) during the first decade of its implementation in order to empower teachers and students through the use of computers and telecommunications (Hepp *et al.*, 1993). This software allows easy access to computers, for exploring educational software (mostly multimedia-based applications), for using email and for participating in regional, national and international educational projects. The software was used as a 'Trojan Horse' for a friendly and non-intimidating first encounter with computers. It was particularly successful in helping to reduce teachers' anxiety towards a technology that was perceived as complex, for experts only, and requiring long hours of technical training in order to start using it effectively. As ICT evolved, this software was replaced by commercial web-based services. However, La Plaza is still used in many schools that do not have free or reliable Internet for low cost e-mail service and because of its simplicity as an application launcher.

Enlaces started to develop web-based services for teachers and students in the mid 1990s, as the Internet started to penetrate Chile. An important push took place in 1998 when a telephone company (Telefónica CTC) donated free Internet access for 10 years to thousands of schools. The early developments evolved into the Chilean educational portal called EducarChile (http://www.educarechile.cl). This portal offers a variety of educational services and databases containing educational resources aligned with the Chilean curriculum. It is designed for teachers, students, parents and researchers and it is linked into a wide network of national and international educational initiatives that contribute content and experiences.

The rural schools

The early years of Enlaces, followed in the mid 1990s by a national expansion, were grounded on a design for urban schools, the arrangement of computers within a special computer room (the ICT lab), training groups of 20 teachers in weekly sessions at their own school, Internet connectivity, frequent technical support, and so on. Although almost 90 per cent of Chilean students attend primary and secondary urban schools; the other 10 per cent study in rural schools that have a very different reality. The Ministry of Education has had a special programme for working with rural schools since 1992. This programme involves methodological and organizational approaches that are suitable for mixed grade classes, and monthly meetings with teachers from nearby schools constituting a community of teachers called Microcenter (San Miguel, 1999). The reality for these schools is outlined below:

- The school has a small population of students (rural schools have an average of 27 students per school).
- Several classes are taught by the same teacher in one classroom (66 per cent of rural schools have just one teacher).
- The number of schools is relatively high (the 3,300 rural schools make up more than one-third of all the schools in the country).
- Most rural schools are located in places with difficult access (no public transportation).
- Most rural schools do have electricity, but 10 per cent of them still do not have regular access to electricity.
- The great majority of rural schools do not have telephone lines (80 per cent).

Enlaces designed a special ICT programme for rural schools in 1999, known as Rural Enlaces (IIE, 2000). One distinctive aspect of this design is that ICT must get inside the classroom from the first day onwards, sometimes the one and only classroom. The computers are placed as an additional 'learning corner' inside the classroom. Rural teachers are used to this approach because they use it to deal with groups of students belonging to different grades. Therefore, this new ICT corner came as a natural expansion of a well known classroom setting and was easily accepted by teachers and students.

Another characteristic of this teacher-training programme is that it has to address schools that might have only one or two teachers and that could be difficult to reach by the trainers because of geographical isolation. To address this challenge, Rural Enlaces created a specialized teacher training team to deal specifically with the rural schools in each Zone Center and also networked these teams. These rural teacher trainers, called facilitators, visit each school once a month and work with the teacher and the students directly inside the classroom. The facilitators make classroom observations and offer models, examples and hints on how to use the ICT corner for pedagogical activities. The facilitator also meets with all the teachers from nearby schools during the established monthly Microcenter meeting. In the first year teachers participate in intensive workshops at the closest university to learn basic ICT skills. This professional development programme has been designed as a progressive process that takes three years, after which Enlaces provides a long-standing support scheme for these schools.

Naturally the Internet connectivity has been more problematic for many of these schools, so it was decided to begin Rural Enlaces with a focus on the pedagogical use of technology inside the classroom where the schools did not have Internet access. In parallel, a central task force is designing a national solution to provide sustainable Internet access to all the rural schools and communities in the future.

Empowering the community

Enlaces is already providing access to the new digital technologies for more than 92 per cent of students all over the country. However, many of their parents do not have access even through they could improve the quality of their life using services provided over the Internet. For example, the agricultural sector has up-to-date figures on the Internet about the seed and cattle markets, machinery, rural electricity and subsidies for the small landowner. Similarly, working mothers can learn about their rights, about new projects in their community, family subsidies, child benefits and other information that is free to all people. In addition, some counties are publishing on the Internet the results of their investments decisions, information on bidding for public work and subsidies. It is recognized that every member of a community may now locate useful information closely related to their life and the place where they live, including youngsters, adults and elders, workers and unemployed.

Therefore, the Ministry of Education started a pilot project in 2001 to open schools with the Enlaces infrastructure to the community. Parents were trained to use the computers and the Internet for their own purposes in the schools by teachers, sometimes with the help of their children. The results of this pilot effort have been outstanding, with a good response from the parents and other members of the community. This stimulated the Ministry to provide incentives to the schools to open their laboratories to more parents and also to other members of the community. By the end of 2003, more than one thousand schools from all over the country should be offering regular courses for adults in their community. The goal is to train more than 250,000 adults in the use of ICT by 2005.

There are two main challenges in this initiative; one is about content and the other about bandwidth. For adults with low levels of literacy, the Internet content should be of direct interest and also easy to understand. Many public services are increasingly conscious about this issue and are beginning to offer well designed user interfaces linked to help desks to assist their users. On the other hand, schools need to improve their connection bandwidth to ensure reasonable waiting times when all parents are using the Internet at the same time. Therefore, the Ministry has committed new resources to improve the connectivity of all schools. Only some pockets of more isolated rural schools will remain without these facilities because of the high costs, and the Ministry is actively investigating satellite technology to overcome this problem. The schools are thus becoming open community centres where adults can attend after school hours and at weekends. As a side effect, parents are assigning more value to the schools. This is important in a developing country where many rural parents still believe that only a few years of education is necessary and that their children should return work with them full time after that. Research also indicates that parents become more interested in what and how their children learn, children are proud because they can teach their parents something useful for their parents' lives, and school owners perceive that their 'customers' are well served (Hepp *et al.*, 2000).

Evaluation

Evaluating is an essential activity in a national programme for introducing ICT in education. It is mainly about stating whether a programme is achieving what it was planned to do and to what extent. A clear definition of what should be evaluated imposes a precise and measurable definition of the goals and helps detecting unrealistic expectations, failures and successes. Different types of evaluations have been conducted for Enlaces. At an early stage, the goal was to research the possible effects that the introduction of ICT in the school would have on students, teachers and on the school organization. Results of these evaluations provided very useful feedback for the strategic design of the project on a larger scale. During the expansion of Enlaces, most evaluations aimed to measure its achievements and more recent evaluations have focused on understanding the way in which teachers and students integrate ICT into their teaching and learning practices.

Results of the initial evaluations (1993–8) in small samples of schools were generally positive. For *students* the technology helped increase their reading comprehension levels, improved their creativity, self-esteem and concentration capacities. For the *teachers*, external evaluations showed that many of them believed that communications via computers improved the quality of the teaching–learning process and that Enlaces was a source of pride that opened doors for teachers' professional development. Other results indicated that participating schools' prestige improved in their communities, especially among parents, and that this led to an increase in enrolments. *School officials* were found to value the increase in equity that the project provided by fitting out schools with equipment that they otherwise would not have been able to acquire.

From a more global perspective, results of evaluations made by UNESCO (1995), the World Bank (1998) and the Agency for International Development (1999) highlighted the Enlaces project as one of the successful programmes in Chilean educational reform. An important point noted was that the project had expanded its coverage to the national level without sacrificing quality or equity. They identified the programme's focus on teachers, the construction of a social network of educators and students facilitated by user-friendly technology and decentralized support, and respect for the participating schools' autonomy and their decisions in the use of these new technologies as factors that contributed to its success.

In 1999, Enlaces conducted a national survey of the Chilean educational ICT infrastructure and its use in schools (Hinostroza *et al.*, 2003) according to the design and implementation of the international study of ICT in schools. This evidence placed Chile in a good position in the international rankings, using several indicators related to ICT in education. Moreover, on many indicators, Chile's results were similar or even better than the ones shown by developed countries such as Japan, Italy and France. More specifically, the survey showed that Chilean ICT policy coordinated with private sector initiatives, such as that of the telecommunication industry, was able to install an internationally competitive infrastructure in Chilean schools (IEA, 2000) including hardware, software and Internet, all of which was being used extensively. One important result of the survey was the widespread implementation of teacher training in the general use of ICT. Nevertheless, some challenges were identified. They related to the need to provide more equipment in both primary and secondary schools and the need to improve the quality of software in primary schools. The survey showed that the goals of using ICT reported by the school principals were related to the implementation of active, collaborative and autonomous learning by the teachers. However, the obstacles mentioned by them included difficulty in integrating ICT into instruction, as well as a lack of teachers' knowledge to do this.

The Chilean Ministry of Education decided to search for answers that could help to characterize innovative uses of ICT in Chilean schools by participating in an international qualitative study in 2000 (IEA, 2000). Seven cases of exemplary use of ICT in Chile were studied in depth and compared to cases in other countries. Hinostroza *et al.* (2002) showed that the innovative uses of ICT in these case studies did not provide evidence of having an impact on students' learning achievement on a large scale, as defined in the national curriculum and measured by the national assessment tests. However, the case studies show that students who participate in ICT projects could learn new content; they had the opportunity to develop abilities defined as cross-curricular and practised ICT related skills. The analysis of the teaching and learning activities highlighted some deficiencies in the way that teachers implement new teaching strategies with ICT and thus indicated the need for further training. The cases did show that innovative teaching practices can have an impact on the students' conception of the world and on the social relations beyond the school, and that the parents' conception of the school was altered favourably. Finally, the results underline the special importance of the way in which the *teachers* plan the use of ICT, through the activity guides that teachers prepared *before* lessons take place, which suggests a change in their role when scaffolding learning.

Conclusions

The Chilean ICT in education initiative Enlaces has become a nation-wide programme after more than a decade of development and now reaches more than 92 per cent of the student population all over the country. Enlaces believes more in using the technology to empower people than in the technology itself, at least in schools where it is the people not the technology who are the principal actors and the teachers the main agents of change.

Placing ICT resources into the schools is an easy task compared with achieving effective uses of ICT by the teachers inside the classroom and impacting on the students' achievements. (Editor's note: The same applies to pre-service teacher education, in which Enlaces' leaders also recognize the need to act.) Subject specific classroom materials and tools are one important contribution of ICT in education, but not the only one. ICT can become a powerful tool for the professional development of teachers, by reducing the isolation of many teachers and students in rural schools and by enhancing every learning environment with a variety of resources available worldwide. ICT in the schools of developing countries represents a unique opportunity for many young-sters who do not have access to technology in their homes or in their community to exercise new skills and learn to use information appli-ances that will be required when they enter the work force or pursue further studies.

Finally, investing in ICT for education in developing countries is an important and delicate decision because of the relative large amount of money that needs to be spent for many years to provide reasonable access to the technology for millions of youngsters and hundreds of thousands of teachers and their communities. The range of resources includes software, computers, Internet and other devices, along with long-standing technical and pedagogical support. There are many options available to countries and regions and yet no one solution fits most cases and local realities. Each strategy also represents a different cost equation. Therefore it is of utmost importance for these countries to take advantage of the experience of many projects and research initia-tives worldwide, as Enlaces did. This chapter provides an important national case study of a systematic approach that developed commun-ities who in turn enhanced the use of digital media and communications in education.

References

Cuban, L. (2001) *Oversold & Underused: Computers in the classroom*, Harvard University Press, Cambridge, MA.

Hepp, P., Alvarez, M., Hinostroza, J. E. and Laval, E. (1993) La Plaza: a software design for an educational network, paper presented at Ed-Media'93 World Conference on Educational Multimedia and Hypermedia, Orlando, FL.

Hepp, P., Rehbein, L., Hinostroza, J. E., Lavel, E. *et al.* (1994) Enlaces: a hyperme-dia based educational network, paper presented at ACM Multimedia: The Second International Conference on Multimedia, San Francisco, CA.

Hepp, P., Lavel, E. and Garrido, R. (2000) Telecentres in Chile: a community access project, paper presented at WebNet 2000 World Conference on the WWW and Internet, San Antonio, TX.

Hinostroza, J. E., Jara, I., Guzmán, A. and Isaacs, S. (2002) Innovative uses of ICT in Chilean schools, *Journal of Computer Assisted Learning*, 18 (4), pp. 459–69.

Hinostroza, J. E. Jara, I. and Gusmán, A. (2003) Achievements during the 90s of Chile's ICT in education program: an international perspective, *Interactive Educational Multimedia*, 6, pp. 78–92.

IEA (1998) [accessed 26 August 2003] SITES Module 1: indicators module, second information technology in education study, International Association for the Evaluation of Educational Achievement [Online] http://www.mscp.edte. utwente.nl/sitesm1/.

IIE (2000) *Enlaces Rural: La informática como un recurso de aprendizaje para todas las escuelas rurales de Chile*, Universidad de La Frontera, Temuco, Chile.

Laval, E. and Hinostroza, J. E. (2002) Chilean schools: the Enlaces network, *TechKnowLogia*, 4 (3), pp. 14–18.

OECD (2001) *Learning to Change: ICT in schools,* Organization of Economic Cooperation and Development, Paris.

OECD (2002) *Measuring the Information Economy,* Organization of Economic Cooperation and Development, Paris.

San Miguel, J. (1999) *Programa de Educación Básica Rural, La Reforma Educacional Chilena,* Editorial Popular, Madrid.

Index

Aalborg University 242, 252, 254, 255
Aarseth, E.: *Cybertext* 77–8;
    Nonlinearity and Literary Theory
    88, 89
access 2, 3, 6, 7, 84, 115–16, 198, 306
Adams 182
adaptive multimedia 52
adult basic skills 7, 131–44
affordances 23–5
Africa 159, 160, 161
Agency for International Development
    308
Aikenhead, G. S.: Cultural aspects of
    learning science 212; Science
    education 212
Alaska 180–1
Alaska, University of 188
Alaska Federation of Natives 188
Alaska Traditional Diet Project 190
Alaskan Native Knowledge Network
    188–9
Allen, P.: Special problems 185–6
All My Children (television) 79
American Indian Art from the Pacific
    Northwest 190
American Indian Higher Education
    Consortium 188-9
American Indians *see* United States of
    America: indigenous peoples
American Psychological Association:
    *Learner-centered Psychological
    Principles* 265
Angola 197, 203
Angus, L.: Families 124, 125, 127
animation 46, 139, 149
Anishinabe clan system 186–91, 192

Antarctica 300
Aristotle 106–7
Arnold, Matthew 86
art 70, 108
Asia 159, 160, 161
Ask Jeeves 70
Association for Computing and
    Information Technology Teaching
    293
Association of American Indian
    Physicians 191
audio recording 199
Austen, Jane 76, 84–5, 90
Australia 6, 269; adult basic skills 131,
    133; CaseNEX 227; children and
    computers 115–30; online courses
    212
Australian Bureau of Statistics: *Year
    Book Australia 2003* 115
Australian National Training
    Authority 212
authentic assessment 126
authoring 33–8
Axel, Gabriel 74

Babette's Feast (film) 74, 91
'Back-to-Basics' criticism 98
Bangladesh 206
Barcelona, University of 48, 242
Barlow, J. P.: *Declaration* 74, 91
Barna, L. M.: Stumbling blocks 245
basic skills *see* adult basic skills
Bates, T.: Cultural and ethical issues
    211–12, 223
Bay Mills Community College 189
Baym, N.: *Tune In, Log On* 90

Belgium 138
Bennett, M. J.: *Intercultural Development Inventory* 231–2
Blade Runner (film) 91
Blurton, C.: *New Directions in Education* 161
Bolter, J. D.: *Writing Space* 88, 89
Bonamie, B.: Reconstructing the teaching of language 99
books: access 41–2; organization 33–8, 41; *see also* text
Booth, S.: *Learning and Awareness* 62, 63, 65
Bovill, M.: *Young People, New Media* 198
Boylan, P.: Learning languages as 'culture' 98
Brewer, Cindy 83
British Columbia, University of 265; Community of Inquiry in Teacher Education 268, 269
Brooks, C.: *Well Wrought Urn* 86
Brown, J. S.: Organizational learning 267
browsers 47
Bruner, J.: *Actual Minds, Possible Worlds* 101; *Acts of Meaning* 101
Burch 47
bureaucracy 91
Bush, George W. 164
business 43
Buzan, T.: *Mind Map Book* 61
Byatt, A. S.: *Possession* 84

Cabri-Géomètre 271
Cambridge Training and Development Ltd 138
Canada 10, 160, 161, 264–76; adult basic skills 131, 133; indigenous peoples 181; online courses 212
Carvin, A.: More than just access 143
case method 8, 9–10, 225–33; video cases 164–78
CaseNex 225–33
Castells, M.: Fourth World of exclusion 3, 7, 84; *Information Age* 2, 84, 96; Introduction to the Information Age 84; space of flows/space of places 2

Catholic University, Santiago 301
CD-ROMs 46, 47, 70, 120, 121
Center for Innovative Learning Technologies 272
Center for Learning Technologies in Urban Schools 269
Centre for the Study of Children Youth and Media 196–7
Certificate in Intercultural Educational Technology 241–2
Cervantes 88
Charles University, Prague 295
Charlier, B.: Les communautés délocalisées d'enseignants 273
chat rooms 68, 71, 72, 197
Cherian, A.: Information technology 186
Chicago 269
Chickasaw Nation 189
children: computer use 5, 6, 57, 115–30; concepts of digital technologies 57–73; gender differences 120; Internet and 57–73, 99, 115–20; refugees 2, 7, 9, 196–210
Children in Communication about Migration (CHICAM) 196–210
Chile 3, 11, 295, 299–311
Cisco Networking Academy Program 211, 213–23
Cisco Systems 9
citizenship 43, 146
CLAIT 70
classical-humanist education 96–7
clubs 196–208
Cobern, W. W.: Cultural aspects of learning science 212
Cochiti Dam 191
cognitive psychology 231
cognitivism *see* constructivism
Cohen, R.: *Les jeunes enfants* 278
coherence 51
collaborative action 257
collaborative learning 98, 251–63
collaborative study groups 237
collective intelligence 4, 40–5
Colombia 197
Comenius Logo 280, 282
communication 97–8; collective 45; media of 16

communicativity 199
communities, intercultural 196–210
communities, online 1–2, 196–210,
   228–9, 235–9
communities of learning 53–5
communities of practice 1, 2, 53–5,
   264–76, 289–98
competence 38
computer assisted language learning
   (CALL) 99, 100
Computer Clubhouse project 279
computers: children's use of 5, 6,
   115–30; home and school use
   compared 5, 6, 57, 125–6
computer-supported collaborative
   learning (CSCL) 251–63
concept mapping 57–72, 61–3,
   63–71
constructivism 52, 100–1, 216–17, 231,
   265, 277
content 97, 98
content-based learning 98
contiguity 51
contrastive rhetoric 106
Cool Edit 280
cooperation 43
cooperative learning 255
Corel Print Office 280
cost 117
Creative Communications 281–3,
   284
creativity 15, 16, 198–9
critique 38
Cuba 227
Cultura project 242
cultural studies 101–3, 107
culture 98; revitalization of 183
culture shock 10, 235–9
curriculum 75, 76, 78, 79, 108, 126, 145,
   147, 150, 152, 156, 157, 162, 199;
   CCNA 215, 221–2; National
   Curriculum (UK) 76, 135; spiral
   215
cyberculture 104
cyber-dystopias 1
cyberspace 91, 99, 109
cyber-utopias 1
Czech Technical University 293–4
Czechoslovakia 197, 289–97

Daele, A.: Les communautés
   délocalisées d'enseignants 273
Daes, E.: *Study* 185, 186
Dallas (television) 181
Darwin, Charles 181
Davis, N. E.: Pedagogy and protocols
   199; Quality @ a distance 242
Davis, T.: Shaping the destiny of
   Native American people 188
de Castell, S.: *Object Lessons* 109
De Kerckhove, D.: *Connected
   Intelligence* 108
Delgado, V.: Technology and Native
   America 183, 192
Denmark 242; CCNA 222; CSCL,
   251–63
Descartes, René 91
design 38–9, 199
Detroit 267, 269
Developmental Model of Intercultural
   Sensitivity 230–1
Dewey, J.: *Experience and Education*
   226–7
Dick, P. K.: *Do Androids Dream of
   Electric Sheep?* 91
digital literacy 55
digital television *see* television
digital video *see* video
digitalization 95–109
Dijkstra, S.: *Multimedia Learning*
   49–50
dilemma discussion 228–9
discourse 126; analysis 101, 103–5,
   107
distance learning 211–12, 227–8, 237
distributed education 228
Dorling Kindersley 34
Douglas, J. Y.: *End of Books* 88–9, 91
Dowling, P. C.: Reading school
   mathematics texts 76; School
   mathematics in late modernity 76;
   Sociology of Mathematics Education
   76
Downes, T.: Children's and Families'
   Use of Computers 119; Children's
   and parents' discourses 118, 119;
   Children's use of computers 118, 119,
   120, 121, 123, 124, 125
Draxler, A.: *Technologies for Education* 9

Dreamcatchers: What is Rez Robics? 190

Duguid, P.: Organizational learning 267

Dull Knife Memorial College 189

dystopia 74

Easter Island 300

Easthope, A.: *Literary into Cultural Studies* 86–7

Ecolab, The 54

EducarChile 305

Education Reform Act (1988) 78

Egan, K.: *Educated Mind* 96

eGroups 273

El Nino 148

e-learning 9, 211–24

Electronic Frontier Foundation 74

Ellis, Kristine 242

email 1, 41, 54, 68, 71, 81, 134, 197, 265

Emin, Tracey 70

Eminem 205

Encarta 121

English for Speakers of Other Languages (ESOL) 136, 138

Enlaces 11, 299–311

Eotvos Lorand University 279

equity 2, 3, 5, 131

Europe: Eastern 160, 161; 'New' 11, 289–98; Western 159, 160, 161

European Commission: CHICAM 196, 198; prisons 138

European SchoolNet 295

European Union: adult basic skills 131; Internet use 115; Upgrade 139

European Union of Women 294

evaluation 259–60

Evanston 269

Excel 148

exclusion 6, 7, 115–16, 131, 134, 135, 138–40, 142, 198

expository teaching 150

fan fiction 84, 90

fans, Internet-based 79–80, 81–3

feminism 104

field awareness 64, 66–7

film 77, 87, 199, 200, 201

First International Congress on the Cultural & Intellectual Property Rights of Indigenous Peoples (1993): Mataatua Declaration 185

Fixico, D.: Ethics and responsibilities 184–5

Flash 47, 280

Florida, University of 242

focal awareness 64, 66–7

Fort Belknap College, Montana 191

forums 54, 167–8, 265

Four Directions project 188–9

France 308; CaseNEX 227; prisons 138

fringe awareness 64, 66–7

FrontPage 280

Fullan, M.: Three stories of education reform 275

Furlong, J. and R.: National Grid for Learning 119

game-playing 7, 118, 119, 120, 121, 124, 135; CD-ROM 57; digital television 140; educational software based on 137; online 57, 72

Gaskin, R.: Beyond the browser 47

Gee, J.: *Social Linguistics and Literacies* 103

Geertz, C.: *Interpretation of Cultures* 101

General Certificate of Secondary Education 68, 70

genetic engineering 95

Geographic Information System 191

Geometers SketchPad 271

Germany 196; after-school clubs 201, 204, 205; CCNA 218, 220, 221; theatre groups 294

Gibson, W.: *Neuromancer* 74, 91

Global Positioning Systems 191

globalization 16, 83, 95, 96, 211, 212, 234; global village 98, 235, 238

'Gone' 83

Gorard, S.: *Lifelong Learning Trajectories in Wales* 141

Gowin, D. B.: *Learning How to Learn* 61

grammar 105

Grammar-Translation method 96

Greece: after-school clubs 201; Internet use 115

Greek 96–7
Greek Council for Refugees 201
Grifalconi, Ann 166
grounded theory 62, 65
group activities 43
Guinea 197, 206

Haddad, W.: *Technologies for Education* 9
Hammer, M. R.: *Intercultural Development Inventory* 231–2
Hannahville Indian School 189
Harris, Judi 274
Harvard Law School 226
Haskell Cultural Center, Lawrence, Kansas 189
Hayles, N. K.: *How We became Posthuman* 91; *Writing Machines* 89
health 190–1
hierarchy 43
Hirsch, E.: *Cultural Literacy* 103
Hong Kong 149
Hopi Cultural Preservation Office: Protocol for research 185
horror films 77
Human Resources Development Canada 264
humanITy: ICT development 142
Hung, D.: Differentiating 54
Hungary 11, 277–88; CCNA 217; Ministry of Informatics and Communication 280
Hutcheon, L.: *Irony's Edge* 104
hypermedia 51
hypertext 41, 51, 74–5, 77, 78, 80, 83–5, 87–9, 90
hypertext markup language (html) 47, 85

image 46, 149; text and 16–39, 51, 55, 100, 107
ImpaCT2 project 58–72
India 227
Indian Nations At Risk Task Force: *Indian Nations at Risk* 180–1
Indians, *see* United States of America: indigenous peoples
indigenous communities 179–95
individual differences 51

industry 43
Informatics Methodology Group 279
informatics teacher training 277–88
information: collective 44; retrieval 41–1
innovation 15, 16
Institute for Knowledge Innovation and Technology 272
Institute of Education, University of London 36–7, 38, 133, 241, 242
intelligence: capitalization of 43; collective 40–5; enrichment of 43
interaction 53, 102, 120, 134, 139, 141, 257, 258
intercultural communication 2, 234–5
intercultural education 225–33, 234–47
International Adult Literacy Survey 131
International Leadership in Educational Technology (ILET) 239–43
Internet 1, 41, 90, 91, 102, 115, 132, 134; access 84, 198; applications transferred to 46; bandwidth 52, 117, 199, 307; cafés 117; children and 57–73, 99, 115–30; Chile 304–5, 306–7, 308; communities of interest 264; cultural technology 108; distribution medium 199; Europe 115, 198; fans 79–80, 81–3; Hungary 278; indigenous peoples 191; IRC 57; learning and 55; literacy and 5–6; literature and 5–6; multimedia 5; protocols 213; teaching and 164–78; Web browsers 47
Internet Explorer 280
intranets 42
Iowa State University 242, 253, 254
Ireland: prisons 138; television 139
Italy 308; after-school clubs 205; CCNA 221
iVisit 272

Jansen, Eva 242
Japan 308; theatre groups 294
JavaScript 47
JDTalk 81–2, 90
Jefferson, Thomas 74
Jenkins, H.: *Textual Poachers* 80

Jenson, J.: *Object Lessons* 109
Jojola, T.: Revision on revisionism 185
Jonassen, D. H.: Manifesto for a constructivist approach 282; *Multimedia Learning* 49–50
JoshDonnaFF 81, 82–3, 90
Joyce, James 76
Joyce, M. 76; *afternoon* 74, 87–9; New stories for new readers; *Other-mindedness* 88; *Of Two Minds* 82
Juneau, D.: Oneida tribal web site 189

Kamira, R.: Te Mata o te Tai 187
Kaplan, R. B.: Cultural Thought Patterns 106
Kenya 197, 206
Kern, R.: *Introduction* 100
knowledge: capitalization of 43; collective 43, 44; enrichment of 43; networked communities 251–63; shaping of 25–7
knowledge economy 117
Knowledge Forum 270, 271, 272
Kramer, M. E.: Competitive advantage of corporate philanthropy 214
Kress, G.: *Literacy in the New Media Age* 55

La Frontera University 301, 303, 304
La Plaza 304
Landeskunde 103
Landow, G. P.: *Hypertext 2.0* 78
language 15, 16
language teaching 95–111
Lanham, R. A.: Electronic word 108; *Electronic Word* 106, 107; Rhetorical paideia 108
laptops 133, 139
LARA project 242
Latin 96–7
Laval University 265, 268, 269, 270, 272
Lave, J.: *Situated Learning* 54, 264, 266
Law, N.: Innovative classroom practices 157
Lazarus, W.: *Online Content for Low-income and Underserved Americans* 117

LCSI (1999) 284–5
learning: apprenticeship 126; collaborative 98, 251–63; collective 44; communities 53–5, 237; content-based 98; cooperative 255; digital technologies and 115–30, 145–63; distance 211–12, 227–8, 237; doing and 126; e-learning 9, 211–24; Internet and 55; learner autonomy 98; learning shops 7; lifelong 98, 264; multimedia 46–56; online 150, 164–78; process-based 98; scaffold 126, 216; semiotic view of 4, 15–39; situated 266; task-based 98, 150; web-based 164–78, 278, 281–3, 284
Leavis, F. R.: *Great Tradition* 86
LeTUS Community 267
Levonen, J.: *Multimedia Learning* 49–50
libraries 117; virtual 188
Lieberman, A.: Network geographies 269
lifelong learning 98, 264
linguistic turn 101, 103, 106
literacy 7, 74–94, 95–111, 126, 131–44, 164–78; digital 55; Internet and 5–6
literary criticism 101
literature 74–94; Internet and 5–6; teaching 95–111
Lithuania 197
Livingstone, S.: *Young People, New Media* 198
local instructors 211–24
logics 23–5
LOGO Microworlds 280
London Academy 244–5
Lubeck, A.: Economic, sociocultural and technological contexts in the New Europe 290
lurkers 54

McAleese, T. M. R.: Manifesto for a constructivist approach 282
McCormick, R.: Information and communications technology 283–4
McGill Network of TeleLearning Professional Development Schools 268, 274
McGill University 265, 268, 272

Magnusson, M.: Technology and pedagogy 215
Mandela, Nelson 229
Mander, J.: In the Absence of the Sacred 181
Mannova, Bozena 294
Martin, J. N.: *Intercultural Communication in Contexts* 234–5, 245
Marton, F.: *Learning and Awareness* 62, 63, 65; Phenomenography 63
Mason, R.: *Globalising Education* 212
materiality 23–5
Max Trax (game) 137
May, J.: *Technological Needs* 180
Mayer, Mercer 166
Mayer, R. E.: *Multimedia Learning* 49–50, 51–3, 55
Mead, G. H.: *Mind, Self, and Society* 226–7
mediation 200–4
memory, collective 44
Micarelli, A.: Learning languages as 'culture' 98
Michigan, University of, 269
Microcenter 305, 306
Microsoft 295; Office 280; Windows 280
MirandaNet 237, 289–97
mobile phones 115, 132, 139, 140
modes 5, 25–7, 51; modal ensembles 28–31; multimodality 28–31, 33–8, 47
Montreal 268
MOOs (MUDs, Object-Oriented) 124
Mora, F.: *Online Content for Low-income and Underserved Americans* 117
Morse, M.: Nature morte 108
Moser, Sir Claus 132–3
Moss, G.: Informal literacies 76
MSN messaging 57, 71
multiliteracies 95, 106
multimedia 46, 48, 51, 102, 107–8; adaptive 52; art 108; interactive 134, 139, 141; Internet and 5; learning 46–56; rhetoric and 107–8
Multimedia Principle, the 51
multimodality *see* modes

Multi-User Dungeons/Domains (MUDs) 78, 124
Mumtaz, S.: Children's enjoyment and perception of computer use 124
Murray, J. H.: *Hamlet on the Holodeck* 79–80
museums, virtual 188
music 70, 71, 149

Nakayama, T. K.: *Intercultural Communication in Contexts* 234–5, 245
National Association for Advisors for Computers in Education 292–3
National Association for Information Technology in Teacher Education 292–3
National Association of Legal Assistants 139
National Center for Education Statistics (Washington, DC): *Stats in Brief* 117
National Indian Telecommunications Institute 191
National Research and Development Centre for Adult Literacy and Numeracy 137–8, 140
Native American Diabetes Initiative 190
Native Americans *see* United States of America: indigenous peoples
Navajo Health Promotions: What is Rez Robics? 190
Negroponte, N.: *Being Digital* 99
Netherlands, The: after-school clubs 205; CaseNEX 227
NETLogo 281–3, 284
Network-Based Language Learning (NBLT) 100
networked communities 251–63
networks 40–5, 91; defined 41; internal 42
New Criticism 86
new economy 95, 96
New London Group, The: Pedagogy of multiliteracies 97, 102, 104, 105, 109
New Reading Disc (CTAD) 138
Nichani, M.: Differentiating 54

Nilakanta, R.: Quality @ a distance 242
'No Child Left Behind' Act (2001) 164
Northwest Indian College 190
Northwestern University 269
Novak, J. D.: *Learning How to Learn* 61
numeracy 7, 131–44

Oneida Indian Nation 190
online intercultural communication and community 196–210
online learning 150, 164–78
order of discourse 105
Organization for Economic Cooperation and Development 115; ICT and the Quality of Learning 146; *Knowledge and Skills for Life* 131
Ostrava, University of 294
'outreach' schemes 139

Paintbrush 121
Paivio, A.: Dual Coding Hypothesis 49, 50; *Mental Representations* 49
Pakistan 197
pen-pals 200
personal digital assistants (PDAs) 132, 139, 140
phenomenography 62, 63–71
Philips, R. B.: Art, 108
Piaget 227, 284
Plato 106
Plowman, L.: 'Primitive Mode of Representation' 47
Poland 294
portals 41
Porter, M. J.: Competitive advantage of corporate philanthropy 214
portfolios, online 257–8
possession 74–94
Post-16 E-learning Strategy Task Force: *Get on with IT* 142
postcolonialism 104
postmodernism 98, 108
post-perspectives 98–9
poststructuralism 78, 87, 104
PowerPoint 217
pragmatics 103, 107
Preston, Christina 294
prisons 7, 133, 138

privacy 76–7
process-based learning 98
Project Cape Town 225–6, 227, 229–32
Project-oriented Project Pedagogy (POPP) 252–3, 255
PROTIC Community of Practice 270, 271
protocols 184–91, 192, 213

quizzes 256

Reading Classroom Explorer 8, 164–78; features 166–8; impact on instructors 169, 171; impact on students 169–71
reading paths 31–3
Real Time study, the 117
redundancy 51
refugee children 2, 7, 9, 196–210
Reinhart Collection 189
relevance 79
renewal, educational 299–311
representation 16, 18, 23–5
REPRÉSENTATION project 57–72
Republic of Pemberley, The 84, 90
retention 50, 53
Reynar, R.: Indigenous people's knowledge and education 181
Rez Robics 190
Rez Robics for Couch Potato Skins 190
rhetoric 102, 105–8; contrastive 106
romantic fiction 76, 77
Rorty, R.: *Contingency, Irony, and Solidarity* 101
Rouet, J. F.: *Multimedia Learning* 49–50
Roy, L.: Information technology 186
Rumble, G.: Globalisation of open and flexible learning 212
Runner (game) 137
Rural Enlaces 305, 306
Russia 197, 203

Salish Kootenai College 189
San Juan Pueblo community 189
Santa Fe Indian School 191
satellite 197
Saussure, Ferdinand de 17
scaffold learning 126, 216

SchoolNet Canada 264, 268, 274;
    GrassRoots Program 268
school organization 42
Schutz: life-worlds 35
science 43, 49; impact 181, 182–3, 212
screen *see* image
Screen Play 117, 118, 119, 125
Scrimshaw, P.: Information and
    communications technology 283–4
Sealaska Corporation 189
search engines 41, 70
semantics 17
Sembill, D.: *Multimedia Learning* 49–50
semiotics 4, 15–39, 103, 105, 107
Shakespeare, William 85
Shank, R.: Case-based teaching 98
Shiva, V.: Reductionism science 181
Sierra Leone 197
signs *see* semiotics
Simon Fraser University, Vancouver
    252
Sims, J. W.: *Boy Electrician* 33–4, 35
simulations 10, 256
Singapore 149
SITES: M1 159; M2 146–62
situated cognition 126
situated learning 266
skills *see* adult basic skills
Skills for Life 132–43
Snyder, I.: Families 124, 125, 127
soap opera 77, 79, 181
Society for Information Technology in
    Teacher Education 11
socio-constructivism 267
socio-economic status (SES) 116
Socrates 227
Soetaert, R.: Communicating
    complexity 99
Somalia 197, 203
Sophists 106
Sorkin, Aaron 82
sound 46
South Africa: CaseNEX 227; CCNA
    218, 220, 222
South America 160, 161
Spain 48; CCNA 220; Cultura 242;
    LARA 242
spatial contiguity 51
speech act theory 103

spheres of thinking 62–3, 64, 65
Sri Lanka 197
Star Trek 77
Steiner, C. B.: Art 108
Still, M.: Pedagogy and protocols 199
Stockbridge-Munsee Band of Mohican
    Indians 191
Storyspace 74
Strijbos, J. W.: Classification model for
    group-based learning 283
structure 260
stygmergy 43
stylistics 107
Sutherland, R.: National Grid for
    Learning 119
Sutherland-Smith, W.: Families 124,
    125, 127
Svensson, L.: Technology and
    pedagogy 215
Sweden: after-school clubs 201; CCNA
    217, 222; Internet use 115; literacy
    and numeracy 131
Swisher, K.: Why Indian peoples
    should be the ones 186
syntax 17

TACT Community 268–72, 273
Tajfun Theatre Group 294
TAPPED-IN 272
Tapscott, D.: *Growing Up Digital* 124
Task-based learning 98, 150
Tate Modern 70
teachers: CHICAM 200; expository
    teaching 150; ICT and 145–63,
    164–78; lack of confidence 145;
    networks and 40–5; 'reinvention'
    146; resistant intellectuals 103; role
    49, 102, 103, 134, 135, 138, 145–63;
    training 164, 302–3
Teaching with Multimedia (TEAM)
    Lab 277–88
TEAM Project 48
teamwork 43
technology 43; impact 181, 182–3,
    212
technology enhanced language
    learning (TELL) 99, 100
technology integrated language
    learning (TILL), 99, 100

technotexts 89
telecollaborative communities 264–76
teleconferencing 272
Telefónica CTC 305
Tele-houses 11, 277–88
TeleLearning Professional
    Development School (PDS) 268–72
TeleLearning-NCE 272
television 115, 118, 132, 139, 140, 197,
    261; fans 81–3; soap opera 77, 79,
    181
temporal contiguity 51
Tewa Language CD-ROM 189
text 46, 52; image and 16–39, 51, 55,
    87, 107
Think.com 237
thinking, collective 43
Thornton, P.: Pedagogy and protocols
    199
timetable 150
Tocqueville, Alexis de 74
Tohono O'odham Community Action
    190
Toronto, University of, 272
tradition 96–7
training, collective 43
transduction 25
transference 50, 53
transmission 43
Trebian, M.: Shaping the destiny of
    Native American people 188
tribal colleges and universities (TCUs)
    188
Tupac 202, 207
Turkle, S.: *Second Self* 124
tutors *see* teachers

Ufi/learndirect 132–43
UKOnline 198
understanding 98
unemployment 131
United Arab Emirates 217, 218, 219
United Kingdom: adult basic skills
    131, 132, 133; after-school clubs
    201–2, 203, 204, 205; CCNA 217, 218,
    219; Department for Education and
    Skills 142; doctorates 78;
    intercultural videos 196–7;
    MirandaNet 289–97; National

Curriculum 76, 135; OFSTED 292;
    online courses 212; prisons 138
United Nations Commission on
    Human Rights 185
United Nations Educational, Scientific
    and Cultural Organization 2, 11,
    308; *ICT in Teacher Education*
    247
United States of America 6, 90, 160,
    161; adult basic skills 131, 133;
    Agency for International
    Development 280; Bureau of Indian
    Affairs 191; CaseNEX 227; children
    and computers 115–30; CSCL
    251–63; Department of Commerce
    115, 117; indigenous peoples 8,
    179–95; Internet use 115; literacy
    164; online courses 212
Upgrade project 139
Usenet 79

video 8, 51, 118, 149, 190, 196, 199,
    200, 207, 225; digital 1
video cases 164–78
video-conferencing 254, 260–1,
    272
video-phones 139
Villanueva, V. Jnr: Sophistry
    106–7
Virginia, University of 226
virtual libraries, 188
virtual museums 188
virtual schools 150
Virtual-U 252, 257, 270
visibility, electronic 78–9, 90
Vygotsky, L. S. 54; *Mind and Society*
    96, 226–7

Wagner, R.: *Hyperstudio* 294
Warschauer, M.: *Introduction* 100
Washington, University of 189
web sites *see* World Wide Web
WebCT 48, 237, 273
Webster College Dictionary 184
Welch, K. E.: *Electric Rhetoric* 107
Weltanshauung 98
Wenger, E.: *Communities of Practice*
    266, 268, 270; *Situated Learning* 54,
    264, 266

West Wing, The (television) 80–3, 90
Whitehead, A. N. 108
Whitt, L.: Cultural Imperialism 182
Wilbur, S. P.: Archaeology of
    Cyberspaces 76
word processing 125, 134
World Bank 11, 300, 308
World War, Second 183
World Wide Web 45, 90, 118, 121, 132,
    134, 254, 261; authoring and
    animation tools 139; browsers 47;
    web-based learning 164–78, 278,
281–3, 284; web sites 35, 37, 41, 48,
    81, 150, 189, 200–4, 264–5
Wright, B.: Pedagogy and protocols
    199
writing *see* literacy *and* text

X-Philes 79

Yahoo! 68, 70, 81, 237, 242
Yellowknife 181

zones of use 62–3, 64, 65, 68